Artificial Intelligence and Society

RIVER PUBLISHERS SERIES IN COMPUTING AND INFORMATION SCIENCE AND TECHNOLOGY

Series Editor:

The "River Publishers Series in Computing and Information Science and Technology" covers research which ushers the 21st Century into an Internet and multimedia era. Networking suggests transportation of such multimedia contents among nodes in communication and/or computer networks, to facilitate the ultimate Internet.

Theory, technologies, protocols and standards, applications/services, practice and implementation of wired/wireless networking are all within the scope of this series. Based on network and communication science, we further extend the scope for 21st Century life through the knowledge in machine learning, embedded systems, cognitive science, pattern recognition, quantum/biological/molecular computation and information processing, user behaviors and interface, and applications across healthcare and society.

Books published in the series include research monographs, edited volumes, handbooks and textbooks. The books provide professionals, researchers, educators, and advanced students in the field with an invaluable insight into the latest research and developments.

Topics included in the series are as follows:-

- Artificial intelligence
- Cognitive Science and Brian Science
- Communication/Computer Networking Technologies and Applications
- Computation and Information Processing
- Computer Architectures
- Computer networks
- Computer Science
- Embedded Systems
- Evolutionary computation
- Information Modelling
- Information Theory
- Machine Intelligence
- Neural computing and machine learning
- Parallel and Distributed Systems
- Programming Languages
- Reconfigurable Computing
- Research Informatics
- Soft computing techniques
- Software Development
- Software Engineering
- Software Maintenance

For a list of other books in this series, visit www.riverpublishers.com

Artificial Intelligence and Society

Editors

Ayan Mukhopadhyay
College of William & Mary, USA

Yevgeniy Vorobeychik
Washington University in St. Louis, USA

River Publishers

Routledge
Taylor & Francis Group
NEW YORK AND LONDON

Published 2026 by River Publishers
River Publishers
Broagervej 10, 9260 Gistrup, Denmark
www.riverpublishers.com

Distributed exclusively by Routledge
605 Third Avenue, New York, NY 10017, USA
4 Park Square, Milton Park, Abingdon, Oxon OX14 4RN

Artificial Intelligence and Society / by Ayan Mukhopadhyay, Yevgeniy Vorobeychik.

Routledge is an imprint of the Taylor & Francis Group, an informa business

ISBN 978-87-4381-205-0 (hardback)
ISBN 978-87-4381-326-2 (paperback)
ISBN 978-87-4381-208-1 (online)
ISBN 978-87-4381-207-4 (master ebook)
ISBN 978-87-4381-210-4 (ePub)

DOI: 10.1201/9788743812074

Contents

Preface

In a span of a few decades, Artificial Intelligence (AI) has moved from a specialized academic pursuit to a technology woven into the fabric of our everyday lives. It now shapes how we travel, how we receive medical care, how we learn, and how we are governed. With this reach has come a corresponding responsibility: to think carefully about where AI helps, where it harms, and what principles should guide its design and deployment.

This book grew out of our conviction that these two conversations, i.e., what AI can do for society, and what society should ask of AI, belong in the same volume. Too often, discussions about AI's social impact are split into parallel tracks: one technical, focused on algorithms and benchmarks, and one normative, focused on ethics and policy. We believe researchers, practitioners, students, and policymakers are best served when these threads are brought together.

Accordingly, the book is organized into two parts. Part I presents a series of tutorial-style chapters on application areas where AI has produced, or has the potential to produce, tangible positive impact: smart transportation, sustainable energy management, social-network-based interventions for vulnerable populations, matching market design, emergency response, disease screening, and security against threats ranging from cyberattacks to wildlife poaching. Each chapter, contributed by leading researchers in the field, introduces the relevant technical foundations and grounds them in concrete deployments. Part II turns to the cross-cutting concerns that arise across every one of these domains: privacy, fairness, adversarial robustness, and the broader landscape of ethics, law, and policy.

We want to point out that this volume is not an exhaustive treatment of the field of AI for social impact. Several important application areas, such as autonomous driving, climate science, and large-scale agriculture, are already covered by excellent existing volumes. Instead, we have prioritized topics where the societal impact is significant, but the published material is comparatively dispersed, and where each chapter can serve as a self-contained tutorial suitable for senior undergraduate or graduate courses.

We are deeply grateful to the contributors who shared their expertise so generously, and to the communities, agencies, and field partners who, through years of collaboration, made the deployments described in these pages possible. We hope this volume offers both a practical resource and an invitation: to do AI research that takes societal impact seriously, and to deploy AI in ways that take seriously the harms it can cause.

Ayan Mukhopadhyay, College of William & Mary
Yevgeniy Vorobeychik, Washington University in St. Louis

Dedicated to our families.

List of Figures

List of Tables

List of Contributors

Ayman, Afiya, *Pennsylvania State University*

Chen, Yixin, *Washington University in St. Louis*

Dubey, Abhishek, *Vanderbilt University*

Fang, Fei, *Carnegie Mellon University*

Kantarcioglu, Murat, *University of Texas at Dallas*

Laszka, Aron, *Pennsylvania State University*

Lee, SangMok, *Washington University in St. Louis*

Liu, Fangqi, *Vanderbilt University*

Mukhopadhyay, Ayan, *College of William & Mary, USA*

Samaranayake, Samitha, *Cornell University*

Sen, Rishav, *Vanderbilt University*

Shen, Weiran, *Renmin University*

Sivagnanam, Amutheezan, *Pennsylvania State University*

T. Kim, Pauline, *Washington University in St. Louis*

Tong, Liang, *Stellar Cyber*

Vorobeychik, Yevgeniy, *Washington University in St. Louis*

Wilbur, Michael, *Vanderbilt University*

Wilder, Bryan, *Carnegie Mellon University*

Yadav, Amulya, *Pennsylvania State University*

Yao, Zhenjie, *Chinese Academy of Sciences*

Yenmez, M. Bumin, *Washington University in St. Louis*

1

Introduction

Ayan Mukhopadhyay[1] and Yevgeniy Vorobeychik[2]

[1]College of William & Mary
[2]Washington University in St. Louis

Abstract

In this opening chapter, we set the stage for the book by describing both the opportunities and risks that artificial intelligence (AI) presents as it becomes increasingly embedded in critical domains such as healthcare, education, transportation, energy, conservation, and security. We argue that researchers and practitioners have a dual responsibility: to push the boundaries of technical innovation while also ensuring that AI systems are deployed in ways that are transparent, fair, and accountable. We begin by explaining the book's structure. In the first half, we share case studies where AI methods—ranging from optimization and reinforcement learning to game theory and deep learning–are applied to concrete societal problems and evaluated in real-world settings. In the second half, we turn to the cross-cutting issues that surface regardless of domain, including questions of privacy, fairness, security, and governance. By weaving together technical depth and social reflection, our goal is to offer both a resource for practitioners who want to understand how AI can be effectively applied to social good and a guide for scholars and policymakers interested in the ethical and institutional frameworks needed to support responsible use.

1.1 The Purpose of this Book

Over the past two decades, artificial intelligence (AI) has profoundly transformed human lives, from reshaping industries to changing our daily activities. In healthcare, AI has revolutionized diagnostics and treatment personalization, enabling early detection of diseases through advanced imaging analysis,

DOI: 10.1201/9788743812074-1

predictive modeling, and analysis of electronic health records [Barragán-Montero et al. 2021, Mehrabi et al. 2015]. For instance, AI algorithms can analyze medical images to identify signs of health conditions (e.g., tumors) with remarkable accuracy, often surpassing human capabilities. AI has also been widely used to improve access to healthcare, e.g., by improving emergency response [Mukhopadhyay et al. 2022] and designing interventions that improve health outcomes in resource-constrained geographies [Bastani et al. 2021, Kehinde et al. 2024, Nair et al. 2022, Verma et al. 2023]. In shaping urban lives, data-driven algorithmic approaches and AI have been widely used in designing smart transportation systems [Alonso-Mora et al. 2017, Li et al. 2021b, Pavia et al. 2024], improving outcomes in social choice problems (e.g., matching students to public schools and medical residents to universities) [Reny 2022], and leveraging social networks for raising public awareness [Yadav et al. 2017c].

AI has also fundamentally reshaped how we lead our personal lives and interact with data-driven technologies. AI-powered virtual assistants such as Siri and Alexa have become ubiquitous, managing tasks ranging from setting reminders to controlling smart home devices, thereby making daily tasks more convenient and personalized. Recommendation algorithms employed by platforms like Netflix and Amazon enhance user experiences by curating content and products tailored to individual preferences. Smartwatches, capable of an extremely large spectrum of applications from monitoring health to facilitating virtual meetings, use recent advances in both the software and hardware industries for AI-based technologies. This pervasive and widespread use of AI has transformed health and medicine, modes of travel, marketplaces, finance and trading, social interactions, and security services. The field of AI is projected to generate more than $300 billion in revenue by 2026, amounting to a forty-fold increase in merely a decade. Leading scientists have referred to AI as the new electricity, with the ability to transform every existing industry and spawn new ones.

The AI research community, in collaboration with experts from other domains, has also used the power of data to address complex societal problems. Indeed, in the last few decades, AI has been used to support the conservation of endangered species, aid drug discovery, improve medical imaging, support emergency and disaster response, design markets for organ exchange, and address homelessness, among other applications. In a comprehensive survey of papers published at top-tier peer-reviewed AI conferences over the last decade, Shi et al. [Shi et al. 2020b] reported that more than 1,000 publications addressed "AI for social good." Indeed, *AI for social good* (AISG) or *AI for societal impact* has emerged as a sub-discipline of AI that studies techniques, algorithms, and mathematical modeling used to tackle complex societal problems using AI and address challenges that AI can pose to society. The sub-discipline has grown rapidly in the last few years and has attracted computer scientists, social scientists, statisticians, policy experts, and government and nonprofit organizations. Leading conferences like the International Conference on Learning Representations (ICLR), Association for the Advancement of Artificial Intelligence Conference (AAAI), Neural Information Processing Systems Conference (NeurIPS), International Joint Conference on Artificial Intelligence (IJCAI), and International Conference on Autonomous Agents and Multiagent Systems (AAMAS) have had special tracks or workshops specifically dedicated to applications of AI that benefit society. In a parallel thrust of exploring the field of AI for society, large technology companies, such as Google and Microsoft, have created dedicated programs and teams that exclusively work on such problems.

This widespread use of AI raises critical concerns about privacy, security, and fairness. AI systems typically learn from vast amounts of data, often including personal user data, posing risks of unauthorized access and misuse. High-profile data breaches and the pervasive collection of user information without explicit consent underscore the potential for privacy violations. The potential risk to user privacy is nuanced — private information can often be reconstructed even when algorithm designers anonymize data used by AI systems. Security concerns are equally pressing, as AI systems can be vulnerable to cyberattacks, which can lead to algorithmic manipulation and data theft. Fairness in AI is another significant concern, as these systems can inadvertently perpetuate and even amplify existing societal inequalities. For example, facial recognition technology has been shown to exhibit disparate performance across demographic groups [Buolamwini and Gebru 2018b]. Research on algorithmic fairness aims to characterize and, where possible, mitigate such bias in the performance of AI tools.

The goal of this edited volume is to summarize the technical and applied contributions made in this field of AI for social good. Given the plethora of work in this domain, it is futile to attempt to summarize all technical components of AI that have contributed to social impact or provide case studies of successful deployments of AI in the field. Instead, we focus on key *verticals*, i.e., application areas, such as urban planning, transportation, health, and conservation, and key *horizontals*, i.e., technical areas, such as combinatorial optimization, deep learning, adversarial machine learning, and decision-theoretic approaches to resource allocation. We collate contributions from leading researchers in AI whose work has not only advanced the algorithmic state-of-the-art in AI but also made significant contributions to society.

The book is divided into two major parts. The first part describes fundamental technical concepts and their applications related to specific application areas (e.g., health, transportation, and others). The second part deals with cross-cutting challenges that exist across all application areas of AI (e.g., privacy and security). Our list of authors includes instructors who have already designed undergraduate and graduate-level courses on AI for social impact and have extensive experience in designing teaching material on this topic. The proposed collection of essays will be suitable for senior undergraduate as well as graduate-level courses. We envision each chapter to be a tutorial that explains relevant technical material and describes case studies and applications from the field.

Part I

Fundamental Concepts and Applications

2

Applications of AI for Social Impact

Ayan Mukhopadhyay[1] and Yevgeniy Vorobeychik[2]

[1]College of William & Mary
[2]Washington University in St. Louis

Abstract

In this chapter, we set the stage for the first part of this book, which focuses on how AI methods have been applied across diverse domains of social importance. We introduce major areas of application, such as healthcare, conservation, transportation, and emergency response, and highlight the methodological foundations that underpin them, such as combinatorial optimization, planning, machine learning, and game theory. Each chapter focuses on an application area, provides a summary of prior work, introduces key technical problems that AI has successfully assisted in solving, and presents real-world use-cases that describe the impact of AI.

2.1 Overview of Part I

In this section of the book, we present contributed chapters and case studies focusing on positive applications of AI for social impact. Instead of presenting chapters focusing on specific theoretical or algorithmic ideas, we present chapters focusing on specific applications. Our rationale for this categorization is three-fold. First, our primary goal in this book is to discuss the societal impact of AI, and it is significantly more natural to discuss (from the writer's perspective) and understand (from the reader's perspective) impact based on application areas than on specific theoretical concepts. Second, excellent textbooks already exist that discuss AI concepts based on theoretical and algorithmic categorizations. Third, the categorization based on application areas naturally entails a coarse categorization based on theoretical concepts.

DOI: 10.1201/9788743812074-3

While this categorization means that some of the key algorithmic ideas might be repeated throughout the chapters, e.g., applications of combinatorial optimization are discussed in transportation (i.e., Chapter 3) as well as in emergency response (i.e., Chapter 7), this categorization will help the reader understand how the exact modeling and algorithmic paradigms have impacted different application areas.

Specifically, this section of the book will discuss applications of AI in transportation, network analysis for AI-augmented Intervention for HIV prevention, the design of matching markets for school admissions, emergency response, smart healthcare, computational game theory for security, and the design of green security games to combat wildlife poaching. While these application areas have seen widespread and impactful use of AI in the last decades, this list is certainly not exhaustive. Our choice of application areas combines the scale of impact (and potential impact in the future) and the lack of detailed discussion about these areas in other edited volumes on AI for social impact. For example, AI has profoundly affected healthcare screening, agriculture, combating climate change, and autonomous driving, among other areas. However, these topics have been extensively discussed [Kaack et al. 2022, Tambe et al. 2023, Yu et al. 2018]. On the other hand, the topics we choose have seen significant positive impacts due to AI but have not been discussed extensively in the "AI for social impact" community.

We will begin this section by discussing how AI has been used to solve the many complex challenges of affordable public transportation. Public transit is critical to social and economic development, and more than 7000 transit agencies serve 60 billion passenger miles each year in the USA. Optimizing transit services is a complex problem, and in Chapter 3, Wilbur et al. discuss how algorithms for solving complex combinatorial optimization and planning problems have helped make public transit more efficient. Then, we continue to explore how AI can be used in urban settings, albeit in a very different context. Then, in Chapter 4, we will stay with a related theme with Liu et al. discussing how principled decision-making under uncertainty can aid in the management of sustainable energy, particularly in the context of electric vehicles. In Chapter 5, Wilder and Yadav discuss how maximizing influence in social networks of people can be used for HIV prevention among homeless youth. While HIV is a major health challenge in general, its prevalence is particularly high among the 4.2 million homeless youth in the USA. Specifically, we will explore how robust optimization techniques can influence youth towards increasing adoption of behaviors protective against HIV spread. Then, in Chapter 6, Lee et al. discuss algorithms for matching market design, which has extensive applications in facilitating public school choices, housing allocation, and specialty matches in the military.

Having looked at influence maximization and matching markets, we will move to a critical piece of infrastructure that links people with essential emergency services, i.e., emergency response by first responders. First responders must respond to various incidents, such as fires, traffic accidents, and medical emergencies, and they must respond quickly to incidents to minimize the risk to human life. This procedure can be improved through data-driven planning, where resources are stationed and dispatched in anticipation of future incidents. Mukhopadhyay discusses how AI-based approaches can improve emergency response in Chapter 7. We will then discuss what is perhaps the most direct use of AI in healthcare, i.e., in disease screening for patients. Deep learning has been particularly useful in this context, and in Chapter 8, Chen et al. discuss how it can be successfully used for liver disease screening.

We end the next section with two applications of computational game theory for security. In Chapter 9, Vorobeychik discusses the fundamentals of computational game theory for security, which has applications in designing security infrastructure for a wide array of practical problems, ranging from airport security to wildlife protection. Wildlife protection is a particularly interesting use case for this class of algorithms since the global scale of the problem is daunting and traditional computational approaches are computationally prohibitive. This topic is explored in Chapter 10, where Shen et al. discuss a specific application of computational game theory in designing patrol strategies for combating illegal poaching of wildlife.

Each chapter consists of a background on the relevant technical material as well as the social challenge that it addresses. We intend these chapters to be tutorial-type essays. Naturally, the use of AI in each of these application areas has seen extensive prior work, and we only cover a portion of it. Each chapter also consists of a list of related work, which we encourage the reader to explore to gain a deeper understanding of prior theoretical, algorithmic, and applied research in the area.

3

AI for Smart Transportation

Michael Wilbur[1], Amutheezan Sivagnanam[2], Afiya Ayman[2], Samitha Samaranayake[3], Abhishek Dubey[1], and Aron Laszka[2]

[1]Vanderbilt University
[2]Pennsylvania State University
[3]Cornell University

Abstract

Public transportation systems worldwide face persistent challenges of efficiency, reliability, and sustainability. In this chapter, we explore how AI-powered approaches can reimagine transportation planning and operations, with particular emphasis on optimization and learning-based methods. We discuss predictive demand modeling, vehicle routing, and multimodal integration, illustrated through case studies on on-demand paratransit services, energy-efficient vehicle assignment, and microtransit operations. These examples demonstrate how AI can lower operational costs, improve system performance, and reduce emissions while managing the trade-offs between efficiency and service coverage. By highlighting the role of AI in advancing both operational effectiveness and energy sustainability, the chapter positions transportation as a critical testbed for understanding how AI can deliver practical improvements in large, complex infrastructure systems.

3.1 Introduction

There are more than 7,000 public transit agencies in the U.S. (and many more private agencies), and together, they are responsible for serving 60 billion passenger miles each year. Additionally, new on-demand modalities including ride-share, bike-share, and e-scooters have been introduced in recent years and transformed the transportation landscape in urban environments.

DOI: 10.1201/9788743812074-4

A well-functioning transit system fosters the growth and expansion of businesses, distributes social and economic benefits, and links the capabilities of community members, thereby enhancing what they can accomplish as a society [Beyazit 2011, Federal Highway Administration 2003, Harvey 2010]. However, the explosion in transportation options and the complicated relationship between public and private offerings present myriad new challenges in the design and operation of these systems. There are also complex, and often competing, operational objectives that complicate the implementation of efficient services. Since affordable public transit services are the backbones of many communities, solving these problems and understanding state-of-the-art methods for AI-driven smart transportation has the potential to strengthen urban communities, address the climate challenge, and foster equitable growth.

Fundamentally, the design of a well-functioning transit system requires solving complex combinatorial optimization problems related to planning and real-time operations. These problems span many well studied fields, from classical line planning to offline and online vehicle routing problems (VRPs). While there are many ways to assess the performance of smart transportation systems, we largely focus on evaluating these systems in the context of optimizing *utilization* (i.e. ridership) and *efficiency* (i.e. reducing operational costs). Increasing utilization requires learning mobility patterns over wide geographical areas and adapting systems to better meet the demand for mobility. It also requires flexible mobility options such as on-demand and multi-modal transportation to adapt to demand in real-time and thus better serve potential passengers. Additionally, more efficient systems alleviate the impact on the environment by reducing emissions and can free resources by reducing costs. Lastly, *coverage* is an important consideration that often competes with utilization and efficiency. Therefore it is important to discuss optimization in the context of *ridership* versus *coverage*, the latter of which is an important consideration in the design of equitable and fair transportation. While the problem of ridership versus coverage is open-ended, there are ways in which these dimensions can be modelled such that transit agencies can better optimize over the objectives that matter most to them.

Efficient transportation systems require making decisions in real-time over large geographical areas and computationally intractable state-action spaces. Due to the intractability of these problems, traditional analytical methods fall short. Therefore, transit agencies have turned to computational approaches that enable large-scale data-driven optimization. AI-driven transportation can address this problem by learning complex abstractions of vast volumes of data to make decisions in a computationally efficient manner at scale and in real-time. However, it requires solving complex challenges in model representation, decision-making under uncertainty, as well as data ingestion and processing.

Since smart transportation is a broad field, we primarily focus on two high-impact modalities: fixed-line and on-demand transportation systems. Fixed-line transportation utilizes vehicles (bus or rail) that traverse predefined routes over the course of a day following fixed schedules. On-demand transportation is a flexible service in which users request rides either in real-time or ahead-of-time, and transportation is provided from origin to destination through ride-share, e-scooters, or bike-share. Additionally, many transit agencies have recently investigated the potential of multi-modal transportation, which provides a more flexible and adaptive transportation model that combines fixed-line and on-demand transportation.

This chapter discusses the primary requirements, objectives, and challenges related to the design of AI-driven smart transportation systems. The major content involves the following:

1. Data sources and data management for AI-driven transportation.
2. An overview of how AI can aid decision-making with a focus on transportation.
3. Computational problems in the transportation domain and AI approaches.

3.2 Context

Large-scale adoption of smart phones and sensing technologies have revolutionized urban mobility in recent years. Led by companies such as Uber, Lyft and Via, new on-demand transportation options such as ride-share, e-scooters, and bike-share have been introduced to complement existing transportation services provided by public transit agencies. As the mobility landscape evolves, public transit agencies are tasked with managing ever more complex systems. To understand the relationship between transportation modalities, we can classify these systems as *on-demand*, *fixed-line*, and *multi-modal* as shown in Figure 3.1.

On-demand transportation provides direct service from origin to destination. These systems are often accessed through a smart-phone application or by calling an agency to schedule trips. Ride-share companies such as Uber and Lyft provide their own smart-phone applications for users to request rides in real-time. Microtransit and paratransit provide similar services but are distinguished by the use of high-capacity vehicles. In these systems, passengers

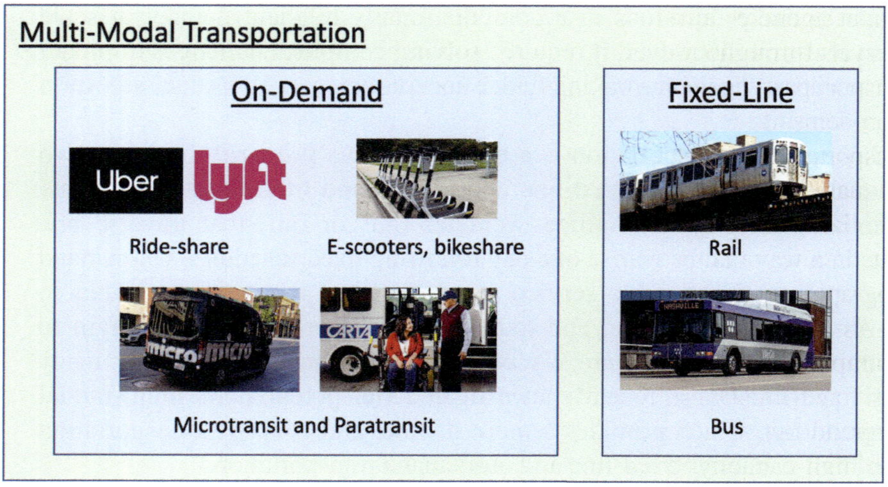

Figure 3.1 Transportation modalities: there is a variety of mobility options in today's urban environments, provided by both public transit agencies and private mobility providers, which can be classified as *on-demand* or *fixed-line*. On-demand transportation provides direct service and is often accessed through a smart-phone application. Fixed-line transportation utilizes mass transit vehicles that service fixed routes and schedules. Multi-modal transportation is a broad categorization that includes any service that combines multiple modes of transit to serve passengers.

typically share rides with several other users, and trip requests can be placed ahead-of-time (for example, a trip can be requested for later in the week at a specific time) or in real-time in the same way as ride-share. These services can be provided by private mobility providers or be managed by a public transit agency. From a city's perspective, microtransit services are available to all residents and can be thought of as a low-cost extension of their public transit system. They can be used for direct point-to-point travel as well as in hybrid transit systems, where the vehicles shuttle passengers to and from fixed-line transit [Salazar et al. 2018]. Similarly, paratransit provides curb-to-curb service for passengers who are unable to use fixed-route transit (e.g. passengers with disabilities) and is often considered a social good or required by law.

Fixed-line transportation is the backbone of urban mobility across many urban centers. These services are provided by public transit agencies and consist of large, mass-transit vehicles such as buses or rail-cars that service fixed routes and schedules. A fixed route is a pre-defined sequence of locations that a vehicle will traverse with a scheduled arrival time at each location.

Transit agencies aim to provide service at each stop at relatively frequent intervals throughout the day. Fixed-line services have high capacity and can transport passengers in a way that is more environmentally friendly compared to on-demand services or personal vehicles. However, in many cities fixed-line transportation struggles to attract a critical mass of passengers while providing adequate coverage to all areas of the city [Wilbur et al. 2020]. Therefore, optimizing these systems is important for increasing ridership and reducing costs in a way that properly serves the needs of passengers spread over wide geographical areas.

As a response to these challenges, public transit agencies have begun revamping their operations in a way that integrates on-demand services with fixed-line transit to provide dynamic coverage in areas where demand is spread out spatio-temporally, making it inefficient to serve these areas with high-capacity, fixed-line services. We can refer to this as *multi-modal* transportation. There are many open challenges to implementing multi-modal transportation systems that are outside the scope of this work. Instead, we focus on optimization methods for on-demand and fixed-line services. *Optimization in this context aims to improve ridership and efficiency while providing adequate service to residents across socio-economic groups.* By optimizing these services, we can better understand how these systems can be integrated more effectively. The most promising way to optimize transportation services is through data collection and analysis. Data enables transit agencies to improve their understanding of their systems to better inform decision-making as well as leverage recent advances in AI to optimize their services, which is the focus of this work.

3.3 Background

Effective solutions are of critical importance in that poorly designed mobility applications can make for unhappy users, increase costs, and in the case of safety critical applications, can affect the livelihood of residents that depend on the system. The goal of these systems is to learn models from data that can aid optimization and support more efficient mobility options. AI-driven smart transportation systems therefore require integrating *data*, *learning*, and *optimization* as shown in Figure 3.2. Each one of these components presents unique challenges that must be addressed when designing smart transportation systems. In this section, we summarize each of these components and how they can be combined to create smart transportation applications.

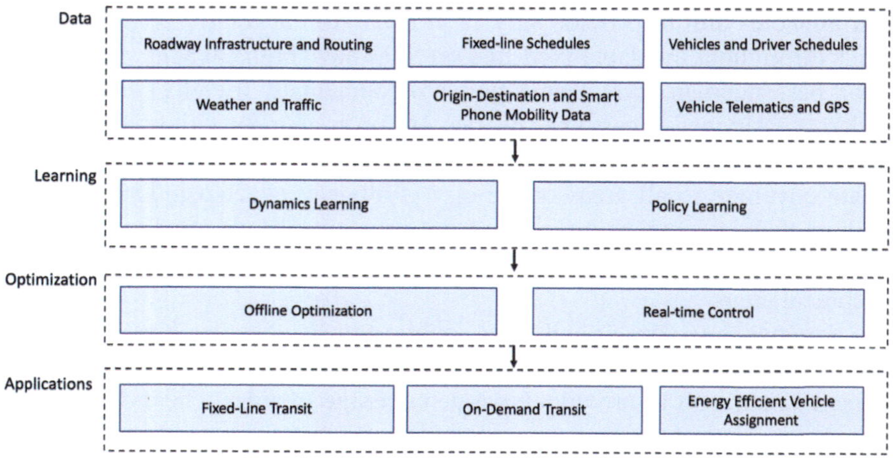

Figure 3.2 AI-driven smart transportation requires integrating data, learning, and optimization to provide smart transportation services and applications for transit agencies and users. These applications aim to optimize *utilization* (i.e. increase ridership) and *efficiency* (i.e. reduce operational costs and emissions).

3.3.1 Data Sources and Sensing

The "data" component refers to the need for high-quality data sources that can be used to generate datasets for training predictive models and to generate data online for real-time applications. In the transportation domain, this data is mostly streamed from various sensors and is spatio-temporal in nature. Therefore, sensor data typically includes a timestamp indicating when the reading was taken, the value of the reading, as well as a spatial component representing where this sensor is located. Sensors can be statically located along roadways or can be dynamic in that they travel over time, e.g. GPS receiver within a vehicle or bus. The spatio-temporal nature of these data sources presents challenges in efficient storage, synthesis, and data retrieval [Aydin et al. 2016, Wang et al. 2019, Wilbur et al. 2021b]. Synthesis requires processing data in a variety of domain-specific formats and at irregular intervals. Raw sensor streams must often be enriched by joining them with infrastructure data, such as the identifier of the road along which a vehicle is travelling.

Data sources can be classified as static or real-time. Static data are datasets related to the road networks, GIS layout, and schedules for the operating regions, while real-time data consists of data streaming from sensors and collected during real-time operations. In this sense, the static data is not fully "static." For instance, both roadway information and fixed-line schedules can change over time. However, the static data in this context is not required to be updated daily in the way that real-time data is. The most common forms of static data used for building smart transportation systems include the following:

- *Roadway Infrastructure and Routing Graphs:* Transportation models require a way to represent the roadway network. A commonly used roadway network data source is OpenStreetMap (OSM). OSM is community-driven and open-source with updates provided by the OSM community with a wide geographic footprint [Haklay and Weber 2008]. Data can be directly downloaded from various mirrors [Topf and Ramm 2020] and is used as the mapping data for a variety of commercial-grade applications. OSM in its raw form consists of *nodes*, which are points with a geographic position (latitude, longitude); *ways*, which are ordered lists of nodes representing linear features such as streets; and *relations*, which define relationships between nodes and ways. Together, these features represent a graph that can be used for mapping or routing. There are numerous open-source projects that provide routing services such as shortest path calculation and travel time estimation using OSM data, including the Open Source Routing Machine (OSRM), OpenTripPlanner, and Valhalla [MapZen 2023, Project-OSRM 2022].
- *Transit Schedules:* The most widely used schema for representing fixed-line routes and schedules is the General Transit Feed Specification (GTFS) [Google 2022b]. GTFS describes a standard format for public transportation schedules and associated geographic information. This includes standard representations for routes, trips, stops, and scheduled arrival times at each stop for buses and subway networks. It also includes geo-spatial shape objects representing routes so that fixed-line transit can be mapped to the operating region. Public transit agencies maintain and publish their own schedules in GTFS format for public consumption. In this way, developers and researchers can write code that consumes GTFS data in an interoperable way that can work across transit agencies and regions, provided that the transit agencies maintain GTFS-compliant data sources.
- *On-Demand Driver Runs:* Some forms of on-demand transportation, particularly those managed directly by public transit agencies, may include scheduling information for vehicles and drivers. For instance, in

the case of micro-transit and para-transit, a transit agency maintains a list of available drivers for a day and the start and end times of their runs. It may also maintain the list of available vehicles including the capacity of each vehicle and which driver-run corresponds to each available vehicle. This contrasts with many commercial ride-share services, such as Uber or Lyft, where there are no fixed schedules for drivers.

Advances in sensing technologies have led to an explosion of real-time streaming data in urban environments. These sensors allow us to monitor transportation systems in real-time and act as a bridge between the physical and cyber domains. They allow us to quantify and monitor the system through data. Real-time data then serves two purposes. First, we can collect sensor data over a time range to generate offline datasets. These offline datasets are joined with the static data and are used to train AI models. Second, the learned models then ingest the sensor data at inference time to make predictions and aid decision-making processes.

The data itself comes in a variety of formats and is typically defined as high-velocity and high-volume. Therefore, the problem of ingesting, processing, storing, and interpreting real-time sensor data in the transportation domain inherits the traditional problems associated with Internet of Things (IoT) analytics [Mohammadi et al. 2018]. Commonly used real-time data sources in the transportation domain are as follows.

- *Vehicle Telematics and GPS:* Vehicle telematics typically consist of physical sensing kits installed in vehicles. These devices can record vehicle dynamics such as speed, acceleration, and tractive or brake torque of a vehicle or flow of vehicles [Chen et al. 2021]. They can also record power consumption and generation which can vary between types of vehicles (e.g. electric, diesel, and hybrid vehicles). AI-driven smart transportation relies heavily on vehicle positioning and trajectory tracking using GPS. GPS readings are streamed in real-time either through GPS-specific devices installed in the vehicle or through mobile applications on smart phones and tablets. In addition to monitoring vehicle locations, GPS trajectories can also be tracked for transit users through user-defined smart-phone applications.
- *Origin-Destination and Smart-Phone Data:* Many optimization applications for smart transportation require origin-destination (OD) datasets which encompass trips for users throughout the day. At a minimum, OD data requires an origin location (where the user originates) and a destination location (where the user ends) for each trip. Optionally

these locations can be timestamped in a way that represents when the user started and or ended the trip. Historical data may also include trajectories which represent geo-points along the trip for the transit user. One publically available source of OD-data is the Longitudinal Employer-Household Dynamics (LEHD) Origin-Destination Employment Statistics (LODES), which is provided by the United States Census Bureau [Bureau 2023]. LODES data includes information related to census groups and tracts where residents live and work, which can be used to investigate demographics and trips between spatial regions within a city or state. There are also commercially available datasets derived from anonymized smart-phone GPS data, which can aid OD generation by provided traffic related to points-of-interest (POIs) [SafeGraph 2023].

- *GTFS Realtime:* GTFS is an open data format used by many transit agencies to represent public transportation schedules and associated geographic information. GTFS Realtime is an extension to the static GTFS schedules that provides up-to-date information about current arrival times, vehicle locations, occupancy, and service alerts to help users better plan their trips [Google 2022a]. The structured nature of GTFS Realtime makes it easy to monitor fixed-line public transit performance in the context of the transit schedules and routes. GTFS Realtime has been incorporated into a variety of commercial-grade applications including Google Maps. GTFS Realtime is typically provided by transit agencies themselves. Compared to raw GPS data, GTFS Realtime is a structured format that is interoperable between agencies and telematics kit providers.
- *Weather:* Weather conditions can have a significant impact on transportation systems including on energy usage and travel delays [Wilbur et al. 2021a]. Raw weather data can be accessed for weather stations throughout the United States from the National Oceanic and Atmospheric Administration (NOAA). Common weather features include temperature, precipitation, atmospheric pressure, wind speed, and wind direction. Various APIs, such as Meteostat [Meteostat 2020], provide easy access to historical as well as real-time NOAA weather data for simple integration into AI pipelines.
- *Traffic:* Traffic congestion and road segment speeds are important features for estimating travel time, routing, and energy prediction in smart transportation applications. Typically these datasets include real-time travel speeds or travel time along roadway segments that must be

tied in some way to the roadway infrastructure. HERE Technologies provides an API for speed recordings for segments of major roads in the form of timestamped speed recordings [Technologies 2022]. Every road segment is identified by a unique Traffic Message Channel identifier (TMC ID). Each TMC ID is also associated with a list of latitude and longitude coordinates, which describe the geometry of the road segment. Additionally, INRIX [INRIX 2022] provides TMC-level traffic information that also is mapped to OSM segments and is therefore easily integrated with OSM-based applications.

3.3.2 Optimization for Transportation

Smart transportation systems require solving computational problems that optimize various objectives, such as ridership, costs, or emissions over time. Optimization problems in this setting can be broadly classified in two categories: offline and real-time. In this section, we will discuss these two settings and the role that learning plays in solving these computationally challenging problems.

3.3.2.1 Offline optimization problems

Offline optimization problems are often solved ahead of time in a batch setting, and they are common in logistics and supply-chain optimization. For example, a package delivery company may need to assign routes to drivers to deliver items the next day. This class of problems is fundamentally combinatorial optimization. Broadly, combinatorial optimization involves finding an optimal solution from a set of feasible solutions, where the set of feasible solutions is discrete or can be reduced to a discrete set; many of these problems are NP-hard. In transportation settings, there are often strict constraints that must be satisfied. For example, in the case of package delivery, there may be certain times of day when the package must arrive at a specific location or a fixed number of vehicles that are available. Therefore, a feasible solution is a solution that satisfies all of the constraints, and an optimal solution is a feasible solution that maximizes the objective. Combinatorial optimization can be modelled as an integer linear program or mixed-integer linear program (MILP) and solved using state-of-the-art heuristic search approaches, such as branch-and-bound or branch-and-cut. While these methods are exact in that they are guaranteed to converge to optimal solutions, they unfortunately reduce to potentially enumerating all feasible solutions, which poses scalability issues.

3.3.2.2 Online optimization problems

Conversely, Online planning refers to optimization problems where decisions must be made sequentially over time. Sequential decision-making is commonly formalized as a Markov decision process (MDP) [Puterman 2014]. An MDP can be specified by a tuple $\{\mathcal{S}, \mathcal{A}, \mathcal{T}, \mathcal{R}, p(s_o)\}$:

- Set of states $\mathcal{S}$ and distribution over the starting state $p(s_0)$.
- Set of actions $\mathcal{A}$.
- Transition function $\mathcal{T} : \mathcal{S} \times \mathcal{A} \rightarrow \mathcal{S}$ takes as input the current state $s_t \in \mathcal{S}$ and an action $a_t \in \mathcal{A}$ at timestep t and returns the next state $s_{t+1} \in \mathcal{S}$.
- Reward function $\mathcal{R} : \mathcal{S} \times \mathcal{A} \times \mathcal{S} \rightarrow \mathbb{R}$.
- The policy $\pi : \mathcal{S} \rightarrow \mathcal{A}$ controls the agent's behaviour by selecting an action given the current state.

The *environment* consists of the transition function and reward function. At each timestep t the environment takes s_t, a_t and returns the next state from $\mathcal{T}(s_{t+1}|s_t, a_t)$ and a scalar reward from $\mathcal{R}(s_t, a_t)$. The objective of sequential decision-making is to select actions given a policy $\pi(a_t|s_t)$ to optimize expected cumulative reward over time.

3.3.3 Learning

The fundamental advantage of learning-based AI methods is their ability to handle high-dimensional state-space and to *learn* decision procedures/control algorithms from data rather than from models. This is advantageous in the transportation domain, where real-world state-action spaces are high-dimensional and manifest as intractable state-spaces for mathematical modeling and analysis. Therefore, we can employ state-of-the-art AI methods to learn abstract representations of these problems to tackle real-world transportation problems. In this section, we discuss two broad categories of learned models: *descriptive* models and *generative* models.

3.3.3.1 Descriptive Models

Descriptive models utilize supervised learning to learn abstract representations of the model environment and are often referred to in the AI literature as discriminative models. The models are trained with labeled data and aim to capture the conditional probability $p(Y|X)$ for input features X and output labels Y. That is, predictive models aim to learn a function $f : X \rightarrow Y$ that maps the input features to output labels. Supervised learning can be separated into two types of problems (or *tasks*): classification and regression. Classification tasks aim learn a function f that maps the input features to labels that are discrete categories. For example, given the features of a transit route and the current state-of-charge for an electric bus, we may want to predict whether the vehicle can service the route without having to re-charge. This would be a binary classification problem. On the other hand, regression tasks map the input features to a continuous label space. For example, given the features of a transit route and the current state-of-charge for an electric bus, we may simply want to predict the energy that will be used for this vehicle to service the route. There are many state-of-the-art methods for learning predictive models, including deep neural networks (DNN).

3.3.3.2 Generative Models

On the other hand, generative models are a class of statistical models that learn the distribution of the environment $P(X)$, or in tasks where labelled data is available, learn the joint probability of $P(X, Y)$. Generative models provide a condensed representation of the environment for building simulators, learning policies through reinforcement learning, or being queried at inference time to simulate future scenarios. Generative models in the transportation domain are particularly important for modelling demand. For example, we might create a generative demand model for representing the spatio-temporal distribution of trip requests for on-demand transportation, which can aid decision-making when assigning vehicles to service new requests in real-time.

3.3.4 AI-Driven Optimization

There are many ways in which we can utilize descriptive and generative models to aid optimization in the transportation domain. For example, take the high-level description of a sequential decision problem, as shown in Figure 3.3, in the context of on-demand ride-share. In on-demand ride-share, at each timestep a new batch of trip requests arrives and must be assigned to vehicles that can service these new requests. The *planning* component refers to algorithms or methods responsible for this assignment at each timestep. In this case, the *environment* refers to the transportation system itself and includes roadways, traffic congestion, weather, trip requests, etc., all of which generate data. The planner and environment interact sequentially, and as discussed in Section 3.3.2, the goal is to select actions that maximize the objective (costs, emissions, and utilization) over time.

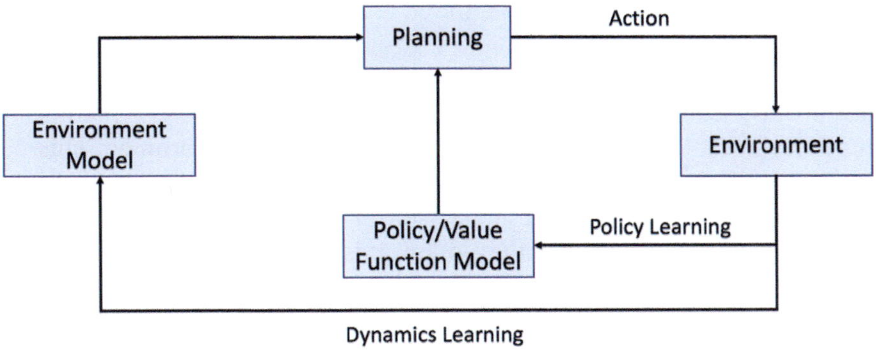

Figure 3.3 Real-time planning for transportation can be modelled as a sequential decision-making problem. Planning requires making decisions over intractably large state-action spaces in stochastic settings. Learning can aid planning by either 1) learning the dynamics of the environment or 2) directly learning or use information from a policy/value network to improve the planning procedure.

Transportation systems are computationally complex, which makes traditional analytical methods intractable in this setting. Therefore, we can utilize AI and machine learning to learn condensed representations through data to aid planning. In Figure 3.3, we highlight two ways to achieve this.

3.3.4.1 Dynamics Learning

Dynamics learning refers to directly learning representations related to the environment itself. Recall from Section 3.3.2.2 that the environment consists of the transition function $\mathcal{T}$ and reward function $\mathcal{R}$. Using these two functions, the environment takes as input the current state s_t and action a_t and returns the next state s_{t+1} and reward r_t. The goal of dynamics learning is to learn the transition function $\mathcal{T}[s_{t+1}|s_t, a_t]$ and/or the reward function $\mathcal{R}[r_t|s_t, a_t]$ through experience. For example, in the context of on-demand ride-share, we could learn a generative model of demand or a traffic congestion model. These environment models can be used to investigate how certain decisions will play out over time and contextualize decisions in light of future scenarios through *planning*. Planning in this context can be a greedy algorithm that simply selects the action with the greatest predicted reward using the reward function or use a combination of the transition and reward functions to look-ahead through online search. A common online search method in this setting is Monte Carlo tree search (MCTS), which we discuss in later sections. This combination of model-learning and planning is often referred to as model-based RL in the RL literature [Moerland et al. 2023].

3.3.4.2 Policy Learning

Alternatively, recent advances in model-free reinforcement learning aim to directly learn policies or value functions that can be embedded directly in the planning component. This can be done with or without an environmental model. For example, recall that the policy π is responsible for selecting an action given the current state with the goal of maximizing reward over time. Therefore, a policy $\mathbb{P}[a_t|s_t]$ can be parameterized and learned directly through experience or simulation. Alternatively, we can learn a value function that estimates the expected future reward from a state given a policy $v_\pi(s) = \mathbb{E}_\pi[r_{t+1} + r_{t+2} + \ldots |S_t = s]$. Model-free RL has proven effective in numerous application domains, including learning to play video games or other camera-input applications where learning a model of the environment is intractable [Arulkumaran et al. 2017]. However, as we will discuss, in the transportation domain a model of the environment can often be learned. In the following sections, we discuss concrete examples of how to combine environment models, policies, and planning to solve unique problems in the transportation domain.

In the U.S., 28% of total energy use is for transportation [EIA 2018]. While public transit services can be very energy-efficient compared to personal vehicles, their environmental impact is significant nonetheless. For example, bus transit services in the U.S. may be responsible for up to 21.1 million metric tons of CO_2 [EPA 2020] emission every year.

Electric vehicles (EVs) can have much lower operating costs and lower environmental impact during operation than comparable internal combustion engine vehicles (ICEVs), especially in urban areas. Unfortunately, EVs are also much more expensive than ICEVs: typically, diesel transit buses cost less than \$500K, while electric ones cost more than \$700K, or close to around \$1M with charging infrastructure. As a result, many public transit agencies can afford only mixed fleets of transit vehicles, which may consist of EVs, hybrid vehicles (HEVs), and ICEVs.

Public transit agencies that operate such mixed fleets of vehicles face a challenging optimization problem. First, they need to decide which vehicles are assigned to serving which transit trips. Since the advantage of EVs over ICEVs varies depending on the route and time of day (e.g., advantage of EVs is higher in slower traffic with frequent stops, and lower on highways), the assignment can have a significant impact on energy use and, hence, on costs and environmental impact. Second, transit agencies need to schedule when to charge electric vehicles because EVs have limited battery capacity and driving range, and may need to be recharged during the day between serving transit trips. Since agencies often have limited charging capabilities (e.g., limited number of charging poles, or limited maximum power to avoid high peak loads on the electric grid), charging constraints can significantly increase the complexity of the assignment and scheduling problem.

In this chapter, we present a novel problem formulation and algorithms for assigning a mixed fleet of transit vehicles to trips and for scheduling the charging of electric vehicles. We developed this problem formulation in collaboration with the Chattanooga Area Regional Transportation Authority (CARTA), the public transit agency of Chattanooga, TN, which operates a fleet of EVs, HEVs, and ICEVs. To solve the problem, we introduce an integer program as well as greedy and simulated annealing algorithms. Our problem formulation applies to a wide range of public transit agencies that operate fixed-route services. Our objective is to minimize energy consumption (i.e., fuel and electricity use), which leads to lower operating costs and environmental impact—as demonstrated by our numerical results. Our problem formulation considers assigning and scheduling for a single day (it may be applied to any number of consecutive days one-by-one), and allows any physically possible re-assignment during the day. Our formulation also allows capturing additional constraints on charging; for example, CARTA aims to charge only one vehicle at a time to avoid demand charges from the electric utility.

Our study is most closely related to the work of Cauwer et al. and of Wickramanayake and Bandara. Cauwer et al. [De Cauwer et al. 2017] use a cascade of ANN and multiple linear regression models as a data-driven energy-consumption prediction method for EVs. Their study uses vehicle monitoring data for two types of vehicles as time series of tuples with location, vehicle speed, and energy-consumption information, such as battery voltage, current, and SoC. Their dataset also includes road-network data, weather data, and an altitude map. Our approach has some similarity to this study. However, we also use traffic data in our model, which we find to be very helpful for diesel prediction. Wickramanayake and Bandara [Wickramanayake and Bandara 2016] assess three different techniques for predicting the fuel consumption of a long-distance public bus. Their time series of tuples include GPS location, bearing, elevation, distance travelled, speed, acceleration, ignition status, battery voltage, fuel level, and fuel consumption.

The authors compare the performance among two ensemble models, random forest and gradient boosting, and one ANN model. However, their study lacks critical parameters, such as road information, traffic, weather, etc.

Perrotta et al. [Perrotta et al. 2017] compare the performance of SVM, RF, and ANN in modeling fuel consumption of a large fleet of trucks. Their features include gross vehicle weight, speed, acceleration, geographical position, torque percentage, revolutions of the engine, activation of cruise control, use of brakes and acceleration pedal, measurement of travelled distance, fuel consumption. The study also integrates some road characteristics. Based on comparison of the RMSE, MAE, and R^2 scores of the prediction, RF gives the best performance. Nageshrao et al. [Nageshrao et al. 2017] model the energy consumption of electric buses based on time-dependent factors such as ambient temperature and speed, battery capacity, total mass, battery parameters, etc. They use a NARX based ANN time series predictor to predict the state of charge of the battery. Gao et al. [Gao et al. 2018] discuss an adaptive wavelet neural network (WNN) based energy prediction. Their study uses features such as day type, temperature, rainfall, the travelled distance, and clarity of the atmosphere. The study groups the trip days based on similar attributes, using Grey Relational Analysis (GRA) and then implements the Adaptive WNN.

There also exist prior efforts to utilize spatial and temporal data to model the energy consumption of bus transit networks and to estimate costs. Wang et al. [Wang et al. 2018a] collect GPS records of vehicle position and vehicle status and GPS location details of bus stops and bus transaction data of passenger fares. Wang et al. [Wang et al. 2017] and Hassold et al. [Hassold and Ceder 2014] obtain historical transaction data. Li et al. [Li et al. 2019], Paul et al. [Paul and Yamada 2014] and Li et al. [Li 2014] gather the distance of each trip in the bus transit network schedule. Santos et al. [Santos et al. 2016] and Zhou et al. [Zhou et al. 2020] make use of publicly available resources, which provide details of average energy costs per unit of energy, emission rate per unit of energy consumption, and consumption rates per unit distance. In contrast to previous efforts, we collect traffic, elevation and weather data in addition to vehicle position and vehicle status data.

3.4 Computational Problems and AI Approaches

In this section, we discuss some key computational problems in which AI has been used in recent work related to transportation.

3.4.1 On-demand Paratransit and Microtransit

Advances in sensing and smart phone adoption have led to rapid expansion of new demand-responsive modes of transportation in recent years such as ride-share (Uber, Lyft), e-scooters, and bike-share. In the case of ride-share, users request trips through a smart-phone application and a vehicle provides direct transportation to the user's requested destination. As users have increasingly utilized demand-responsive services in this way, public transportation agencies are looking for ways to make their own transportation options more demand-responsive and dynamic. One way in which transit agencies can make their systems more responsive is through microtransit. Microtransit offers door-to-door service with high-capacity vehicles. Similarly, paratransit service is a socially beneficial curb-to-curb transportation service provided by public transit agencies for passengers who are unable to use fixed-route transit (e.g. passengers with disabilities). Paratransit is often required by law and comes with its own unique set of design challenges.

Both paratransit and microtransit are forms of ride-pooling, which can be defined as a direct transportation service that allows trips to be pooled together in a way that users can share rides with other passengers. By allowing passengers to share trips, ride-pooling has the potential to overcome inefficiencies with traditional ride-share—particularly by reducing vehicle miles travelled (VMT) [Séjourné et al. 2018, Sivagnanam et al. 2022]. However, the design and implementation of ride-pooling systems has numerous challenges. First, the problem is computationally complex and involves solving complex allocation problems in real time. Second, the environment is highly uncertain and dynamic in that traffic, weather, and the distribution of requests can change rapidly over time.

Ride-pooling is a dynamic version of the vehicle routing problem (DVRP) with stochastic trip requests. In this setting, some customer requests may be known at the time of planning while others are unknown, and some stochastic information may be available about potential future requests. When a new trip request or batch of trip requests arrive, these requests must be assigned to vehicles that can serve these requests without violating the VRP constraints. Both microtransit and paratransit include standard constraints, such as that pickups must occur before dropoffs, and each passenger can be served by only one vehicle. Since paratransit primarily focuses on serving passengers with disabilities, paratransit services operate under the Americans with Disabilities Act (ADA), which enforces time windows as a hard constraint, unlike on-demand microtransit services, thereby requiring strict adherence to such constraints which must be taken into account.

There are many highly efficient myopic solutions available for the ride-pooling problem. State-of-the-art myopic assignment utilizes shareability graphs to generate a large number of feasible solutions and then batch assigns requests to vehicles through an integer linear program (ILP) [Alonso-Mora et al. 2017]. These methods are highly efficient and can solve the assignment problem to near-optimality at each decision-epoch, but since they do not take into account future information, they may not be optimal when evaluated over the course of a full day. However, the availability of stochastic information and environment models presents an opportunity to utilize AI to learn more non-myopic solutions that can make decisions in the context of expected future demand and environment conditions. There are two primary methods for designing non-myopic solutions to the DVRP. First, we can utilize historical trip requests and demand to build a simulator that can be used to train a value function that encodes the value of a future state in the context of expected reward over the entire day [Joe and Lau 2020]. This approach can be categorized as model-free reinforcement learning and is computationally efficient at run-time. However, it requires a large amount of high-quality data for the simulator and can perform poorly when real-time conditions deviate greatly from historical patterns. The second approach is to utilize dynamics learning to create a generative demand model that can be used with online search to evaluate current actions in the context of future scenarios [Wilbur et al. 2022]. This method is more adaptive to changing environment dynamics at run-time since traffic and demand models can be updated based on current conditions. However, this approach is less scalable since it requires computationally intensive online search to run at each decision epoch.

3.4.2 Prediction of Energy Usage

Transportation accounts for 28% of total energy consumption in the U.S. [EIA 2018], leading to significant environmental consequences such as urban air pollution and greenhouse gas emissions. Shifting from personal vehicles to public transit systems offers a substantial opportunity to reduce energy usage and environmental impact. However, public transit itself consumes substantial energy, with U.S. bus services alone emitting around 19.7 million metric tons of CO2 annually [Office of Transportation and Air Quality 2019]. The adoption of electric vehicles (EVs) can help decrease the environmental impact, but their higher costs result in a combination of EVs, hybrids, and internal combustion engine vehicles (ICEVs) in transit agency fleets. This creates a challenging optimization problem for transit agencies: determining which vehicles should be assigned to specific transit trips. Since the advantages of EVs over ICEVs vary depending on factors like route and time of day (e.g., EVs are more beneficial in slower traffic with frequent stops and less advantageous on highways), the assignment of vehicles can significantly affect energy use and, consequently, environmental impact. The heart of operational optimization of a transit agency lies in the challenge of precisely forecasting the electricity and fuel consumption of transit vehicles. Accurate prediction of electricity and fuel consumption for transit vehicles is difficult due to various factors like vehicle type, traffic conditions, and road characteristics. Leveraging sensor-based technologies, data analytics, and machine learning can address these challenges, allowing the development of a comprehensive framework for route-level energy prediction in public transit.

Within this subsection, we introduce an innovative framework designed for data-driven offline energy consumption prediction at the route level [Ayman et al. 2020, 2022]. Our framework is specifically tailored for mixed-vehicle transit fleets, considering diesel (ICEV), hybrid, and electric vehicles to accommodate the operational diversity of the fleet. To evaluate its efficacy, we utilize real-world data obtained from the bus fleet of a public transit authority from a midsize city in the U.S.

3.4.2.1 Data Processing Framework

Before applying machine-learning models for energy usage prediction, we must process the time series data recorded from the vehicles by cleaning it, generating samples with a fixed-dimension feature space, and incorporating data from other sources, including traffic and weather data. For each bus, the recorded data is a series of datapoints, numbered $i = 0, 1, 2 \ldots$, where each datapoint is a tuple of a timestamp TS_i, a location L_i, etc. For EVs, each datapoint i includes a battery current A_i, a battery voltage V_i, a battery state of charge ($\%$), and a charging cable status (0 or 1). For diesel and hybrid vehicles, instead of battery data, datapoint contains fuel usage in gallons. First, we filter out specific data points in our analysis to achieve our objective of predicting energy usage. First, we exclude data recorded when a bus is either waiting in the garage or undergoing charging. We also remove data points where the charging cable status indicates active charging (for electric vehicles).

In order to create labels for our supervised energy prediction model, we estimate the energy usage from the recorded vehicle data. For diesel buses, we can determine the amount of fuel consumed between two consecutive data points by calculating the change in the total fuel used. For electric buses, estimating energy usage is more intricate. The state of charge values, recorded with limited precision, can be used to approximate energy usage. However, for accurate values, we rely on estimates derived from recorded battery current (A) and voltage (V) values. Instantaneous power usage (in Watts) at any given time can be computed as the product of A and V. We estimate the energy used (in Joules), denoted as E_i, between consecutive data points ($i - 1$) and (i) using $E_i = A_i \cdot V_i \cdot (TS_i - TS_{i-1})$. Here, TS_i represents the timestamp of data point i in seconds. This formula provides highly accurate estimates since current and voltage values are recorded at least once per second. To ensure the validity of our estimates, we conducted comparisons against changes in SoC across numerous data points, confirming their unbiased nature.

One of the important steps in the data processing framework is *cleaning and mapping the GPS location to roads*. The recorded vehicle locations, based on GPS, inherently contain noise. Some locations may fall on streets or parking lots where buses cannot traverse, posing challenges for accurate distance calculations and integration with other data sources. To mitigate this noise, we combine the recorded vehicle locations (L_i) with a street-level map obtained from OpenStreetMap (OSM) [Haklay and Weber 2008]. OSM represents roads using disjoint segments known as OSM features, each with unique identifiers and properties. To align the vehicle locations with the street-level map, we employ two novel methods: a heuristic algorithm and a machine-learning approach. For mapping recorded locations (L_i) to OSM segments (road segments), we consider nearby OSM segments based on geographical distance. We create an R-tree spatial index for the street-level map and intersect it with a bounding disk around L_i. This intersection yields a set of potential road segments, which we filter based on road types suitable for buses. For the heuristic approach, we count the number of preceding and following locations near each nearby segment and select the segment with the most nearby locations. For the machine-learning approach, rather than directly outputting the correct segment from the nearby candidate segments, we estimate their likelihood using a regression model. The model incorporates variables such as distance between the location and the candidate OSM segment, road type, and distances to the set of preceding and following locations. The model outputs a value between 0 and 1, indicating the likelihood of correct mapping. We apply the regression model to each nearby candidate segment and select the one with the highest likelihood for mapping the location.

For evaluating the accuracy of different approaches for mapping noisy locations to OSM features, we first generate routes using a street-level map, selecting locations precisely on the roads, and then introduce random noise to these locations (noise is generated from a two-dimensional Gaussian

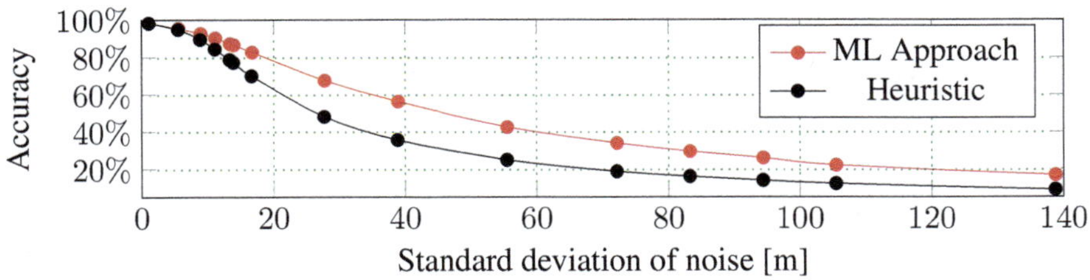

Figure 3.4 Accuracy of mapping noisy locations to road segments using heuristic and machine-learning approach. Accuracy is measured as the fraction of locations that are mapped to the correct road segment.

distribution with zero mean).[1] The standard deviation of the noise is varied from 1 meter to 140 meters in both directions. Finally, we map the noisy locations to road segments using both the heuristic and machine-learning approaches with decision tree regression. Accuracy is measured as the ratio of correctly mapped locations. In Fig. 3.4, the accuracy of both approaches is compared across different levels of noise. At the lowest noise level (1.1 meters), both the heuristic algorithm and the machine-learning approach achieve accuracy above 98%. As expected, the accuracy of both approaches decreases as the noise level increases. However, the machine-learning approach outperforms the heuristic algorithm at higher noise levels.

Once we map the location traces to road segments, we can generate samples by dividing the time series data into segments based on the traveled road segments. Each sample represents a maximal continuous travel on a specific road segment and includes the starting and end locations, starting and end times, and the sum of energy used during the travel. To accurately calculate the distance traveled for each sample, we obtain the geometry of the corresponding road segment from OSM and identify the line segments that the bus actually traveled. The distance traveled for each sample is calculated based on the partial distance on the starting line segment, the complete distance of the intermediate line segments, and the partial distance on the ending line segment.

Finally, we incorporate additional features for the prediction model. These features encompass elevation changes within the samples, weather-related attributes like temperature, humidity, visibility, precipitation, and wind speed,

[1]The synthetic location traces are solely used for evaluating the mapping approaches, as we require ground-truth segments. However, for training and evaluating energy-use prediction, we utilize real location traces obtained from vehicles.

as well as traffic data such as the speed ratio between actual speed and free-flow speed.

3.4.2.2 Prediction Models

For prediction of energy usage, we apply three different machine-learning models: artificial neural network, linear regression, and decision tree regression. The input to the energy prediction models (i.e., the training or test set) consists of samples, where each sample is a tuple of distance traveled, road-type features, elevation change, weather features, traffic features, and energy used as the target. Before training and testing, we map categorical variables (e.g., road type) to binary features via one-hot encoding. We train all three models to minimize *mean squared error* (MSE).

For our neural-network-based models, we use feed-forward deep neural networks with one input layer, multiple hidden layers, and one output layer. Sigmoid activation is used in the hidden layers, and linear activation is used in the output layer for both diesel and electric. The models are optimized with the *Adam* optimizer [Kingma and Ba 2014] and a learning rate of 0.001, implemented using Keras [Chollet et al. 2015], a high-level API of TensorFlow. We use standard multiple linear regression and decision tree regression [Scikit-learn Developers] as other prediction models. For implementing the models, we use the implementation provided by the *scikit-learn* Python library. Decision tree regression builds a tree structure based on the training samples, where each node represents a decision based on the value of a feature variable, and leaf nodes provide predictions. We opted for neural networks due to their exceptional predictive capabilities, a fact supported by our numerical findings. In comparison, linear and decision tree regression techniques do not exhibit the same level of performance, although their outcomes are more straightforward to comprehend and articulate. For instance, linear regression highlights the direct relationship between input variables and target features, providing a clear understanding of their influence.

3.4.2.3 Numerical Evaluation

Comparison of Prediction Models for Short trips

We assess the performance of three machine-learning models in predicting energy usage for short trip segments. These segments pose a challenge due to their limited distance and duration. Fig. 3.5 displays the results in terms of mean squared error (MSE) for all three models for both diesel and electric vehicles. The artificial neural network (ANN) demonstrates

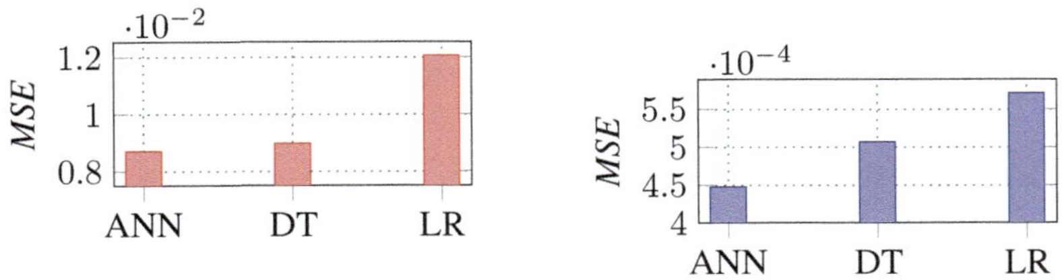

(**a**) *Electric* (**b**) *Diesel*

Figure 3.5 Comparison of different energy prediction models based on *mean squared error* (MSE) for electric and diesel vehicles.

superior performance compared to the other models, both for electric and diesel vehicles.

Comparison of Prediction Models for Longer Trips

We also examine the performance of our models in predicting energy usage for longer trips. To accomplish this, we segment our time series into extended durations, ranging from 10 minutes to 6 hours. We generate a collection of examples for each trip duration and utilize our models to predict energy consumption for each example. Subsequently, we compare the sum of these predictions with the actual energy usage recorded for the entire trip. Fig. 3.6 shows the relative prediction error for trips of various lengths. When analyzing various trip lengths, we observe that the average error values, computed across multiple trips, tend to be lower for longer trips. This is an expected outcome because with larger sample sizes, the individual errors of numerous samples cancel each other out when using an unbiased prediction model. In the case of diesel vehicles, we discover that the artificial neural network (ANN) consistently outperforms the other models across all trip lengths, exhibiting

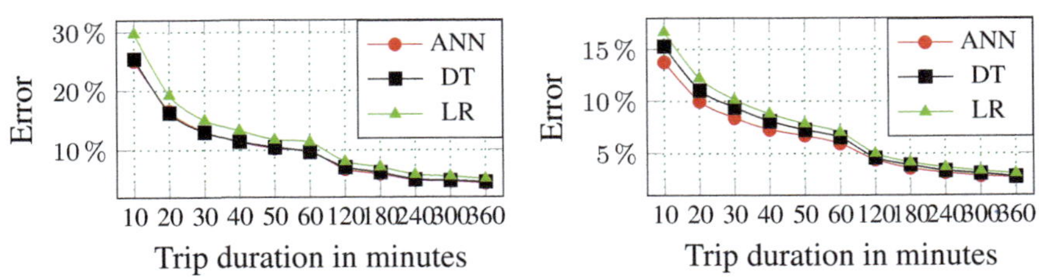

(**a**) Electric (**b**) Diesel

Figure 3.6 Energy prediction error for longer trips, consisting of many samples, with neural network (ANN), decision tree (DT), and linear regression (LR).

significant improvement. However, for electric vehicles, both the ANN and decision tree (DT) models perform equally well for the majority of trip lengths.

3.4.3 Energy-Efficient Vehicle Assignment

3.4.3.1 Problem Formulation

Vehicles

We consider a transit agency that operates a set of *buses* $\mathcal{V}$. Note that we will use the terms *bus* and *vehicle* interchangeably. Each bus $v \in \mathcal{V}$ belongs to a *vehicle model* $M_v \in \mathcal{M}$, where $\mathcal{M}$ is the set of all vehicle models in operation. We divide the set of vehicle models $\mathcal{M}$ into two disjoint subsets: liquid-fuel models $\mathcal{M}^{\text{gas}}$ (e.g., diesel, hybrid), and electric models $\mathcal{M}^{\text{elec}}$. Based on discussions with CARTA, we assume that vehicles belonging to a liquid-fuel model can operate all day without refueling. On the other hand, vehicles belonging to an electric model have limited battery capacity, which might not be enough for a whole day. For each electric vehicle model $m \in \mathcal{M}^{\text{elec}}$, we let C_m denote the *battery capacity* of vehicles of model m.

Locations

Locations $\mathcal{L}$ include bus stops, garages, and charging stations in the transit network.

Trips

During the day, the agency has to serve a given set of *transit trips* $\mathcal{T}$ using its buses. Based on discussions with CARTA, we assume that locations and time schedules are fixed for every trip. A bus serving trip $t \in \mathcal{T}$ leaves from trip origin $t^{\text{origin}} \in \mathcal{L}$ at time t^{start} and arrives at destination $t^{\text{destination}} \in \mathcal{L}$ at time t^{end}. Between t^{origin} and $t^{\text{destination}}$, the bus must pass through a series of stops at fixed times; however, since we cannot re-assign a bus during a transit trip, the locations and times of these stops are inconsequential to our model. Finally, we assume that any bus may serve any trip. Note that it would be straightforward to extend our model and algorithms to consider constraints on which buses may serve a trip (e.g., based on passenger capacity).

Charging

To charge its electric buses, the agency operates a set of *charging poles* $\mathcal{CP}$, which are typically located at bus garages or charging stations in practice. We let $cp^{\text{location}} \in \mathcal{L}$ denote the location of charging pole $cp \in \mathcal{CP}$.

For the sake of computational tractability, we use a discrete-time model to schedule charging, which divides time into uniform-length *time slots* $\mathcal{S}$. A time slot $s \in \mathcal{S}$ begins at s^{start} and ends at s^{end}. A charging pole $cp \in \mathcal{CP}$ can charge $P(cp, M_v)$ energy to one electric bus v in one time slot. We will refer to the combination of a charging pole $cp \in \mathcal{CP}$ and a time slot $s \in \mathcal{S}$ as a *charging slot* (cp, s); and we let $\mathcal{C} = \mathcal{CP} \times \mathcal{S}$ denote the set of charging slots.

Non-Service Trips

In addition to serving transit trips, buses may also need to travel between trips or to charging poles. For example, if a bus must serve a trip that departs from a location different from the destination of the previous trip, the bus must first drive to the origin of the subsequent trip. An electric bus may also need to drive to a charging pole after serving a transit trip to recharge, and then drive from the pole to the origin of the next transit trip. We will refer to these deadhead trips, which are driven outside of revenue service, as *non-service trips*. We let $T(l_1, l_2)$ denote the non-service trip from location $l_1 \in \mathcal{L}$ to $l_2 \in \mathcal{L}$; and we let $D(l_1, l_2)$ denote the time duration of this non-service trip.

3.4.3.2 Solution Space

Our primary goal is to assign a bus to each transit trip. Additionally, electric buses may also need to be assigned to charging slots to prevent them from running out of power.

Solution Representation

We represent a solution as a *set of assignments* $\mathcal{A}$. For each trip $t \in \mathcal{T}$, a solution assigns exactly one bus $v \in \mathcal{V}$ to serve trip t; this assignment is represented by the relation $\langle v, t \rangle \in \mathcal{A}$. Secondly, each electric bus v must be charged before its battery state of charge drops below the safe level for operation. A solution assigns at most one electric bus v to each charging slot $(cp, s) \in \mathcal{C}$; this assignment is represented by the relation $\langle v, (cp, s) \rangle \in \mathcal{A}$. We assume that when a bus is assigned for charging, it remains at the charging pole for the entire duration of the corresponding time slot.

Constraints

If a bus v is assigned to serve an earlier transit trip t_1 and a later trip t_2, then the duration of the non-service trip from $t_1^{\text{destination}}$ to t_2^{origin} must be less than or equal to the time between t_1^{end} and t_2^{start}. Otherwise, it would not be possible to serve t_2 on time. We formulate this constraint as:

$$\forall t_1, t_2 \in \mathcal{T};\ t_1^{\text{start}} \leq t_2^{\text{start}};\ \langle v, t_1 \rangle \in \mathcal{A};\ \langle v, t_2 \rangle \in \mathcal{A} : \\ t_1^{\text{end}} + D(t_1^{\text{destination}}, t_2^{\text{origin}}) \leq t_2^{\text{start}} \tag{3.1}$$

Note that if the constraint is satisfied by every pair of consecutive trips assigned to a bus, then it is also satisfied by every pair of non-consecutive trips assigned to the bus.

We need to formulate similar constraints for non-service trips to, from, and between charging slots:

$$\begin{aligned}
&\forall t \in \mathcal{T};\ (cp, s) \in \mathcal{C};\ t^{\text{start}} \leq s^{\text{start}};\ \langle v, t\rangle, \langle v, (cp, s)\rangle \in \mathcal{A}: \\
&\qquad t^{\text{end}} + D(t^{\text{destination}}, cp^{\text{location}}) \leq s^{\text{start}} \qquad (3.2) \\
&\forall t \in \mathcal{T};\ (cp, s) \in \mathcal{C}; t^{\text{start}} \geq s^{\text{start}};\ \langle v, t\rangle, \langle v, (cp, s)\rangle \in \mathcal{A}: \\
&\qquad s^{\text{end}} + D(cp^{\text{location}}, t^{\text{origin}}) \leq t^{\text{start}} \qquad (3.3) \\
&\forall (cp_1, s_1), (cp_2, s_2) \in \mathcal{C}; s_1^{\text{start}} \leq s_2^{\text{start}}; \langle v, (cp_1, s_1)\rangle, \langle v, (cp_2, s_2)\rangle \in \mathcal{A}: \\
&\qquad s_1^{\text{end}} + D(cp_1^{\text{location}}, cp_2^{\text{location}}) \leq s_2^{\text{start}} \qquad (3.4)
\end{aligned}$$

We also need to ensure that electric buses never run out of power. First, we let $\mathcal{N}(\mathcal{A}, v, s)$ denote the set of all non-service trips that bus v needs to complete by the end of time slot s according to the set of assignments $\mathcal{A}$. In other words, $\mathcal{N}(\mathcal{A}, v, s)$ is the set of all necessary non-service trips to the origins of transit trips that start by s^{end} and to the locations of charging slots that start by s^{end}. Next, we let $E(v, t)$ denote the amount of energy used by bus v to drive a transit or non-service trip t. Then, we let $e(\mathcal{A}, v, s)$ be the amount of energy used by bus v for all trips completed by the end of time slot s:

$$e(\mathcal{A}, v, s) = \sum_{t \in \mathcal{N}(\mathcal{A}, v, s)} E(v, t) + \sum_{t \in \mathcal{T},\ \langle v, t\rangle \in \mathcal{A},\ t^{\text{end}} \leq s^{\text{end}}} E(v, t) \qquad (3.5)$$

Similarly, we let $r(\mathcal{A}, v, s)$ be the amount of energy charged to bus v by the end of time slot s:

$$r(\mathcal{A}, v, s) = \sum_{(cp, \hat{s}) \in \mathcal{C},\ \langle v, (cp, \hat{s})\rangle \in \mathcal{A},\ \hat{s}^{\text{end}} \leq s^{\text{end}}} P(cp, M_v) \qquad (3.6)$$

Since a bus can be assigned for charging only to complete time slots, the minima and maxima of its battery level will be reached at the end of time slots. Therefore, we can express the constraint that the battery level of bus v must always remain between 0 and the battery capacity C_{M_v} as

$$\forall v \in \mathcal{V}, \forall s \in \mathcal{S}:\ 0 < r(\mathcal{A}, v, s) - e(\mathcal{A}, v, s) \leq C_{M_v}. \qquad (3.7)$$

Note that we can provide vehicles with an initial battery charge by adding "virtual" charging slots before the day begins.

3.4.3.3 Objective

Our objective is to minimize the energy use of the transit vehicles. We can use this objective to minimize both environmental impact and operating costs by applying appropriate cost factors to the energy use of liquid-fuel and electric vehicles. We let K^{gas} and K^{elec} denote the unit costs of energy use for liquid-fuel and electric vehicles, respectively. Then, by applying the earlier notation $e(\mathcal{A}, v, s)$ to all vehicles, we can express our objective as

$$\min_{\mathcal{A}} \sum_{v \in \mathcal{V}:\, M_v \in \mathcal{M}^{\text{gas}}} K^{\text{gas}} \cdot e(\mathcal{A}, v, s_\infty) + \sum_{v \in \mathcal{V}:\, M_v \in \mathcal{M}^{\text{elec}}} K^{\text{elec}} \cdot e(\mathcal{A}, v, s_\infty) \tag{3.8}$$

where s_∞ denotes the last time slot of the day.

3.4.3.4 Algorithms

Since this optimization problem is NP-hard, we first present an integer program to find optimal solutions for smaller instances. Then, we introduce efficient greedy and simulated annealing algorithms, which scale well for larger instances. Due to a lack of space, we include less important subroutines in [Sivagnanam et al. 2021].

3.4.3.5 Integer Program

Variables

Our integer program has five sets of variables. Three of them are binary to indicate assignments and non-service trips. First, $a_{v,t} = 1$ (or 0) indicates that trip t is assigned to bus v (or that it is not). Second, $a_{v,(cp,s)} = 1$ (or 0) indicates that charging slot (cp, s) is assigned to electric bus v (or not). Third, $m_{v,x_1,x_2} = 1$ (or 0) indicates that bus v takes the non-service trip between a pair x_1 and x_2 of transit trips and/or charging slots (or not). Note that for requiring non-service trips (see Eqs. (3.1) to (3.4)), we will treat transit trips and charging slots similarly since they induce analogous constraints. There are also two sets of continuous variables. First, $c_s^v \in [0, C_{M_v}]$ represents the amount of energy charged to electric bus v in time slot s. Second, $e_s^v \in [0, C_{M_v}]$ represents the battery level of electric bus v at the start of time slot s (considering energy use only for trips that have ended by that time). Due to the continuous variables, our program is a mixed-integer program.

Constraints

First, we ensure that every transit trip is served by exactly one bus:

$$\forall t \in \mathcal{T} : \sum_{v \in \mathcal{V}} a_{v,t} = 1$$

Second, we ensure that each charging slot is assigned at most one electric vehicle:

$$\forall (cp, s) \in \mathcal{C} : \sum_{\forall v \in \mathcal{V}:\ M_v \in \mathcal{M}^{\text{elec}}} a_{v,(cp,s)} \leq 1$$

Next, we ensure that Eqs. (3.1) to (3.4) are satisfied. We let $F(x_1, x_2)$ be *true* if a pair x_1, x_2 of transit trips and/or charging slots satisfies the applicable one from Eqs. (3.1) to (3.4); and let it be *false* otherwise. Then, we can express these constraints as follows:

$$\forall v \in \mathcal{V}, \forall x_1, x_2, \neg F(x_1, x_2) : a_{v,x_1} + a_{v,x_2} \leq 1$$

When a bus v is assigned to both x_1 and x_2, but it is not assigned to any other transit trips or charging slots in between (i.e., if x_1 and x_2 are consecutive assignments), then bus v needs to take a non-service trip:

$$m_{v,x_1,x_2} \geq a_{v,x_1} + a_{v,x_2} - 1 - \sum_{x \in \mathcal{T} \cup \mathcal{C}:\ x_1^{\text{start}} \leq x^{\text{start}} \leq x_2^{\text{start}}} a_{v,x}$$

Note that if x_1 ends at the same location where x_2 starts, then the non-service trip will take zero time and energy.

Finally, we ensure that the battery levels of electric buses remain between zero and capacity. First, for each slot s and electric bus v, the amount of energy charged c_s^v is subject to

$$c_s^v \leq \sum_{(cp,s) \in \mathcal{C}} a_{v,(cp,s)} \cdot P(cp, M_v).$$

Then, for the $(n+1)th$ time slot s_{n+1} and for an electric bus v, we can express variable $e_{s_{n+1}}^v$ as

$$\begin{aligned} e_{s_{n+1}}^v = e_{s_n}^v + c_{s_n}^v - & \sum_{t \in \mathcal{T}:\ s_n^{\text{start}} < t^{\text{end}} \leq s_n^{\text{end}}} a_{v,t} \cdot E(v,t) \\ - & \sum_{x_1,x_2:\ s_n^{\text{start}} < x_2^{\text{start}} \leq s_n^{\text{end}}} m_{v,x_1,x_2} \cdot E(v, T(x_1,x_2)) \end{aligned}$$

where s_n is the $(n)th$ slot. Note that since $e_s^v \in [0, C_{M_v}]$, this constraint ensures that Eq. (3.7) is satisfied.

Objective

We can express Eq. (3.8) as minimizing

$$\sum_{v \in \mathcal{V}} K^{M_v} \left[\sum_{t \in \mathcal{T}} a_{v,t} \cdot E(v,t) + \sum_{x_1, x_2 \in \mathcal{T} \cup \mathcal{C}} m_{v,x_1,x_2} \cdot E(v, T(x_1, x_2)) \right]$$

where K^{M_v} is K^{elec} if $M_v \in \mathcal{M}^{\text{elec}}$ and K^{gas} otherwise.

3.4.3.6 Greedy Algorithm

Next, we introduce a polynomial-time greedy algorithm. The key idea of this algorithm is to choose between assignments based on a *biased cost* instead of the actual cost.

Biased Energy Cost

Our greedy approach uses Algorithm 1 to compute a *biased energy cost* of assigning a bus v to a transit trip or charging slot x. If x is a transit trip (i.e., $x \in \mathcal{T}$), then the base cost of the assignment is $E(v,x)$. If x is a charging slot, then the base cost is zero. To compute the actual cost, the algorithm checks if bus v is already assigned to any earlier (or later) transit trips or charging slots. If it is, then it factors in the cost of the moving trip m_{prev} (and m_{next}) from the preceding (and to the following) assignment x_{prev} (and x_{next}). Finally, the algorithm adds a bias to the actual cost based on the waiting time between

---

Algorithm 1: BiasedCost$(\mathcal{A}, v, x, \alpha)$

---

if $x \in \mathcal{T}$ **then**
  | *cost* $\leftarrow E(v,x)$
else
  | *cost* $\leftarrow 0$
Earlier $= \left\{\hat{x} \in \mathcal{T} \cup \mathcal{C} \,\middle|\, \langle v, \hat{x}\rangle \in \mathcal{A} \wedge \hat{x}^{end} \leq x^{start}\right\}$
if *Earlier* $\neq \emptyset$ **then**
  | $x_{prev} = \text{argmax}_{\hat{x} \in \textit{Earlier}}\, \hat{x}^{end}$
  | $m_{prev} \leftarrow T\left(x_{prev}^{destination}, x^{origin}\right)$
  | *cost* $\leftarrow$ *cost* $+ E(v, m_{prev}) + \alpha \cdot \left(x^{start} - x_{prev}^{end}\right)$
Later $= \left\{\hat{x} \in \mathcal{T} \cup \mathcal{C} \,\middle|\, \langle v, \hat{x}\rangle \in \mathcal{A} \wedge x^{end} \leq \hat{x}^{start}\right\}$
if *Later* $\neq \emptyset$ **then**
  | $x_{next} = \text{argmin}_{\hat{x} \in \textit{Earlier}}\, \hat{x}^{start}$
  | $m_{next} \leftarrow T\left(x^{destination}, x_{next}^{origin}\right)$
  | *cost* $\leftarrow$ *cost* $+ E(v, m_{next}) + \alpha \cdot \left(x^{end} - x_{next}^{start}\right)$
Result: *cost*

---

x^{end}_{prev} and x^{start} (if x_{prev} exists) and between x^{end} and x^{end}_{next} (if x_{next} exists). By adding these waiting times to the cost with an appropriate factor $\alpha > 0$, we nudge the greedy selection towards increasing bus utilization and minimizing layovers.

Algorithm 2 shows our iterative greedy approach for assigning transit trips and charging slots to buses. The algorithm begins by computing the biased assignment cost for each pair of a bus v and transit trip t using **BiasedCost**$(\mathcal{A}, v, t, \alpha)$. Starting with an empty set $\mathcal{A} = \emptyset$, the algorithm then iteratively adds assignments $(v, t) \in \mathcal{V} \times \mathcal{T}$ to the set, always choosing an assignment with the lowest biased cost **BiasedCost**$(\mathcal{A}, v, t, \alpha)$ (breaking ties arbitrarily). After each iteration, the biased costs $\mathcal{E}$ for the chosen vehicle v are updated by **Update**, which also adds charging slot assignments as necessary (see [Sivagnanam et al. 2021]). The algorithm terminates once all trips are assigned (or if it fails to find a solution). The time complexity of **Update** is $\mathcal{O}(|\mathcal{T}| \cdot |\mathcal{V}| + |\mathcal{T}| \cdot |\mathcal{C}| \cdot |\mathcal{X}| \ln |\mathcal{X}|)$, where $\mathcal{X} = \mathcal{T} \cup \mathcal{C}$. Since typically $|\mathcal{T}| \gg |\mathcal{V}|$, the complexity can be simplify into $\mathcal{O}(|\mathcal{T}| \cdot |\mathcal{C}| \cdot |\mathcal{X}| \ln |\mathcal{X}|)$. Accordingly, the time complexity of the greedy algorithm is $\mathcal{O}\left(|\mathcal{T}|^2 \cdot |\mathcal{C}| \cdot |\mathcal{X}| \ln |\mathcal{X}|\right)$.

Providing affordable public transit services is crucial for communities to ensure residents carry out daily activities such as employment, education, and other services without interruption. Unfortunately, transit agencies are facing inefficiency in utilizing transit resources, which results in high operating costs and environmental impact. Further, replacing traditional internal-combustion engine vehicles (ICEVs) with electric vehicles (EVs) can reduce energy costs and environmental impact. But due to the high upfront costs of EVs, transit agencies tend to use mixed fleets of vehicles (i.e. EVs and ICEVs). To efficiently utilize the mixed fleets of vehicles, transit agencies must optimize how they assign each vehicle to serve a transit trip and ensure EVs are charged

---

Algorithm 2: Greedy$(\mathcal{V}, \mathcal{T}, \mathcal{C}, \alpha)$

$\mathcal{A} \leftarrow \emptyset$
$\mathcal{E} \leftarrow \{\langle v, t\rangle \mapsto$ **BiasedCost**$(\mathcal{A}, v, t, \alpha) \mid v \in \mathcal{V}, t \in \mathcal{T}\}$
while $|\mathcal{T}| > 0$ **and** $\min[\mathcal{E}] \neq \infty$ **do**
    MinimumCostAssignments $\leftarrow \text{argmin}(\mathcal{E})$
    $\langle v, t\rangle \leftarrow$ **first**(*MinimumCostAssignments*)
    $\mathcal{A} \leftarrow \mathcal{A} \cup \{\langle v, t\rangle\}$
    $\mathcal{T} \leftarrow \mathcal{T} \setminus \{t\}$
    $\mathcal{E}, \mathcal{A} \leftarrow$ **Update**$(\mathcal{A}, \mathcal{T}, \mathcal{C}, \mathcal{E}, v, t, \alpha)$
    ▷ update cost values $\mathcal{E}$ and and add charging slots to the assignments as necessary
Result: $\mathcal{A}$

---

in a timely manner for uninterrupted services, which is a challenging problem for transit agencies with large transit networks [Sivagnanam et al. 2021]. Because the advantage of using EVs inplace of ICEVs differs based on the route and time of the day. For example, EVs can be good at more traffic with frequent stops compared to be used on highways. Further, transit agencies have limited charging capabilities (i.e. number of charging poles, maximum power to consume at charging station to avoid high peak loads on the electric grid) which makes the problem more challenging.

3.4.3.7 Problem Formulation

We begin the mathematical formulation by defining a transit network, which includes a set of locations $\mathcal{L}$ such as bus stops, garages, and charging stations. Transit agency operates a set of *buses* $\mathcal{V}$, with the assistance of the transit network to serve the day-to-day transit services. Each bus $v \in \mathcal{V}$ belongs to a *vehicle model* $M_v \in \mathcal{M}$, and $\mathcal{M}$ is the set of all vehicle models in operation. Further, we divide vehicle models $\mathcal{M}$ into two disjoint subsets based on the energy source as liquid-fuel models $\mathcal{M}^{\text{gas}}$ (e.g. diesel, hybrid) and electric models $\mathcal{M}^{\text{elec}}$. Electric model ($m \in \mathcal{M}^{\text{elec}}$) has limited battery capacity (C_m) and may require charging during operational hours. On the other hand, liquid-fuel models can operate without refueling throughout the day. Every day the transit agencies must serve a set of *transit trips* $\mathcal{T}$ using its buses. Each trip $t \in \mathcal{T}$ starts from the origin $t^{\text{origin}} \in \mathcal{L}$ at t^{start}, then passes through a set of stops at fixed arrival and departure times, and finally reaches the destination $t^{\text{destination}} \in \mathcal{L}$ at t^{end}.

The transit agency installs a set of *charging poles* $\mathcal{CP}$ (generally at the depot) to charge electric buses. To better facilitate the operation of each charging pole $cp \in \mathcal{CP}$, the day can be divided into uniform-length disjoint *time slots* $\mathcal{S}$, where each slot $s \in \mathcal{S}$ begins at s^{start} and ends at s^{end}. We combine the set of charging poles and slots and obtain the charging slots $\mathcal{CS} = \mathcal{CP} \times \mathcal{S}$. Each electric bus ($v \in \mathcal{V} \wedge M_v \in \mathcal{M}^{\text{elec}}$) can be charged at any unassigned charging slot ($cs \in \mathcal{CS}$) at a time, as long the electric bus v can reach the charging pole without running out of charge in the battery.

In between two transit trips $x_1, x_2 \in \mathcal{T} \bigcup \mathcal{CS}$ (or between a transit trip and a charging slot, or between two charging slots for electric buses), the bus may be required to move from destination for the previous trip x_1 to the origin of the following trip x_2. Such trips can be defined as *non-service trips* since they are not directly contributing to serving passengers but are required for the operation of the buses throughout the day. Each on-service trip can be defined by $T(l_1, l_2)$ where the trips start at the location $l_1 \in \mathcal{L}$ and end at the location $l_2 \in \mathcal{L}$.

Solution

We define the solution as a set of trip assignments where each transit trip is assigned to exactly one bus $v \in \mathcal{V}$ and a set of charging assignments of the electric bus to the combination of a charging pole $cp \in \mathcal{CP}$ and specific slot $s \in \mathcal{S}$ on the charging pole.

Constraints

The solution must respect the following real-world constraints: Every bus can serve only one trip at a time; A bus can serve two trips consecutively (or an electric bus can serve a trip and assign to a charging), if the bus has enough time to move from the destination of the first trip to origin of the second trip before the start time of the second trip; Every electric bus needs to have enough energy before serving every assigned trip; Only one electric bus can be charged in particular charging pole at a particular slot; the energy charged by electric bus is capped at the maximum capacity of the battery.

Objective

In the energy-efficient vehicle assignment, we aim to reduce the energy use of transit vehicles. We express our objective as

$$\min_{\mathcal{A}} \sum_{v \in \mathcal{V}:\, M_v \in \mathcal{M}^{\text{gas}}} K^{\text{gas}} \cdot e(\mathcal{A}, v) + \sum_{v \in \mathcal{V}:\, M_v \in \mathcal{M}^{\text{elec}}} K^{\text{elec}} \cdot e(\mathcal{A}, v)$$

where $e(\mathcal{A}, v)$ be the amount of energy used by bus v for all trips completed at the end of the day and K^{gas} and K^{elec} denote the unit costs of energy used for liquid-fuel and electric vehicles

3.4.3.8 Computational Approaches

One way to solve the above problem is using an integer program (IP). Although the IP provides the optimal solution for smaller problem instances, the problem becomes computationally intractable for larger problem instances. In this sub-section, we introduce a greedy (to provide an initial solution) and simulated annealing-based metaheuristics approach that solves the larger problem instances in polynomial time.

Greedy Algorithm

In this algorithm, we follow an iterative process where we greedily choose an assignment between all possible assignments based on assigning a bus v to a transit trip or charging slot x instead of the base energy cost to serve the request. Biased cost comprises three main costs (i) base energy cost (base energy cost for charging slot is 0), (ii) the cost associated with moving the bus from the destination of the previous trip to the origin of the current trip, or vice versa, (iii) the wait time between the end of the previous trip to the beginning of the current trip or vice versa. The algorithm at the beginning computes the biased cost for the pairs of vehicles and trips. Then follows the iterative process, choosing the assignment with the lowest biased cost in each iteration. Then the algorithm updates the costs of remaining unassigned trips with respect to the vehicle used in the previous assignment. The algorithm follows the iterative process until all the requests are assigned or fail to find a solution.

Simulated Annealing Algorithm

The algorithm starts with the solution from the greedy algorithm and performs an iterative random search where the algorithm generates a random neighbor to the current solution in each iteration. Generating the random neighbor follows an iterative process where the algorithm randomly chooses the two vehicles in each iteration, splits their operational hours into two halves, and tries to swap the assignment between two vehicles. The algorithm to generate a random neighbor terminates after enough swapping iterations are performed. Since simulated annealing is an anytime algorithm, it can be configured to run until a fixed time.

3.4.3.9 Numerical Results

This section discusses the numerical results using the computational approach presented in the earlier sections. First, we obtain the GTFS, vehicles, and charging pole data from a real-transit agency (i.e. Chattanooga Area Regional Transportation Authority (CARTA)). To evaluate the algorithm's effectiveness presented earlier, we obtain real-world GTFS data from CARTA. Since routes for the non-service trips are not specified as part of GTFS, we obtain the routes using Google Directions API. Based on the GTFS data and routes obtained from Google Directions API, we compute the energy consumption for serving the transit and non-service trips using EVs and ICEVs based on the energy estimation described in the earlier Section 3.4.2. After that, we feed the energy optimization into our computational approaches and run experiments.

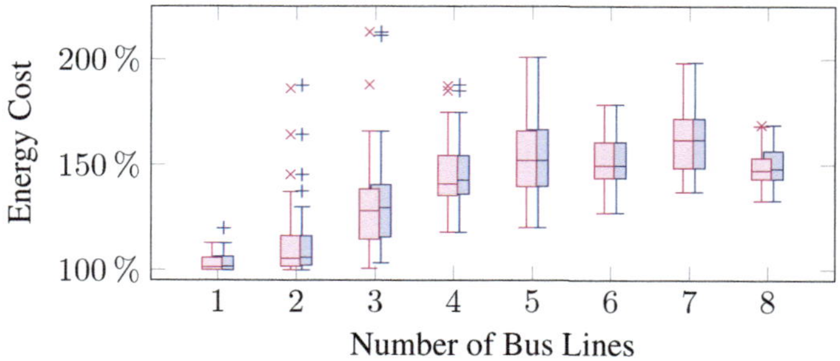

Figure 3.7 Energy cost for operating transit services based on the assignment obtained from simulated annealing and the greedy algorithm compared to optimal assignments using IP.

Solution quality

Based on the experiments on how well our heuristic and meta-heuristic minimize the energy cost compared to the Integer program, we observe that our solution approaches can restrict the solution quality to be within the range of 1.5 to 1.6, even for larger instances. For reference, you can look at the Fig. 3.7, which provides the energy cost of the solution obtained by our heuristic approaches compared to IP in percentages when serving 1-12 bus lines with exactly 10 trips using 3 EVs and ICEVs 5 times as the number of bus-lines capped at 50 ICEVs (i.e. for the scenario with 11 and 12 bus lines we only consider 50 ICEVs)

3.5 Future Considerations

Efficient transportation systems require making decisions in real-time in complex environments. Historically, public transit systems rely on human intuition and analysis to design fixed schedules ahead of time. New demand-responsive modalities such as ride-share, microtransit, and paratransit use control algorithms to match trip requests to vehicles in real-time to provide on-demand service. Next generation systems increasingly aim to leverage AI to automate and increase efficiency across modalities using data. In this chapter, we discussed methodologies for leveraging AI in transportation and provided some concrete examples of computational problems in this space.

A major consideration for transit agencies is to increase utilization of fixed-line public transit. Public transit is highly efficient in terms of energy and emissions per passenger particularly compared to private cars and ride-share. Therefore, to combat climate change it is important to continue investigating ways to increase ridership on fixed-line services. One important future consideration is the potential of multi-modal, hybrid transportation systems that combine on-demand systems with fixed-line service in a way that uses on-demand mobility to serve the first-mile-last-mile (FMLM) to and from fixed-line. These systems have the potential to combine the best parts of demand-responsive and fixed-line services in a way that increases fixed-line utilization by expanding access to more residents.

Autonomy in general has great potential to improve mobility options in urban environments. We already discussed autonomy at the system level, e.g. in the context of designing real-time ride-share and ride-pooling algorithms or optimizing trip-vehicle assignment for fixed-line. Moving forward, there is great potential for improving control systems for autonomous vehicles. At a system level, autonomous vehicles have the potential to reduce accidents as well as traffic, thereby increasing safety and efficiency [Lichtlé et al. 2022, Stern et al. 2018]. As these systems become more capable it will be important for transit agencies to adapt to solve increasingly complicated control and optimization problems that arise from operating mixed fleets that include conventional as well electric and autonomous vehicles.

Acknowledgements

The authors will like to acknowledge the collaborative efforts of Dr. Ayan Mukhopadhyay, Vanderbilt University and Mr. Philip Pugliese from Chattanooga Area Regional Transportation Authority. The work presented here has been sponsored in part by the National Science Foundation through 1952011 and Department of Energy through awards DE-EE0008467 and DE-EE0009212. Any opinions, findings, and conclusions or recommendations expressed in this material are those of the author(s) and do not necessarily reflect the views of the National Science Foundation and Department of Energy.

4

AI for Sustainable Energy Management

Fangqi Liu[1], Rishav Sen[1], Abhishek Dubey[1], and Ayan Mukhopadhyay[2]

[1]Vanderbilt University
[2] College of William & Mary

Abstract

As renewable energy sources and electric vehicles proliferate, managing energy efficiently under uncertainty has become critical. This chapter focuses on optimization challenges in electric vehicle (EV) charging and vehicle-to-building (V2B) integration, formalizing them as sequential decision-making problems under uncertainty. It introduces algorithmic frameworks, including reinforcement learning, online planning with Monte Carlo methods, and model predictive control, explaining how each can be applied to balance user preferences with system-level energy goals. The chapter also emphasizes the human and institutional dimension, discussing incentive design and negotiation protocols that encourage user participation and alignment with social objectives. By bridging technical depth with socio-economic considerations, the chapter illustrates a path toward scalable, user-centric, resilient, and efficient energy management systems.

4.1 Introduction

The rapid rise in urban energy demand, the proliferation of electric vehicles (EVs), and the volatility of electricity pricing have created a pressing challenge for building energy management: how to minimize operational costs while ensuring reliability, resilience, and sustainability [Lund et al. 2017, Ma et al. 2013, Sioshansi 2011]. Commercial and institutional buildings, in particular, face steep demand charges due to sharp peaks in electricity consumption, costs

DOI: 10.1201/9788743812074-5

that are exacerbated when energy use aligns with periods of maximum grid stress [Sundstrom and Binding 2012, Zhou et al. 2016]. At the same time, the accelerating adoption of EVs has introduced a vast, distributed network of mobile energy storage across urban environments. When equipped with bidirectional charging, these EVs can serve as both consumers and suppliers of energy, transforming buildings from passive grid users into intelligent, interactive energy hubs [Kempton and Tomić 2005, Tushar et al. 2018].

Vehicle-to-Building (V2B) systems harness this opportunity by integrating EVs with smart buildings, allowing buildings to strategically charge vehicles when electricity is inexpensive or renewable generation is abundant, and discharge stored energy back into the building during periods of high demand or price spikes [Sortomme and El-Sharkawi 2011, Tushar et al. 2018, Zhou et al. 2016]. This dynamic interaction not only flattens building load curves and reduces costly demand charges but also enhances grid stability, supports renewable energy adoption, and provides backup power during grid stress events [Sortomme and El-Sharkawi 2011, Tushar et al. 2018, Zhou et al. 2016]. The societal benefits are substantial: V2B systems can reduce carbon emissions, defer expensive grid upgrades, and bolster the resilience of critical infrastructure, especially in settings such as office complexes, campuses, and community centers where energy demand and EV presence are high [Kempton and Tomić 2005, Lund et al. 2017].

Yet, unlocking the full potential of V2B systems is far from straightforward. The optimization problem is inherently complex, requiring the coordination of numerous heterogeneous EVs and chargers, each with unique capabilities, constraints, and user preferences, over extended billing cycles [Liu et al. 2025, Ma et al. 2013, Sen et al. 2025, Sundstrom and Binding 2012]. The system must operate under multiple, interdependent sources of uncertainty: stochastic building loads driven by weather and occupancy, unpredictable EV arrivals and departures, fluctuating electricity prices, and diverse charging needs. These factors create a high-dimensional, multi-agent decision environment that traditional optimization methods—such as deterministic scheduling, linear programming, or static rule-based control—struggle to address, as they often assume perfect foresight and cannot adapt to real-time changes [Kumar et al. 2020].

Artificial Intelligence (AI) provides a powerful set of tools to address these challenges. Techniques from sequential decision-making, such as Markov decision processes (MDPs) [Puterman 1994], reinforcement learning (RL) [Sutton and Barto 2018], online planning algorithms like Monte Carlo tree search (MCTS) [Browne et al. 2012] and model predictive control [Holkar and Waghmare 2010], support principled reasoning under uncertainty, account for delayed rewards, and model complex agent interactions. These methods can integrate forecasts, learn from historical data, and adapt to changing system conditions, enabling energy decisions that are both responsive and forward-looking. In the context of Vehicle-to-Building (V2B) systems, AI can determine when and how much each vehicle should charge or discharge, while respecting individual constraints and improving collective performance.

This chapter explores the V2B optimization problem through the lens of AI for social impact. We begin in Section 4.2 by formally describing the problem and its unique challenges. Section 4.3 presents forecasting methods for predicting key sources of uncertainty in V2B scenarios, such as building load and EV behavior. In Section 4.4, we introduce advanced AI-based strategies for online EV charging decision-making under environmental uncertainty. These include learning-based approaches such as reinforcement learning (RL) and online planning methods like MCTS, along with techniques to enhance their performance, including action masking based on domain knowledge and policy guidance using mixed-integer linear programming (MILP). Section 4.5 explores the human dimension, focusing on strategies for user incentives that encourage flexibility in charging requirements to reduce the building's overall energy cost. Throughout, we draw on insights from recent research and real-world testbeds to illustrate how AI-driven V2B systems can deliver scalable, socially beneficial solutions for future urban energy management.

4.2 Problem Definition and Challenges

Our problem setting involves a large commercial building equipped with multiple EV charging stations powered by the grid. These chargers fall into two categories: unidirectional chargers, which draw electricity from the grid to charge vehicles, and bidirectional chargers, which can both charge EVs and discharge stored energy back into the building. When an EV arrives, it is assigned to an available charger if one is free. Each EV provides its expected departure time and charging requirement, typically specified in terms of its required state of charge (SoC) before departure. We use v to index each EV and denote its required departure SoC by e_v^{req}.

The goal of the system is to periodically determine the optimal charging and discharging rates for all chargers in order to minimize the building's total electricity bill, while simultaneously satisfying each EV's charging requirements. Operationally, the building makes energy management decisions every 15 minutes, aligned with typical utility billing intervals and enabling frequent adjustments [Sen et al. 2025]. At each decision interval, the system determines how much power should flow through each EV charger. This decision is represented by a charging-rate vector: $\mathbf{u}_t = [P_1(t), P_2(t), \ldots, P_N(t)]$, for N chargers, where $P_i(t)$ denotes the power allocated to charger i at time $t \in [0, T]$, representing the full billing cycle. A positive value indicates charging (drawing power from the grid), while a negative value indicates discharging energy back into the building, which is only applicable to bidirectional chargers. Each power rate must lie within the allowable bounds: $\underline{P}_i \leq P_i(t) \leq \overline{P}_i$, where $\underline{P}_i$ and $\overline{P}_i$ represent the minimum and maximum allowable power for charger i.

In a V2B system, the presence of bidirectional chargers effectively transforms EVs into mobile energy storage units, offering significant potential to reduce the building's total electricity cost. This cost includes two main components: demand charges, calculated based on the peak power consumption over a billing cycle (typically one month), and energy consumption charges, which vary depending on time-of-use pricing (e.g., off-peak vs. peak hours). Mathematically, the total electricity bill, consisting of cumulative energy cost and peak demand charge, is defined as:

$$\begin{aligned}\text{TotalBill}(\{\mathbf{u}_t\}_{t=0}^{T}) = &\sum_{t=0}^{T} \left(B(t) + \sum_{i=1}^{N} P_i(t) \right) \times \theta_E(t)\Delta t \\ &+ \max_{t\in[0,T]} \left(B(t) + \sum_{i=1}^{N} P_i(t) \right) \times \theta_D, \end{aligned} \tag{4.1}$$

where $B(t)$ denotes the baseline building load at time t, $P_i(t)$ represents the power allocated to charger i, $\theta_E(t)$ is the electricity price at time t, θ_D denotes the demand charge rate, Δt is the length of each time interval, and N is the total number of chargers.

To ensure user satisfaction, we introduce a penalty for all EVs that arrive during the billing cycle and depart without reaching their required state of charge (SoC). The SoC of each vehicle evolves over time based on its assigned charging rate, following energy dynamics governed by the system's time-varying control decisions [Sen et al. 2025]. The final objective is to minimize the sum of the total electricity bill and the aggregated SoC penalties across all EVs:

$$\min_{\{\mathbf{u}_t\}_{t=0}^{T}} \text{TotalBill}(\{\mathbf{u}_t\}_{t=0}^{T}) + \lambda \sum_{v} \left| e_v^{\text{dep}} - e_v^{\text{req}} \right|,$$

where e_v^{dep} denotes the actual SoC of EV v at departure, and λ is a penalty coefficient balancing operational cost with user satisfaction.

Solving the online EV charging decision-making problem presents a range of challenges stemming from both **system uncertainty** and structural complexity. EV behavior, including arrival times, departure times, and charging requirements, varies significantly across users and days. The building's energy load is influenced by occupancy patterns and weather conditions, making it difficult to forecast accurately. In addition, electricity prices fluctuate throughout the day and month due to changing market conditions and grid demand. These uncertainties make it infeasible to rely on perfect foresight, requiring adaptive control methods that can operate under incomplete and evolving information [Liu et al. 2025, Sen et al. 2025]. In addition to uncertainty, several structural factors further complicate the problem. The **state and action space** grows rapidly with the number of EVs and chargers, especially in the presence of **heterogeneous hardware** such as unidirectional and bidirectional chargers, which have differing capabilities and constraints. This combinatorial complexity limits the scalability of classical optimization methods. The objective function also involves significant **long-term coupling**, particularly due to demand charges, where a single short-term decision can affect the maximum power draw over the entire billing cycle. Finally, the system must meet strict **real-time requirements**, in which control decisions are made at short intervals and computational runtime is a critical concern.

These challenges motivate the use of advanced AI-based methods. We first introduce generative models for forecasting the stochastic events in the V2B scenario, including EV arrivals, departures, and building load fluctuations. We then explore multiple techniques to address the large action space and long-term reward dependencies, which pose significant challenges for learning-based approaches such as RL and MCTS. To improve learning efficiency, we apply *action masking* to eliminate infeasible actions based on domain knowledge and incorporate *policy guidance* by leveraging high-quality exploration strategies to enhance training samples [Liu et al. 2025]. For MCTS-based control, we utilize *action pruning* to reduce the branching factor and apply *decentralized planning* to improve scalability by distributing computation across local agents [Sen et al. 2025]. We further leverage a realistic V2B simulator, OPTIMUS, which enables rigorous design and evaluation of charging policies and operational scenarios in a controlled, reproducible environment [Talusan et al. 2024].

4.3 Forecasting

Effective operation of V2B systems relies on accurate forecasting of both building load and EV behavior. These forecasts enable the system to anticipate future states and make informed charging and discharging decisions under uncertainty. We train predictive models using real-world data collected from EV manufacturers and building energy logs to capture realistic dynamics. The resulting forecasting pipeline generates time-indexed samples of building load, electricity prices, and stochastic EV behavior, which serve as key inputs to the control framework. Next, we present representative models used in this pipeline.

EV Behavior Forecasting. To capture the stochastic nature of EV behavior, we employ a suite of probabilistic models trained on 22 months of real-world telemetry data. These models predict key behavioral attributes, including arrival patterns, state-of-charge (SoC) levels, and dwell durations: (i) **Arrival counts per interval** are modeled using a zero-inflated negative binomial (ZINB) regression, with features such as date, day of the week, hour, and cyclical encoding of time-of-day. The model achieves a pseudo-R^2 of 0.34, indicating that calendar and diurnal patterns explain a substantial portion of the variability. (ii) **Arrival SoC** is captured using beta regression with day-of-week and cyclical time features, effectively reproducing the empirical distribution of arrival SoC levels, as evidenced by strongly negative AIC values. (iii) **Departure SoC** is modeled using a second beta regression conditioned on the arrival SoC, day of the week, and time features. Conditioning on arrival SoC significantly improves model fit (AIC -1801). (iv) **Stay duration** is estimated using a Weibull survival model, with hazard rates dependent on the day of the week and arrival time. The model achieves a concordance index of 0.71, indicating strong predictive accuracy.

Building load is forecasted using autoregressive (AR) models trained on the previous month of building meter data. These models are highly effective, achieving day-ahead mean absolute percentage error (MAPE) typically ranging from 2% to 10%. To simulate real-world variability, zero-mean Gaussian noise calibrated to this error range is added to the predicted load, ensuring that **EV behavior** remains the dominant source of uncertainty. **Electricity prices** are assumed to follow pre-published utility rate schedules, which are treated as known one day in advance.

Decoupling Sampling from Decision-Making. A key observation, confirmed by the building operator, is that EV arrival and departure times are governed solely by user schedules and remain unaffected by prior charging decisions or building load. This property allows the system to *pre-sample* all EV arrivals, initial SoC levels, and dwell durations at the start of each episode. As a result, the generative forecasting process becomes fully decoupled from the control policy, enabling the controller to focus exclusively on meeting SoC targets at minimum cost without influencing future EV availability.

Scenario Generation and Robustness. To support both training and evaluation of control policies under uncertainty, we construct a rich scenario set by sampling 100 distinct monthly billing episodes per calendar month. These episodes incorporate varied realizations of building load, electricity prices, EV behaviors, and charger configurations, and are divided evenly into training and test sets. This scenario-based approach ensures that policies are evaluated across a wide range of plausible futures. Importantly, we find that the proposed MC-MPC framework exhibits strong robustness: even when building load forecast noise is increased threefold, performance remains stable, highlighting the framework's resilience to forecasting errors.

Estimated Peak Power for Demand Charges. To guide demand charge control, the system estimates a monthly reference peak power level $\hat{P}_{\max}$ by solving all training scenarios using an MILP-based offline optimization. The 99th percentile of the resulting peak power values is then used as a penalty threshold during online decision-making. This threshold provides a realistic and conservative target, helping the controller mitigate demand charge violations while accounting for variability across episodes.

By combining predictive modeling, decoupled sampling, and rigorous scenario generation, the system effectively anticipates and adapts to uncertainty in user behavior, building demand, and electricity pricing. These capabilities underpin efficient, equitable, and resilient V2B energy management, supporting broader goals of cost reduction, grid reliability, and sustainable electrification.

4.4 Online EV Charging Optimization

The V2B optimization problem is fundamentally a stochastic control problem, in which the decision-maker must optimize charging decisions over time in the presence of exogenous uncertainty. At each decision point, the system must determine charging and discharging rates for a heterogeneous fleet of EVs, while accounting for user-specified SoC requirements, dynamic building loads, and complex electricity pricing that includes both energy and demand charges. These decisions must be made under uncertainty and over long horizons-often spanning an entire month. To formalize this problem, we model it as an MDP that captures the key system dynamics and cost objectives.

4.4.1 Classical Approaches

Before the advent of advanced AI-driven and search-based methods, V2B optimization was typically addressed using a variety of heuristic scheduling policies. These approaches are attractive for their simplicity and computational efficiency, but they often fall short in handling uncertainty, heterogeneity, and long-term objectives.

MaxCharge: This policy simulates the real-world default: all connected EVs are charged at the maximum possible rate until they reach their battery's maximum SoC. While simple, MaxCharge can lead to excessive peak demand charges and often fails to meet user SoC requirements for short-stay vehicles, especially when charger resources are limited [Sen et al. 2025].

ReqCharge: Similar to MaxCharge, ReqCharge charges all connected EVs as quickly as possible, but only until each vehicle's user-specified required SoC is reached. This approach reduces unnecessary overcharging but still ignores building load constraints, demand charges, and the opportunity to optimize charging timing [Sen et al. 2025].

Early Deadline First (EDF): EDF is a classical real-time scheduling policy that prioritizes EVs with the nearest departure times [Chen et al. 2012]. At each decision point, charging resources are allocated first to those vehicles whose deadlines (departure times) are soonest. While EDF can reduce missed SoC targets for urgent vehicles, it does not consider the flexibility of vehicles with later departures or the potential for demand charge reduction.

Least Laxity First (LLF): LLF extends EDF by prioritizing EVs based on their laxity: the difference between the time remaining until departure and the time required to reach the required SoC at the current charging rate [Xu et al. 2016b]. Vehicles with the least slack are charged first, ensuring that those at greatest risk of missing their SoC targets are prioritized. LLF can outperform EDF in environments with high variability in stay durations and charging needs, but, like other heuristics, it does not explicitly optimize for building-level objectives such as peak shaving or cost minimization.

Despite their practical utility, these heuristics are inherently myopic and unable to anticipate future events or adapt to real-time uncertainty in arrivals, departures, and building load.

4.4.2 Markov Decision Process Model

We define the MDP with the following components:
State. The system state includes temporal indicators (e.g., current time slot, day of the week), building-level data (e.g., current power consumption, historical daily peaks, and a dynamically estimated peak target), and EV-specific attributes (e.g., current and required SoC, time remaining until departure, and energy needs of each connected EV). These features are distilled into a compact, informative state representation that enables efficient learning.

Action. At each time step, the controller selects continuous-valued charging and discharging rates for all chargers. This formulation allows flexible power control tailored to each EV's needs and system conditions.

State Transition. State transitions are governed by EV arrivals and departures, updates to SoC based on charging actions, and evolving building power usage. The estimated peak power is incrementally updated to reflect the building's evolving demand profile, which is critical for managing demand charges.

Reward. The reward function encodes a trade-off between three objectives: (i) meeting EV charging goals (ensuring the required SoC is reached), (ii) minimizing energy costs, and (iii) avoiding increases in demand charges by staying below the estimated peak. These components are weighted to reflect operational priorities and encourage cost-effective, user-compliant behavior.

The learned policy selects actions based on the current state to maximize cumulative reward over the entire billing cycle. To solve this MDP and obtain a policy that maps states to optimal charging actions, we introduce several algorithmic approaches, including RL, MCTS, and control-based methods such as Model Predictive Control (MPC). These approaches are designed to address the challenges posed by continuous action spaces, long-horizon objectives, and dynamic uncertainty.

4.4.3 Reinforcement Learning-Based Approach

We begin by introducing a reinforcement learning (RL)-based approach. To solve the V2B control problem under uncertainty, we adopt a reinforcement learning framework [Liu et al. 2025] built upon the Deep Deterministic Policy Gradient (DDPG) algorithm [Lillicrap et al. 2015], which is well-suited for continuous control in high-dimensional, stochastic environments. The DDPG backbone enables the agent to learn a policy that maps system states to real-valued charging and discharging actions, with the objective of minimizing long-term operational costs. To improve learning efficiency and solution quality, we integrate two key enhancements: action masking and policy guidance.

Action masking ensures the feasibility of policy-generated actions by applying domain-specific constraints during training [Huang and Ontañón 2020, Kanervisto et al. 2020]. The actor network outputs raw charging actions, which are then masked using a differentiable procedure grounded in operational knowledge of the EV and building environment. The masking logic accounts for factors such as EV connection status, required SoC before departure, bidirectional charging capability, peak demand avoidance, and charger power limits. For example, EVs that are disconnected receive zero charging power, while connected EVs are restricted from overcharging beyond their required SoC or discharging below minimum thresholds. By enforcing these rules dynamically, the agent avoids wasting learning effort on invalid or ineffective actions. Importantly, the entire masking procedure is differentiable–built on operations like *ReLU*, *min*, and *max*–allowing gradients to flow through the modified action outputs during backpropagation. This ensures stable and efficient learning without violating action constraints.

Policy guidance improves exploration by leveraging a mixed-integer linear programming (MILP) solver to compute near-optimal actions for selected training episodes. Leveraging the decoupling of sampling and decision-making (Section 4.3), the generative model pre-samples all stochastic elements, such as EV arrivals, SoC requirements, and building load, prior to training. This enables each training episode to be treated as a deterministic instance with a known sequence of future events. Given this fixed sample, the V2B control problem becomes a deterministic MILP that minimizes energy and demand costs while satisfying SoC and charger constraints. The resulting optimal actions are then stochastically injected into the RL replay buffer alongside actions generated by the actor network. This hybrid sampling enriches the learning experience with structured, high-quality trajectories, guiding the RL agent toward more efficient policies and avoiding poor local minima [Levine and Koltun 2013]. Empirically, this guidance significantly accelerates convergence and improves final policy performance, particularly in long-horizon settings with sparse rewards. Importantly, although future information is used during training, the final learned policy remains fully real-time and model-free at inference.

Empirical Results. We evaluate our proposed RL framework using nine months of real-world data (May 2023-Jan 2024) collected from a commercial smart building equipped with 15 heterogeneous chargers provided by a major

EV manufacturer. We evaluate our RL-based policy against a set of heuristic baselines, including the real-world fast-charging policy, laxity- and deadline-based schedulers, and variants that adjust charging based on available power and urgency. These baselines prioritize either minimal charging to ensure SoC requirements or aggressive charging when power is available. Our RL policy outperformed all heuristics in 8 out of 9 months, achieving a significantly lower average total cost ($1,442.2) over 9 months compared to the real-world strategy. This demonstrates the advantage of combining deep reinforcement learning with domain-informed enhancements for effective and scalable V2B energy management.

While RL is well-suited for optimizing long-term rewards in the V2B charging problem, it has inherent limitations. In particular, RL policies can be sensitive to training data and struggle to generalize to rare or unforeseen events not present during training. Examples include abnormal EV departures (e.g., significantly earlier than declared) or unexpected charger failures. To address these limitations, we explore an alternative online decision-making approach based on MCTS. Unlike RL, which relies on offline training, MCTS performs online planning from the current state using simulated rollouts. While it still depends on a generative model, its real-time, adaptive nature makes it more robust to abnormal and unpredictable events.

4.4.4 Dynamic Uncertainty Handling via Online Planning

MCTS with Domain Knowledge. MCTS is a powerful planning algorithm for sequential decision-making under uncertainty. It builds a lookahead search tree by simulating trajectories from the current state, enabling the selection of actions that balance short-term gains with long-term outcomes. However, classical MCTS methods are computationally intensive and struggle to meet real-time decision-making requirements, particularly in large, continuous action spaces such as V2B energy management.

To address these limitations, [Sen et al. 2025] introduces a Domain-Knowledge Guided Monte Carlo Tree Search (DG-MCTS) algorithm that integrates domain knowledge to enhance efficiency and effectiveness. DG-MCTS leverages domain-specific heuristics, such as the Least Laxity First (LLF) scheduling rule, which prioritizes EVs with the least time until departure, ensuring that urgent charging needs are met first. At each decision epoch, DG-MCTS generates a small set of promising actions using LLF and related heuristics, then augments this set with randomly sampled actions to maintain exploration. This dramatically reduces the effective action space, allowing the search to focus on high-value regions while still retaining the flexibility to discover novel strategies.

DG-MCTS builds a forward-looking search tree, simulating the outcomes of each candidate action under sampled future scenarios (episodes). The tree is expanded using the Upper Confidence Bound applied to Trees (UCT) algorithm, balancing exploration and exploitation. During rollouts, a trickle-charging policy is used as the default, charging each EV at the minimum rate needed to meet its SoC target by departure. This combination of heuristic guidance and stochastic simulation enables DG-MCTS to efficiently plan over long horizons, capturing the delayed effects of demand charges and rare peak events.

A defining feature of the V2B problem is the presence of multiple, interacting sources of uncertainty: EV arrivals and departures, user SoC requirements, building load, and electricity prices. The DG-MCTS framework addresses this by operating in an *online* fashion: at each decision epoch, it uses the latest forecasts and observed data to update its plans. Uncertainty is handled by sampling multiple plausible future scenarios (episodes) from generative models, allowing the controller to select actions that are robust across a range of possible futures.

Decentralized MCTS (dMCTS). To further improve scalability as the number of EVs and chargers grows, this paper [Sen et al. 2025] introduces a decentralized version, dMCTS. In dMCTS, each charger or EV agent constructs its own search tree and makes local decisions based on a "criticality score", prioritizing vehicles with the most urgent charging needs (i.e., the least laxity). This decentralized approach substantially reduces computation time to 15.38 seconds per decision (versus 23.75 seconds for centralized DG-MCTS) and scales more efficiently for larger deployments. This decentralized approach offers a practical pathway for real-time V2B control in large-scale deployments, where computational efficiency and scalability are as critical as optimality.

Temporal Decomposition and Root Parallelization. To manage the long planning horizons (e.g., monthly billing cycles), DG-MCTS decomposes the problem into daily subproblems, while maintaining a running estimate of the monthly peak power. Root parallelization is used to sample multiple episodes in parallel, each representing a unique realization of future uncertainty. The final action is chosen by averaging scores across all sampled trees, ensuring robustness to rare events and outliers.

Empirical Results. In real-world experiments using data from EV manufacturers' testbed, DG-MCTS consistently outperformed classical heuristics (such as MaxCharge, ReqCharge, LLF, and EDF) and RL baselines in both total cost and peak shaving, while maintaining comparable rates of missed SoC targets. For example, over eight months, DG-MCTS achieved the lowest monthly total cost in six months, with average monthly bills ranging from $5,195.53 to $8,512.24, compared to MaxCharge, which ranged from $6,827.50 to $9,402.73. DG-MCTS also achieved strong peak shaving, with an average reduction of -5.17 ± 13.67 kW in peak demand, compared to 94.02 ± 46.60 kW for MaxCharge. The number of cars with missing SoC under DG-MCTS was 43.82 ± 30.98, comparable to LLF (40.47 ± 30.67) and much lower than RL (207.34 ± 60.29). In terms of computation, DG-MCTS required an average of 23.75 seconds per decision, while the decentralized variant (dMCTS) was faster at 15.38 seconds per decision, with only a small increase in total cost. Under increased uncertainty (e.g., larger departure windows or more daily arrivals), DG-MCTS and dMCTS remained robust, outperforming all heuristic baselines in both cost and computation time [Sen et al. 2025]. These results highlight that DG-MCTS, through dynamic uncertainty handling, domain-guided action pruning, and robust scenario sampling, delivers significant cost savings and operational reliability for V2B systems in real-world, uncertainty-laden environments. The results also show a clear trade-off: centralized DG-MCTS offers the best performance but is computationally intensive; dMCTS is faster and more scalable but sacrifices some optimality; and we need to strike a balance, achieving high performance and robustness with minimal computation time, making it the preferred choice for real-world, large-scale V2B systems.

While DG-MCTS and dMCTS significantly accelerate online decision-making, they still face limitations in handling large-scale problems, such as managing 300 chargers, where the action space grows exponentially, making exploration increasingly intractable. At the same time, RL-based approaches, though efficient once trained, may struggle with robustness when facing unforeseen events or distributional shifts. To address these challenges, we next explore a control-based solution: *stochastic Model Predictive Control (SMPC)*. In our V2B context, we implement this as *Monte Carlo Model Predictive Control (MC-MPC)*, which performs real-time optimization over sampled future trajectories. Unlike RL, which requires extensive offline training, or MCTS, which can become computationally expensive, MC-MPC provides a more robust and adaptable approach for online planning. This makes it well-suited to high-dimensional, uncertain, and time-sensitive environments.

4.4.5 Fast and Robust Online Control via Monte Carlo MPC

The MC-MPC framework operates by gathering a large set of plausible future scenarios for each control step, sampling from generative models of building load and EV behavior (arrivals, departures, SoC requirements) [Liu et al. 2025]. By leveraging parallel scenario sampling, temporal decomposition, and statistical peak estimation, MC-MPC can deliver robust, near-optimal decisions in real time, even as uncertainty and system size increase. In practice, MC-MPC achieves comparable or better performance than DG-MCTS and dMCTS, while operating within strict real-time constraints (often under 10 seconds per decision for similar problem sizes). This makes MC-MPC particularly attractive for large, real-world V2B deployments, where both speed and robustness are critical [Sen et al. 2025].

As discussed earlier, building load forecasts are produced using autoregressive models fitted to recent meter data, with calibrated Gaussian noise added to match observed day-ahead forecast errors (typically 2–10% MAPE). EV arrivals are modeled using a zero-inflated negative binomial (ZINB) regression, while SoC and stay durations are sampled from beta regression and Weibull survival models, respectively. This approach ensures that each scenario reflects realistic, data-driven uncertainty in both exogenous building load and user-driven EV patterns.

For each scenario, MC-MPC simulates the system forward over the relevant horizon (typically a day), evaluating candidate control actions (charging/discharging rates) at each step. The optimization objective is to minimize the expected total bill—including both energy and demand charges—while ensuring all EVs meet their required SoC at departure. Critically, the demand charge is shaped by the highest instantaneous power draw over the entire billing period, a long-term, non-myopic constraint that is notoriously difficult for traditional MPC to handle. MC-MPC addresses this by estimating a target peak power threshold $\hat{P}_{\max}$ for each month, computed as the 99th percentile of peak power values from offline MILP solutions across sampled episodes. This statistical target is then used to penalize actions that risk exceeding the demand charge threshold, steering the online controller toward robust peak management.

Temporal Decomposition and Sampling. To further restrict computation time, MC-MPC decomposes the monthly billing horizon into daily subproblems, solving for each day independently but with the global demand charge constraint enforced via the estimated $\hat{P}_{\max}$. At each control step, many (more than 30) scenarios are sampled and evaluated together, leveraging modern multi-core hardware. This combined evaluation ensures that the controller's chosen action is robust across a wide range of possible futures, not just a single forecast trajectory. The final action is selected as the best-performing candidate across all scenarios, thereby mitigating the risk of overfitting to any single realization of uncertainty. Here, decoupling decision-making from sampling allows the MC-MPC controller to pre-sample all future EV behaviors for each scenario. The controller can then focus exclusively on optimizing charging and discharging actions to meet SoC targets and minimize costs, without needing to model or influence future EV availability. This decoupling not only simplifies the control architecture but also greatly improves computational efficiency and robustness.

Empirical Performance and Robustness. Experiments on real-world data from a Silicon Valley testbed demonstrate that MC-MPC achieves near-optimal performance in both cost and demand charge reduction. Across eight months of evaluation, MC-MPC (implemented as DG-MCTS) achieved an average monthly total cost of $\$7{,}756 \pm \$1{,}261$, consistently outperforming the real-world MaxCharge baseline, which ranged from \$6,827 to \$9,403, and other heuristic policies. In terms of peak shaving, MC-MPC reduced peak demand by an average of 27.91 ± 16.82 kW compared to MaxCharge, directly lowering demand charges for the building.

Crucially, MC-MPC maintained high user satisfaction: the number of cars departing with unmet SoC was low (43.8 ± 31 out of thousands of sessions), and all cars received at least their required SoC in most episodes. The approach was robust to both epistemic and aleatoric uncertainty—when building load forecast noise was tripled to simulate highly uncertain predictions, MC-MPC's performance remained strong, with only a modest increase in total cost and no significant rise in missed SoC cases. Computation times were kept practical, averaging 0.99 seconds per decision for MC-MPC, which scales efficiently as the number of chargers and EVs increases. These results underscore MC-MPC's ability to deliver reliable, cost-effective, and user-centric V2B operation under real-world uncertainty.

Summary of Insights. The MC-MPC framework exemplifies how modern AI and optimization can deliver robust, scalable, and real-time control for V2B systems. By combining scenario-based planning, temporal decomposition, statistical peak estimation, and parallelization, MC-MPC ensures that high-quality decisions are made within strict time constraints, even as uncertainty and system scale increase. This approach is a blueprint for deploying AI in other large-scale, uncertainty-laden societal systems where both speed and robustness are paramount.

4.5 Managing User Incentives: Behavioral Modeling and Negotiations

A central challenge in deploying V2B systems at scale is ensuring sustained user participation and aligning system-level optimization with individual user preferences. While minimizing energy and demand charges is the technical goal, practical success depends on incentive and negotiation mechanisms that balance operational efficiency with fairness and user engagement [Fatima et al. 2006, Kuang et al. 2017, Liu et al. 2025, Nicholas R. Jennings 2001, Sen et al. 2025, Tanguy et al. 2016, Zhang and Augenbroe 2018].

Incentive Design and User Participation. Incentive mechanisms in V2B typically include monetary compensation for unmet SoC, discounted charging, or priority access for flexible users. If users repeatedly experience unmet SoC or perceive the system as unfair, participation drops, undermining grid and cost benefits [Sen et al. 2025, Tanguy et al. 2016]. To prevent this, V2B optimization frameworks explicitly penalize unmet SoC, with penalties set higher than marginal energy costs, ensuring user satisfaction is prioritized [Liu et al. 2025, Tanguy et al. 2016, Zhang and Augenbroe 2018].

Negotiation and Behavioral Modeling. Advanced V2B systems increasingly employ negotiation protocols, drawing from multi-agent systems and energy market literature [Fatima et al. 2006, Nicholas R. Jennings 2001]. These protocols allow the system and users to iteratively adjust incentives and schedules in real time. For example, if a user's SoC cannot be met, the controller can offer alternatives: higher compensation, delayed departure, or future priority. Such negotiation can be modeled as a bargaining game, contract menu, or auction, and has been shown to improve both fairness and efficiency in EV charging and broader resource allocation settings [Fatima et al. 2006, Kuang et al. 2017, Nicholas R. Jennings 2001]. Behavioral models, often learned from historical data, capture user-specific patterns such as flexibility, tolerance for unmet charging, and likelihood of accepting alternative offers. These models inform both scenario generation in stochastic MPC and the reward structure in RL-based controllers, ensuring user preferences are reflected in the optimization [Kuang et al. 2017, Sen et al. 2025].

Empirical and Societal Impact. Empirical studies confirm that explicit incentives and negotiation mechanisms maintain high user participation and satisfaction, even under uncertainty [Kuang et al. 2017, Tanguy et al. 2016]. By aligning user incentives with system objectives and enabling negotiation, V2B systems achieve robust, scalable, and user-centric energy management, supporting both operational efficiency and social acceptance.

4.6 Conclusion

In this chapter, we discussed how data-driven and AI-based techniques can be used for energy sustainability by solving V2B optimization: making real-time, long-horizon decisions under uncertainty to minimize the total electricity bill while meeting EV charging requirements. We modeled the problem as an MDP that captures the dynamic interactions between charging decisions, EV behavior, and building load. To solve this MDP, we explored three algorithmic approaches. RL enhanced with action masking and policy guidance learns long-term strategies but is sensitive to training data and less adaptable to rare events. DG-MCTS enables robust online planning but faces scalability challenges. MC-MPC addresses these limitations by sampling realistic future scenarios and optimizing actions in real time, offering both robustness and scalability. Together, these methods form a practical toolkit for V2B energy management, balancing performance, adaptability, and computational efficiency. Finally, we emphasized the importance of user participation, highlighting incentive design and negotiation protocols that elicit greater behavioral flexibility (e.g., adjusting charging requirements or departure times), enabling further cost reductions and enhancing system effectiveness.

5

Developing and Deploying an AI-Augmented Intervention for HIV Prevention in Youth Experiencing Homelessness

Bryan Wilder[1] and Amulya Yadav[2]

[1]Carnegie Mellon University
[2]Pennsylvania State University

Abstract

Youth experiencing homelessness face elevated risks of HIV infection, and traditional prevention interventions have struggled to reach them effectively. In this chapter, we describe CHANGE, a computationally guided peer-leader intervention that leverages AI to improve outreach and health outcomes. Drawing on influence maximization theory, we present algorithms to identify peer leaders in social networks who could most effectively diffuse protective behaviors. We also present results from a clinical trial comparing this AI-augmented approach with traditional degree-centrality selection and show that the algorithmic method is significantly more effective at promoting protective practices. The chapter not only details the technical design but also narrates the process of partnering with practitioners to ensure that interventions were culturally and socially appropriate. It stands as a powerful example of how rigorous AI design, combined with sensitive real-world deployment, can yield lasting public health impact.

5.1 Introduction

Each year, an estimated 4.2 million young people in the United States experience some form of homelessness [Morton et al. 2018]. This population faces a range of serious health risks, among which elevated HIV prevalence is

DOI: 10.1201/9788743812074-6

particularly salient. Existing estimates indicate HIV prevalence rates between 2–11% [Young and Rice 2011], representing levels up to ten times higher than those observed among youth with stable housing [National HCH Council 2012].

One frequently proposed approach to promoting positive behavioral change in high-risk populations is the *peer change agent* model. This framework centers on identifying and engaging peer leaders from within the population of youth experiencing homelessness (YEH) to act as advocates for HIV awareness and prevention. The use of peer leaders has been widely discussed in the public health and social science literature, reflecting the influential role of peer relationships in shaping risk behaviors among YEH, including behaviors associated with HIV transmission [Green Jr et al. 2013, Rice et al. 2010, 2012]. Peer change agent strategies have demonstrated success in prior HIV prevention interventions conducted in other settings [Medley et al. 2009]. At the same time, several high-profile interventions have failed to achieve their intended outcomes [Group et al. 2010], with some scholars suggesting that these shortcomings may stem from the criteria used to select peer leaders [Schneider et al. 2015]. Traditionally, the dominant approach in the public health literature has been to identify peer leaders based on their popularity within social networks, typically operationalized as individuals with the highest number of social ties [Kelly et al. 1997] (i.e., the highest-degree nodes). This raises a critical question: are highly connected youth necessarily the most effective peer leaders for disseminating HIV prevention messages? Importantly, this issue extends well beyond HIV prevention, as comparable social network-based interventions are widely employed across fields such as development, medicine, and education [Banerjee et al. 2013, Kim et al. 2015, Paluck et al. 2016, Valente and Pumpuang 2007].

Related challenges concerning information diffusion in social networks have also been studied extensively within computer science. A central example is the *influence maximization* problem, introduced by [Kempe et al. 2003], which seeks to determine how to select a limited set of initial "seed" nodes in a network so as to maximize the spread of information. This problem has generated substantial attention in the theoretical computer science and artificial intelligence literature, leading to a large body of work focused on algorithmic and computational advances [Borgs et al. 2014, Chen et al. 2009, 2010, Goyal et al. 2011, Tang et al. 2014]. However, to the best of our knowledge, prior research has not meaningfully linked this computational literature on influence maximization to the design and implementation of network-based interventions in public health and related domains. Much of the existing computational research has emphasized the development of highly efficient algorithms for application to large-scale social media platforms, often motivated by advertising or marketing use cases, whereas practitioners in health-focused interventions have generally not adopted explicit algorithmic strategies for optimizing peer leader selection. This disconnect between theoretical developments and applied practice may be further compounded by the fact that most influence maximization models assume access to detailed data—such as complete network structures and well-specified stochastic models of information diffusion—that are rarely available in real-world public health settings.

This chapter presents findings from a project that seeks to connect advances in computational influence maximization with the design and execution of real-world public health interventions. Conducted by an interdisciplinary team of computer scientists and social workers, the project involved the development, deployment, and evaluation of an HIV prevention intervention for youth experiencing homelessness (YEH) in which peer leaders were selected using algorithmic methods. The intervention was refined over multiple years through an iterative process that alternated between algorithm development and small-scale pilot studies to assess feasibility and practicality. The resulting system, termed CHANGE (CompreHensive Adaptive Network samplinG for social influencE), was ultimately assessed through a large-scale clinical trial that enrolled 713 participants over two years across three geographic locations. The study design compared outcomes from interventions planned using CHANGE with those based on the conventional public health approach of selecting peer leaders according to the highest degree centrality (DC), as well as with an observation-only control condition (OBS). *Findings from the clinical trial show that CHANGE substantially outperformed the standard DC-based approach in promoting the adoption of behaviors that reduce the risk of HIV transmission.* To our knowledge, this study represents the first empirically validated demonstration that AI-driven methods can enhance the effectiveness of social network-based health interventions. More broadly, the project illustrates the importance of translating "AI for Social Good" research into deployed interventions that are rigorously evaluated in real-world settings.

The chapter proceeds as follows. We begin with a review of relevant prior work, spanning both computational research and applied intervention studies. We then introduce a computational formalization of the peer leader selection problem. Next, we provide a high-level overview of the CHANGE system developed to address this challenge, referring readers to earlier technical publications for detailed algorithmic treatments [Wilder 2018, Wilder et al. 2018a,b]. We subsequently describe the design and implementation of the clinical trial, followed by a presentation and analysis of the trial outcomes. Finally, we reflect on key lessons learned throughout the project that may inform future efforts to design and deploy AI-supported interventions in public health contexts.

5.2 Related Work

A substantial body of work in computer science has focused on the influence maximization problem. Much of this research has focused on designing computationally efficient algorithms for very large social networks [Borgs et al. 2014, Chen et al. 2009, 2010, Goyal et al. 2011, Tang et al. 2014], typically under the assumption that both the underlying network structure and the model governing information diffusion are fully known. More recent studies have relaxed these assumptions by proposing methods to learn or explore unknown network or diffusion parameters. However, such approaches generally rely on extensive repeated interaction with the system. For instance, algorithms that estimate parameters of an unknown diffusion model [Du et al. 2014, He et al. 2016, Kalimeris et al. 2018, Narasimhan et al. 2015, Pouget-Abadie and Horel 2015] often require observing hundreds of diffusion cascades on the same network. In the context of public health interventions, collecting data at this scale is infeasible, as a single intervention cycle may span several months. Related work has examined bandit-based formulations in which an algorithm repeatedly selects sets of seed nodes and observes the resulting diffusion outcomes [Chen et al. 2013, Wang and Chen 2017, Wen et al. 2017]. These methods similarly tolerate suboptimal performance in early rounds in exchange for improved outcomes over time, an assumption that is incompatible with domains where waiting through dozens or hundreds of rounds is impractical. Consequently, such techniques are better suited to settings like online social networks and advertising, where large datasets and repeated experimentation are readily available.

The computational work most closely aligned with our approach addresses robust variants of the influence maximization problem [Chen et al. 2016a, He and Kempe 2018, Lowalekar et al. 2016], extending earlier research on robust submodular maximization [Krause et al. 2008]. Our method for robust submodular optimization, outlined below, differs from these prior approaches primarily in its use of a fractional relaxation of the optimization problem, rather than relying on repeated applications of greedy algorithms for discrete submodular maximization. This design choice improves computational efficiency while maintaining robustness guarantees.

Parallel to the computational literature, there exists a broad body of research on social network-based interventions across public health [Kim et al. 2015, Valente and Pumpuang 2007], clinical medicine [Young et al. 2003], international development [Banerjee et al. 2013, Cai et al. 2015], and education [Paluck et al. 2016], among other domains. Common intervention strategies include selecting individuals with high degree centrality (as in the baseline condition of our trial), selecting participants at random, or relying on peer nominations to identify influential individuals. Empirical findings regarding the relative effectiveness of these approaches have been mixed. For example, [Kim et al. 2015] report little to no advantage of nomination-based selection over random assignment for certain outcomes, whereas [Banerjee et al. 2019] find statistically significant benefits from nomination-based methods. In contrast, [Chin et al. 2018] introduce improved statistical techniques for comparing seeding strategies and conclude that nomination-based approaches do not yield measurable performance gains. Complementing these empirical results, [Akbarpour et al. 2018] demonstrate theoretically that, in some network models, recruiting a modestly larger number of influencers at random may outperform strategies that depend on detailed network mapping. Our contribution builds on this literature by developing and empirically testing an algorithmic framework that integrates elements reminiscent of nomination-based strategies—specifically, the collection of partial information about network structure—with robust optimization methods that jointly select the entire set of influencers, a feature absent from previously evaluated approaches. Results from our clinical trial show statistically significant improvements over the standard strategy of selecting high-degree nodes, offering, to our knowledge, the first real-world evidence that systematic algorithmic optimization can lead to superior outcomes in social network-based health interventions.

5.3 Problem Description

We represent the population of youth as the vertex set of a graph $G = (V, E)$, where edges encode social connections. The goal is to select a subset of youth $S \subseteq V$ to serve as peer leaders, subject to the constraint $|S| \leq k$. From an applied perspective, this constraint captures the practical limitation that peer leaders must undergo an intensive training and support process. The objective is to maximize the expected total number of youth who are reached with HIV prevention information, as quantified by an objective function $f(S)$. This function reflects the behavior of a stochastic process governing information diffusion over the network, described in more detail below. The resulting optimization problem, $\max_{|S| \leq k} f(S)$, corresponds to the classical influence maximization formulation. Under standard assumptions about information diffusion dynamics, the function f is submodular, meaning that the marginal benefit of adding an additional peer leader decreases as the size of S grows. Although computing an exact optimum is NP-hard, a straightforward greedy procedure is known to achieve a $(1 - 1/e)$ approximation guarantee [Kempe et al. 2003].

A widely adopted specification of the diffusion process is the independent cascade model. In this setting, when a node becomes informed, it has a single opportunity to pass the information to each of its neighbors, succeeding with probability p independently across edges. The diffusion unfolds in discrete rounds: at each time step, newly informed nodes attempt to activate their neighbors, and the process terminates once no further activations occur. The value of $f(S)$ is defined as the expected number of nodes that ultimately receive the information when the nodes in S are seeded at the beginning of the process, with the expectation taken over the randomness inherent in the diffusion dynamics.

The classical formulation of the influence maximization problem effectively ends at this point. In the course of developing an algorithmic framework suitable for deployment in public health settings, however, we encountered a number of additional challenges that arise before, during, and after the scenario typically assumed in standard influence maximization. Addressing these challenges led to a sequence of new algorithmic questions, which have been studied across multiple publications in the AI literature [Hu et al. 2018, Rice et al. 2018, Wilder 2018, Wilder et al. 2017, 2018a,b, Yadav et al. 2015, 2016a,b,c, 2017a,b,c, 2018a,b,c]. In what follows, we outline three key stages required to operationalize an influence maximization-based intervention in real-world field settings.

The first challenge concerns the acquisition of information about the underlying network structure G. Much of the prior influence maximization literature assumes that the social network is known *a priori*. While this assumption may be reasonable for online platforms, our objective is to spread information through networks defined by in-person interactions among youth at a physical service center. Pilot studies further indicated that data derived from online social networks such as Facebook provided a poor approximation of these real-world connections: not all youth maintained Facebook accounts, and even among users, online friendships frequently failed to reflect actual social ties within the drop-in center. As a result, network data must instead be collected through face-to-face interviews, during which social workers ask youth to identify individuals with whom they interact regularly. This process is both labor-intensive and costly, often requiring a week or more of sustained effort by trained staff. Consequently, the initial algorithmic task is to determine which nodes to query to elicit network information. Formally, the algorithm is permitted to issue up to M queries, each of which reveals the incident edges of the selected node. These queries may be adaptive, meaning that the selection of the ith node to query can depend on the information obtained from queries to nodes $1, \dots, i-1$.

Second, the partially observed network information is leveraged to identify an initial set of peer leaders. This step most closely aligns with the classical influence maximization formulation, but it introduces an additional source of uncertainty: the propagation probability p is unknown. In contrast to online platforms, where large volumes of historical data may be available to estimate such parameters (see related work), no comparable data source exists in this setting. To address this limitation, we define an uncertainty set $\mathcal{U}$ consisting of plausible values of p that are consistent with prior knowledge. In the CHANGE system, $\mathcal{U}$ was instantiated as a discretization of the interval $[0, 1]$, reflecting substantial uncertainty about the true diffusion probability. The objective is to identify a seed set S that performs well across all scenarios in $\mathcal{U}$. Formally, this requirement gives rise to the following robust optimization problem:

$$\max_{|S| \leq k} \min_{p \in \mathcal{U}} \frac{f(S, p)}{OPT(p)}$$

where $OPT(p) = \max_{|S| \leq k} f(S, p)$ denotes the optimal value achievable if the propagation probability p were known in advance. The normalization by $OPT(p)$ serves to encourage solutions that approximate the optimal performance uniformly across all values of $p \in \mathcal{U}$, while avoiding degenerate solutions in which the inner minimization is dominated by trivially small values of p. Because $OPT(p)$ is constant with respect to the choice of S, the ratio $\frac{f(S,p)}{OPT(p)}$ retains submodularity as a function of S. Nonetheless, robust optimization over submodular objectives is considerably more challenging than optimizing a single submodular function; indeed, such problems are provably inapproximable in full generality [Krause et al. 2008], necessitating the use of tractable relaxations rather than exact solutions.

The third stage concerns the adaptive recruitment of peer leaders after an initial candidate set S has been selected. In practice, not all youth who are invited to participate ultimately attend the training sessions. Various obstacles may prevent attendance, such as incarceration or a lack of transportation resources. To capture this uncertainty, we assume that each invited youth attends with probability q, independently of others. Based on observations from pilot studies, we set $q = 0.5$. For a fixed propagation probability p, the resulting objective function is denoted $f(S, p, q)$, which incorporates expectation over both sources of randomness: the stochastic realization of which invited nodes successfully become peer leaders and the subsequent diffusion of information through the network. As shown in prior work [Wilder et al. 2018b], the inclusion of this additional uncertainty preserves the submodularity of f.

Given variability in attendance and practical constraints on training capacity, recruitment is conducted over multiple rounds rather than in a single step. Importantly, the selection of peer leaders in round t may depend on which individuals were successfully recruited in earlier rounds $1, \ldots, t-1$. In each round t, a set of candidates S_t is chosen subject to a round-specific budget constraint $|S_t| \leq k_t$, after which the outcomes of recruitment are observed. This adaptive process is repeated for a total of T rounds.

5.4 System Design

Our complete intervention planning framework is referred to as CHANGE. The system was first introduced in [Wilder et al. 2018b], and the version described here closely follows that original formulation. The primary difference lies in the robust optimization component, which was subsequently refined and presented in [Wilder 2018]. In the following sections, we outline the CHANGE framework in detail, organizing the presentation to correspond directly to the stages of the problem formulation described above.

5.4.1 Network sampling

CHANGE employs a straightforward yet intuitively grounded heuristic to determine which nodes should be queried to obtain partial information about the network structure. In the discussion section, we briefly revisit earlier work that explored a more theoretically sophisticated approach, along with the reasoning behind ultimately adopting a simpler strategy in practice. The selected method divides the total query budget M evenly into two stages. During the first stage, each query targets a node drawn uniformly at random from the population. In the second stage, each query is paired with one from the first stage and targets a node chosen uniformly at random from among the neighbors of the previously sampled node. This two-step procedure is motivated by the friendship paradox, which notes that individuals with higher degrees are disproportionately likely to appear when sampling random neighbors [Feld 1991]. As a result, the approach balances two competing goals: the initial random sampling promotes broad coverage across the network, while the subsequent neighbor-based sampling biases queries toward highly connected individuals who can reveal substantial additional information about network structure.

5.4.2 Robust optimization

We next outline how CHANGE addresses uncertainty in model parameters within a single planning stage, before turning to the multi-stage setting that incorporates uncertain attendance. As noted earlier, max-min optimization of submodular objectives is NP-hard to approximate to within any nonzero factor [Krause et al. 2008], making direct solutions infeasible. To obtain tractable performance guarantees, we therefore adopt a relaxation of the original problem. Let $\mathcal{I}$ denote the collection of all feasible seed sets (i.e., all subsets S such that $|S| \leq k$), and let $\Delta(\mathcal{I})$ represent the space of probability distributions over $\mathcal{I}$, corresponding to the $|\mathcal{I}|$-dimensional simplex. Our approach focuses on solving the relaxed optimization problem

$$\max_{D \in \Delta(\mathcal{I})} \min_{p \in \mathcal{U}} \mathrm{E}_{S \sim D} \left[\frac{f(S,p)}{OPT(p)} \right], \tag{5.1}$$

which permits the algorithm to choose a distribution over feasible solutions and assesses worst-case performance in expectation with respect to this distribution. From a game-theoretic perspective, this corresponds to allowing the algorithm to employ a mixed strategy rather than committing to a single pure strategy. During deployment, a specific seed set is drawn from the distribution D. While this guarantees strong performance only in expectation over the random draw—and does not yield ex-post guarantees for any particular sampled set due to the intrinsic hardness of the original max-min formulation—empirical results suggest that this approach is effective in practice. In particular, sampling multiple candidate sets from D and selecting the best-performing one typically yields outcomes that closely match, and in some cases exceed, the expected value implied by the distribution.

Our solution to this problem, presented in detail in [Wilder 2018], relies on a compact representation of the space of distributions by tracking only the marginal probability with which each node is selected, rather than explicitly representing the exponentially large collection of possible subsets. Using this representation, the algorithm solves a fractional relaxation of the original discrete max-min optimization problem through a stochastic first-order method tailored to the structural properties of the objective function. Once a solution to the fractional relaxation has been obtained, established rounding techniques for submodular maximization are applied to generate random feasible sets consistent with the inferred distribution. This overall approach yields a $(1 - 1/e)^2$-approximation guarantee for Problem 5.1, which can be further strengthened to a $(1 - 1/e)$ approximation with additional refinements, although we found such refinements to be unnecessary in practice.

5.4.2.1 Multi-stage intervention with attendance uncertainty

We address the multi-stage structure of the intervention by repeatedly solving a robust optimization problem at each stage. At every step, the objective is evaluated in expectation over which invited peer leaders ultimately attend, while conditioning on the peer leaders who were successfully recruited in earlier stages. Formally, at stage $t > 1$, we solve

$$\max_{D \in \Delta(\mathcal{I})} \min_{p \in \mathcal{U}} \mathrm{E}_{S_t \sim D} \left[\frac{f(S_t \cup S_1 \cup ... \cup S_{t-1}, p, q)}{\max_{|S^*| \leq k} f(S^* \cup S_1 \cup ... \cup S_{t-1}, p, q)} \right]$$

where $S_1 ... S_{t-1}$ denote the sets of peer leaders who were successfully recruited in each previous stage. As shown in [Wilder et al. 2018b], the objective function f remains submodular with respect to S_t, which allows us to preserve the approximation guarantees established for the single-stage setting at each individual stage of the process. Moreover, [Wilder et al. 2018b] demonstrates that the overall multi-stage formulation satisfies the property of *adaptive submodularity*. Specifically, for any fixed value of the parameter p, repeatedly solving

$$\max_{D \in \Delta(\mathcal{I})} \mathrm{E}_{S_t \sim D} \left[\frac{f(S_t \cup S_1 \cup ... \cup S_{t-1}, p, q)}{\max_{|S^*| \leq k} f(S^* \cup S_1 \cup ... \cup S_{t-1}, p, q)} \right]$$

at each stage t and selecting the corresponding set S_t yields an approximation guarantee with respect to the optimal adaptive policy for choosing a sequence of sets $S_1 ... S_t$, again assuming a fixed p. A more detailed treatment of these theoretical results is provided in [Wilder et al. 2018b].

5.5 Study Design

We now turn to the empirical component of the project and describe the design of the clinical trial. All study procedures received approval from our institution's Institutional Review Board. The trial was designed to evaluate the relative effectiveness of two approaches for selecting peer leaders: the CHANGE system described above and the standard public health practice based on degree centrality (DC), which selects youth with the highest number of social connections. In addition, an observation-only control condition (OBS) was included, yielding three study arms in total. The trial was implemented at three drop-in centers serving youth experiencing homelessness (YEH)—My Friend's Place,[1] Safe Place for Youth,[2] and Los Angeles LGBT Center[3]—all located in Los Angeles, USA. These drop-in centers offer essential services to YEH, including meals, clothing, case management, and mobile HIV testing. Given the high level of transience within the YEH population, most clients at a given center disengage within approximately six months. To account for this turnover, each of the three intervention conditions was deployed once at each center, resulting in nine total deployments, each involving a distinct cohort of youth. Deployments at the same center were spaced at least six months apart. Youth were permitted to enroll in the study only once; thus, individuals who remained at a center across multiple deployments were included only during their first enrollment attempt. Implementing each condition at each center helped control for variation in demographic composition and other contextual factors associated with differences across service sites.

Each of the nine deployments followed an identical study protocol. Figure 5.1 summarizes the number of youth who were recruited and subsequently retained at each phase of the study, disaggregated by study arm.

Each deployment proceeded through four phases. First, youth were recruited at the drop-in center over the course of one week to participate in the study. All participants provided informed consent prior to enrollment. Participants completed a baseline survey that collected information on demographic characteristics, sexual behaviors, and HIV-related knowledge. Demographic measures included age, sex assigned at birth, gender identity, race and ethnicity, and sexual orientation. Participants were also asked about their current living situation and relationship status.

[1] https://www.myfriendsplace.org/
[2] https://www.safeplaceforyouth.org/
[3] https://lalgbtcenter.org/

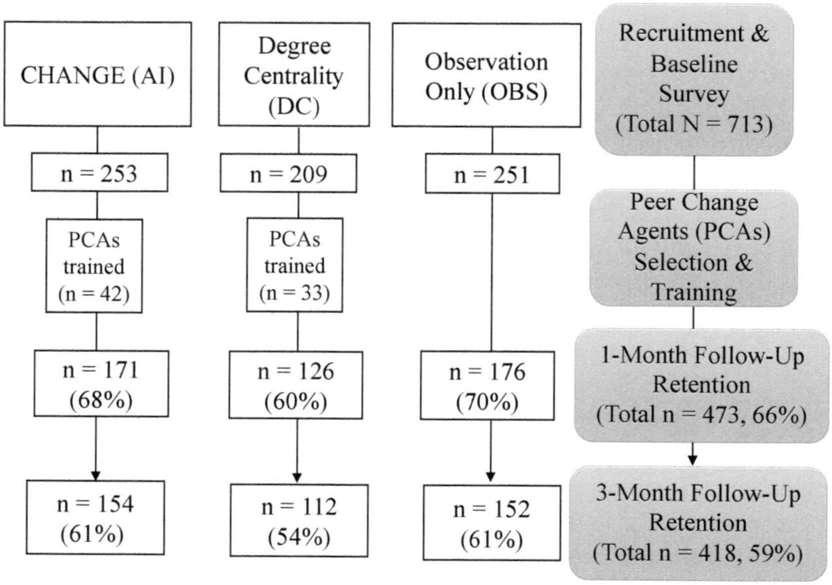

Figure 5.1 Number of participants recruited and retained in each arm of the study.

Second, peer leaders were selected and trained in the CHANGE and DC study arms. Training sessions typically included approximately four youth per session, with three to four sessions conducted per deployment, depending on attendance. Overall, roughly 15% of surveyed participants in each deployment were trained as peer leaders. In the CHANGE arm, network information was collected from approximately 20% of participants, sampled according to the procedure described earlier. In the DC arm, a complete network survey was administered to identify individuals with the highest degree, ensuring that the comparison condition reflected the strongest possible implementation of the standard public health approach.

Third, trained peer leaders were given a three-month period to disseminate HIV prevention messages within their social networks. During this time, peer leaders participated in seven weekly 30-minute check-in sessions with members of the research team. These sessions emphasized reinforcement of successful outreach efforts, as well as discussion of challenges, problem-solving strategies, and future goals. All peer leaders attended at least one check-in session, with the most common level of participation being five sessions. Peer leaders received $60 in compensation for completing the initial training and $20 for each check-in session attended.

Fourth, follow-up surveys were administered to the original study participants recruited in the first phase. These surveys assessed the same domains as the baseline instrument. Changes in self-reported sexual behaviors between baseline and follow-up constituted the primary outcome measures used to evaluate intervention effectiveness. All outcomes were self-reported; established best practices were employed to reduce bias, including self-administered surveys completed on tablets and assurances of participant anonymity, both of which are known to mitigate social desirability bias when reporting sensitive behaviors. Any residual bias would be expected to affect all study arms similarly, including the observation-only control condition.

The training component of the peer change agent intervention was delivered by two or three facilitators from the social work research team and lasted approximately four hours (one half-day). Training was interactive in format and organized into six 45-minute modules covering the peer leader role, sexual health, HIV prevention, communication skills, leadership development, and self-care. Peer leaders were encouraged to promote regular HIV testing and consistent condom use through conversations with their social contacts at the drop-in center.

5.6 Study Results

We next report the findings from the clinical trial. We begin by describing the outcome measures and the statistical analysis approach, and then present the primary results.

5.6.1 Outcome Variables

Two primary outcome variables were compared across the study arms. The first was condomless anal sex (CAS), measured using a survey item that asked whether participants had engaged in anal sex without a condom at least once during the previous month. The second was condomless vaginal sex (CVS), measured using a parallel survey item asking whether participants had vaginal sex without a condom at least once during the previous month. Both CAS and CVS represent key behavioral risk factors for HIV transmission and therefore serve as direct indicators of the intervention's effectiveness in achieving meaningful health-related outcomes.

5.6.2 Statistical Methodology

We now discuss statistical methods for analyzing the results of an experiment like the one conducted. The goal of such methods is to analyze the *treatment effect*, or the difference in some outcome attributable to the intervention that individuals are assigned to. In our case, the treatment effects we would like to estimate are the expected reduction in the likelihood of engaging in condomless sex due to inclusion in either the CHANGE or the degree centrality arm of the study compared to no intervention, i.e., the control group.

To briefly review, there are two principal ways of analyzing the results of a field trial under "normal" circumstances (where the ways in which our setting is "abnormal" will be clarified later). The first method is to simply average the outcomes of participants in each arm of the trial and report confidence intervals or p-values based on simple formulas for the mean of IID random variables. The second common method is to specify a statistical model (often linear) for the outcome as a function of pre-treatment covariates (e.g., demographic variables) as well as the treatment assignment. This can help improve the precision of the estimated treatment effect (i.e., lower its variance) when the pre-treatment covariates are correlated with the outcome. Although the simple sample mean estimator is unbiased, randomization is expected to create differences in the pre-treatment covariates of individuals assigned to different arms, which creates variance. A model-based analysis helps reduce this variance by controlling for these random baseline differences (at the potential cost of introducing bias under some circumstances if the model is misspecified). See [Sheldon 2000] for a more detailed discussion. Approaches based on regression adjustments (typically with linear or logistic models) are very common in applied settings such as medicine and public health because the reduction in variance from controlling for covariates is sufficiently great that it is viewed as worthwhile to accept some potential bias from model misspecification.

Our setting deviates from the standard picture in that our measurements are not all IID. In fact, the IID assumption fails in two notable ways. First, the very premise of the study is that participants will be influenced by one another. This is a form of *interference*, where the outcomes of participants within the same group will be correlated via the spread of behaviors among them. This means that attempts to treat the responses as independent will produce overly optimistic confidence intervals. In the most pessimistic scenario, the effective number of independent samples we see could be as low as one sample per network, if the respondents within each network were perfectly correlated.

Reality lies somewhere in the middle, where participants within the same network are imperfectly correlated, meaning that we have less information than if all of their responses were independent, but nevertheless more than if there if the entire network were completely correlated.

Second, we make multiple post-treatment measurements of the same individual (at one and three months after the intervention). These measurements are also correlated with one another, since we expect there to be (unobserved) characteristics of each individual person that influence their outcomes across time. Again, while these data points are not fully independent, we may still nevertheless be able to increase the precision of our estimates by jointly analyzing all of the responses instead of limiting ourselves to the smaller sample collected at a fixed time point.

A wide range of methods have been proposed in statistics, econometrics, and epidemiology to accommodate these structured forms of dependencies between observations. We do not provide a comprehensive treatment of these methods here, but we offer an overview of their main advantages and disadvantages as they pertain to the setting at hand.

One family of methods starts with one of the usual estimators discussed above but attempts to correct for interference (either within individuals or within networks) in the confidence intervals or p-values that are associated with the estimates. Effectively, we should think of our estimator as having higher variance due to the fact that some of our observations are correlated with one another, leading to wider confidence intervals. This idea is instantiated via a particular method for approximating the sampling variance of the treatment effect estimator. It is often referred to as "clustered standard errors" because it produces standard errors that account for the clustering of observations into groups within which correlations are possible. Clustered standard errors are an extension of the standard "sandwich estimator" of the variance of an estimand. Asymptotically, the sandwich estimator will produce consistent estimates of the standard errors of the estimator, which, for an asymptotically normal estimator, can in turn be translated into confidence intervals or p-values. This asymptotic validity is a desirable property that does not require distributional assumptions about the data (beyond those on the model or design that underlie the cluster structure). However, these methods are potentially problematic for our circumstances because we have only nine groups—too small for asymptotics to be meaningful—and simulation experiments have shown that the sandwich estimator may perform poorly in this few-clusters regime.

A second family of methods goes by a variety of names – random or mixed effects models, hierarchical models, multi-level models, etc. [Gelman 2006]. These methods impose stronger distributional assumptions on the data. In particular, they model the data as drawn from a statistical model (typically linear) that contains a shared random error term across all observations within the same group, in contrast to the standard regression model, where error terms are independent across observations. This shared error induces correlations in observations within the group. Consider an example where the groups correspond to the nine different networks we intervene in. Intuitively, we can think of the shared error as modeling that, while the expected outcomes of individuals in a given network will depend on their covariates and treatment assignments through whatever regression equation is specified, the individuals in a given network will tend to all deviate from their expected outcomes in the same direction, depending on whether their shared diffusion process spread more or less widely than expected. The shared error term is typically modeled as drawn from a normal distribution and must be uncorrelated with the covariates of individuals in the group. If these assumptions are satisfied, we have more powerful statistical tools at our disposal with which to analyze the results. These can take the form of either frequentist hypothesis tests (after fitting the model with maximum likelihood) or Bayesian analyses, which produce a full posterior over the parameters of interest.

Our analysis employs a Bayesian mixed-effects model, as this allows us to obtain a full posterior distribution over the treatment effect in a manner that accounts for the small number of clusters (i.e., avoids potentially inappropriate asymptotic approximations). For each outcome variable, we specified a regression model that included terms capturing the effect of participation in each study arm—our primary estimand of interest—along with a set of control variables designed to adjust for demographic differences and baseline variation in risk behaviors across arms. The demographic controls included age, sex assigned at birth, transgender identity, LGBQ identity, an interaction between male sex and LGBQ identity, race, committed relationship status, housing status, and drop-in center. In addition, we included a "time" covariate to account for temporal changes affecting the overall study population independent of assignment to a particular intervention arm. Together, these covariates help disentangle the causal impact of the intervention from both pre-existing differences between study arms and broader time trends unrelated to the intervention. Because the outcomes of interest are binary, the models were estimated using a logistic link function.

We further incorporated random effects to account for potential dependence among observations, as noted previously. Specifically, we included one random effect at the participant level and one at the intervention-group level, reflecting the nested structure of the data. Let x_i denote the covariate vector for individual i, $a_{\text{CHANGE},i}$ indicate assignment of individual i to the CHANGE arm, $a_{\text{DC},i}$ indicate assignment to the DC arm, $c(i)$ denote the intervention group associated with individual i, p_i indicate whether individual i was selected as a peer leader, and β represent the model parameters. The resulting model takes the following form:

$$\begin{aligned}\text{logit}(y_{it}) = {} & \beta_{\text{cov}} x_i + \beta_{\text{CHANGE}} \cdot t \cdot a_{\text{CHANGE},i} \\ & + \beta_{\text{DC}} \cdot t \cdot a_{\text{DC},i} + \beta_{\text{PL}} \cdot t \cdot p_i + \epsilon_i + \epsilon_{c(i)} + \epsilon_{it}.\end{aligned}$$

Within this framework, the log-odds of the outcome y_{it} are determined by several distinct components. First, individual-level covariates contribute through a set of coefficients denoted by β_{cov}. Second, assignment to a study arm contributes via parameters β_{CHANGE} and β_{DC}, corresponding to the CHANGE and DC conditions, respectively. These effects enter the model through interactions between treatment assignment and time, thereby capturing changes in outcomes over time for individuals assigned to each intervention arm. Third, we account for outcome changes among participants selected as peer leaders, independent of intervention arm, by including an interaction between time and peer leader status, with coefficient β_{PL}. This term allows us to distinguish improvements attributable to direct participation as a peer leader from broader spillover effects within the population. Finally, the model includes random effects ϵ_i and $\epsilon_{c(i)}$, which capture correlation among repeated observations from the same individual and among individuals within the same intervention group, respectively. The term ϵ_{it} represents an independent error component for each observation.

We also evaluated an alternative Mundlak-Chamberlain specification, which relaxes standard random-effects assumptions by permitting $\epsilon_{c(i)}$ to be correlated with group-level means of the covariates [Chamberlain 1982, Mundlak 1978]. This alternative formulation produced estimates that were substantively indistinguishable from those of the primary model. All analyses were conducted within a Bayesian framework, with posterior inference performed using rstan [Stan Development Team 2023]. Posterior distributions over the parameters of interest were obtained using the default weakly informative priors provided by rstan.

We report results using both 90% and 95% credible intervals for the estimated model parameters. For the treatment effects corresponding to the

CHANGE and DC arms, we additionally present posterior distributions of the relative risk. These relative risk estimates marginalize over the distribution of other covariates in the study population, thereby capturing the average probability of a given outcome among participants assigned to a particular intervention arm relative to those in the control condition. For instance, a relative risk of 80

Outcome data were available only for participants who completed follow-up surveys, resulting in missing observations due to attrition, which is common in studies involving youth experiencing homelessness. Among the 713 participants who completed the baseline survey, 245 (34%) did not complete the 1-month follow-up, 300 (42%) missed the 3-month follow-up, and 180 (25%) missed both follow-up assessments. Importantly, attrition was not statistically significantly associated with either CAS or CVS, suggesting that participants included in the follow-up analyses were not systematically over- or under-represented with respect to baseline levels of risk behavior.

5.6.3 Results

We now report the primary findings from the statistical analysis, summarized in Figure 5.2. As illustrated in the figure, there is little evidence for baseline differences across study arms or for improvements over time that are independent of the intervention. Specifically, the credible intervals for all parameters corresponding to baseline differences and time effects include 0 for both outcomes.

For condomless anal sex (CAS), we observe a reduction over time in the CHANGE arm, with a posterior median relative risk of 0.58 (95% CrI: 0.35–0.93). A relative risk of 0.58 implies that, according to the model estimates, a youth enrolled in the CHANGE arm has a 42% lower probability of engaging in CAS compared to a youth in the observation-only control group. In other words, holding baseline characteristics constant—including baseline CAS behavior—participants receiving the CHANGE intervention exhibit a substantially reduced likelihood of CAS following the intervention relative to comparable youth who did not receive the intervention. In the DC arm, the posterior median relative risk was 0.70, suggesting a possible improvement; however, the 95% credible interval included 1 (95% CrI: 0.39, 1.15), indicating that a reduction in CAS cannot be established with high confidence.

Turning to the second outcome, condomless vaginal sex (CVS), the estimated median relative risk for the CHANGE arm was 0.73, with a 95% credible interval narrowly including 1 (95% CrI: 0.50, 1.01). As shown in

Figure 5.2, the corresponding 90% credible interval excluded 1. For the DC arm, the estimated median relative risk was 0.84 (95% CrI: 0.54, 1.21).

Overall, these results indicate that CHANGE led to improvements in HIV-related risk behaviors with high posterior probability, with at least a 97.3% probability of improvement for both outcomes. The DC intervention showed a tendency toward reduced risk behaviors, but the posterior distributions did not rule out null or negative effects at the 90% credible interval level. Because the analysis explicitly controlled for whether participants were selected as

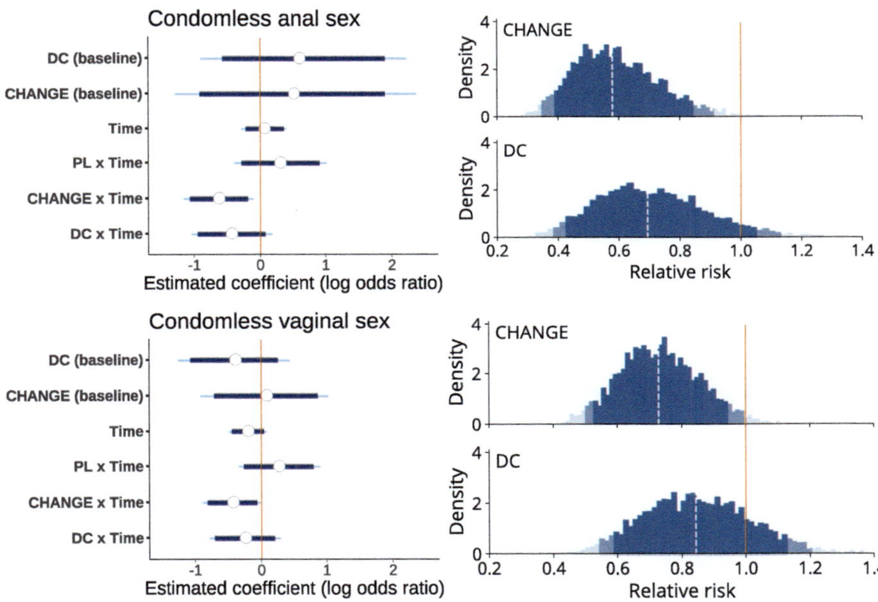

Figure 5.2 Posterior estimates for the CAS (top) and CVS (bottom) outcomes. Left: credible intervals for estimated coefficients in the linear mixed effects model. Thick lines denote 90% credible intervals, thin lines denote 95% credible intervals, and circles denote the posterior median. Right: posterior distribution of the relative risk post-intervention for each treatment arm. Shaded regions denote the 90% and 95% credible intervals, with the dashed line giving the posterior median. In the left-hand figure, the "baseline" category measures pre-existing differences between the groups (relative to the observation-only group) on enrollment in the study. The "Group x Time" category measures the estimated per-unit-time impact of participating in each arm of the intervention (relative to the observation-only group, and after controlling for both demographics and baseline behaviors). "PL x Time" refers to improvement over time in youth selected to be peer leaders across either arm of the intervention. "Time" gives the estimated contribution of a trend over time independent of which arm of the study a participant was enrolled in.

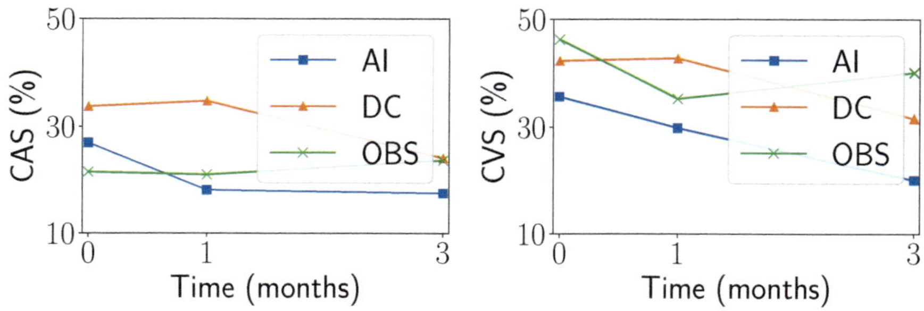

Figure 5.3 Average value of each outcome variable at each point in time for the three arms. These plots show the results without any statistical processing, while the analysis above attempts to control for pre-existing differences between participants in each arm.

peer leaders, the estimated treatment effects reflect changes at the level of the broader population, including youth who did not serve as peer leaders. This pattern provides evidence that the intervention generated spillover effects from directly trained peer leaders to other youth in the network, consistent with the intended mechanism of action.

A complementary perspective emerges from direct inspection of the average outcome values by study arm over time (Figure 5.3). These descriptive trends suggest that behavioral improvements in the CHANGE arm occurred more rapidly than in the DC arm: most of the reduction in risk behaviors for CHANGE is evident by the one-month follow-up, whereas comparable improvements in the DC arm are not fully realized until the three-month assessment. The speed of impact is particularly important in this context for two reasons. First, earlier adoption of protective behaviors can immediately reduce HIV transmission risk in a highly vulnerable population. Second, high levels of transience among YEH imply that a meaningful fraction of participants may no longer be engaged with a drop-in center by the end of a three-month intervention period. Taken together, these findings suggest that the AI-augmented intervention implemented through CHANGE may offer an additional advantage over standard degree-based peer leader selection by producing faster and more immediate behavioral change.

5.7 Discussion

This project provides empirical evidence that AI-based methods can enhance the effectiveness of social network interventions in public health. In particular, we observed significant reductions in HIV risk behaviors in groups where the intervention was planned using the CHANGE system, whereas no statistically significant behavioral changes were detected when the conventional public health approach of selecting high-degree individuals was applied. Beyond these specific findings, we aim for the experiences accumulated over the course of this project to offer transferable insights into how AI research can be productively directed toward social good. Recent work has sought to articulate general principles for AI for Social Good research [Floridi et al. 2020, Tomašev et al. 2020]. Our discussion complements these efforts by grounding recommendations in the practical realities of deploying a community-level intervention. While much of the existing discourse appropriately emphasizes ethics, data privacy, and trust-building, our experience suggests that equal attention should be paid to the operational challenges involved in translating AI methods into real-world impact. We highlight five lessons from this process.

First, effective projects begin by engaging closely with domain experts to identify where AI can meaningfully contribute. This work did not originate from a preconceived plan to apply influence maximization to peer leader selection. Instead, this direction emerged organically through sustained collaboration between researchers in AI and social work, who jointly identified an opportunity where algorithmic support was both feasible and likely to improve outcomes. *Projects are less likely to succeed when AI researchers begin with a preferred technique and then search for a suitable application.*

Second, data availability proved to be the primary bottleneck for the AI components of the intervention. Much of the existing computational literature on influence maximization assumes access to detailed information, including full network structure and well-specified diffusion models. In practice, none of this information was readily available for youth experiencing homelessness, nor is it likely to be accessible in many public health contexts. Moreover, collecting such data directly is time-intensive and costly, placing an unsustainable burden on organizations attempting to deploy interventions independently. Consequently, a substantial portion of the technical contribution of this work involved developing methods that substantially reduce the amount of data required for effective intervention planning. *Designing algorithms that minimize or eliminate data requirements is critical for creating AI systems that can be deployed in community health settings.*

Third, simplicity in system design is highly valuable. Prior to developing CHANGE, we explored a more theoretically sophisticated algorithm for network data collection that offered provable guarantees for certain classes of graphs [Wilder et al. 2018a]. However, this approach required many sequential, interdependent queries, making it difficult to implement in practice. In settings involving youth experiencing homelessness, it is often challenging to locate specific individuals at specific times, and interruptions can derail tightly coupled processes. More generally, algorithms that require frequent back-and-forth interaction with the external environment introduce multiple points of failure that are not captured in formal models. This notion of simplicity differs from how simplicity is often framed in AI for Social Good discussions, which typically emphasize *explainability* [Floridi et al. 2020] or *methodological* simplicity [Tomašev et al. 2020], such as favoring established techniques over novel ones. While both are valuable, our experience suggests that neither was a first-order requirement in this setting. Instead, what mattered most was that the system's interface with the real world was simple, robust, and resilient, even if the internal optimization was complex. *We argue that this form of operational simplicity deserves greater emphasis in AI for Social Good research.*

Fourth, small-scale pilot deployments were essential precursors to the larger clinical trial. We conducted multiple pilot studies, each involving a single drop-in center, to test early versions of the system [Wilder et al. 2018b, Yadav et al. 2016b, 2017c]. These pilots surfaced critical challenges that would have been difficult to anticipate otherwise. For example, we quickly learned that relying on Facebook data to infer social networks was ineffective for this population, and that in-person network data collection required substantial effort. We also observed high rates of nonattendance among invited peer leaders, necessitating adaptive recruitment strategies. Resolving these issues proved central to the eventual success of the intervention and constituted much of the technical challenge of the project. *Many of these obstacles would likely have remained invisible without testing algorithms in the environments where they were intended to operate.* It was also invaluable for computer scientists on the research team to be physically present during pilot deployments, both to better understand the context and to assist with early coordination of algorithmic decision-making.

Fifth, sustained community engagement and trust were indispensable. Beyond the core research team, the project depended on collaboration with multiple stakeholders, including leadership and staff at each participating drop-in center. Their support was necessary to host the study, recruit participants, and allocate space and resources. To facilitate ongoing communication, we convened a community advisory board composed of representatives from the centers and members of the research team, which met regularly to discuss study progress, explain methodological choices, and share insights relevant to broader center activities. Equally important were the youth themselves. Participation required disclosure of highly sensitive information, including HIV risk behaviors and social relationships. For youth experiencing homelessness—who may be especially wary of authority figures—trust-building was critical. Two factors were particularly influential. First, the social work members of the research team had longstanding relationships with the community, having provided services at these centers for over a decade. Second, transparency regarding data use was essential. We found that youth were significantly more willing to disclose social connections when researchers proactively explained how this information would be used, including the role of algorithmic selection of peer leaders. *Because the peer change agent model is fundamentally about empowering youth to effect change in their communities, this ethos should also guide how AI systems are designed and deployed in community contexts.*

We hope that this project contributes a concrete example to a broader research agenda focused on developing AI techniques that meaningfully advance health and equity. Considerable work remains. Even within the domain of social network interventions, future research could explore alternative intervention designs, such as approaches that seek to reshape network structure by fostering supportive ties, methods for further reducing data requirements through the use of administrative or auxiliary data, and deeper investigation into the mechanisms linking information diffusion to behavioral change. Nonetheless, the results of this clinical trial demonstrate that AI has the potential to substantially enhance the quality and effectiveness of services delivered to some of the most vulnerable populations in our communities.

Acknowledgments

This work was supported by the Army Research Office (MURI W911NF1810208) and the California HIV/AIDS Research Program.

6

Algorithms for Matching Market Design

SangMok Lee and M. Bumin Yenmez

Washington University in St. Louis

Abstract

Market design applies algorithmic and economic principles to create fair and efficient allocation mechanisms in contexts such as school choice, housing, and organ donation. This chapter introduces the theoretical foundations of matching algorithms, focusing on the Deferred Acceptance mechanism and its extensions. We demonstrate how these algorithms can incorporate fairness constraints, diversity objectives, and efficiency adjustments, and explore their application in real-world systems, such as public school assignments. The chapter illustrates how careful algorithmic design can balance stakeholder preferences, equity considerations, and systemic efficiency.

6.1 Introduction

The purpose of this chapter is to introduce the literature on market design, specifically the design of algorithms for economic applications. The literature is vast, so we focus on the so-called **school choice problem**. More generally, the question is how to allocate items that have priorities. Besides public school choice, other applications include university housing allocation, where different buildings give priority to students with different seniorities, and specialty matches in the military. We demonstrate how economists have designed and improved a matching algorithm, and how the algorithm can be generalized to accommodate a more complex priority structure that includes factors such as student diversity.

DOI: 10.1201/9788743812074-7

6.2 Basic Matching Algorithms

Most public school districts in the US assign students to their neighborhood schools. However, large school districts such as those in NYC, Chicago, and San Francisco allow students and families to choose public schools outside their neighborhoods. We study how to design an algorithm for a public school choice program, should we decide to implement one.[1] Most of the results in this section are from the inspiring work of Abdulkadiroğlu and Sönmez [2003].

6.2.1 Illustrative Example

We explain the main results using the following illustrative example. Formal models and results are provided in 6.2.2.

Example 6.1. *Consider a school district with three students, i_1, i_2, i_3, and three schools, s_1, s_2, s_3. Each school can accommodate only one student. Students have preferences over schools, and schools have priorities over students as follows.*

i_1	i_2	i_3
s_2	s_1	s_1
s_1	s_3	s_2
s_3	s_2	s_3

s_1	s_2	s_3
i_1	i_3	i_1
i_2	i_1	i_2
i_3	i_2	i_3

For example, student i_1's most preferred school is s_2, followed by s_1, with s_3 being the least preferred. School s_1 gives the highest priority to student i_1, followed by students i_2 and i_3. In practice, school priorities are determined by their districts. A student's higher priority for a school can be due to factors such as an older sibling already attending the school or the proximity of the student's home to the school.

The district's goal is to assign students to schools. The design objectives are efficient and fair placements, and an easy-to-understand procedure. Different algorithms can be used to produce an assignment.

The Immediate-Acceptance (IA) algorithm, also known as the (old) Boston algorithm, was once common practice. The algorithm operates in steps. In the first step, students apply to their top-choice schools. If rejected, they apply to their next choices in the following step. Matches made in each step are permanent, and subsequent steps start with unmatched students and schools

[1] There is a debate regarding the pros and cons of having a public school choice program [Harris and Fessenden 2017], but we will set it aside.

with empty seats. In 6.1, i_1 proposes to s_2 and is admitted. The other students propose to s_1; using s_1's priority ranking, i_2 is admitted, and i_3 is rejected, concluding the first step. In the second step, only i_3 and s_3 remain unmatched, so they match with each other. The outcome is $\{(i_1 - s_2), (i_2 - s_1), (i_3 - s_3)\}$

In the IA algorithm, students who apply to competitive schools first take the risk of losing the opportunity to be matched with their next preferred schools if they are rejected by their top choices. In the scenario described above, if student i_3 had reported a preference where s_2 is listed first, they could have been admitted to that school based on the priority for s_2. Hence, while the IA algorithm itself is easy to understand, deciding what preference to report to the algorithm is a difficult question for students and their families. It is crucial for i_3 to understand the level of competitiveness at s_1. Student i_1 needs to anticipate that i_3 might choose to apply to s_2 first, making s_2 more competitive. In this case, i_1 could be rejected by s_2 and matched poorly with s_3, so i_1 may want to skip their top choice and consider other less competitive options.

Abdulkadiroğlu and Sönmez [2003] propose two alternative algorithms. Unlike the IA algorithm, both alternatives are known to be **strategy-proof**, meaning that truthfully reporting preferences is always optimal for each student, irrespective of the preferences reported by other students. Strategy-proofness makes it straightforward for students to decide what preferences to report.

The first proposal is the Deferred-Acceptance (DA) algorithm, also called the Gale-Shapley algorithm. The DA algorithm is almost identical to the IA algorithm but defers matches in each step until the end of all steps. This allows students who have been rejected by their most preferred schools to move down their rank-order lists and potentially displace previously matched students. In 6.1, the DA algorithm works as follows. In Step 1, student i_1 applies for s_2 and is tentatively admitted. Other students apply for s_1, and i_2 is tentatively admitted, whereas i_3 is permanently rejected. In the next step, i_3 applies for s_2 and displaces i_1, which subsequently, in the following step, applies for s_1 and displaces i_2. In the last step, i_2 applies to s_3 and gets matched. The algorithm outputs the matching $\{(i_1 - s_1), (i_2 - s_3), (i_3 - s_2)\}$. The 'deferred' acceptances let students apply for their most preferred schools first and make the algorithm strategy-proof.

The second alternative algorithm is the Top Trading Cycles (TTC), which also operates in multiple steps. In each step, each student points to their top-choice school from schools with an empty seat, and each school points to its highest-ranked student. This creates a graph with at least one cycle. The algorithm then removes students in cycles and reduces the capacities of schools in cycles by one, matching the removed students to the schools they pointed to. The next step proceeds with unmatched students and schools with empty seats. If the TTC algorithm is run for 6.1, in the first step, i_1 points to s_2, which points to i_3, who points to s_1, forming a cycle back to i_1. Accordingly, $(i_1 - s_2)$ and $(i_3 - s_1)$ are matched. In the second step, the only remaining student i_2 and school s_3 point to each other, forming a cycle, and get matched. TTC is also strategy-proof because if a student matches in step k, the first $k-1$ steps remain unchanged regardless of the student's reported preferences. The student obtains the most preferred school remaining until step k, so there is no reason not to report truthfully.

Let's compare the DA outcome with the TTC outcome:

$$\text{DA} = \{(i_1 - s_1), (i_2 - s_3), (i_3 - s_2)\},$$
$$\text{TTC} = \{(i_1 - s_2), (i_2 - s_3), (i_3 - s_1)\}.$$

The DA outcome is inefficient, because two students (i_1 and i_3) can match strictly better, and no student matches worse by switching to the TTC outcome. The TTC algorithm is known to always produce an efficient matching. However, the TTC outcome is unfair. Student i_2 is matched to s_3, while a more preferred school s_1 is matched to i_3, who has a lower priority for s_1 than student i_2. Imagine that student i_2 lives next to s_1 and has a high priority for the school, but ends up matched to a far-away school s_3, while the school s_1 is assigned to a lower-priority student i_3. Such a match would be considered unfair. In contrast, the DA algorithm is known to always produce a fair matching.

Ultimately, the choice between DA and TTC comes down to fairness versus matching efficiency.

6.2.2 Formal Model and Results

A school choice problem is defined by $\{I, S, (\succ_i)_{i \in I}, (q_s)_{s \in S}, (P_s)_{s \in S}\}$. Here, I is a finite set of students (or individuals) and S is a finite set of schools. For each school s, a positive integer q_s represents the school's capacity. Each student i has a strict preference ranking $\succ_i$ over schools, and each school s has a strict priority ranking P_s over individual students. We assume that all students and schools rank each other, and there is enough overall capacity to accommodate all students, i.e., $\sum_s q_s \geq |I|$. These assumptions ease the exposition but are not necessary for the results in this section.

A **matching** $\mu : I \to S$ must satisfy the capacity constraint: the number of students matched to a school s does not exceed the school capacity q_s (mathematically, $|\{i : \mu(i) = s\}| \leq q_s$). We extend a student's preferences over schools as preferences over matchings, such that for matchings μ and ν, we have $\mu \succeq_i \nu$ if $\mu(i) \succ_i \nu(i)$ or $\mu(i) = \nu(i)$.

A matching μ is **Pareto efficient** if there is no other matching $\nu \neq \mu$ such that $\nu \succeq_i \mu$ for every student i, ensuring that no student becomes worse off and at least one student is strictly better off. A matching μ is **stable** if (1) there are no student i and school s such that $s \succ_i \mu(i)$ and $|i' : \mu(i') = s| < q_s$ (**non-wastefulness**), and (2) there are no students i, i' and school s such that $s \succ_i \mu(i)$, $iP_s i'$, and $\mu(i') = s$ (**no justified envy**). A wasteful matching is not Pareto efficient, and a matching with justified envy is considered unfair.

Note that schools' priorities are determined by a school district, but students' preferences are privately known and have to be reported to the district. Accordingly, a school district needs to choose an algorithm (often called a mechanism) that takes rank order lists (ROLs) from students and produces a matching. We denote an algorithm by ϕ and its output by $\phi(\succ)$ if students report $\succ = (\succ_i)_{i \in I}$. Since student preferences are privately known, the ROLs need not coincide with students' true preferences.

An algorithm ϕ is **strategy-proof** if for any student i, any pair of preferences $\succ_i$ and $\succ_i'$, and other students' preferences $\succ_{-i} = (\succ_j)_{j \neq i}$, we have $\phi(\succ_i, \succ_{-i}) \succeq_i \phi(\succ_i', \succ_{-i})$.

We present the definition of the Deferred-Acceptance algorithm below. The DA algorithm underlies algorithms currently used in many school districts. For the other two algorithms—Immediate Acceptance (IA) and Top Trading Cycle (TTC)—we believe the description using 6.1 above suffices, and thus we omit their definitions.

The Deferred-Acceptance Algorithm

There are multiple steps of proposals and selections. Initially, no one is matched.

Step 1 Each student proposes to their highest-ranked school. Each school tentatively accepts the highest-priority students among all proposals it has received until the capacity is full and rejects the rest (if any remain).

Step t Each rejected student in Step $t - 1$ proposes to the next-ranked school. Each school tentatively accepts the highest-priority students among all proposals that it has received so far up to capacity and rejects the rest.

Abdulkadiroğlu and Sönmez [2003] obtained the following results:

Theorem 6.1. *1. The IA algorithm is not strategy-proof; however, the DA and TTC algorithms are strategy-proof.*

2. The DA algorithm produces a matching that is stable but may be Pareto inefficient.

3. The TTC algorithm produces a Pareto efficient matching but may have justified envy.

6.3 Efficiency-Adjusted DA (EADA)

Many school districts have recently started using variations of the DA algorithm. Choosing the DA algorithm over TTC essentially prioritizes fairness over matching efficiency. One recent development in school choice design aims to enhance matching efficiency by adjusting the DA algorithm and tolerating some degree of unfairness.

The following adjustment to the DA algorithm was originally proposed by Kesten [2010] and later redefined more intuitively by Tang and Yu [2014].

The idea is for a school district to obtain a student's consent to relinquish priorities, thereby enabling the planner to improve Pareto efficiency by starting from the outcome of the DA algorithm.

Example 6.2. *(Example 3 of Kesten [2010]) There are five schools, denoted as $s_1, \ldots, s_5$, and five students, denoted as $i_1, \ldots, i_5$. School s_5 has two seats, while the other schools have only one seat. Preferences and priorities are given as follows.*

i_1	i_2	i_3	i_4	i_5	i_6
s_2	s_3	s_3	s_1	s_1	s_4
s_1	s_1	s_4	s_2	s_5	s_1
s_3	s_5	s_2	s_4	$\vdots$	s_3
$\vdots$	$\vdots$	$\vdots$	$\vdots$		s_2
					s_5

,

s_1	s_2	s_3	s_4	s_5
i_2	i_3	i_1	i_4	$\vdots$
i_1	i_6	i_6	i_3	
i_5	i_4	i_2	i_6	
i_6	i_1	i_3	$\vdots$	
i_4	$\vdots$	$\vdots$		
i_3				

For the given school choice problem, the DA algorithm operates as follows:

Step	s_1	s_2	s_3	s_4	s_5
Step 1	$\underline{i_5}$, i_4	$\underline{i_1}$	$\underline{i_2}$, i_3	$\underline{i_6}$	
$\vdots$	$\vdots$	$\vdots$	$\vdots$	$\vdots$	$\vdots$
Final assignment	$\underline{i_2}$	$\underline{i_3}$	$\underline{i_1}$	$\underline{i_4}$	$\underline{i_5}$, $\underline{i_6}$

In Step 1, students i_5 and i_4 initially propose to s_1. School s_1 permanently rejects i_4 and tentatively accepts i_5.

A school is considered **underdemanded** in a matching μ if no student prefers the school to their assignment under μ. In the above example, only s_5 is underdemanded in the DA matching.

Now, we are ready to state the algorithm proposed by Kesten [2010].

Efficiency Adjusted Deferred Acceptance Algorithm (EADA) Each student chooses either "consent" or "not".

- Round 0: Run DA (Call it Round-0 DA).
- Round 1:
  1. Identify underdemanded schools at the Round-0 DA matching μ, and finalize assignments for these schools.
  2. For each removed student i who does not consent, and for each $(s, j) \in S \times I$ such that $s \succ_i \mu(i)$ and iP_sj, remove s from j's preference list.
  3. Then, run DA with the remaining students and schools (call it Round-1 DA).
- Repeat until all schools are removed.

Now we demonstrate how the EADA algorithm works.

Example 6.3. *(EADA, when i_5 does not consent, and other students consent)*

1. *Round 0: DA.*
2. *Round 1: Due to s_5 being underdemanded, assignments for i_5 and i_6 to s_5 are finalized. As i_5 does not consent and prefers s_1 to s_5 ($s_1 \succ_{i_5} s_5$), s_1 is removed from the lists of students j with $i_5 \succ_{s_1} j$. Specifically, s_1 is removed from the lists of i_3 and i_4. The revised preference lists and Round-1 DA are:*

i_1	i_2	i_3	i_4
s_2	s_3	s_3	s_2
s_1	s_1	s_4	s_4
s_3	s_5	s_2	$\vdots$
$\vdots$	$\vdots$	$\vdots$	

,

Step	s_1	s_2	s_3	s_4
1		i_1, $\underline{i_4}$	$\underline{i_2}$, i_3	
2	$\underline{i_1}$			$\underline{i_3}$
Outcome	$\underline{i_1}$	$\underline{i_4}$	$\underline{i_2}$	$\underline{i_3}$

3. *Round 2: both s_1 and s_4 are under-demanded, leading to final assignments for these schools to i_1 and i_2, respectively. Both students chose to consent.*

4. *Round 3: The DA assigns s_2 and s_3 to i_4 and i_2, the same as in the Round-2 DA.*[2]

Since student i_6 consents, an efficiency-improving trade is possible at Round-0 DA outcome among the remaining agents and schools. However, i_5 does not consent, so an efficiency-improving trade between i_1 and i_4 at the Round-1 DA matching is not allowed. Student i_5 opposes i_4 being assigned to s_1 while i_5 is assigned to a less preferred school.

The assignment of a student by EADA is independent of whether the student consents or not. This result is intuitive because EADA uses a student's consent only after finalizing the student's assignment.

A matching μ is **constrained efficient** if it has no justified envy among non-consenting students and is not Pareto dominated by any such matching.

Theorem 6.2. *The EADA outcome is Pareto efficient when all students consent and is constrained efficient, otherwise.*

6.4 Generalization of DA

In this section, we provide a generalized version of DA. Previously, we assumed each school had a priority ranking over students and a capacity, so that, from a set of students, the school admits students according to the priority ranking until the capacity is filled or all proposed students are chosen. However, in practice, schools can have more complicated admissions rules. For example, schools may have diversity or affirmative action policies. Our treatment is based on [Hatfield and Milgrom 2005], [Roth and Sotomayor 1990], and [Chambers and Yenmez 2017].

To illustrate this point, consider the setting in 6.1. Let i_1 and i_2 be female students and i_3 a male student. Suppose now that s_1 has a capacity of two and has preferences for diversity based on gender. When s_1 considers only the priority ranking of students if all students apply, then it would admit $\{i_1, i_2\}$ because both of them have a higher priority than i_3. However, both admitted students are female, and, therefore, the admitted set lacks diversity based on gender. Therefore, s_1 may consider admitting i_3 instead of i_2, so the admitted set would be $\{i_1, i_3\}$ that has one female student and one male student. One way of implementing affirmative action or diversity policies is to *reserve* seats for students belonging to target groups [Echenique and Yenmez 2015, Ehlers et al. 2014, Hafalir et al. 2013]. In the example, s_1 may reserve one seat for

[2]Round 3 could be omitted in a simpler version of EADA in Tang and Yu [2014].

female students and one seat for male students. From any set of students, s_1 would first admit the female student with the highest priority (if a female student is in the set) and the male student with the highest priority (if a male student is in the set). Then the school admits students of the highest priority from the remaining students to fill its empty seats.

We introduce the following notion to model schools with complicated admissions rules. The **choice rule** of school $s \in S$ is given by a function $Ch_s : 2^I \to 2^I$, which maps each nonempty set $I' \subseteq I$ of students to a subset $Ch_s(I') \subseteq I'$ of chosen students such that the number of chosen students does not exceed the capacity, that is, $|Ch_s(I')| \leq q_s$. The choice rule of a school governs how students are admitted.

We can now define DA when schools have choice rules as follows.

Generalized Deferred Acceptance Algorithm (DA)

Step 1. Each student proposes to their most preferred school. Each school s considers the set of proposals that it receives, say $I_1(s)$. It tentatively accepts $Ch_s(I_1(s))$. It permanently rejects all other students. If there is no rejection, then stop.

Step $t \geq 2$. Each student who is rejected at Step $t-1$ proposes to her most preferred school among the ones that have not rejected her yet. If there is no such school, then she is assigned to her outside option (i.e., she is unassigned). Each school s considers the set of students that it tentatively accepted at Step $t-1$ together with students who have proposed at Step t, say $I_t(s)$. It tentatively accepts $Ch_s(I_t(s))$, and permanently rejects other proposals. If there is no rejection, then stop.

In this more general school choice setting, stability can be defined as follows: A matching $\mu : I \to S$ is **stable** if (i) for each $s \in S$, $Ch_s(\mu^{-1}(s)) = \mu^{-1}(s)$ (**individual rationality**) and (ii) there exist no $s \in S$ and $i \in I$ such that $s \succ_i \mu(i)$ and $i \in Ch_s(\mu^{-1}(s) \cup \{i\})$ (**no blocking pairs**).[3]

Stable matchings need not exist in general. Therefore, we make the following assumption: Choice rule Ch_s satisfies **path independence** if, for every $I', I'' \subseteq I$, $Ch_s(I' \cup I'') = Ch_s(Ch_s(I') \cup Ch_s(I''))$. The choice rule that reserves seats for students belonging to target groups satisfies path independence.

Theorem 6.3. *Suppose that school choice rules satisfy path independence. Then the generalized DA produces a stable matching.*

[3]Note that individual rationality for students is trivially satisfied in our setting because we assume that each student finds all schools more preferred than being unassigned.

Different versions of this result have appeared in the literature. See [Chambers and Yenmez 2017] for a proof using the properties of path-independent choice rules.

Even when school choice rules are path-independent, the generalized DA need not be strategy-proof. We make the following assumption to get strategy-proofness: Choice rule Ch_s satisfies **the law of aggregate demand** if, for every $I', I'' \subseteq I$, $I' \supseteq I''$ implies $|Ch_s(I')| \geq |Ch_s(I'')|$. The choice rule that reserves seats for target groups also satisfies the law of aggregate demand.

Theorem 6.4. *Suppose that school choice rules satisfy path independence and the law of aggregate demand. Then the generalized DA is strategy-proof.*

See [Hatfield and Milgrom 2005] for a version of this result.

In the setting with school choice rules, [Ehlers and Morrill 2020] provide a generalization of EADA when all students consent and study its properties. Their definition is based on a novel concept of *irrelevance* of a student for a match. Using this concept, they define the generalized EADA mechanism and show that it is Pareto efficient.

6.5 Discussion

6.5.1 Applications

In June 2005, the Boston School Committee voted to replace the IA algorithm with the DA algorithm. The city implemented DA in the following school year and has since used this mechanism for allocating K-12 public school seats. The IA algorithm compelled many parents to engage in an "admissions game" regarding their children's future, motivating the district to adopt a strategy-proof algorithm. Economists proposed two algorithms: variations of DA and TTC, but officials chose DA over TTC because they were uncomfortable with the concept of trading priorities. Despite TTC's strategy-proofness, the term "trading priorities" could mislead families into thinking they should strategically rank schools where they have the highest priorities for potential trades [Abdulkadiroğlu et al. 2005a].

In 2002, the New York City Department of Education faced significant challenges in assigning rising high school students to over 500 programs: approximately 30% of nearly 100,000 students were assigned to schools not listed in their preferences, and the system was susceptible to strategic manipulation. Consequently, the NYC DOE Director of Strategic Planning explored adapting a variation of the DA algorithm used for the US Medical Match to a new high school matching process [Abdulkadiroğlu et al. 2005b].

A similar reform occurred in Chicago. In 2009, the district abandoned a version of the IA algorithm used for allocating seats at selective high schools. Chicago Public Schools officials discovered that "high-scoring kids were being rejected simply because of the order in which they listed their college prep preferences." After preferences were submitted under the IA algorithm but before placements were announced, officials requested students resubmit their preferences under a version of the DA algorithm.

Subsequently, many other school districts in the US and internationally have adopted variations of the DA algorithm.

6.5.2 Further Development

The generalized DA has been adopted by many school districts, but efficiency adjustment has not. One reason is that the EADA algorithm is not strategy-proof, and the efficient adjustment depends on students' consent. In an extreme case, there could be no adjustment to DA if no student consents.

The concern about the non-strategy-proof nature of EADA may be mitigated in large school districts. In such settings, it is challenging for an individual student to deduce how to misreport their rank order to secure a more preferred school, as the matching process is influenced in a complex manner by the reports of many other students. Regarding voluntary consents, Ehlers and Morrill [2020] and Reny [2022] propose alternative approaches to achieving the same efficiency adjustment without seeking students' consent.

Ehlers and Morrill [2020]

Perhaps we may consider a match between a student i and a school s **legal**, even in the presence of justified envy, if there is no legal way of assigning students to schools where i and s are matched. Then, whether a matching is legal or not depends on the legality of other matchings. Thus, legality seems to be a property of a set of matchings rather than an individual matching.

Let's consider an example with three students and their preferences as follows:

i_1	i_2	i_3	s_1	s_2	s_3
s_1	s_2	s_1	i_2	i_1	i_3
s_2	s_1	s_2	i_3	i_2	i_2
s_3	s_3	s_3	i_1	i_3	i_1

A unique stable matching is $\mu = \{(i_1 - s_2), (i_2 - s_1), (i_3 - s_3)\}$. Through Pareto improvement, we obtain $\nu = \{(i_1 - s_1), (i_2 - s_2), (i_3 - s_3)\}$. Whether the matching ν is legal or not depends on what other matchings are legal. Thus, legality is a property of a set of matchings. We would consider the set $\{\mu, \nu\}$ legal because μ has no justified envy, and although ν has a justified envy $(i_3 - s_1)$, this pair never forms in a legal matching. Note that ν is a constrained efficient legal matching.

A legal set of matchings is defined similarly to a von Neumann-Morgenstern stable set. A matching ν **blocks** a matching μ if there exists (i, s) such that $\nu(i) = s$ (matched in ν), $s \succ_i \mu(i)$, and iP_sj for some $j \in \mu^{-1}(s)$ (justified envy in μ). A set of matchings L is **legal** if and only if: (i) any $\mu \notin L$ is blocked by some $\nu \in L$, and (ii) for any $\mu, \nu \in L$, ν does not block μ.

Ehlers and Morrill [2020] shows that a unique legal set of matchings exists. Furthermore, a Pareto-efficient legal matching exists, which coincides with the outcome of EADA when all students consent.

Reny [2022]

A similar approach can consider a matching with justified envy as socially acceptable. Suppose a matching μ has justified envy. It means that the matching μ violates a student i's priority: i prefers a school s over $\mu(i)$, while the school is matched to a student i' who has a lower priority for school s than student i. We say that matching μ is **neutrally blocked** by ν if (1) $\nu \succ_i \mu$, and (2) $\nu \succeq_j \mu$ for every j whose priority is violated by ν. If μ is neutrally blocked by ν, there is no reason not to take ν instead of μ, because even though some student j finds ν unfair (their priority is violated in ν), they still find it weakly better than μ.

A matching μ is **priority neutral** if it is not neutrally blocked. A priority-neutral matching μ may simply have no justified envy. If not, some student i's priority is violated. However, if a district attempts to make student i strictly better by considering an alternative matching ν, there must be an agent j who gets worse off and whose priority gets violated in ν. This argument allows a district to justifiably choose matching μ.

Reny [2022] finds that the set of priority-neutral matchings is a subset of Ehlers and Morrill [2020]'s legal set of matchings. Moreover, there exists a unique constrained efficient priority-neutral matching, which also coincides with the outcome of EADA when all students consent.

7

AI for Emergency Response

Ayan Mukhopadhyay

College of William & Mary

Abstract

Emergency services operate under uncertainty and time pressure, where small improvements in forecasting and response can save lives. This chapter surveys the application of AI methods to incident forecasting, real-time detection, and dynamic resource allocation across domains such as firefighting, medical emergencies, and disaster response. It encompasses predictive modeling of incident hotspots, the integration of sensor and call data for rapid detection, and the optimization-based deployment of emergency resources in real-time. Special attention is given to handling uncertainty and adapting to evolving conditions during emergencies. The chapter illustrates how AI can reduce response times, allocate resources more efficiently, and ultimately enhance public safety. We conclude with reflections on the practical and ethical considerations of deploying predictive models in high-stakes environments.

7.1 Introduction

First responders must respond quickly to incidents such as fires, traffic accidents, and medical emergencies to minimize the risk to human life [Jaldell 2017]. However, with rapid urbanization and increasing traffic volume, the losses due to emergency incidents are on the rise [Mukhopadhyay et al. 2022], and emergency incidents still cause thousands of deaths and injuries and result in losses worth billions of dollars directly or indirectly each year [Hattis 2015]. Emergency management deals with proactively mobilizing resources to reduce response time and ensure that communities can recover from the effects of incidents such as accidents and fires. Emergency response management can be divided into five major components: 1) mitigation, 2) preparedness, 3)

DOI: 10.1201/9788743812074-8

detection, 4) response, and 5) recovery [Department of Homeland Security 2019, Mukhopadhyay 2019, Mukhopadhyay et al. 2022]. Mitigation is the process of ensuring the long-term safety of people and property, partly by understanding when and where future incidents can occur. This process leads to the development of predictive models for risk and incident occurrence. Preparedness involves creating the necessary infrastructure for emergency response, such as optimizing the locations for responders, ambulances, and police vehicles, and designing response plans. The detection process involves automated algorithms to detect incidents to improve the response speed, e.g., traffic cameras can detect accidents even before they are reported. Response involves dispatching responders when incidents happen or are about to occur. Lastly, the recovery phase ensures that impacted individuals and the community can cope with the after-effects of incidents. These stages are interlinked, with one stage often being a prerequisite to another. For example, predictive models learned in the preparedness stage are used to guide planning approaches in the response stage. These inter-dependencies must be taken into account while designing emergency management pipelines.

The design of an emergency response pipeline is often governed by the type of incident in consideration; e.g., the nature of the response differs between large-scale disasters such as hurricanes, wildfires, and floods, and everyday incidents such as road accidents and crimes. In this chapter, we focus on the latter category of incidents, which enables us to explore in depth several sub-problems in this area. While such incidents are more common, they cause massive damage. The daily death toll globally from road accidents is 3,200, which translates to more than a million deaths annually [Center of Disease Control and Prevention 2019]. The sheer volume of calls that first responders receive for emergency medical services (EMS) is also staggering; more than 240 million EMS calls are made annually in the United States alone [National Emergency Number Association 2019]. First responder agencies have designed principled approaches to deal with such a large number of incidents. In the last few decades, principled data-driven approaches have been used to complement such efforts, and we will explore how artificial intelligence can be used to improve emergency response. One way to optimize resource allocation in emergency response is to proactively allocate resources (e.g., ambulances and fire trucks) spatially and temporally in anticipation of incidents. Indeed, considerable attention has been devoted to studying emergency response from a principled data-driven perspective [Erkut et al. 2008, Knight et al. 2012, McCormack and Coates 2015, Mukhopadhyay et al. 2017]. This chapter is organized as follows. First, we will begin with a general problem formulation for emergency response, largely based on prior work by Mukhopadhyay et al. [Mukhopadhyay et al. 2022]. Then, we will explore data-driven approaches to forecasting and detecting incidents, followed by how responders can be stationed and dispatched in anticipation of future incidents. Throughout the chapter, we will use road accidents as a case study.

7.2 Problem

Emergency response enables first responders to physically travel to the spatial location of incidents, such as road accidents, to provide care, first aid, and transport to hospitals, among other services. While the nature of resources varies based on the type of incident and call for service, we provide an abstraction that is based on the commonalities among different incident types. The general problem structure is based on prior work by Mukhopadhyay et al. [Mukhopadhyay et al. 2022]. Given a spatial area of interest S, we assume that incidents occur in space and time through some *true* function f_{True}. This function, as in other learning problems, is unknown. Instead, the decision-maker observes a set of samples (possibly noisy) drawn from an incident arrival distribution. We denote these samples, available to us in the form of a *dataset*, are denoted by D, and can be represented as a vector of tuples $\{(s_1, t_1, k_1, w_1), (s_2, t_2, k_2, w_2), \ldots, (s_n, t_n, k_n, w_n)\}$, where s_i, t_i, and k_i denote the location, time of occurrence, and reported severity of the ith incident, respectively, and $w_i \in \mathbb{R}^m$ represents a vector of features associated with the incident. The vector w can consist of spatial, temporal, or spatio-temporal features, capturing covariates potentially affecting the occurrence of incidents. For example, consider the occurrence of road accidents. The set w, in such a scenario, typically includes determinants of accidents captured by features such as weather, traffic volume, and time of day. The problem of incident prediction can then be stated as learning the parameters θ of a function over a random variable X conditioned on w. We denote this function by $f(X \mid w, \theta)$. The random variable X represents a measure of incident occurrence such as a *count* of incidents (the number of incidents in S during a specific time period) or *time* between successive incidents. The decision-maker seeks to find the *optimal* parameters θ^* that best describe D. This can be formulated as a maximum likelihood estimation (MLE) problem or an equivalent empirical risk minimization (ERM) problem.

The function $f(X \mid w, \theta)$, therefore, captures the likelihood (or risk) of incident occurrence given a specific set of relevant features. Given such a model, the next part of designing an emergency response pipeline is planning in anticipation of future incidents, which involves allocating (or stationing) responders strategically and dispatching them as incidents occur. This problem can be modeled by the optimization problem $\max_y G(y \mid f)$, where y represents the decision variable (e.g., the location of emergency responders in space), G is a utility function, and f is the model of incident occurrence. For example, G might measure the total coverage (spatial spread) of the responders or the expected response time to incidents. Therefore, given a model of incident occurrence f, the decision-maker's goal is to maximize the utility defined by G. The optimization can be represented as a sequential stochastic control process and modeled by a Markov decision process (MDP) [Kochenderfer 2015, Mukhopadhyay et al. 2018]. Such a formulation can tackle the temporal nature of the response and is particularly relevant for finding a general mapping (i.e., a policy) for response stationing and dispatch. The second approach is to directly model the allocation problem as a single-shot optimization problem according to a specific measure of interest, e.g., one way to model resource stationing is maximizing the coverage of emergency responders [Church and ReVelle 1974, Gendreau et al. 1997, Mukhopadhyay et al. 2017, Toregas et al. 1971].

Emergency response pipelines were traditionally designed to initiate response *after* an incident was reported, e.g., via 911 calls in the USA. However, in practice, there is a delay between an incident and its reporting. This loss of time can be detrimental to the response, especially in life-threatening incidents such as accidents. This gap can be bridged by using incident detection or extraction models that automatically detect incidents using crowdsourced and sensor data. For example, traffic cameras can be used to detect accidents as soon as they occur. Mathematically, this process involves learning a function E which takes relevant data u as input (for example, video data from a traffic camera) and outputs information about an event (for example, the location of an accident). This can be represented as $\bar{z} = E(u)$, where $\bar{z}$ denotes an estimate of variable z. In event extraction, z can denote any variable related to the incident, such as the location of the incident, the extent of the damage, the number of people involved, and so forth.

7.3 Forecasting Incidents

The most important aspect of using data-driven approaches for emergency response is to understand *where* and *when* incidents are likely to occur. There is a plethora of prior work in this domain, ranging from using the historical frequency of incidents to learn an empirical distribution [Deacon et al. 1974] to using neural networks that use heterogeneous features [Vazirizade et al. 2021]. Early approaches often used linear regression models [Frantzeskakis et al. 1994, Jovanis and Chang 1986] to predict the number of likely incidents in an area. However, such models fail to capture the discrete and strictly positive nature of incident counts. Moreover, they also fail to account for the sporadic nature of emergency incidents [Joshua and Garber 1990, Miaou and Lum 1993]. An alternate approach is to use Poisson models, which have been used widely to forecast incidents such as road accidents [Bonneson and McCoy 1993, Joshua and Garber 1990, Jovanis and Chang 1986, Lord et al. 2005, Maher and Summersgill 1996, Sayed and Rodriguez 1999]. Poisson models can also suffer from two disadvantages in this context: first, they assume that the expected value of the response variable (count of incidents) is equal to its variance. This assumption does not usually hold in practice with emergency data [Lord et al. 2005, Mukhopadhyay et al. 2022]. Second, such models fail to adequately take into account the prevalence of zero counts in real-world data pertaining to emergency incidents. Consider data collected for road accidents at an hourly frequency; most roads do not experience accidents every hour, and as a result, such data often has very high sparsity [Lord et al. 2005, Mukhopadhyay et al. 2022, Vazirizade et al. 2021]. To tackle these problems, zero-inflated Poisson models and zero-inflated negative binomial models are often used [Mukhopadhyay et al. 2022]. Another approach to account for high sparsity in data is to use resampling-based approaches. For example, it is possible to either over-sample the positive labels (i.e., the occurrence of incidents) or under-sample the lack of incidents to balance a dataset [Vazirizade et al. 2021].

The availability of big data has resulted in the creation of richer feature sets, which in turn have enabled the usage of more complex algorithmic models for incident forecasting. For example, neural networks and ensemble learning have been extensively used in the context of forecasting road accidents [Abdel-Aty et al. 2008, Abdelwahab and Abdel-Aty 2002, Bao et al. 2019, Chang 2005, Pande and Abdel-Aty 2006, Riviere et al. 2006, Yu and Abdel-Aty 2014, Zhu et al. 2018]. An important consideration of developing complex models is data collection and feature engineering. Emergency incidents are caused by a variety of factors; it is recommended that model designers collaborate with domain experts to identify the determinants of specific types of incidents. However, such data is often available at different temporal and spatial scales. For example, while traffic data can be mined in (almost) real-time, demographic data is typically available over much larger time intervals. Similarly, traffic data can be mapped to a graph (e.g., the existing road network), whereas demographic data is usually available over a grid or census tracts. Therefore, model designers often need to harmonize the heterogeneous data into the same spatial and temporal scale before learning models. Broadly, features for incident prediction (especially in the context of roadway accidents) can be divided into temporal, spatial, or a combination of both [Mukhopadhyay et al. 2022]. For example, a commonly used feature in incident prediction approaches is the time of day or the season (e.g., summer or winter), which are examples of temporal features. The geometry of a specific road segment, on the other hand, is a spatial feature, as it is a property of a specific spatial unit. Spatio-temporal features measure spatial properties that change with time, such as traffic congestion on a particular road segment.

Finally, in addition to using a rich variety of features, model designers must account for additional checks to ensure that models accurately represent the underlying process of incident occurrence. For example, unobserved heterogeneity can arise in a model when features that are not recorded in the data affect the occurrence of incidents or are correlated to observed features [Mannering and Bhat 2014, Mukhopadhyay et al. 2022]. Similarly, data collection can be biased for many reasons. For example, in the example of roadway accidents, vehicle crashes with no severe injuries are often under-reported, thereby causing sampling bias [Yasmin et al. 2014]. Such biases can be particularly detrimental when data-driven approaches are used for law enforcement, where existing enforcement practices can produce biased data against specific communities or spatial areas.

7.4 Detecting Incidents

Emergency response to an event can only be dispatched after the concerned agency (e.g., the fire department) is notified about the event. Traditionally, the pipeline for emergency response relied on manual notification, i.e., either the victim of the event or a passerby would call a helpline number (e.g., 911) to request assistance. However, the delay between when an event actually occurs and when assistance is requested can be critical in practice. For example, consider a road accident where the victim is severely injured and unable to call for assistance; waiting for a passerby to call 911 could be life-threatening for the victim. However, modern cities are now equipped with various modalities of data streams and sensors that can be used to detect such events quickly (even before they are reported). For example, consider a fire in an urban area. Residents who observe the fire can report it on social media (even before they call an official helpline). Similarly, road accidents can be detected by traffic cameras. The goal of designing incident detection pipelines in emergency response is to use heterogeneous data to detect the occurrence of events in order to reduce the overall time for response.

While event detection can focus on various modalities of data, the three most commonly used (and promising) modalities are the following: using text data from social media (e.g., from applications such as Twitter), video or image data (e.g., data from traffic cameras), and crowdsourced event reports (e.g., from applications such as Waze). In general, there are two subtasks in event detection for emergency response [Mukhopadhyay et al. 2022]: 1) the first task seeks to identify the occurrence of the event and relies on "triggers" that aid detection; e.g., a social media post containing words such as *accident* or *crash* could be used as triggers. Naturally, complex models leverage more abstract patterns to detect incidents. 2) The second task deals with identifying information about the incident, e.g., where the incident has happened, what is the most likely time of occurrence, how many people (or structures) are involved, and so on. Natural Language Processing (NLP) techniques have been widely used to extract event information from social media text data. One of the traditional approaches to tackle this problem is to use feature engineering [Ahn 2006, Grishman et al. 2005, Ji and Grishman 2008]. First, the input data (text) is converted into a sequence of tokens. Then, for each token, various features such as lexical and syntactic features are extracted. These features are then used to learn a classifier. One limitation of this approach is that social media text is often unstructured and has informal grammar. Recently, deep neural networks have become an attractive choice as no manual feature engineering is required [Chen et al. 2015b, Nguyen et al. 2016].

Event extraction is also possible from video and image data, especially from traffic cameras, which can be used to track and monitor congestion and detect incidents that need response [Chang et al. 2016, Gan et al. 2015, Li et al. 2020, Ma et al. 2017]. For example, Gan et al. [Gan et al. 2015] use a CNN, pre-trained on a large corpus of openly available image data, to perform keyframe detection. More recently, there has been work that proposes a new approach that projects the structured semantic representations from the combination of textual and visual data into a common space, which then aids learning [Li et al. 2020]. Finally, Event detection from crowdsourced event reporting data has also garnered interest in recent years, and several first responder agencies have started using applications such as Waze [Crisis Response, European Emergency Number Association 2018]. Senarath [Senarath et al. 2021] leverage crowdsourced data to detect roadway accidents and point out that the accuracy of detection has a trade-off with spatial and temporal localization. Moreover, it is imperative to consider that practitioners might focus on different metrics for effective deployment (e.g., reduced number of false alerts and a balance between precision and recall) than standard metrics such as accuracy.

7.5 Responding to Incidents

Responding to incidents is the most consumer-facing component of the emergency responder pipeline. However, a critical prerequisite of response is resource allocation, i.e., optimizing resources spatially and temporally in anticipation of incidents. This anticipation, or forecast, is fed to the allocation in the form of a prediction model, which we discussed previously in section 7.3. As pointed out by Mukhopadhyay et al. [Mukhopadhyay et al. 2022], the distinction between allocation and response can be unclear, as a solution to the allocation problem can implicitly define a response strategy. For example, consider an allocation problem whose solution minimizes the expected response times to incidents defined by a distribution f. Responders such as fire trucks or ambulances can be stationed based on this solution. When an incident occurs, the closest available responder may be dispatched, a response strategy often employed by first responders. However, several nuances must be considered: dispatching the closest responder does not necessarily minimize response times over the long term, and the severity of the incident may dictate which responder to dispatch. The problem of responder dispatch seeks to address such questions in a principled manner.

The allocation problem is often formulated as a *single-shot* combinatorial optimization problem that seeks to maximize metrics such as the spatial coverage of the allocated responders [Church and ReVelle 1974, Toregas et al. 1971] or the probability of patient survival [Erkut et al. 2008, Knight et al. 2012]. The two canonical formulations that maximize coverage are the Location Set Covering Problem (LSCP) [Toregas et al. 1971] and the Maximal Covering Location Problem (MCLP) [Church and ReVelle 1974]; the former seeks to find the least number of facilities (e.g., fire stations) that *cover* all spatial areas that need service (e.g., based on municipal jurisdiction), the latter maximizes the overall area covered by a given number of facilities. It is also common to add secondary goals as constraints to the coverage problem, such as an upper bound on the maximum time an incident must wait before a responder arrives on the scene [Mukhopadhyay et al. 2017, Silva and Serra 2008]. Two major shortcomings of using the facility location problem to allocate emergency responders are the strong assumptions that responders are always available at their locations and a facility is able to account for the entire area that it *covers*. To tackle this challenge, several extensions have been proposed, such as the Double Standard Model (DSM) [Gendreau et al. 1997], which posits that while every area must have *some* coverage, some areas, e.g., the ones with the majority of incidents, have greater coverage. There is also extensive work on probabilistic coverage models, which model the stochastic nature of station availability [Daskin 1983, Revelle and Hogan 1989].

While allocation problems are typically formulated as integer linear programs, the response problem is a sequential decision-making problem under uncertainty: as incidents occur over time, responders must be dispatched, and their distribution must be readjusted given uncertainty about the occurrence of future incidents. This problem is typically modeled as a Markov decision process (MDP), which is a natural model for discrete-time stochastic control processes [Kochenderfer 2015]. The decision-maker's goal is to choose an *action* (e.g., which responder to dispatch) given a *state*; the state subsumes relevant information of interest, e.g., how many responders are available, what is the expected demand for responders, and so on. The MDP is often solved by learning an optimal policy, which is a mapping from states to actions that maximizes expected utility or minimizes expected cost. The cost function can be constructed based on domain expertise, and in its simplest version, could simply be the time taken for response.

Early work on using MDPs to tackle emergency response leverage continuous-time MDPs, which assume that the time between the world transitioning from one state to another is memoryless [Carter et al. 1972, Keneally et al. 2016]. While this framework provides computational convenience, real-world problems violate these assumptions; for example, the time required for an ambulance to travel to the scene of an incident is not memoryless. Mukhopadhyay et al. [Mukhopadhyay et al. 2018] relax this assumption by considering a semi-Markovian decision process. Although this framework is more challenging due to the absence of closed-form transition functions in the MDP, it is better suited to emergency response, and historical data can be used to learn the transition distribution. Often, learning a policy for the MDP is intractable due to the large state and action spaces inherent in emergency response. In such situations, decision-makers can leverage online planning, where instead of learning a general mapping from all states to actions, the goal is to quickly compute a near-optimal action for the current state of the world [Mukhopadhyay et al. 2019]. Other approaches to tackle the large state and action space include decentralized [Pettet et al. 2020b] and hierarchical planning [Pettet et al. 2020a], which decompose the planning problem into smaller sub-problems that are solved independently. For example, one approach to hierarchical planning is to identify spatial regions (similar to jurisdictions) within a city and solve an independent MDP for each region.

An important consideration in designing response strategies is the importance of a *greedy dispatch* strategy depending on the severity of some categories of incidents. In practice, our conversations with first responders revealed that the ethical and legal constraints under which first responders operate could dictate that the closest available responder be dispatched to critical incidents, even when such a dispatch strategy is proven to be sub-optimal in the long run. Since the exact severity of an incident is difficult to gauge in practice, first responders often leverage a greedy dispatch strategy for a wide array of incidents. To ensure that the overall expected response time does not suffer too much, Pettet et al. [Pettet et al. 2020a] propose dynamic reallocation with greedy dispatch; in such an approach, when an incident occurs, and a call for emergency service is required, the closest responder is always dispatched. However, the allocation of responders is periodically re-adjusted to account for temporal changes or the unavailability of responders in some regions. Dynamic reallocation has been shown to improve response times in emergency response simulations.

7.6 Conclusion

Emergency response is a critical piece of infrastructure required around the globe. First responders face the daunting challenge of responding to an increasing number of calls for service with limited budgets and time. Artificial intelligence and data-driven decision-making can learn complex abstractions from historical data to enable first responders to make better decisions in practice. While automated decision-making cannot (at least yet) replace the invaluable domain expertise of first responders, principled automated approaches for prediction, detection, and response are being adopted by cities across the world to expedite and improve emergency response.

8

AI for Smart Healthcare

Zhenjie Yao[1] and Yixin Chen[2]

[1]Chinese Academy of Sciences
[2]Washington University in St. Louis

Abstract

Healthcare is a domain where AI, and specifically, deep learning, has shown enormous promise. However, this domain also presents unique challenges in terms of safety, interpretability, and clinical integration. In this chapter, we review core neural architectures–convolutional networks, recurrent networks, graph neural networks, autoencoders, and generative adversarial networks–and discuss their suitability for different biomedical data types. We then present a detailed case study on liver disease screening, where densely connected deep neural networks were trained on liver function test indicators to classify disease status. The chapter draws lessons about the strengths and limitations of deep learning in healthcare, emphasizing issues of scalability, interpretability, and generalization across populations. We conclude by reflecting on how to bridge research innovations with real-world deployment in clinical settings, ensuring both effectiveness and trustworthiness.

8.1 Introduction

In the era of big data, information has become more valuable than ever. At the same time, rapid advances in information technology have greatly enhanced our ability to process data. This trend is especially evident in the healthcare sector. Traditional healthcare data are collected, standardized, and stored in information systems such as HIS (Hospital Information System), LIS (Laboratory Information System), and PACS (Picture Archiving and Communication System). These systems contain a wide range of information,

DOI: 10.1201/9788743812074-9

including patient demographics, medical records, imaging data, laboratory results, medications, procedures, and diagnoses. Emerging technologies, such as wearable devices, medical websites, and genetic testing, have further expanded the types, scale, and richness of healthcare data. Intelligent analysis of these data can support diagnosis, treatment planning, clinical decision-making, prescription optimization, disease prediction, and evaluation of therapeutic outcomes. Consequently, extracting meaningful knowledge from the massive volume of healthcare data has become an urgent and essential task.

Deep learning (DL) originated around the early 2000s. In recent years, it has surpassed traditional machine learning methods by a wide margin in tasks such as image recognition, speech recognition, and natural language processing [LeCun et al. 2015]. This remarkable success highlights its powerful capability to model complex and high-dimensional data. Today, deep learning has been increasingly applied across a broad range of domains, achieving impressive results in many areas. Among these, healthcare has emerged as one of the most promising and impactful fields for deep learning applications.

The application of deep learning in healthcare has led to many remarkable advancements. Building upon its success in computer vision and image processing, deep learning techniques have been effectively extended to medical image analysis, where they are widely used for image segmentation, recognition, and lesion detection. This has inspired a large body of research in medical image processing, resulting in the publication of hundreds of papers over the past 5 years. Comprehensive reviews of deep learning in medical image analysis have already been provided by Litjens et al. [2017] and Greenspan et al. [2016]. However, healthcare encompasses much more than medical imaging. Researchers have increasingly applied deep learning to other types of healthcare data, achieving significant performance improvements across various tasks. This chapter focuses on healthcare applications beyond medical image processing. Yao et al. [2018] offered an early and comprehensive survey of deep learning applications in healthcare. Here, we introduce additional recent developments, including applications of novel neural network architectures, with the aim of providing readers with a clearer understanding of the current landscape in this rapidly evolving field.

8.2 Deep Learning

Neural networks (NNs) trace their origins back to the 1940s and were first implemented as the perceptron in the 1950s [Rosenblatt 1957], a biologically inspired linear classifier. The perceptron marked the first wave of NN research. However, early neural networks demonstrated limited performance, and the perceptron's inherent constraints soon became evident. The field was revitalized in the 1980s with the introduction of the multi-layer perceptron (MLP) and the backpropagation (BP) algorithm [Rumelhart et al. 1988, Werbos 1974], which together initiated the second wave of NN research. At that time, typical neural networks consisted of three layers—an input layer, a hidden layer, and an output layer—collectively referred to as shallow models. Although these advances improved performance, neural networks were soon overshadowed by other machine learning techniques, particularly Support Vector Machines (SVMs), in the 1990s. LeCun et al. introduced convolutional neural networks (CNNs) with multiple hidden layers [LeCun et al. 1998], while Hinton et al. [2006] demonstrated the feasibility of training deep neural networks, broadly defined as neural networks with more than two hidden layers. The rapid expansion of the internet and mobile technologies enabled the collection of massive datasets. Combined with advances in hardware, these changes paved the way for the third wave of NN research.

Since the mid-2010s, numerous deep neural network architectures have been developed and applied across a wide range of domains. In this chapter, we categorize these deep networks into five groups and introduce each in turn. Further details on these architectures can be found elsewhere [LeCun et al. 2015, Ravì et al. 2017].

Deep Neural Networks (DNN). For clarity, in this chapter, the term *deep NN* refers to all types of deep learning models, while *DNN* specifically denotes the conventional neural network architecture with more than two hidden layers, as illustrated in Fig. 8.1. Training DNNs is inherently challenging, as they are particularly susceptible to the vanishing gradient problem—a phenomenon in which gradients (or errors) become extremely small when propagated backward through many layers, rendering the early layers difficult to train. Addressing these challenges has driven the rapid development of deep learning.

AutoEncoder networks (AE). An AutoEncoder (AE) is an unsupervised learning model. Unlike supervised models, its output layer does not produce class labels but instead aims to reproduce the input data—or a noisy version of it. The training objective of an AE is to reconstruct the original input as accurately as possible. From an information theory perspective, this reconstruction process seeks to preserve all information contained in the input, effectively minimizing information loss. The encoder component generates a compressed representation that retains the most essential information from the original data, serving as its low-dimensional representation. Because this

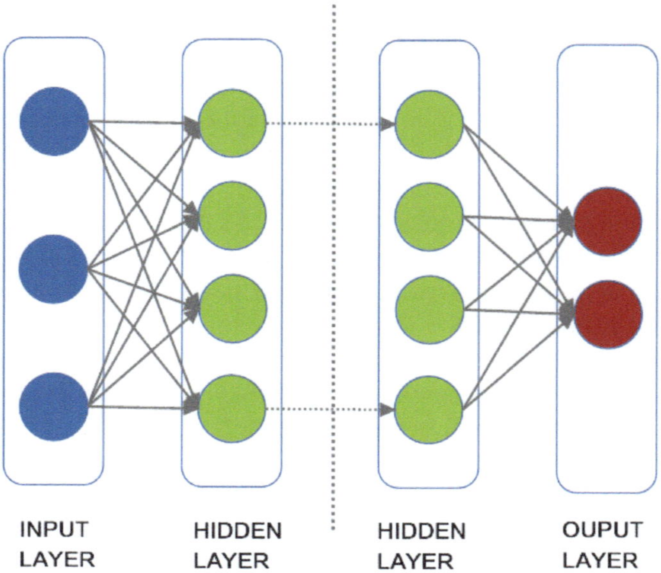

Figure 8.1 Architecture of DNN.

representation is both compact and discriminative, AutoEncoders are highly effective for feature extraction. Consequently, many researchers have applied AEs to extract meaningful features from various types of healthcare data [Al Rahhal et al. 2016, Danaee et al. 2016, Miotto et al. 2016, Xu et al. 2017].

Restricted Boltzmann Machines (RBMs) and related Networks (DBN and DBM). The Restricted Boltzmann Machine (RBM) [Hinton and Sejnowski 1986] is a variant of the Boltzmann Machine inspired by concepts from statistical thermodynamics, where neural variables take values between 0 and 1. A key restriction imposed on the Boltzmann Machine is that it forms a bipartite graph structure, in which visible and hidden units are fully connected across layers but have no intra-layer connections. This structural simplification makes the RBM significantly easier to train compared to the original Boltzmann Machine. Two major deep neural network frameworks, Deep Belief Networks (DBN) [Hinton et al. 2006] and Deep Boltzmann Machines (DBM) [Salakhutdinov and Hinton 2009], are derived from RBMs. Both DBNs and DBMs are typically initialized through layer-wise greedy training of stacked RBMs, followed by fine-tuning using target labels.

Convolutional Neural Networks (CNN). A Convolutional Neural Network (CNN) consists of alternating convolutional and pooling layers, which provide robustness to variations such as translation, rotation, and scaling [LeCun et al. 1998]. CNNs are among the most widely used deep learning models, and their breakthrough performance on the ImageNet dataset [Krizhevsky et al. 2012] marked a major turning point in the rise of deep learning research. Although originally designed for image recognition tasks [LeCun et al. 1998], CNNs can be effectively applied to any data that are fixed, ordered, and spatially or temporally correlated. For instance, they can process one-dimensional time sequences of fixed length, and their architecture can be naturally extended to handle three-dimensional data such as video.

Recurrent Neural Networks (RNN). In general, all the networks discussed above operate as static models with fixed input structures. In contrast, the Recurrent Neural Network (RNN) [Williams and Zipser 1989] is a dynamic model, where the output depends not only on the current input but also on the previous hidden states. However, RNNs suffer from the same vanishing gradient problem as other deep networks. Moreover, RNNs also experience gradient decay over time, which hampers their ability to capture long-term dependencies. To address this issue, Hochreiter and Schmidhuber [1997] introduced the Long Short-Term Memory (LSTM) architecture, which replaces standard RNN nodes with gated memory units. Later, Chung et al. [Chung et al. 2014] proposed the Gated Recurrent Unit (GRU), a simplified variant of LSTM that achieves comparable performance. RNN-based models have achieved remarkable success in a variety of sequential data processing tasks, such as speech and language modeling [Hinton et al. 2012].

Attention. The attention mechanism in neural networks is designed to identify and emphasize the most relevant information within input features, a technique that is especially useful when inputs involve long sequences of tokens (such as with natural language). The attention mechanism can function as a standalone network, as exemplified by the *Transformer* architecture in modern language models [Vaswani et al. 2017], or it can be integrated into other neural network architectures to enhance their performance by guiding the model's focus towards critical information.

Generative Adversarial Network (GAN). A Generative Adversarial Network (GAN) primarily consists of two components: a generator, which serves as the generative model, and a discriminator, which acts as the discriminative model. These two networks are trained in an adversarial manner: the generator aims to produce data that are indistinguishable from real samples, while the discriminator seeks to differentiate between genuine and synthetic data. Through this adversarial training process, the GAN effectively learns the underlying data distribution [Goodfellow et al. 2014].

Graph Neural Networks (GNN). Graph Neural Networks (GNNs) are designed for graph-structured data modeling, focusing on learning node representations by iteratively aggregating information from neighboring nodes [Bruna et al. 2013, Hamilton et al. 2017]. GNNs excel at capturing complex relationships and dependencies within networked data. They have achieved remarkable success in various tasks such as graph classification, node classification, and link prediction, and have been widely applied in domains including recommender systems [Ying et al. 2018], computer vision [Yan et al. 2018], and internet traffic forecasting [Yao et al. 2021].

8.3 A Review of AI in Healthcare Applications

In this section, we review a number of applications of deep learning in healthcare.

Electronic Health Records (EHRs) are systematized collections of patient-centered health information in digital form, encompassing a wide range of healthcare-related data. Mehrabi et al. [2015] explored temporal patterns and association rules among diagnosis codes by modeling each patient's records as a matrix of temporal clinical events, where rows represent ICD-9 diagnosis codes and columns represent years of diagnosis. They constructed a Deep Boltzmann Machine (DBM) with three hidden layers, using each patient's diagnosis matrix as the visible input layer. Miotto et al. [2016] proposed *Deep Patient*, an unsupervised representation learning framework based on a three-layer Stacked Denoising Autoencoder (SDAE) that learns patient embeddings from EHR data. The learned representations were evaluated by predicting patients' risk of developing various diseases on a dataset of 76,214 test patients, achieving an AUC of 0.773, compared to 0.695 for the best conventional method—demonstrating significant improvement. Rajkomar et al. [2018] conducted a large-scale analysis of EHR data by converting it into temporally ordered clinical events, which served as input for deep learning models across four predictive tasks: inpatient mortality, 30-day unplanned readmission, length of stay, and discharge diagnosis. Three different network architectures were developed, and their ensemble achieved consistent AUC improvements over enhanced conventional scoring systems commonly used in hospitals. Yao et al. [2020] applied a densely connected neural network for liver disease screening, using demographic information and laboratory test results from EHRs to assess the likelihood of liver disease.

Choi et al. [2020] designed a *Graph Convolutional Transformer* to uncover hidden structural relationships within EHR data while performing supervised prediction tasks. Their model consistently outperformed previous approaches across multiple prediction benchmarks, demonstrating its effectiveness as a general-purpose representation learning framework for EHR data. Dernoncourt et al. [2017] developed the first deep learning-based de-identification system using an LSTM architecture. Evaluated on the two largest publicly available de-identification datasets, the model outperformed state-of-the-art systems, achieving an F1-score of 99.23%, with recall of 99.25% and precision of 99.06% on the MIMIC dataset. Finally, Torfi and Fox [2020] proposed *corGAN*, a correlation-capturing Generative Adversarial Network designed to generate synthetic healthcare records. By combining Convolutional GANs and Convolutional Autoencoders, corGAN effectively captured correlations among adjacent medical features in the data representation space. The generated synthetic data demonstrated comparable performance to real data across various machine learning tasks, including classification and prediction.

Time-series signals such as Electrocardiography (ECG) and Electroencephalography (EEG) are noninvasive recordings of the body's electrical activity and play a vital role in physiological monitoring and diagnosis. Yao et al. [2017] developed the first deep learning model for atrial fibrillation detection, known as the *Multi-scale Convolutional Neural Network (MCNN)*. In their approach, R-waves were first detected from ECG signals, and the resulting RR interval sequences (intervals between successive R-waves) were used as inputs to the MCNN. The algorithm was evaluated on both public and private datasets, achieving state-of-the-art performance on the public benchmark. Rajpurkar et al. [2017] constructed the largest ECG dataset to date, comprising 64,121 ECG recordings collected from 29,163 patients using a single-lead wearable monitor. They trained a 34-layer ResNet to classify 14 rhythm types (13 arrhythmia and one normal rhythms), achieving cardiologist-level performance in arrhythmia detection. Wulan et al. [2020] introduced three deep learning models for ECG signal generation and proposed a quantitative evaluation framework to assess the performance of ECG generative models. Schirrmeister et al. [2017] investigated a range of deep convolutional neural network architectures for decoding imagined and executed movements directly from raw EEG signals. Experimental results on four movement classes demonstrated that CNN-based methods significantly outperformed the widely used *Filter Bank Common Spatial Pattern (FBCSP)* algorithm. Liu et al. [2021] proposed a *Three-Dimensional Convolutional Attention Neural Network*

(3DCANN) for EEG-based emotion recognition. The model comprises a spatio-temporal feature extraction module and an EEG channel attention weighting module, effectively capturing dynamic relationships among multi-channel EEG signals and their spatial dependencies over time.

Social media data capture users' online activities and can provide valuable insights for monitoring mental health status and detecting Adverse Drug Reactions (ADRs). Benton et al. [2017] developed a deep Multi-Task Learning (MTL) neural network for ten prediction tasks, including suicide risk, seven mental health conditions, neurotypicality, and gender classification, using Twitter data as input. The MTL model was compared with Single-Task Learning (STL) baselines, and results demonstrated that MTL significantly outperformed STL across all tasks—for instance, achieving an AUC of 0.848 for suicide prediction. Dong et al. [2021] proposed an end-to-end *semi-supervised Graph Instance Transformer (SS-GIT)*, integrating multiple instance learning with contrastive self-supervised learning to predict early indicators of generalized anxiety disorder and depression under weak supervision. Experiments on a mobile sensing dataset showed that SS-GIT outperformed the best baseline by 6.7% in ROC-AUC. Zhang et al. [2021] introduced an *Adversarial Neural Network with Sentiment-aware Attention (ANNSA)* for ADR detection in social media data. The proposed sentiment-aware attention mechanism extracts word-level sentiment features and learns task-relevant information through a task-specific loss function. Their results revealed that sentiment features significantly enhance ADR detection performance.

Wearable devices are smart electronic systems worn on the body that continuously capture physiological and behavioral data. Ravi et al. [2016] proposed a deep learning-based human activity recognition framework designed for accurate and real-time classification on low-power wearable devices. To reduce computational demands, they adopted a constraint-aware Convolutional Neural Network (CNN) to analyze spectral representations of sensor data for activity recognition. Aliamiri and Shen [2018] employed a wearable device equipped with a photoplethysmography (PPG) sensor to develop a portable, non-intrusive, and low-cost system for atrial fibrillation (AF) monitoring and detection. Their end-to-end CNN-based model effectively filtered out low-quality signals and achieved reliable AF detection performance. Zhang et al. [2017] proposed a deep learning framework that used a sparse autoencoder (SAE) for feature extraction and logistic regression for emotion recognition, relying solely on respiration data collected from wearable devices. The model achieved approximately 80% accuracy in emotion classification. A key limitation of deep learning models for wearable applications is their high computational complexity, which poses challenges for deployment on devices with limited battery life, memory, and processing capacity. Therefore, an appropriate trade-off between performance and resource consumption is essential for practical implementations.

Deep learning has become a powerful tool for molecular structure analysis in drug discovery and compound screening. Unterthiner et al. [2015] developed *DeepTox*, a deep learning system that normalizes chemical compound representations and uses a large set of chemical descriptors as input features. A five-layer Deep Neural Network (DNN) was trained to predict compound toxicity. Evaluations on a dataset of 12,000 environmental chemicals and drugs demonstrated that DeepTox outperformed conventional machine learning methods across 12 different toxicity endpoints. Cheung and Moura [2020] applied Graph Neural Networks (GNNs) to predict molecular properties relevant to identifying potential drug candidates capable of inhibiting SARS-CoV-2. By modeling the molecular topologies, their approach achieved promising preliminary results on two COVID-19-related datasets. Li et al. [2021a] introduced *Drug3D-Net*, a grid-based 3D Convolutional Neural Network (3D-CNN) integrated with a spatial-temporal gated attention module to model the geometric structure of molecules for molecular property prediction. The network effectively captures spatial and geometric features through 3D convolution operations, leading to improved performance in molecular prediction tasks.

Genomic analysis plays a crucial role in cancer detection and survival prediction. Kumardeep et al. [Chaudhary et al. 2017] investigated survival outcomes among subgroups of hepatocellular carcinoma (HCC) patients by integrating multi-omics data from multiple patient cohorts. They developed a deep learning model based on an autoencoder, trained on data from 360 HCC patients obtained from The Cancer Genome Atlas (TCGA) database. Their analysis revealed that mutations in the *TP53*, *KRT19*, *EPCAM*, and *BIRC5* genes, as well as activation of the Wnt and Akt signaling pathways, were strongly associated with patient survival. These findings were validated across five external datasets encompassing diverse cohorts and omics types. This study represented the first application of deep learning for identifying multi-omics features predictive of differential survival in HCC patients, demonstrating the potential of such workflows for prognosis prediction.

Table 8.1 categorizes several deep learning (DL) models applied in healthcare into *general* and *specific* types. General models are versatile architectures applicable to a wide range of tasks and capable of handling diverse data formats. In contrast, specific models are designed for targeted

Table 8.1 Insights of DL in healthcare

Architecture	Applications	Scope	Comments
DNN	EHR, EEG, Community, Drug, Genomics	General	Conventional, various tasks
AE	EHR, ECG, Community, Wearable, Drug, Genomics	General	Feature extraction, usually combined with other models
DBN & DBM	EHR, ECG, EEG, Wearable	General	Various tasks, sometimes as feature extractor
CNN	EHR, ECG, EEG, Wearable, Drug	Specific	Uniformly sampled data, such as image & time series
RNN	EHR, ECG, Wearable	Specific	Sequences
Attention	EHR, ECG, EEG, Community, Drug	–	Performance improvement, usually combined with other models
GAN	EHR, ECG, Drug	General	Data augmentation & anonymization
GNN	EHR, Community, Drug	Specific	Graph structure data

applications, with their input data and structural design tailored to a particular problem domain.

The Deep Neural Network (DNN) is a general-purpose model that has been applied across nearly all types of tasks. As discussed in Section 8.2, the Autoencoder (AE) is primarily an unsupervised learning model used for feature extraction. However, it is often combined with supervised models to perform specific tasks. Due to its versatility, the AE is considered one of the most general deep learning architectures, applicable to a wide range of domains. Similarly, Deep Belief Networks (DBN) and Deep Boltzmann Machines (DBM) are also general models. The Generative Adversarial Network (GAN) is another general framework, widely used for data augmentation, anonymization, and synthetic data generation across diverse data types.

The attention mechanism can operate as an independent structure (as in the Transformer) or be integrated with other models such as DNNs, CNNs, RNNs, or GNNs. Its scope and functionality largely depend on the architecture with which it is combined.

In contrast, models such as CNN, RNN, and GNN are typically task-specific architectures. The Convolutional Neural Network (CNN) excels at processing uniformly sampled data, such as images or signals. The Recurrent Neural Network (RNN) is designed for sequential data—including speech, language, and text—and can be readily extended to other temporal sequences, such as EHR data. The Graph Neural Network (GNN) is specialized for graph-structured data, effectively modeling physical or abstract relationships among entities.

8.4 Liver Disease Screening Based on Densely Connected Deep Neural Networks

In this section, we present our work as an example which applies Deep Neural Networks (DNNs) to liver disease screening [Yao et al. 2020]. The screening task is formulated as a binary classification problem, where individuals diagnosed with liver disease are labeled as positive examples, and those without the disease are labeled as negative examples. The objective is to determine whether a subject is positive or negative based on their Liver Function Test (LFT) results. The clinical diagnoses provided by physicians are used as the ground truth to evaluate the model's performance.

8.4.1 LFT

Due to the liver's diverse physiological functions, a wide variety of Liver Function Tests (LFTs) and corresponding indicators exist. For the purpose of large-scale screening, we utilize only the most commonly used LFT indicators. The selected indicators are summarized in Table 8.2, which lists their names, healthy reference ranges, and measurement units. In total, 11 primary LFT indicators (such as ALT, AST, and TBIL) and 2 derived indicators (AST/ALT and A/G) are included. These indicators are integral components of routine medical examinations, ensuring that the proposed model can be readily applied to large-scale liver disease screening.

8.4.2 Dataset and Preprocessing

The dataset used in this study was collected from a hospital in northwestern China, containing Liver Function Test (LFT) records from 2015 to 2018. In total, 84,685 samples were initially obtained. After excluding samples with missing values, 76,914 valid LFT records were retained for analysis. Among these, 43,572 samples were from male subjects and 33,329 from female subjects. The dataset includes 64,226 healthy samples and 12,688 samples diagnosed with varying degrees of liver disease. The patients' ages range from 1 to 95 years, with an average age of 55.1 ($\pm$ 14.2) years. To the best of our

Table 8.2 Summary of the selected LFT indicators

Indicators	**Healthy range**	**Unit**
Alanine aminotransferase(ALT)	1.00–40.00	U/L
Aspartate aminotransferase(AST)	1.00–45.00	U/L
AST/ALT	0.00–1.15	NULL
Total bilirubin(TBIL)	3.42–20.50	μmol/L
Direct bilirubin(DBIL)	0.10–6.84	μmol/L
Indirect Bilirubin(IB)	2.00–12.00	μmol/L
Alkaline phosphatase(ALP)	15.00–142.00	U/L
Glutamyl transpeptidase(r-GT)	11.00–50.00	U/L
Total protein(TP)	60.00–80.00	g/L
Albumin(ALB)	35.00–55.00	g/L
Globulin(GLOB)	20.00–30.00	g/L
Albumin/Globulin(A/G)	1.50–2.50	NULL
Cholinesterase(CHE)	4500–13000	U/L

knowledge, this represents the largest LFT dataset ever analyzed—over 100 times larger than those used in previous studies.

For liver disease screening, we utilized 15 features, including gender, age, and 13 LFT indicators listed in Table 8.2. All features are numerical, except for gender, which was encoded as 1 for male and 0 for female. Each feature was normalized using Equation 8.1 to ensure consistent scaling across variables.

$$x_{ij} = \frac{x_{ij} - \bar{x_i}}{\mathrm{std}(x_i)}, \tag{8.1}$$

where x_{ij} is the value of the ith feature of the jth sample, x_i is the vector composed by ith feature of all the samples, $\bar{x_i}$ is the mean value of x_i and $\mathrm{std}(x_i)$ is its standard deviation.

8.4.3 DenseDNN

We propose a novel deep neural network architecture, the *Densely Connected Deep Neural Network (DenseDNN)*. The overall structure of DenseDNN is illustrated in Figure 8.2a. Because the numerous inter-layer connections can make the visualization complex, Figure 8.2b presents an equivalent, simplified representation of the architecture. The preprocessed features serve as the input layer to the DenseDNN. As shown in the figure, the architecture differs from that of a conventional DNN. Specifically, DenseDNN contains four hidden layers (denoted by $h1$, $h2$, $h3$, and $h4$). Each hidden layer receives input not only from its immediate predecessor but from all preceding layers.

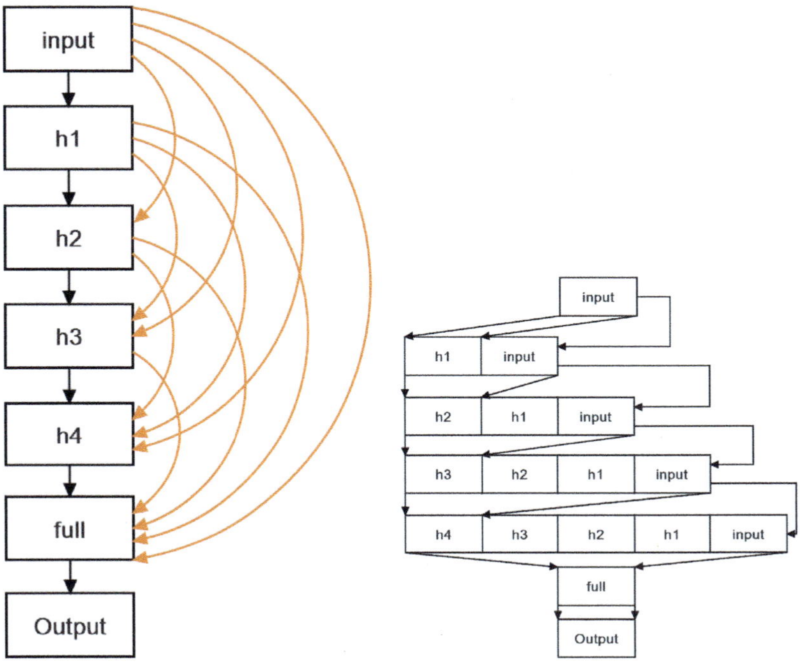

(a) DenseDNN (b) Equivalent architecture

Figure 8.2 Overall architecture of the densely connected DNN.

As illustrated in Figure 8.2a, unlike standard DNNs that connect layers sequentially, DenseDNN introduces dense shortcut connections (highlighted in orange) across all layers, including the input, hidden, and fully connected layers. These direct connections ensure that every layer receives inputs from all preceding layers and, in turn, contributes its output to all subsequent layers. This design shortens the information flow path between intermediate and output layers, thereby mitigating the vanishing gradient problem and enhancing information propagation during both forward and backward passes.

8.4.4 Implementation Details of DenseDNN

The input layer of the DenseDNN consists of 15 neurons, each corresponding to one feature. The network contains four densely connected hidden layers, each comprising 512 neurons. Every hidden layer includes dense connections, utilizes the tanh activation function, and applies dropout regularization with a rate of 0.5. The fully connected layer contains 1024 neurons, also with a dropout rate of 0.5, and employs the sigmoid activation function. The output layer is a softmax layer with two neurons, representing the classification outcomes: liver disease and no liver disease.

The DenseDNN architecture is primarily characterized by two key hyper-parameters: (1) the width of the hidden layers (i.e., the number of neurons per layer) and (2) the dropout rate. Various combinations of these parameters were tested, as described in Section 8.5.3, and the configuration reported above produced the best overall performance.

8.5 Results and Discussions

8.5.1 Measuring Effectiveness

To measure the performance of the proposed method for liver disease screening, we use the standard sensitivity (Sen), specificity (Spec), Detection Rate (DR), False Alarm Rate (FAR) and accuracy (Acc) metrics. These are defined as:

$$Sen = TP/(TP + FN), \tag{8.2}$$

$$Spec = TN/(TN + FP), \tag{8.3}$$

$$DR = Sen, \tag{8.4}$$

$$FAR = 1 - Spec, \tag{8.5}$$

$$Acc = (TP + TN)/(TP + FN + TN + FP), \tag{8.6}$$

where TP (True Positives) denotes the number of positive samples correctly identified as positive, FN (False Negatives) represents the number of positive samples incorrectly classified as negative, TN (True Negatives) is the number of negative samples correctly identified as negative, and FP (False Positives) refers to the number of negative samples incorrectly classified as positive. In general, the objective of an effective detection model is to minimize the False Alarm Rate (FAR) while maximizing the other four performance metrics.

The test results were obtained using a 5-fold cross-validation strategy. The network was trained using Adam, an efficient stochastic gradient-based optimizer [Kingma and Ba 2014], with a batch size of 1024.

8.5.2 Reference Models

For comparison, we also evaluated Logistic Regression (LR), Random Forests (RF), and a conventional Deep Neural Network (DNN) on the same dataset.

LR is one of the most widely used statistical analysis methods in clinical data modeling, while RF is a popular machine learning algorithm known for its robustness and interpretability. A conventional DNN architecture serves as a baseline model to assess the effectiveness of the proposed DenseDNN architecture. In the conventional DNN, the dense inter-layer connections are removed. Its architecture consists of an input layer, multiple hidden layers, a fully connected layer, and an output layer, where each layer receives input only from its immediately preceding layer.

8.5.3 Parameter Settings

We evaluated two key hyperparameters of the DenseDNN architecture: (1) the width of the hidden layers (i.e., the number of neurons per layer) and (2) the dropout rate. Different values for both parameters were systematically tested to determine their impact on model performance. The Area Under the Curve (AUC) of the Receiver Operating Characteristic (ROC) curve was used as the quantitative performance metric, with larger AUC indicating better detection performance.

Table 8.3 presents the AUC results of DenseDNN with varying hidden layer widths, where the dropout rate was fixed at 0.5. As shown, the models with 512 and 1024 neurons per hidden layer achieved the highest AUC values: 0.8919 and 0.8922, respectively. Given their comparable performance, a width of 512 neurons was selected to reduce model complexity.

Table 8.3 Comparison of different widths.

width	64	128	256	512	1024	2048
AUCs	0.8851	0.8881	0.8904	0.8919	0.8922	0.8911

Table 8.4 summarizes the AUC results for different dropout rates, with the hidden layer width fixed at 512 neurons. The highest AUC was obtained with a dropout rate of 0.5. Therefore, this value was adopted for all subsequent experiments.

Table 8.4 Comparison of different dropout rates.

Dropout rate	0.3	0.4	0.5	0.6	0.7
AUCs	0.8812	0.8891	0.8919	0.8904	0.8856

8.5.4 Learning Curves

Figure 8.3 illustrates the learning curves of the two types of DNNs for both the training and validation sets. The horizontal axis represents the number of epochs, while the vertical axis denotes the cross-entropy loss, defined as

$$C = \frac{1}{n}\sum_{i=1}^{n}[y_t \ln y_p + (1 - y_t)\ln(1 - y_p)], \tag{8.7}$$

where y_t is the true label, and y_p is the predicted label. For comprehensive evaluation, we trained the model for more epochs to get a complete learning curve.

As shown in Figure 8.3, the training loss for both models decreases steadily with increasing epochs. The DenseDNN exhibits a sharper decline in loss compared to the conventional DNN, and a noticeable gap between the two curves emerges and widens as training progresses. After 600 epochs, the training loss of DenseDNN reaches approximately 0.24, whereas that of the DNN remains around 0.265.

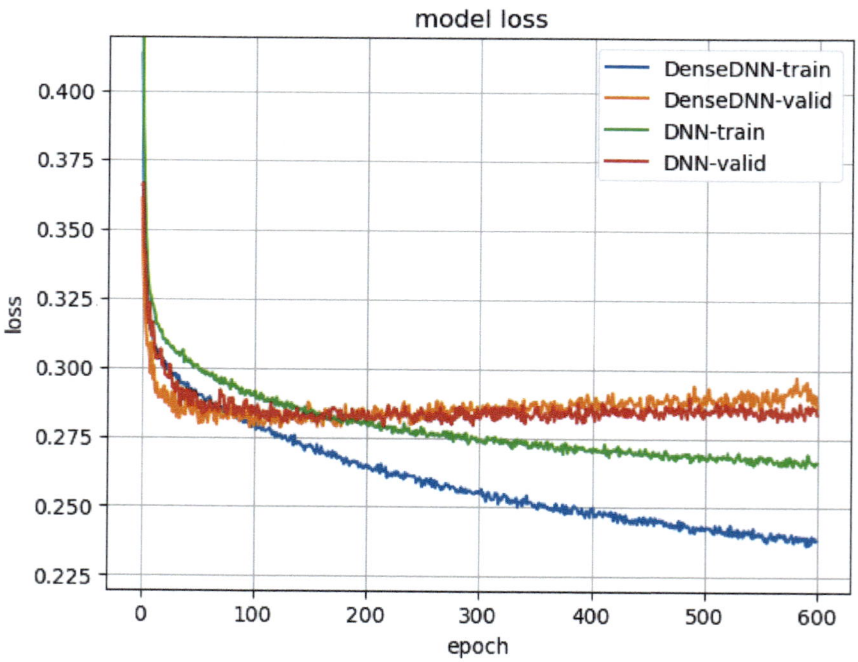

Figure 8.3 Learning curves of the neural networks

Table 8.5 Comparison of AUCs.

Model \ Epochs	100	200	300	400	500	600
DNN	0.8831	0.8867	0.8884	0.8896	0.8897	0.8897
DenseDNN	0.8881	0.8919	0.8929	0.8930	0.8935	0.8933

On the validation set, the losses of both models converge to approximately 0.28, after which no significant improvement is observed. However, DenseDNN again shows a faster convergence, reaching this loss value in about 90 epochs, while the DNN requires around 160 epochs. After approximately 350 epochs, the validation loss of DenseDNN increases slightly—an indication of moderate overfitting. Despite this, the validation loss remains generally stable, suggesting that the overfitting is not severe and may even contribute to better generalization.

Because DenseDNN's loss decreases more rapidly, it is easier to train than the conventional DNN. This improvement can be attributed to the dense shortcut connections, which shorten the information flow path between layers, accelerating error propagation and enhancing the overall training efficiency.

To determine the optimal number of training epochs, both models were trained for 600 epochs, and the AUC values were evaluated at different training stages using the test sets. As shown in Table 8.5, the AUC of both models generally increases with the number of training epochs. For instance, the AUC of the DNN improves from 0.8831 at 100 epochs to 0.8897 at 500 epochs, but shows no further gain at 600 epochs. Similarly, the DenseDNN achieves an AUC of 0.8881 at 100 epochs, peaks at 0.8935 at 500 epochs, and slightly declines when training extends to 600 epochs. These results suggest that 500 epochs yield the best test performance for both models. However, as indicated by the learning curves in Figure 8.3, the optimal range based on validation performance is between 160 and 350 epochs. The discrepancy arises from differences between the validation and test sets. Although the test results indicate that 500 epochs produce the best fit, in practice, the test set is not available during training. Therefore, model selection should rely on validation performance, which points to 160–350 epochs as the most appropriate range. In the following experimental setup, both models were trained for 200 epochs.

8.5.5 Comparison with Conventional Methods

The ROC curves of DenseDNN, DNN, Random Forests (RF), and Logistic Regression (LR) for liver disease detection are shown in Figure 8.4. As illustrated, for each model, the detection rate increases with the false alarm rate. The corresponding AUC values are provided in Table 8.6. Among the evaluated models, LR demonstrates the poorest performance, with a substantial gap between its ROC curve and those of the other models. The AUC of LR is 0.7977, whereas the AUCs of RF, DNN, and DenseDNN are 0.8790, 0.8867, and 0.8919, respectively.

Additionally, we compared the detection performance of the three machine learning models. As shown in Figure 8.4, the ROC curves of the deep learning models (DenseDNN and DNN) are consistently higher than that of the Random

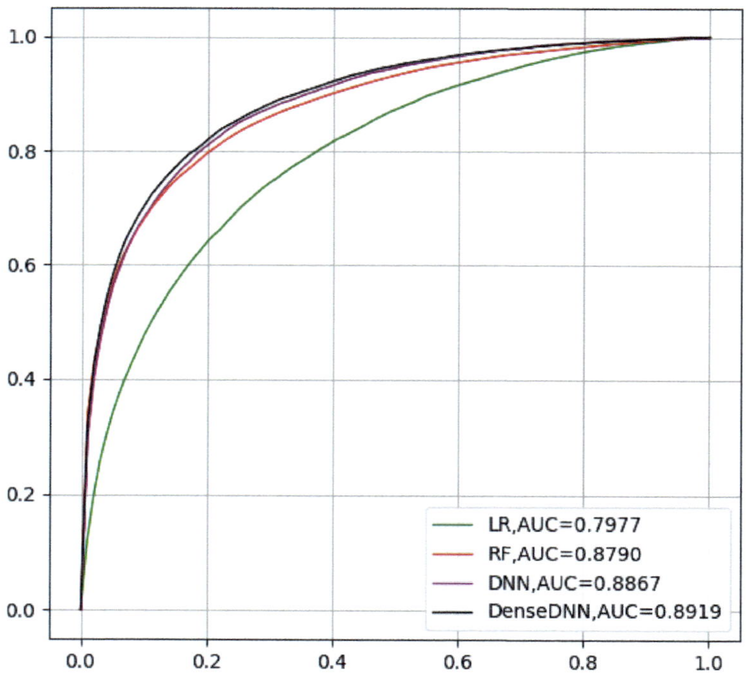

Figure 8.4 ROC curves of different models for liver disease screening

Table 8.6 Prediction performance of different models for liver disease screening

Model	Sen with different Specs					AUC
	0.95	0.90	0.85	0.80	0.75	
LR	0.3412	0.4794	0.5690	0.6416	0.7003	0.7977
RF	0.5724	0.6857	0.7517	0.7986	0.8353	0.8790
DNN	0.5643	0.6884	0.7604	0.8116	0.8517	0.8867
DenseDNN	**0.5840**	**0.7068**	**0.7737**	**0.8204**	**0.8565**	**0.8919**

Forest (RF), with a noticeable margin. The AUC values of DenseDNN, DNN, and RF are 0.8919, 0.8867, and 0.8790, respectively, indicating that deep learning models achieve superior performance compared to traditional machine learning methods. Between the two deep learning models, DenseDNN consistently outperforms DNN, with its ROC curve lying above that of the conventional DNN throughout. The corresponding AUCs (0.8919 vs. 0.8867) confirm the advantage of the proposed architecture. Based on the ROC curves and AUC results, we conclude that the DenseDNN architecture provides a significant performance improvement over both conventional machine learning models and standard deep neural networks in the liver disease screening task.

The specificity (Spec), sensitivity (Sen), and AUC values for all models are summarized in Table 8.6. Five reference specificity levels—0.95, 0.90, 0.85, 0.80, and 0.75—were selected for comparison. Across all specificity values, DenseDNN achieves the highest sensitivity, whether at high or low specificity levels. Its AUC of 0.8919 is greater than that of all other models, confirming its superior detection capability.

8.6 Challenges and Limitations

Although deep learning models have demonstrated remarkable success across a wide range of healthcare applications, major challenges remain. We summarize these below.

Data. Deep neural network (DNN) models are inherently data-driven, with a number of parameters far exceeding those of conventional machine learning models. Consequently, they require large volumes of data for effective training. However, in healthcare applications, data collection is often challenging—datasets containing even 10,000 samples are considered large, yet remain relatively small compared to benchmarks such as ImageNet, which includes over 14 million images. Moreover, healthcare data are frequently imbalanced. In disease screening tasks, for example, cases with the target condition are typically much fewer than those from healthy populations. Constructing a large, representative dataset is therefore both crucial and time-consuming.

Interpretability. In many machine learning tasks, the primary focus is typically on achieving high model accuracy, with less emphasis on understanding the underlying decision process. Although feature map visualizations can provide some insight into intermediate representations, most deep neural networks remain end-to-end black-box models with limited interpretability. However, interpretability is crucial in healthcare applications, where understanding why a model makes a particular prediction is as important as the prediction itself. Clinicians must be able to identify risk factors and determine appropriate treatments based on transparent reasoning. To address this challenge, Che et al. [2015] proposed Interpretable Mimic Learning, a method for distilling knowledge from deep neural networks into more interpretable models. Similarly, Lundberg and Lee [2017] introduced an interpretation approach based on Shapley values, which quantify the marginal contribution of each feature to the model's prediction. These methods provide valuable pathways toward improving model transparency. Nevertheless, data visualization remains one of the most effective tools for facilitating the interpretation and understanding of deep learning models in healthcare.

Data representation. In many traditional machine learning tasks, such as image classification, the data are relatively homogeneous and well-structured. In contrast, healthcare data, particularly Electronic Health Records (EHRs), are typically irregular, heterogeneous, and poorly structured. Additionally, missing values are common; for example, vital signs recorded manually in hospitals frequently contain incomplete entries. Currently, EHR data are commonly represented as temporal event matrices, with missing values handled through simple interpolation methods [Cheng et al. 2016, Mehrabi et al. 2015]. Developing more effective data representations could substantially improve model performance in such applications.

Generalization ability. In many application domains, the training and testing datasets share similar underlying distributions. Consequently, the learned models tend to generalize well. However, in many healthcare applications there is a significant gap between the distributions of training and testing data. For instance, a model trained on data from American patients may not generalize effectively to Chinese populations [Yao et al. 2017]. In such cases, transfer learning offers a powerful approach to adapt models across different populations and datasets, thereby improving generalization and robustness.

Computational complexity. Deep neural networks (DNNs) are computationally complex machine learning models, requiring substantial time, memory, and processing resources. The vast number of operations involved can make model training and inference expensive. This issue becomes particularly critical for wearable devices, which are constrained by limited memory, computational power, and battery capacity.

Model compression offers a possible solution. For example, Chen et al. [2015a] proposed techniques to compress deep neural networks, significantly reducing storage requirements while largely preserving generalization performance. Another promising direction involves developing energy-efficient hardware accelerators tailored for deep learning. For instance, on several representative neural network layers, the DaDianNao system achieved up to 450.65× speedup compared to a GPU, while reducing energy consumption by an average factor of 150.31× across 64 chips [Chen et al. 2016b].

8.7 Conclusion

In this chapter, we surveyed the applications of deep learning in healthcare, covering diverse domains such as Electronic Health Records (EHR), Electrocardiography (ECG), Electroencephalography (EEG), community healthcare, wearable device data, drug discovery, and genomic analysis. Across these areas, deep learning has demonstrated remarkable performance and adaptability. Moreover, we introduced DenseDNN, a novel neural network architecture designed for liver disease screening based on Liver Function Test (LFT) data. The proposed DenseDNN jointly learns representations from all layers through dense shortcut connections, which enhance feature extraction and improve information flow during both forward propagation and backpropagation. This design led to more efficient training and effective prediction.

Overall, deep learning holds great promise in driving innovation within the healthcare industry. Its unparalleled capability for representation learning makes it a powerful tool for analyzing clinical and biomedical data. A promising future direction lies in leveraging deep learning to integrate and analyze multi-dimensional, heterogeneous, and unstructured personal data, including demographics, diet, lifestyle habits, sleep patterns, mental health, medical imaging, vital signs, medications, and laboratory tests. Such data fusion has the potential to enable breakthroughs in personalized, data-driven healthcare decision-making.

9

Computational Game Theory for Security

Yevgeniy Vorobeychik

Washington University in St. Louis

Abstract

Security applications often involve strategic interactions between defenders and adversaries, making game theory a natural framework for modeling these interactions. In this chapter, we introduce Stackelberg security games and their extensions to network settings, stochastic environments, and adversarial patrolling. Applications include airport and border security, cyber defense, and the protection of critical resources. We also review algorithmic advances that allow efficient equilibrium computation in large-scale security games, a critical step for real-world deployment. Beyond the mathematical foundations, we also discuss the challenges of translating theoretical models into practice.

9.1 Introduction

Security, or protection from harm, is a central social good, crucial for thriving organizations and communities. In security, harm comes not spontaneously, but as a result of deliberate vicious acts by a malicious party or parties. For example, home security protects residents against unwanted intrusions, security in an airport entails protection against threats of violence by organized terror groups, while cybersecurity in an organization means protection against sabotage by parties who may aim to reduce the organization's competitiveness or harm its reputation. The interaction between the *defender*, who strives to protect a collection of assets, and an *attacker*, who aims to achieve some malicious goal that likely leads to direct or indirect harm to these assets, is thus endemic in security encounters. Game theory, which is a mathematical

DOI: 10.1201/9788743812074-10

framework for modeling interactions among strategic (self-interested) agents whose actions impact one another, has emerged as an important framework for modeling such defender-attacker interactions in security. Computational game theory, which uses AI (mostly, optimization) techniques for computing solutions in games, provides us with the capability to connect such modeling approaches to practical security deployment solutions. This is the subject of the present chapter.

An important conceptual step in game-theoretic modeling for security is to frame the interaction between the defender and attacker as sequential, with the defender first deploying ("committing" to) its defense strategy, and the attacker then responding to deployed defense in deciding on the attack strategy. A formal representation for this structure of interaction is as a Stackelberg game, in which a leader (in our case, the defender) chooses a strategy first, and the follower (the attacker) chooses thereafter, upon observing the leader's strategy. While alternative modeling frameworks abound, the Stackelberg model has had considerable practical impact [Abbas et al. 2017, Fang et al. 2015, Tambe 2011], and will therefore be the primary focus of this chapter.

We begin this chapter by describing a formal model first of Stackelberg games (Section 9.2), and then their particular variations common in security settings, *Stackelberg security games* (Section 9.3), along with solution techniques for these. Subsequently, we consider a particular class of security problems in which the defender aims to *interdict* a path taken by an attacker through a network (Section 9.4). We broaden this first to consider attackers as decision makers in a dynamic setting, and, finally, study security interactions in dynamic environments in which the defender commits to a *policy*, formalized as *stochastic Stackelberg games*, with adversarial patrolling problem providing a concrete application of this modeling framework (Section 9.5).

9.2 Stackelberg Games

Let us start with Stackelberg games, generally. Consider two players, a leader (L) and a follower (F). Both L and F have sets of actions, A_L and A_F, respectively, along with their respective utility functions $u_L(a_L, a_F)$ and $u_F(a_L, a_F)$. Throughout, we assume that $A_L \cup A_F$ is finite. Let σ_L be a probability distribution over A_L, with $\sigma_L(a) \geq 0$ the associated probability of $a \in A_L$. Thus, $\sum_{a \in A_L} \sigma_L(a) = 1$. It is common to refer to σ_L as the leader's *mixed strategy*. We can extend utility functions to be functions of σ_L by taking the expectations with respect to this distribution, i.e.,

$$u_L(\sigma_L, a_F) = \sum_{a \in A_L} \sigma_L(a) u_L(a, a_F) \quad \text{and}$$
$$u_F(\sigma_L, a_F) = \sum_{a \in A_L} \sigma_L(a) u_F(a, a_F).$$

The follower is presumed to observe σ_L, but, crucially, *not the actual realization of random draws a from it*, and then respond by choosing a strategy $b \in A_F$. In particular, we assume that the follower chooses a strategy that is a *best response* $\phi(\sigma_L)$ to σ_L, that is,

$$\phi(\sigma_L) \in \text{argmax}_{b \in A_F}\, u_F(\sigma_L, b). \tag{9.1}$$

Our notation here already makes explicit that a best response strategy of the follower explicitly depends on the observed leader strategy σ_L; indeed, this dependence is what makes this game Stackelberg in nature, and the full strategy space of the follower in this game is the space of all functions that map σ_L to follower actions b.

At this point, one may observe that our formalization of the best response in Equation (9.1), we have effectively assumed that the follower need not consider randomized strategies. Indeed, it is not difficult to show that in the game model we consider here, there always exists a deterministic best response. Intuitively, if a randomized strategy puts non-zero weight on multiple follower actions, we can do no worse than shifting all of this weight to the action which yields the highest follower utility.

A common solution concept for Stackelberg games is a *Stackelberg equilibrium*, in which the follower chooses a best response strategy $\phi(\sigma_L)$, while the leader chooses σ_L to maximize its strategy *given the follower's best response* ϕ. Formally, (σ_L^*, ϕ) is a Stackelberg equilibrium if ϕ is the follower's best response in the sense of Equation (9.1), and $\sigma_L^* \in \arg\max_{\sigma \in \Delta_L} u_L(\sigma, \phi(\sigma))$, where Δ_L is the simplex (i.e., the set of all probability distributions) over A_L.

A limitation of a Stackelberg equilibrium is that the follower may have many ways to break ties, and the particular choices could be somewhat arbitrary. It is common, therefore, to make use of a refinement, referred to as the *Strong Stackelberg equilibrium (SSE)*, in which the follower breaks ties in the leader's favor (commonly justified using the argument that the leader can induce this to be a strict best response for the follower by simply slightly changing the strategy σ_L). Specifically, (σ_L^*, ϕ) form an SSE if

$$\sigma_L^* \in \text{argmax}_{\sigma \in \Delta_L; \phi(\sigma) \in \arg\max_{b \in A_F} u_F(\sigma, b)}\, u_L(\sigma, \phi(\sigma)). \tag{9.2}$$

It turns out that computing SSE amounts to solving a collection of linear programs. The idea is this. Let us fix a follower strategy $b \in A_F$, and ask the following question: how can the leader maximize utility while at the same time incentivizing the follower to choose b (i.e., while b is constrained to be the follower's best response)? The solution to this problem can be formulated as the following linear program:

$$\max_{\sigma \geq 0} \sum_{a \in A_L} \sigma(a) u_L(a, b) \tag{9.3a}$$

$$\text{subject to :} \tag{9.3b}$$

$$\sum_{a \in A_L} \sigma(a) = 1 \tag{9.3c}$$

$$\sum_{a \in A_L} \sigma(a) u_L(a, b) \geq \sum_{a \in A_L} \sigma(a) u_L(a, b') \quad \forall b' \in A_F \setminus b. \tag{9.3d}$$

Of course, there may be no solution to the linear program (LP) (9.3) for particular choices of b, but that simply means that it is not possible for the leader to have b be the follower's best response (e.g., if b is dominated by other choices the follower has). However, suppose we solve it for every possible strategy $b \in A_F$, with the associated solution σ^b and leader utility $u_L(\sigma^b, b)$. Whenever LP (9.3) is infeasible, define σ^b arbitrarily and $u_L(\sigma^b, b) = -\infty$. Then $\sigma^* = \sigma^{b^*}$, where $b^* \in \operatorname{argmax}_b u_L(\sigma^b, b)$. In other words, we simply choose the solution to the LP corresponding to the opponent strategy b for which the leader's solution yields the highest leader utility.

The Stackelberg game model above presumes that the leader has complete information about the follower, and vice-versa. An important generalization is to consider a leader's uncertainty about the follower's utility function, u_F, which we refer to as a *Bayesian Stackelberg game*. Specifically, suppose that there is a finite set of follower *types*, Θ. Each type $\theta \in \Theta$ is a parameter of the follower's utility function, which now takes the form $u_F(a_L, a_F; \theta)$ (with the extension to $u_F(\sigma_L, a_F; \theta)$ exactly as above). Let p_θ be the probability that the follower is of type θ; we suppose that although the leader does not know the actual type, the distribution itself is common knowledge. Let $\phi(\sigma; \theta)$ be the follower's *best response* strategy, which is now parametrized by θ, and is characterized by $\phi(\sigma; \theta) \in \operatorname{argmax}_{b \in A_F} u_F(\sigma, b; \theta)$. The leader then maximizes its expected utility, $\sum_{\theta \in \Theta} p_\theta u_L(\sigma, \phi(\sigma, \theta))$, over randomized strategies σ. Now, we can again seek a SSE solution to this problem. However, the approach above where we solve multiple linear programs, one for each possible follower action, no longer works: since each follower type can take any of the actions, we must solve $|\Theta|^{|A_F|}$ linear programs in the worst case!

Instead, we can compute an SSE of a Bayesian Stackelberg game using the following mixed-integer linear program (MILP):

$$\max_{\sigma \geq 0} \sum_{\theta \in \Theta} p_\theta u_\theta \tag{9.4a}$$

$$\text{subject to :} \tag{9.4b}$$

$$\sum_{a \in A_L} \sigma(a) = 1 \tag{9.4c}$$

$$\sum_{b \in A_F} x(b, \theta) = 1 \quad \forall \theta \in \Theta \tag{9.4d}$$

$$u_\theta - \sum_{a \in A_L} \sigma(a) u_L(a, b) \leq (1 - x(b, \theta))Z \quad \forall b \in A_F, \theta \in \Theta \tag{9.4e}$$

$$0 \leq v_\theta - \sum_{a \in A_L} \sigma(a) u_F(a, b) \leq (1 - x(b, \theta))Z \quad \forall b \in A_F, \theta \in \Theta. \tag{9.4f}$$

In this MILP, u_θ denotes the expected utility of the leader when the follower's type is θ, while v_θ denotes the corresponding expected utility for the follower. Since the leader does not actually know the follower's type, the objective also takes the expectation with respect to the probability distribution over the follower types. Turning to constraints, their main role is to compute the best response strategy $\phi(\sigma; \theta)$ of the follower. We encode it using a binary vector $x(b, \theta)$ such that $x(b, \theta) = 1$ whenever b is the follower's *actual* best response. Note that it depends on σ implicitly insofar as the strategy σ of the leader is itself being computed by the MILP. Constraints (9.4f) actually do the work of computing the follower's best response for each type θ, while Constraints (9.4e) use the best response strategies x of the follower to compute the leader's associated expected utility. In both of the sets of constraints above, Z is a large constant that we take conceptually to be $Z = \infty$.

9.3 Stackelberg Security Games

The Stackelberg game model can be applied to security settings directly as follows. Let the leader be the defender, with A_L the set of defender strategies, and the follower the attacker, with A_F the set of possible attacks. The machinery we developed goes through directly. As it turns out, however, there is more to say here.

Let us make the sets of strategies for the defender and attacker more concrete. In particular, let T be the set of targets that need to be defended from a possible attack. Suppose that the defender can defend—or *cover*—at most r targets at a time; that is, the defender has r protection resources (e.g., security guards). Then a defender strategy is a subset $C \subset T$ such that $|C| \leq r$, and the strategy set A_L is the set of all possible such subsets of targets. Similarly, if the attacker has L resources to attack the targets in T, the set of attack strategies A_F is the set of all subsets of T of size at most L. Even if we suppose that both players saturate their resource use, both A_L and A_F grow exponentially in the number of targets. Consequently, the approaches developed above, which require us to enumerate the entire A_L and A_F will not scale. This means that we must exploit problem structure to develop effective approaches to practical security game models.

Let us add some structure to the utility functions. Let U_i^c be the utility the defender receives when a target i is attacked while it is covered by the defender, and V_i^c the associated utility of the attacker. Similarly, define U_i^u and V_i^u to be the utilities of the defender and attacker, respectively, when target i is attacked while it is not covered by the defender. Commonly, one alternatively defines $R_i^d > 0$ and $P_i^d < 0$ as the reward of the defender if the attacked target i is covered and defender's penalty if it is not covered, and similarly $R_i^a > 0$ the reward to the attacker if i is uncovered and penalty $P_i^a < 0$ when it is covered. Thus, $U_i^c = R_i^d$, $U_i^u = P_i^d$, $V_i^c = P_i^a$, and $V_i^u = R_i^a$. Next, suppose that the attacker can only attack a single target; that is, $L = 1$, and the attacker strategy set is just the set of targets T. Further, suppose that instead of a hard constraint r on the number of defense resources, the defender incurs a cost c for each time it uses a resource to cover a target. Let us also represent the defender's choice as a coverage vector $d \in \{0,1\}^n$, where $n = |T|$ is the number of targets, and let σ be the probability distribution over d (i.e., the defender's mixed strategy). The defender's expected utility is then

$$u_D(\sigma, i) = \sum_d \sigma(d) \left((d_i U_i^c + (1 - d_i) U_i^u) - c \sum_i d_i \right).$$

If we define $x_i \in [0, 1]$ as the probability of covering target i induced by the mixed strategy σ, we can rewrite the utility as

$$u_D(q, i) = x_i U_i^c + (1 - x_i) U_i^u - c \sum_i x_i.$$

Consequently, we no longer need to explicitly reason about the mixed strategy over all possible coverage vectors, but just over target-specific coverage probabilities x_i, aggregated into a vector x. This means that despite the combinatorial underlying strategy space of the defender, we can actually compute a SSE of the Stackelberg security game of this form in polynomial time using multiple LPs just as above, where each LP corresponding to a particular target i of an attack has the following form:

$$\max_x \quad x_i U_i^c + (1 - x_i) U_i^u - c \sum_i x_i \tag{9.5a}$$

$$\text{subject to :}$$

$$0 \leq x_i \leq 1 \quad \forall i \in T \tag{9.5b}$$

$$x_i V_i^c + (1 - x_i) V_i^u \geq x_{i'} V_{i'}^c + (1 - x_{i'}) V_i^u \quad \forall i' \in T \setminus i. \tag{9.5c}$$

The key idea above is that we replace a hard constraint on the defender's resource use with a soft cost function that in principle allows unlimited resources. This approach can be adapted in a straightforward way to consider a constraint that the number of resources used *in expectation* is bounded by r instead of the soft cost function. What does not work, however, is a hard constraint that *in every realization* of coverage vectors we can use at most r resources. In fact, imposing such a constraint effectively prevents us from using this compact representation of the problem, and we now must again enumerate all coverage vectors d.

But what if we do wish to impose a hard constraint that we can use at most r resources? It is often the case that there is little flexibility on this account: for example, we cannot hire new security staff if it happens that our utilization exceeds the current staff. The problem of inducing the attacker to choose a particular target i to attack then becomes

$$\max_{\sigma \geq 0} \quad \sum_d \sigma(d) u_D(d, i) \tag{9.6a}$$

$$\text{subject to :}$$

$$\sum_d \sigma(d) = 1 \tag{9.6b}$$

$$\sum_d \sigma(d) \Delta V(d, i, i') \geq 0 \quad \forall t' \in T, \tag{9.6c}$$

where $\Delta V(d, i, i') = d_i V_i^c + (1 - d_i) V_i^u - d_{i'} V_{i'}^c - (1 - d_{i'}) V_{i'}^u$ and the consideration set of vectors d is restricted to those that involve the use of r resources (since we always wish to saturate resource use in this context, there is no need to include those using fewer than r resources). This set is exponential in the number of targets $|T|$. Nevertheless, we can make use of the problem structure here to avoid explicitly enumerating all variables $\sigma(d)$. Specifically, since the number of constraints is linear in the number of targets, we actually know that the support of the solution σ (i.e., the set of configurations d with $\sigma(d) > 0$) is also going to be linear in $|T|$ [Bertsimas and Tsitsiklis 1997]; the trick is just to find it. To do this, we can use a technique called *column generation*, in which we begin with an arbitrary small subset of l resource assignments $\hat{D} = \{d_1, \ldots, d_l\}$, and solve the linear program (9.6) considering only these. Suppose $\hat{\sigma}(\hat{D})$ is the resulting optimal solution. We can use this solution to compute the *reduced cost* of the standard form analog of this linear program [Bertsimas and Tsitsiklis 1997]. We now construct this standard form analog and derive the expression for reduced cost. First, we add slack variables $\lambda_{i'}$ to each of the inequality constraints to turn these into equality constraints, obtaining

$$\sum_d \sigma(d)\Delta V(d,i,i') - \lambda_{i'} = 0 \quad \forall\, t' \in T.$$

Let $u(i)$ be a vector associated with the security resource configurations in $\hat{D}$, and let $\Delta V(i,i')$ be a vector of $\Delta V(d,i,i')$ for all $d \in \hat{D}$. Turning each constraint into matrix-vector notation, we obtain

$$1^T\sigma = 1$$

for the first constraint, where 1^T is a row vector of 1s, and

$$\Delta V(i,i')^T\sigma - \lambda_{i'} = 0$$

for the rest. Let λ be a vector of all slack variables $\lambda_{i'}$. Define a matrix B as follows. Let the first row be $a_1 = [1^T, 0]$, where the number of 1s is the number of variables, and let each subsequent row be $a_{i'} = [\Delta V(i,i'), -1]$. Finally, define $b = [1, 0^T]^T$, where 0^T is a vector of $|T|$ 0s. The problem can then be rewritten as

$$\min_{\sigma,\lambda\geq 0} \quad -u(i)^T\sigma \tag{9.7a}$$

$$\text{subject to :}$$

$$B[\sigma,\lambda]^T = b. \tag{9.7b}$$

From this standard form, we can then derive the expression for reduced cost associated with an arbitrary resource assignment d' that is not in $\hat{D}$ as follows. First, an optimal solution to the linear program (9.7) over variables in $\hat{D}$ will compute the set of variables d for which $\sigma(d) > 0$. Let $\hat{B}$ be the submatrix of B with the associated columns, and let $u_{\hat{B}}(i)$ be the associated components of $u(i)$. Let $[\alpha, \beta] = u_{\hat{B}}(i)^T \hat{B}$, where α is a scalar and β a vector with one element for each target t'.

$$\bar{c}_{d'} = -d'_i U_i^c - (1 - d'_i)U_i^u - \alpha - \sum_{i'} \beta_{i'}(d'_i V_i^c + (1 - d'_i)V_i^u - d'_{i'} V_{i'}^c - (1 - d'_{i'})V_{i'}^u).$$

Let $\bar{\beta} = \sum_{i'} \beta_{i'}$. Then this expression can be slightly simplified to

$$\bar{c}_{d'} = -d'_i(U_i^c + \bar{\beta}V_i^c) - (1 - d'_i)(U_i^u + \bar{\beta}V_i^u) - \alpha + \sum_{i'} \beta_{i'}(d'_{i'} V_{i'}^c + (1 - d'_{i'})V_{i'}^u).$$

Our goal is now to minimize the reduced cost, which is equivalent to solving the following integer linear program (ILP):

$$\min_{d'} \quad d'_i(U_i^u - U_i^c + \bar{\beta}(V_i^u - V_i^c)) - \sum_{i'} d'_{i'}\beta_{i'}(V_{i'}^u - V_{i'}^c) \tag{9.8a}$$

$$\text{subject to :}$$

$$\sum_i d'_i = r \tag{9.8b}$$

$$d'_i \in \{0, 1\} \quad \forall i \in T. \tag{9.8c}$$

Moreover, if for an optimal solution d' of this optimization problem we find that $\bar{c}_{d'} \geq 0$, we know that the solution we obtained in the last iteration is in fact optimal, and we can stop the column generation process. The power of this approach is that while ILPs are NP-hard to solve in general, in practice we can often solve them effectively and quickly using state-of-the-art ILP solvers.

9.4 Security Games on Networks

So far, we have studied both the rather general Stackelberg game model, and its specialization to security games with independent targets. One important class of problems in security entails preventing, or *interdicting*, the flow of malicious activity on network. In its classical form, this problem is known as *network interdiction* [Cormican et al. 1998, Smith and Song 2020]. Many variations of this problem have been explored; here, I describe one of the first, *deterministic network flow interdiction* [Wood 1993], which well illustrates the main idea.

Consider a network $G = (V, E)$ where V is the set of nodes and E the set of (directed) edges, with a particular edge denoted by $(i, j) \in E$. Additionally, we associate each edge (i, j) with a capacity u_{ij}. Suppose that a malicious actor aims to solve the *network flow* problem over this network, maximizing the total amount of flow (of goods, malicious activity, etc) between a source node $s \in V$ and a target node $t \in V$. Assume for the moment that both s and t are known. The problem of maximizing total flow from s to t can be represented as the following linear program [Bertsimas and Tsitsiklis 1997, Wood 1993]:

$$\max_{x} \quad x_{ts} \tag{9.9a}$$
$$\text{subject to :}$$
$$\sum_j x_{sj} - \sum_j x_{js} - x_{ts} = 0 \tag{9.9b}$$
$$\sum_j x_{ij} - \sum_j x_{ji} = 0 \quad \forall i \in V \setminus \{s, t\} \tag{9.9c}$$
$$\sum_j x_{tj} - \sum_j x_{jt} + x_{ts} = 0 \tag{9.9d}$$
$$0 \leq x_{ij} \leq u_{ij} \quad \forall (i, j) \in E \tag{9.9e}$$
$$x_{ts} \geq 0, \tag{9.9f}$$

where x_{ij} represents flows along edges $(i, j) \in E$ and x_{ts} is an artificial edge added to the network, going from t to s.

The network interdiction problem involves removing a subset of edges S from E, subject to a budget constraint, so as to minimize the maximum network flow as computed by the above linear program with edges restricted to $E \setminus S$. Suppose that removing an edge (i, j) incurs a cost c_{ij}, and let C be the total budget on cutting edges. We can encode this network interdiction problem as follows:

$$\min_{y} \max_{x} \quad x_{ts} \tag{9.10a}$$
$$\text{subject to :}$$
$$\sum_j x_{sj} - \sum_j x_{js} - x_{ts} = 0 \tag{9.10b}$$

$$\sum_j x_{ij} - \sum_j x_{ji} = 0 \quad \forall i \in V \setminus \{s,t\} \tag{9.10c}$$

$$\sum_j x_{tj} - \sum_j x_{jt} + x_{ts} = 0 \tag{9.10d}$$

$$0 \leq x_{ij} \leq u_{ij}(1 - y_{ij}) \quad \forall (i,j) \in E \tag{9.10e}$$

$$\sum_{ij} c_{ij} y_{ij} \leq C \tag{9.10f}$$

$$x_{ts} \geq 0 \tag{9.10g}$$

$$y_{ij} \in \{0,1\} \quad \forall (i,j) \in E, \tag{9.10h}$$

where y_{ij} represents the choice of edges that are cut. Finally, we can note that the inner maximum flow problem admits a dual linear program, and after taking the dual and linearizing the objective, we obtain the following integer linear program for network interdiction:

$$\min_{y,\alpha,\beta} \sum_{ij} u_{ij}\beta_{ij} \tag{9.11a}$$

$$\text{subject to :}$$

$$\alpha_i - \alpha_j + \beta_{ij} + y_{ij} \quad \forall (i,j) \in E \tag{9.11b}$$

$$\alpha_t - \alpha_s \geq 1 \tag{9.11c}$$

$$\sum_{ij} c_{ij} y_{ij} \leq C \tag{9.11d}$$

$$y_{ij}, \alpha_i, \beta_{ij} \in \{0,1\} \quad \forall i \in V, (i,j) \in E. \tag{9.11e}$$

The problem of network interdiction has received a great deal of attention over the years, with many variations of the setting above explored, including problems which are not zero-sum (that is, when the interdictor's goals are not necessarily in opposition to the adversary) [Jain et al. 2011], uncertainty (e.g., about the s, t source and destination nodes) [Cormican et al. 1998, Pay et al. 2019], etc. In the end, the general problem structure tends to closely resemble the basic network flow interdiction problem above.

One substantive variation of network interdiction is *plan interdiction*, in which the goal of the defender is to prevent the attacker from achieving its goals, which the latter attempts to accomplish by solving a dynamic decision problem. A number of variations of this problem have been explored [Letchford and Vorobeychik 2013, Panda and Vorobeychik 2017, 2018, Vorobeychik and Pritchard 2020]; here we describe a very general setting—Markov decision process (MDP) initial state interdiction problem (MDPSI) which admits a relatively simple solution approach.

Formally, the MDPSI is defined by 1) an MDP $\mathcal{M} = \{S, A, r(s,a), \gamma\}$, where $S, A, r(s,a)$, and γ are the state space, action space, reward function, and the discount factor of an infinite-horizon discounted MDP which the attacker is solving, respectively, and 2) interdiction costs $\rho(s'_0, s_0) = \sum_j \rho_j |s'_{j0} - s_{j0}|$ of modifying an initial state s_0 into s'_0, where ρ_j is the cost of modifying variable j. Note that this cost can also capture inability to modify specific state variables (the corresponding $\rho_j = \infty$). We assume that the game is zero-sum (modulo interdiction costs), so that the defender aims to minimize the sum of discounted attacker rewards. Define $V(s_0, \pi)$ as the attacker's value function for a policy π starting at state s_0 in MDP $\mathcal{M}$. Let Π be the set of deterministic stationary policies of the MDP. The defender then solves

$$\min_{s'_0 \in S} V(s'_0) + \rho(s'_0, s_0), \tag{9.12}$$

where $V(s)$ is the optimal value function of the MDP. The key observation is that the optimal policy is *independent* of the interdiction decision s'_0, since the optimal policy of an MDP is independent of starting state. Consequently, we can decompose this problem into two parts: first, we compute or approximate the value function $V(s)$, and second, fix $V(s)$ and solve the optimization problem (9.12). The former can be done using standard reinforcement learning techniques, while the latter can subsequently be done using, for example, gradient-based methods (if the value function is differentiable in input state s).

9.5 Stochastic Stackelberg Games and Adversarial Patrolling

The Stackelberg game models discussed so far assume that the attacker is aware of the probability with which each target is covered by the defender, but remains ignorant of the defender's actual sequence of moves. For instance, the defender may follow a fixed but randomly generated patrolling schedule; however, the attacker is assumed to be unable to observe the defender's real-time location during the patrol. In many realistic domains, such as operations by the US Coast Guard [An et al. 2011], this assumption may not hold, since attackers could feasibly observe the ongoing patrol (e.g., coast guard vessels are often visible). Therefore, a more realistic formulation in such contexts would permit the attacker to observe both the defender's randomized policy (i.e., the probability distribution over possible moves) and the defender's current position. This setting can be modeled as an *adversarial patrolling game* (APG). APGs, in turn, constitute a special instance of *discounted stochastic Stackelberg games (DSSGs)*. We first introduce the general framework of DSSGs and then describe the specific APG model.

9.5.1 Stochastic Discounted Stackelberg Games

Two-player infinite-horizon DSSGs involve one player who is a "leader" and the other who is a "follower", just as in general Stackelberg games. The leader commits to a *policy* that becomes known to the follower who plays a best-response policy. These games have a finite state space S, finite action spaces A_L for the leader and A_F for the follower, payoff functions $u_L(s, a_l, a_f)$ and $u_F(s, a_l, a_f)$ for leader and follower respectively, and a transition function $T_{ss'}^{a_l a_f}$, where $s, s' \in S$, $a_l \in A_L$ and $a_f \in A_F$. The discount factors are $\gamma_L, \gamma_F < 1$ for the leader and follower, respectively. Finally, $\beta(s)$ is the probability that the initial state is s.

The history of play at time t is $h_t = \{s_1 a_{l,1} a_{f,1} \cdots s_{t-1} a_{l,t-1} a_{f,t-1} s_t\}$ where t denotes time. Let Π and Φ be the set of nonstationary and non-Markov policies (i.e., mappings from histories to distributions over actions) for the leader and follower, respectively. Let u_L and u_F denote the utility functions for leader and follower respectively. For arbitrary policies $\pi \in \Pi$ and $\phi \in \Phi$,

$$u_L(s, \pi, \phi) = \mathbb{E}\Big[\sum_{t=1}^{\infty} \gamma_L^{t-1} u_L(s_t, \pi(h_t), \phi(h_t)) | s_1 = s\Big],$$

where the expectation is over the stochastic evolution of the states, and where (abusing notation)

$$u_L(s_t, \pi(h_t), \phi(h_t)) = \sum_{a_l \in A_L} \sum_{a_f \in A_F} \pi(a_l | h_t) \phi(a_f | h_t) u_L(s_t, a_l, a_f),$$

with $\pi(a_l|h_t)$ the probability of leader-action a_l in history h_t under policy π, and $\phi(a_f|h_t)$ the probability of follower-action a_f in history h_t under policy ϕ. The utility of the follower, $u_F(s, \pi, \phi)$, is defined analogously.

For any leader policy $\pi \in \Pi$, the follower plays the best-response policy defined as

$$\phi_\pi^{BR} \in \arg\max_{\phi \in \Phi} \sum_s \beta(s) u_F(s, \pi, \phi).$$

The leader's optimal policy is then

$$\pi^* \in \arg\max_{\pi\in\Pi} \sum_s \beta(s) u_L(s, \pi, \phi_\pi^{BR}).$$

Together $(\pi^*, \phi_{\pi^*}^{BR})$ constitute a Stackelberg equilibrium (SE). If, additionally, the follower breaks ties in the leader's favor, these are a Strong Stackelberg equilibrium (SSE).

A natural question arises: is the leader's optimal policy in a DSSG guaranteed to be Markov stationary (that is, only depend on current state)? Turns out, it is not, as the following example illustrates. Suppose that the DSSG has three states, i.e., $S = \{1, 2, 3\}$, and the leader and the follower have two actions each, $A_L = \{U, D\}$ for the leader and $A_F = \{L, R\}$ for the follower. Let initial state be $s = 1$ and suppose that the following transitions happen deterministically and independently of either player's decisions: $T_{12} = 1$, $T_{23} = 1$, $T_{33} = 1$, that is, the process starts at state 1, then moves to state 2, then, finally, to state 3, which is an absorbing state. In state $s = 1$ only the follower's actions have an effect on payoffs, which is as follows: $u_L(1, \cdot, L) = -M$, $u_L(1, \cdot, R) = 0$, $u_F(1, \cdot, L) = \epsilon$, $u_F(1, \cdot, R) = 0$, where M is an arbitrarily large number and $\epsilon << M$. In state $s = 2$, in contrast, only the leader's actions have an effect on payoffs: $u_L(2, U, \cdot) = u_L(2, D, \cdot) = 0$, $u_F(2, U, \cdot) = -M$, $u_F(2, D, \cdot) = 0$. Suppose that the discount factors $\gamma_L = \gamma_F$ are close to 1. First, note that a Markov stationary policy for the leader would be independent of the follower's action in state 2, and, consequently, the follower's best response is to play L, giving the leader a payoff of $-M$. On the other hand, if the leader plays the following non-Markov policy: play U when the follower plays L and D otherwise, the follower's optimal policy is to play R, and the leader receives a payoff of 0. Since M is arbitrarily large, the difference between an optimal and best stationary policy is arbitrarily large.

The consequence of the fact that the leader's optimal policy can have arbitrary dependence on history is that DSSGs are extremely difficult to solve, except in special cases, such as when the game is zero-sum (in which case it is equivalent to a stochastic game, which can be solved in polynomial time [Littman 1994]).

Next, we consider the important special case of APGs [Vorobeychik et al. 2012, 2014], and present solution techniques for these.

9.5.2 Adversarial Patrolling Games

An *adversarial patrolling game (APG)* is formalized by $\{T, U_i^c, U_i^u, V_i^c, V_i^u, \gamma, G\}$, where T is the set of n targets patrolled by the defender, U_i^c and U_i^u are defender's utilities if an attacker attacks a target $i \in T$ when it is patrolled and not, respectively, while V_i^c and V_i^u are the corresponding attacker utilities, $\gamma \in (0, 1)$ is the discount factor (in some cases, we also allow $\gamma = 1$), and $G = (T, E)$ is a graph with targets as vertices and E the set of directed edges constraining defender patrolling moves between targets. It is useful to consider the representation of this graph as an adjacency matrix B, where $B_{ij} = 1$ if and only if there is an edge from target i to target j.

The game proceeds over a sequence of steps in which the defender moves between targets (subject to the constraints imposed by G), while the attacker decides on both the timing of the attack, as well as its target. The defender's (stochastic) patrolling policy π can in general be an arbitrary function from the full observed history (i.e., the sequence of targets patrolled in the past) to a probability distribution over the targets to move to next. We assume that the attacker knows π. At each time step t the attacker observes the defender's current location i and may choose to wait or to attack an arbitrary target $j \in T$. An attacker who chooses to wait at time t receives no immediate utility, while attacking a target j gains the attacker V_i^c if it is covered by the defender at time $t + 1$ and V_i^u if it is not. We denote the attacker's policy by ϕ. We say that a policy (π or ϕ) is *Markovian* if it only depends on the current location of the defender, and we call it *stationary Markovian* if it additionally has no dependence on time.

US Coast Guard's Patrolling Problem as an APG: The United States Coast Guard (USCG) is responsible for protecting critical infrastructure along the nation's coasts, ports, and inland waterways. For a given port with multiple potential targets that an adversary might attack, the USCG carries out patrols aimed at detecting adversaries and safeguarding these assets. However, although adversaries may be able to observe patrol patterns, the USCG's limited security resources prevent continuous coverage of all locations at all times [An et al. 2011]. Within the APG framework, the USCG serves as the defender, while a terrorist organization (for instance) acts as the attacker, capable of conducting surveillance, observing the patrols' current positions, and inferring the stochastic patrolling policy being used.

We now note that adversarial patrolling games can be naturally formulated as DSSGs. In particular, the states in an APG correspond to the set of targets T, along with an absorbing state s. At each state, the defender's available actions consist of the targets j that can be reached within a single time step, while the attacker's possible actions are to either *wait* or *attack*. (For now, we assume that the expected utilities associated with an attack can be computed; we will address the question of which targets are attacked later.) State transitions in this model are deterministic, given the players' actions: if the attacker decides to attack, the system transitions to the absorbing state s; otherwise, the next state is fully determined by the defender's chosen move. Finally, when the attacker chooses to wait, our baseline formulation assumes that both players receive zero reward.

9.5.3 Solving Zero-Sum APGs

Consider a special case of zero-sum APGs, where $U_i^c = -V_i^c$ and $U_i^u = -V_i^u$. In this case, APGs (and associated DSSGs) become equivalent to *stochastic games*, since the order of player moves is no longer important. A particularly important consequence is that while in general SSE solutions to DSSGs need not be in Markov stationary policies (as our example above illustrated), stochastic games always have equilibria that are Markov stationary [Filar and Vrieze 1997]. Thus, for zero-sum APGs, we can focus exclusively on stationary policies, and denote by π_{ij} the (stationary) probability that the defender moves from target i to j.

Since an APG is a special case of a stochastic game, we can adapt the nonlinear programming formulation proposed by Filar and Vrieze [1997] for computing Nash equilibria in general zero-sum stochastic games to our specific setting. A minor but useful modification to their formulation, which we introduce here, is the explicit inclusion of constraints on the defender's feasible actions as defined by the underlying graph G.

$$\pi_{ij} \leq B_{ij} \quad \forall\, i, j \in T. \tag{9.13}$$

Let v_i be the expected attacker value of starting in state i. We can formulate the defender's problem as the following mathematical program:

$$\min_{\pi, v} \sum_i v_i \tag{9.14a}$$

$$\text{subject to}:$$

$$\pi_{ij} \geq 0 \qquad \forall\, i, j \in T \tag{9.14b}$$

$$\sum_j \pi_{ij} = 1 \qquad \forall\, i \in T \tag{9.14c}$$

$$\pi_{ij} \leq B_{ij} \qquad \forall\, i, j \in T \tag{9.14d}$$

$$v_i \geq (1 - \pi_{ij})V_j^u + \pi_{ij}V_j^c \quad \forall\, i, j \in T \tag{9.14e}$$

$$v_i \geq \gamma \sum_j \pi_{ij} v_j \qquad \forall i \in T. \tag{9.14f}$$

Constraints (9.14b) and (9.14c) restrict the defender policy to be a valid probability distribution. The key constraints (9.14e) and (9.14f) are best understood by fixing the defender policy π, in which case the attacker faces an MDP. The right-hand-side of Constraint (9.14f) is the expected value of waiting (for which the immediate reward is 0). The constraints then arise because the value v_i of state i is the expected utility of making the best action choice, and minimizing the objective ensures that these values bind to *some* action in every state. While this formulation is a non-convex non-linear program, it turns out that all local optima are also global optima [Filar and Vrieze 1997].

9.5.4 Solving General-Sum APGs

The approach above for effectively computing equilibria in zero-sum APGs relies strongly on the particular structure of the zero-sum game. We now present a general formulation of the problem of computing SSE in APGs which does not require the game to be zero sum. First, let $\beta(i)$ be the distribution over the initial location of the defender (which in many cases may simply be a fixed initial location). Let $v_d(i)$ be the defender's value (expected discounted cumulative reward) of the defender being in location i, and let $v_a(i)$ be the attacker's value when the defender is at location i. For the attacker, we now also need to explicitly represent their policy best response. We again use ϕ to denote the attacker's policy, but our notation for it will be somewhat different than earlier. Specifically, we use ϕ_{ij} to denote the decision of the attacker whether or not to attack a location (target) j when the defender is at location i, and ϕ_{iw} to indicate whether the attacker chooses to wait when seeing the defender in location i (treating the decision to wait is effectively an artificial target w). The full mixed-integer non-linear program (MINLP) for solving general-sum APGs can be represented as follows:

$$\max_{\pi, \phi, v_a, v_d} \sum_i \beta(i) v_d(i) \tag{9.15a}$$

s.t. :

$$\pi_{ij} \geq 0 \quad \phi_{ij} \in \{0, 1\}, \phi_{iw} \in \{0, 1\} \qquad \forall\, i, j \in T \tag{9.15b}$$

$$\sum_j \pi_{ij} = 1 \quad \sum_j \phi_{ij} + \phi_{iw} = 1 \qquad \forall\, i \in T \tag{9.15c}$$

$$\pi_{ij} \leq B_{ij} \qquad \forall\, i, j \in T \tag{9.15d}$$

$$v_i \geq (1 - \pi_{ij})V_j^u + \pi_{ij}V_j^c \quad \forall\, i, j \in T \tag{9.15e}$$

$$v_i \geq \gamma \sum_j \pi_{ij} v_j \qquad \forall i \in T \tag{9.15f}$$

$$0 \leq v_a(i) - [(1 - \pi_{ij})V_j^u + \pi_{ij}V_j^c] \leq (1 - \phi_{ij})Z \qquad \forall i, j \in T \tag{9.15g}$$

$$v_a(i) - \gamma \sum_j \pi_{ij} v_a(j) \leq (1 - \phi_{iw})Z \qquad \forall\, i \in T \tag{9.15h}$$

$$v_d(i) - [(1 - \pi_{ij})U_j^u + \pi_{ij}U_j^c] \leq (1 - \phi_{ij})Z \qquad \forall i, j \in T \tag{9.15i}$$

$$v_d(i) - \gamma \sum_j \pi_{ij} v_d(j) \leq (1 - \phi_{iw})Z \qquad \forall\, i \in T. \tag{9.15j}$$

Note that this representation echoes back to our solution of Bayesian Stackelberg games in Section 9.2; in particular, the nature of the constraints used to compute the attacker's best response has very much the same structure.

Much as we can represent the general-sum APGs equilibrium computation as a MINLP, that is of only marginal help: such problems are extremely challenging to solve in practice. Even if we were to discretize the defender's policy π, turning this into a mixed-integer linear program, the resulting problems are still difficult to solve. Indeed, scalable approaches for solving general sum APGs—and all the more so, DSSGs—remain elusive.

9.6 Conclusion

Computational game theory for security has been a very active field of research for a number of years now, and the volume of both modeling and computational approaches far exceeds what can be reasonably covered in a short chapter. Consequently, this chapter was scoped somewhat narrowly on a collection of models and computational methods for several classes of Stackelberg security games. It is nevertheless worth specifically mentioning two important paradigms that the chapter has ignored entirely. First, there is now considerable and important line of work on game-theoretic models of deception in security settings. Some of this work pertains to the strategic deployment of honeypots [Anwar and Kamhoua 2022, Garg and Grosu 2007, Kiekintveld et al. 2015], while other efforts consider problems involving choosing configurations of devices on a network as well as deceptive presentation of such configurations [Schlenker et al. 2018b, Shi et al. 2020, Thakoor et al. 2019, Wu et al. 2021]. Second, there is much work that aims to relax the assumption of perfectly rational behavior by adversaries. In this line of work, a common consideration is the merging of behavioral game-theoretic models with Stackelberg-style approaches for computing optimal defender strategies [Abbas et al. 2017, Nguyen et al. 2013, Yang et al. 2013].

10

Green Security Game and Community Engagement

Weiran Shen[1] and Fei Fang[2]

[1]Renmin University
[2]Carnegie Mellon University

Abstract

Wildlife conservation is increasingly threatened by illegal poaching, where rangers must protect vast areas with limited resources. In this chapter, we apply computational game theory to design patrol strategies that take into account poachers' adaptive behavior. We integrate adversary modeling with randomized patrol planning, producing strategies that are both unpredictable and robust. Field deployments in conservation areas demonstrate the effectiveness of these approaches, showing measurable improvements in wildlife protection. The chapter highlights the broader role of AI in conservation science, where predictive analytics and decision optimization can support biodiversity on a large scale. We close by reflecting on the importance of interdisciplinary collaboration among computer scientists, conservationists, and policymakers to ensure the lasting success of such interventions.

10.1 Introduction

While game-theoretic and algorithmic approaches have been developed to combat illegal activities such as poaching and overfishing in green security domains, existing research in AI and computational game theory has largely overlooked a key factor: community engagement. In practice, law enforcement agencies often recruit local community members as informants who

DOI: 10.1201/9788743812074-11

can provide valuable intelligence—such as the locations of ongoing illegal activities—to support patrol operations.

In this chapter, we address this gap by introducing a novel two-stage security game model that explicitly incorporates community engagement. Our model represents the informant-attacker social network as a bipartite graph and models attacker behavior using a level-l response framework inspired by cognitive hierarchy theory. We establish the computational complexity of the problem and present exact, approximate, and heuristic algorithms for informant selection and patroller allocation against level-l ($l < \infty$) attackers. For level-∞ attackers, we propose a new algorithm that transforms the defender's optimization problem—originally framed as a parameterized fixed-point computation—into a bi-level optimization problem, where the inner level is a linear program and the outer level contains only a linear number of variables and a single linear constraint. Finally, we conduct extensive experiments to evaluate the effectiveness and efficiency of the proposed algorithms.

10.2 Background

Although safeguarding natural resources is critical for environmental sustainability, chronic underfunding often results in very low densities of law-enforcement personnel (hereafter defenders) responsible for combating illegal activities such as wildlife poaching and overfishing (hereafter attacks).

Weak or insufficient sanctions enable attackers to engage in frequent offenses [Le Gallic and Cox 2006, Leader-Williams and Milner-Gulland 1993], which further complicates effective detection and deterrence through patrols. To enhance patrol efficiency, enforcement agencies frequently rely on community informants and allocate defensive resources based on the intelligence they provide [Linkie et al. 2015].

Because attackers often come from the same local communities, their actions can be observed by informants through regular social interactions. As a result, informant tips frequently contain detailed information about ongoing or imminent illegal activities and, if available to defenders, can directly guide the allocation of limited defensive resources. Indeed, community engagement is identified by the World Wildlife Fund as one of the six pillars toward zero poaching [WWF 2015]. Its importance extends beyond environmental conservation and applies to other domains—such as combating urban crime—where community cooperation plays a crucial role [Gill et al. 2014, Tublitz and Lawrence 2014].

Prior work in computational game theory has produced models and algorithms to help defenders distribute scarce resources in the presence of strategic adversaries, with applications in traffic enforcement [Rosenfeld and Kraus 2017], preventing oil siphoning [Wang et al. 2018b], deceiving cyber attackers [Schlenker et al. 2018a], protecting critical infrastructure [Pita et al. 2008], and fighting wildlife crime [Fang et al. 2017]. However, none of these studies incorporate the crucial dimension of community engagement.

Community engagement introduces several fundamentally new challenges that have not been addressed in prior work. First, the defender must decide not only how to patrol but also whom to recruit as informants. Second, multiple attackers may operate simultaneously, and the presence of informants creates interdependencies among their outcomes: a tip about one attacker can alter the defender's patrol strategy and thereby influence others. Third, the combinatorial structure of informant tips leads to an exponential representation of the defender's strategy space, making the search for an optimal strategy extremely difficult. Fourth, attackers may learn and adapt to observed patrol patterns over time.

In this chapter, we address this gap by introducing the first two-stage security game model that explicitly incorporates community engagement. The model represents social connections between potential informants and attackers using a bipartite graph. In the first stage, the defender selects informants subject to a budget constraint. In the second stage, the defender allocates protection across targets based on tips received from the recruited informants. Drawing inspiration from the quantal cognitive hierarchy model [Wright and Leyton-Brown 2014], we adopt a level-l response model for attackers, capturing iterative reasoning and the mutual influence between attacker behavior and the defender's resulting marginal strategy.

Our second contribution provides complexity results and algorithms for computing an optimal defender strategy against level-l ($l < \infty$) attackers. We prove that selecting the optimal set of informants is NP-hard.

Building on sampling techniques, we introduce an approximation algorithm for computing the optimal patrol strategy and a heuristic algorithm for determining which informants to recruit. For expository clarity, we primarily present the algorithms for level-0 attackers and briefly outline their extension to level-l ($0 < l < \infty$) attackers in the final section of the chapter.

Our third contribution is a novel algorithm for computing the optimal defender strategy against level-∞ attackers. This setting is particularly challenging: an attacker's strategy can influence the defender's marginal strategy, which in turn affects the attackers' responses, and level-∞ attackers are defined via a fixed-point formulation. Consequently, the defender's utility depends critically on solving a parameterized fixed-point problem.

A naïve mathematical-programming formulation of the problem is prohibitively large to solve. Instead, we reduce the formulation to a bi-level optimization problem in which both levels are substantially more tractable. Specifically, the inner-level problem becomes a linear program, and the outer-level problem involves only a linear number of variables and a single linear constraint.

Finally, we conduct extensive experiments to evaluate our methods. We compare the running time and solution quality of the different algorithms, demonstrating that our bi-level optimization approach outperforms the algorithm adapted from prior work. We also compare level-0 attackers with a scenario involving insider threats (i.e., attackers who know which informants have been recruited). For this case, we formulate the problem as a mathematical program and solve it using an adapted algorithm from earlier research. Our results show that the defender suffers a significant utility loss when insider threats are ignored and a naïve attacker model (level-0) is still assumed.

10.3 Literature Review

Community engagement has been extensively examined in criminology. Duffy et al. [2015], Moreto [2015], and Smith and Humphreys [2015] analyze the role of community participation in wildlife conservation, while Linkie et al. [2015] and Gill et al. [2014] demonstrate the positive impacts of community-oriented strategies. However, these studies do not provide mathematical models that capture the strategic interaction between defenders and attackers.

Informant recruitment has also been studied through evolutionary game-theoretic models to understand societal attitudes toward crime. For example, Short et al. [2013] formulate recruitment planning as an optimal control problem that accounts for limited resources and budget. In contrast, our work emphasizes the synergy between community engagement and the allocation of defensive resources, aiming to jointly optimize informant recruitment and defensive deployment.

In security contexts, Stackelberg Security Games (SSGs) have been applied to a broad range of problems [Tambe 2011], with variants incorporating alarm systems, surveillance cameras, and drones that provide real-time information [Basilico et al. 2017, Guo et al. 2017, Ma et al. 2018]. Unlike these sensor-based systems, informants provide tips that depend on their social connections—an essential aspect of community engagement not captured in previous SSG formulations.

Beyond fully rational attacker models, boundedly rational behavioral models such as quantal response (QR) [McKelvey and Palfrey 1995, Yang et al. 2012] and subjective-utility quantal response [Nguyen et al. 2013] have also been explored in SSG research. Our model and solution approach are compatible with most existing behavioral frameworks in the SSG literature, though, for expository clarity, we focus primarily on the QR model.

10.4 Model

This section introduces the two-stage green security game with community engagement. The central innovation, compared with existing models, is the incorporation of informants from local communities. These informants can be recruited and trained by the defender to provide tips about ongoing or impending attacks.

Following existing works on SSG [Jain et al. 2010, Korzhyk et al. 2011], we consider a game with a set of targets $T = [n] = \{1, \ldots, n\}$. The defender has r units of defensive resources and each can protect (or cover) one target with no scheduling constraint, while attacker chooses a single target to attack. If target i is attacked, the defender (resp. attacker) receives $R_i^d > 0$ (resp. $P_i^a < 0$) if it is covered, otherwise receives $P_i^d < 0$ (resp. $R_i^a > 0$).

Recruited informants can offer the defender tips about the specific targets of ongoing or upcoming attacks, though the frequency and usefulness of these tips may vary due to heterogeneity in the informants' social connections. We model the interactions and connections between potential informants X and potential attackers Y using a bipartite graph $G_S = (X, Y, E)$ with $X \cap Y = \emptyset$. We further assume that the defender has access to a list of potential attackers, which may be provided by the conservation site manager, as the deployment of the approach depends on the manager's domain knowledge, experience, and understanding of the social ties within the community.

When an attacker decides to carry out an attack, any informant who has previously interacted with that attacker may know the intended target location. Formally, for each $v \in Y$, we assume that v initiates an attack with probability p_v, but that the specific target remains unknown without informant reports. We further assume that each attacker acts independently. Each edge $(u, v) \in E$ is associated with an information-sharing intensity w_{uv}, which represents the probability that informant u reports attacker v's activity, conditioned on v launching an attack and u being recruited.

We assume that the game proceeds in two stages. In the first stage, the defender recruits k informants. In the second stage, the defender receives tips from these informants and allocates r units of defensive resources. The defender's objective is to maximize the expected utility, defined as the sum of the utilities obtained from each potential attack. Let U denote the set of recruited informants in the first stage, where $|U| \leq k$, and $V = \{v \mid \exists u \in U, (u, v) \in E\}$ denotes the set of attackers that are connected with at least one informant in U. We represent tips as a vector of disjoint subsets of attackers $\mathbf{V} = (V_1, \ldots, V_n)$, where V_i is the set of attackers who are reported to attack target $i \in T$ such that $V_i \subseteq V, V_i \cap V_j = \emptyset$ for any $i, j \in T$ with $i \neq j$. An attacker v is *reported* if there exists $i \in T$ such that $v \in V_i$, otherwise he is *unreported.* We use $V_0 = \bigcup_{i \in T} V_i$ to denote the set of reported attackers. It is possible that $V_0 = \emptyset$, and we say the defender is *informed* if $V_0 \neq \emptyset$. Note that $\mathbf{V}$ is a compact representation of the tips received by the defender as it neglects the identity of the informants. Since we assume that all informant tips are accurate, we do not need to keep track of informant identities.

In practice, tips are infrequent, and the defender is typically very protective of informants. As a result, attackers are generally unaware of the presence of informants unless a significant insider threat exists. Patrols can be categorized into two types: routine patrols and ambush patrols, with the latter triggered by informant tips. Ambush patrols are costly, often requiring rangers to wait for extended periods in hopes of intercepting a poacher. When no tip is received, the defender follows a routine patrol strategy $\mathbf{x}_0 = (x_1, \ldots, x_n)$, where x_i denotes the probability of covering target i. Under this assumption, the defender should adopt a strategy $\mathbf{x}_0$ that is optimal against the Quantal Response (QR) model, which can be computed by adapting the method of Yang et al. [2012]. When informed, the defender instead deploys a strategy $\mathbf{x}(\mathbf{V})$ tailored to the tip $\mathbf{V}$. We assume that each attacker who chooses to attack a target responds to the defender's strategy according to the QR model.

We define $\mathsf{QR}(\mathbf{x}') := (q'_1, \ldots, q'_n)$, where q'_i is the probability of attacking target i defined by

$$q'_i = \frac{\exp\left(\lambda\left[x'_i P^a_i + (1 - x'_i) R^a_i\right]\right)}{\sum_{j \in T} \exp\left(\lambda\left[x'_j P^a_j + (1 - x'_j) R^a_j\right]\right)}, \tag{10.1}$$

and $\mathbf{x}'$ is the attacker's *subjective belief* of the coverage probabilities. In the above equation, $\lambda \geq 0$ is the precision parameter [McKelvey and Palfrey 1995], which is assumed known throughout the chapter. We discuss the relaxation of some of the assumptions mentioned above in Section 10.10.

10.4.1 Level-l Response Model

Motivated by the high cost of ambush patrols and drawing inspiration from cognitive hierarchy theory, we introduce a level-l response model to characterize attacker behavior.

When the informants' report intensities are negligible, the attackers are almost always faced with the routine patrol $\mathbf{x}_0$. But when the informants' report intensities are not negligible, the attackers' behavior will change the marginal probability that a target is covered. Thus we assume that level-0 attackers just play the quantal response against the routine patrol $\mathbf{x}_0$: $\mathbf{q}^0 = \mathsf{QR}(\mathbf{x}_0)$. Then the defender will likely get informed with different tips $\mathbf{V}$, and respond with $\mathbf{x}(\mathbf{V})$ accordingly. Over time, the attackers will learn about the change in the frequency that a target is covered. We denote the induced defender's marginal strategy at level 0 by $\hat{\mathbf{x}}^0 = \mathsf{MS}(\mathbf{x}_0, \mathbf{x}, \mathbf{q}^0)$. After observing $\hat{\mathbf{x}}^0$ at level 0, level-1 attackers will update their strategies from $\mathbf{q}^0$ to $\mathbf{q}^1 = \mathsf{QR}(\hat{\mathbf{x}}^0)$. Similarly, attackers at level l ($0 < l < \infty$) will use quantal response against the defender's marginal strategy at level $l-1$, i.e., $\mathbf{q}^l = \mathsf{QR}(\hat{\mathbf{x}}^{l-1})$, where $\hat{\mathbf{x}}^{l-1} = \mathsf{MS}(\mathbf{x}_0, \mathbf{x}, \mathbf{q}^{l-1})$. In Section 10.7, we also define level-∞ attackers.

Denote by $\mathsf{DefEU}(U)$ the defender's optimal utility when they recruit a set of informants U and use the optimal defending strategy. The key questions raised given this model are (i) how to recruit a set U of at most k informants and (ii) how to respond to the provided tips to maximize the expected $\mathsf{DefEU}(U)$?

10.5 Defending against Level-0 Attackers

In this section, we first address the case in which all attackers are level-0, providing both complexity results and algorithms for selecting an optimal set of informants. Designing efficient algorithms for this computationally difficult problem is particularly challenging due to the combinatorial nature of tip generation and the exponentially large space of possible informant selections. Moreover, in the general setting, attackers are heterogeneous, and the defender does not know which attackers will be reported, making the computation of $\mathsf{DefEU}(U)$ even more challenging.

10.5.1 Complexity Results

Let $\mathbf{q}^0 = (q_1, \ldots, q_n)$. Before presenting our complexity results, we first define some useful notations. Given the set of informants U and the tips $\mathbf{V} = (V_1, \ldots, V_n)$, we denote by $\tilde{p}_v(V_0)$ the probability of $v \in Y$ attacking a target given V_0 such that $V_0 = \bigcup_{i \in T} V_i$. We can compute $\tilde{p}_v(V_0)$ with

$$\tilde{p}_v(V_0) = \begin{cases} 1 & v \in V_0 \\ \frac{(1-\tilde{w}_v)p_v}{(1-\tilde{w}_v)p_v+1-p_v} & v \in V \setminus V_0 \\ p_v & v \in Y \setminus V \end{cases},$$

where $\tilde{w}_v = 1 - \prod_{(u,v)\in E, u\in U}(1 - w_{uv})$ is the probability of v being reported conditioned on that v attacks. Given V_0 and $t_i = |V_i|$ reported attacks on each target i, we compute the expected utility of covering i by $\mathsf{EU}_i^c(t_i, V_0) := \left(t_i + q_i \sum_{v\in Y\setminus V_0} \tilde{p}_v(V_0)\right) R_i^d$. The expected utility $\mathsf{EU}_i^u(t_i, V_0)$ of not covering i can also be computed similarly. Then, the expected gain of covering the target can be written as $\mathsf{EG}_i(t_i, V_0) := \mathsf{EU}_i^c(t_i, V_0) - \mathsf{EU}_i^u(t_i, V_0)$.

Theorem 10.1. *When the defender is informed by informants U, the optimal allocation of defensive resources can be determined in $O(|Y| + n)$ time given the tips $\mathbf{V} = (V_1, \ldots, V_n)$.*

Given the tips provided by the recruited informants, the defender can determine the optimal allocation of resources by greedily protecting the targets with the highest expected gains. However, the problem of computing the optimal set of informants remains hard.

Theorem 10.2. *Computing the optimal set of informants to recruit is NP-Hard.*

10.5.2 Finding the Best Informants

We now develop both exact and heuristic informant-selection algorithms to identify the optimal set of informants. To determine the U that maximizes $\mathsf{DefEU}(U)$, we first focus on computing $\mathsf{DefEU}(U)$. We present a dynamic-programming-based algorithm for exact computation, along with approximate algorithms.

10.5.2.1 Calculating $\mathsf{DefEU}(U)$

Let DefEU_0 be the defender's expected utility when using the optimal patrol strategy against a single attacker in the case with no informants, which can be obtained by using the algorithms introduced by Yang et al. [2012]. Then $\mathsf{DefEU}(U)$ can be explicitly written as

$$\mathsf{DefEU}(U) = \Pr[V_0 = \emptyset]\mathsf{DefEU}_0 + \Pr[V_0 \neq \emptyset]$$

$$\times \mathbb{E}\left[\sum_{i\in[n]} \mathbf{x}_i(V)\mathsf{EG}_i(t_i, V_0) + \mathsf{EU}_i(t_i, V_0)\middle| V_0 \neq \emptyset\right].$$

Directly computing $\mathsf{DefEU}(U)$ with the above equation is formidable due to exponentially many tip combinations. However, it is possible to reduce the amount of enumerations by handling the calculation carefully. We first develop an Enumeration and Dynamic Programming-based Algorithm (EDPA) to compute the exact $\mathsf{DefEU}(U)$ as shown in Algorithm 3.

First, we compute the defender's utility when they are not informed. Next, we turn to the computation of the total utility $\mathsf{DefEU}'(U)$ in the case where the defender is informed. By linearity of expectation, $\mathsf{DefEU}'(U)$ is just the sum of the expected utilities contributed by all targets. Thus, we restrict our attention to the expected utility of a single target i. For each target i, Algorithm 3 enumerates all possible types of tips. We denote each tip type by a tuple (t_i, V_0), which specifies the set of reported attackers $V_0 \neq \emptyset$ and the number of these attackers t_i who are reported to be targeting location i. The probability of observing (t_i, V_0) can be expressed as follows:

$$\Pr(t_i, V_0|U) = P_{V_0}\binom{|V_0|}{t_i} q_i^{t_i}(1-q_i)^{|V_0|-t_i},$$

where

$$P_{V_0} = \prod_{v\in V_0}(\tilde{w}_v p_v) \prod_{v\in V\setminus V_0}(1-\tilde{w}_v p_v) \tag{10.2}$$

is the probability that V_0 is the set of reported attackers given U. Let $P_{i,r}$ denote the probability that target i is among the r targets with the highest expected gain, conditioned on (t_i, V_0) and U. For any (t_i, V_0), the expected contribution of target i to $\mathsf{DefEU}'(U)$ is:

$$\begin{aligned}
&\Pr(t_i, V_0|U)\cdot \mathsf{EU}_i(t_i, V_0) + P_{V_0}\binom{|V_0|}{t_i} q_i^{t_i}\cdot P_{i,r}\mathsf{EG}_i(t_i, V_0)\\
=&P_{V_0}\binom{|V_0|}{t_i} q_i^{t_i}\left[(1-q_i)^{|V_0|-t_i}\mathsf{EU}_i(t_i, V_0) + P_{i,r}\mathsf{EG}_i(t_i, V_0)\right].
\end{aligned}$$

We can then compute $\mathsf{DefEU}'(U)$ by summing over all possible $t_i, V_0 \neq \emptyset$.

The calculation of $P_{i,r}$ is all that remains. This can be done efficiently using dynamic programming (Algorithm 4). Let $f(s, x, y)$ be defined so that $y!\cdot f(s, x, y)$ equals the probability of observing y reported attacks among

Algorithm 3: Calculate $\mathsf{DefEU}(U)$.

$\mathsf{EU} \leftarrow 0$;
forall *possible sets of reported attackers* $V_0 \subseteq V$ **do**
  $P_{V_0} \leftarrow \prod_{v \in V_0} (\tilde{w}_v p_v) \prod_{v \in V \setminus V_0} (1 - \tilde{w}_v p_v)$;
  if $V_0 = \emptyset$ **then**
    $\mathsf{EU} \leftarrow \mathsf{EU} + P_{V_0} \sum_{v \in Y} \tilde{p}_v(V_0) \mathsf{DefEU}_0$;
    Continue to line 2;
  for *target* $i \in T$ *and* $0 \leq t_i \leq |V_0|$ **do**
    Calculate $f(\cdot)$ given $|V_0|, i, t_i$;
    $\mathsf{EG}_i \leftarrow (t_i + q_i \sum_{v \in Y \setminus V_0} \tilde{p}_v(V_0))(R_i^d - P_i^d)$;
    $\mathsf{EU}_i^u \leftarrow (t_i + q_i \sum_{v \in Y \setminus V_0} \tilde{p}_v(V_0)) P_i^d$;
    $P_{i,r} \leftarrow (|V_0| - t_i)! \, (\sum_{x=0}^{r-1} f(s, x, |V_0| - t_i))$;
    $\mathsf{EU} \leftarrow \mathsf{EU} + P_{V_0} \binom{|V_0|}{t_i} q_i^{t_i} \cdot P_{i,r} \cdot \mathsf{EG}_i$;
    $\mathsf{EU} \leftarrow \mathsf{EU} + P_{V_0} \binom{|V_0|}{t_i} q_i^{t_i} (1 - q_i^{t_i}) \mathsf{EU}_i^u$;
$\mathsf{DefEU}(U) \leftarrow \mathsf{EU}$;

the first s targets, with x of those targets having expected gain greater than EG_i, conditioned on tips of type (t_i, V_0). Thus, $f(s, x, y)$ can be expressed succinctly as:

$$f(s, x, y) = \sum_{\substack{a_1 + \cdots + a_s = y, \\ \sum_{j=1}^{s} \mathbf{1}_{[\mathsf{EG}_{i_j}(a_j, V_0) > \mathsf{EG}_i(t_i, V_0)]} = x}} \frac{q_{i_1}^{a_1} q_{i_2}^{a_2} \cdots q_{i_s}^{a_s}}{a_1! a_2! \cdots a_s!},$$

which can be calculated using dynamic programming. We compute $f(s, x, y)$ by counting the number of s-partitions of the integer y, while also accounting for the constraint imposed by the limited resources. To evaluate $f(s, x, y)$, we enumerate a_s as $\tilde{y}$ and compare $\mathsf{EG}_{i_s}(a_s, V_0)$ with $\mathsf{EG}_i(t_i, V_0)$. If $\mathsf{EG}_{i_s}(a_s, V_0) > \mathsf{EG}_i(t_i, V_0)$, we consult $f(s - 1, x - 1, y - \tilde{y})$; otherwise, we use $f(s - 1, x, y - \tilde{y})$. Thus, we have $P_{i,r} = (|V_0| - t_i)! \left(\sum_{x=0}^{r-1} f(s, x, |V_0| - t_i) \right)$. Therefore, the time complexity for Algorithms 3 and 4 is $O(2^{|Y|} n^2 r |Y|^3)$ and $O(nr|Y|^2)$, respectively.

Since EDPA runs in exponential time, we introduce approximation methods to estimate $\mathsf{DefEU}(U)$. Let $\mathsf{DefEU}(U, C)$ denote the defender's utility estimate obtained by restricting Algorithm 3 to subsets V_0 with $|V_0| < C$. We refer to this truncated estimation method as C-TRUNCATED. We now show that $\mathsf{DefEU}(U, C)$ closely approximates the exact value $\mathsf{DefEU}(U)$ when the probability of many simultaneous attacks is small. Formally, suppose the

Algorithm 4: Calculate $f(\cdot)$ given $|V_0|, i, t_i$.

$\mathsf{EG}_i \leftarrow (t_i + q_i \sum_{v \in Y \setminus V_0} \tilde{p}_v(V_0))(R_i^d - P_i^d)$;
Initialize $f(s, x, y) \leftarrow 0$ for all s, x, y;
$f(0,0,0) \leftarrow 1$;
for s *in* $[1, n-1]$, x *in* $[0, \min(s, r)]$, y *in* $[0, |V_0| - t_i]$ **do**
  for $\tilde{y}$ *in* $[0, y]$ **do**
    $\mathsf{EG}_{i_s} \leftarrow (\tilde{y} + q_{i_s} \sum_{v \in Y \setminus V_0} \tilde{p}_v(V_0))(R_{i_s}^d - P_{i_s}^d)$;
    if $\mathsf{EG}_{i_s} > \mathsf{EG}_i$ **then**
      $f(s, x, y) \leftarrow f(s, x, y) + \frac{q_{i_s}^{\tilde{y}}}{\tilde{y}!} f(s-1, x-1, y-\tilde{y})$;
    else
      $f(s, x, y) \leftarrow f(s, x, y) + \frac{q_{i_s}^{\tilde{y}}}{\tilde{y}!} f(s-1, x, y-\tilde{y})$;

expected number of attacks is bounded by a constant C', i.e., $\sum_{v \in Y} p_v \leq C'$. Then, for any $C > C'$, the quantity $\mathsf{DefEU}(U, C)$ serves as an approximation of $\mathsf{DefEU}(U)$ with a bounded error.

Lemma 10.1. *Assume that $\sum_{v \in Y} p_v \leq C'$ and $|P_i^d|, |R_i^d| \leq Q$, the error of estimation $|\mathsf{DefEU}(U, C) - \mathsf{DefEU}(U)|$ for $C > C'$ is at most:*

$$Q \cdot \exp\left(\frac{-2(C - C')^2}{|Y|}\right)\left(C + \frac{1}{1 - \exp\left(-4(C - C')/|Y|\right)}\right).$$

By applying analyses similar to those for Algorithms 3 and 4, we can verify that the time complexity of C-TRUNCATED is $O(n^2 r |Y|^{C+3})$. However, when $\sum_{v \in Y} p_v$ is large, we must choose $C > \sum_{v \in Y} p_v$ for C-TRUNCATED in order to obtain a high-quality estimate; otherwise, the approximation error may become unbounded. To address this limitation, we introduce an alternative sampling-based method, M-SAMPLING, which estimates $\mathsf{DefEU}(U)$ for general cases without imposing any restriction on $\sum_{v \in Y} p_v$. Rather than enumerating all possible sets V_0 as in EDPA, M-SAMPLING draws T i.i.d. samples of the reported-attacker set, where each sample V_0 is drawn with probability P_{V_0}. The estimate of $\mathsf{DefEU}(U)$ is then obtained by averaging over these samples. A sample V_0 can be generated using the following procedure:

1. Let $V_0 = \emptyset$ initially;
2. For each $v \in V$, add v to V_0 with probability $\tilde{w}_v p_v$;
3. Return V_0 as a sample of the set of reported attackers.

From Equation (10.2), the above sampling process is consistent with the distribution of V_0. M-SAMPLING returns an estimation of $\mathsf{DefEU}(U)$ in $O(Mn^2 r |Y|^3)$ time.

Proposition 10.1. *Let* $\mathsf{DefEU}^{(T)}(U)$ *be the estimation of* $\mathsf{DefEU}(U)$ *given by M-SAMPLING using* T *samples. We have:* $\lim_{T\to\infty} \mathsf{DefEU}^{(T)}(U) = \mathsf{DefEU}(U)$

10.5.2.2 Selecting Informants U

Given the algorithms for computing $\mathsf{DefEU}(U)$, a straightforward way of selecting informants is through enumeration (denoted by SELECT).

When using C-TRUNCATED as a subroutine to compute $\mathsf{DefEU}(U)$, the solution quality of the selected set of informants is guaranteed by the following theorem.

Theorem 10.3. *Assume that* $\sum_{v\in Y} p_v \le C'$ *and* $|P_i^d|, |R_i^d| \le Q$. *Let* U_{OPT} *and* U' *be the optimal set of informants and the one chosen by C-TRUNCATED. Then for* $C > C'$, *the error* $|\mathsf{DefEU}(U_{\mathsf{OPT}}) - \mathsf{DefEU}(U')|$ *can be bounded by:*

$$2Q \cdot \exp\left(\frac{-2(C-C')^2}{|Y|}\right)\left(C + \frac{1}{1-\exp(-4(C-C')/|Y|)}\right).$$

Proposition 10.2. *Using M-SAMPLING to estimate* DefEU, *the optimal set of informants can be found when* $M \to \infty$.

Algorithm 5: $\mathsf{Search}(U')$.

```
if |U'| = k then
    Update OPT with (U', DefEU(U'));
    return;
u1 ← arg max_{u∈X} DefEU(U' ∪ {u});
u2 ← arg max_{u∈X\{u1}} DefEU(U' ∪ {u});
Search(U' ∪ {u1}), Search(U' ∪ {u2});
```

Based on existing results in submodular optimization [Nemhauser et al. 1978], one may expect a greedy algorithm that step by step adds an informant that leads to the largest utility to work well. However, the set function $\mathsf{DefEU}(U)$ in our problem violates submodularity and such greedy algorithm will not guarantee an approximation ratio of $1 - 1/e$. Consider the following example:

Example 10.1. *Consider a network* $G_S = (X, Y, E)$ *where* $X = \{u_1, u_2\}$, $Y = \{v_1, v_2, v_3\}$, $E = \{(u_1, v_2), (u_2, v_3)\}$, $p_v = 1\,\forall v \in Y$ *and* $w_{uv} =$

$1\,\forall(u,v) \in E$. There are 2 targets $T = \{1,2\}$, where $R_i^d = i$, $P_i^d = -10^{-8} \approx 0$ for any $i \in T$. Letting $\lambda = 0$ yields $q_i = 0.5$. The defender has only 1 resource. We can see that $\mathsf{DefEU}(\emptyset) = \mathsf{DefEU}(\{1\}) = \mathsf{DefEU}(\{2\}) = 3$, $\mathsf{DefEU}(\{1,2\}) = \frac{1}{4}(2+0.5) + \frac{1}{4}(4+1) + \frac{1}{2}(2+1) = 3.375$. *As a result,* $\mathsf{DefEU}(\{1,2\}) + \mathsf{DefEU}(\emptyset) > \mathsf{DefEU}(\{1\}) + \mathsf{DefEU}(\{2\})$.

Therefore, we propose GSA (Greedy-based Search Algorithm) for the selection of informants as shown in Algorithm 5. GSA starts by calling $\mathsf{Search}(\emptyset)$. While $|U'| < k$, $\mathsf{Search}(U')$ expands the current set of informants U' by adding u_1, u_2 to U' and recursing, where u_1 and u_2 are the two informants that give the largest marginal gain in DefEU (line 4-5); Otherwise, it updates the optimal solution with U' (line 1-3).

We identify a tractable case to conclude the section.

Lemma 10.2. *Given the set of recruited informants U, the defender's expected utility* $\mathsf{DefEU}(U)$ *can be computed in polynomial time if $w_{uv} = 1\,\forall(u,v) \in E$. When k is a constant, the optimal set of informants can be computed in polynomial time.*

This represents the case where the informants have strong connections with a particular group of attackers and can get full access to their attack plans. We refer to the property of $w_{uv} = 1$ for all u, v as SISI (Strong Information Sharing Intensity). Denote by ASISI (Algorithm for SISI) the polynomial-time algorithm described in Lemma 10.2. We provide detailed descriptions of ASISI in Algorithm 6 and Algorithm 7.

We summarize the time complexity of all algorithms for computing the optimal U in Table 10.1.

10.6 Defending Against Level-l Attackers

In Section 10.5, we studied the setting with only level-0 attackers and presented algorithms for selecting the optimal set of informants to recruit. In this section, we demonstrate how those methods extend naturally to scenarios involving level-l attackers.

Once $\hat{\mathbf{x}}^{,l-1}$ is given, the vector $\mathbf{q}^l$ can be computed directly, as can DefEU_l, the defender's expected utility when using $\mathbf{x}_0$ against a single level-l attacker. To obtain the solution, we simply replace DefEU_0 and $\mathbf{q}^0$ with DefEU_l and $\mathbf{q}^l$, respectively, and then apply Algorithm SELECT or GSA. To compute $\hat{\mathbf{x}}^{,l-1}$, the remaining task is to evaluate $\mathsf{MS}(\mathbf{x}_0, \mathbf{x}, \mathbf{q}^i)$ for each $i < l$. The marginal probability that each target is covered can be computed analogously to the procedure used in EDPA.

Algorithm 6: Calculate $\mathsf{DefEU}(U)$.

Expand polynomial $\prod_{v \in V}(1 - p_v + p_v x) = \sum_{j=0}^{|V|} P_j x^j$;
$\mathsf{EU} \leftarrow 0$;
forall *possible number of reported attackers* $0 \le t_O \le |V|$ **do**
  if $t_O = 0$ **then**
    $\mathsf{EU} \leftarrow \mathsf{EU} + P_{t_O} \sum_{v \in Y} p_v \mathsf{DefEU}_O$;
    Continue to line 3;
  for *target* $i \in T$ *and* $0 \le t_i \le t_O$ **do**
    Calculate $f(\cdot)$ given t_O, i, t_i;
    $\mathsf{EG}_i \leftarrow (t_i + q_i \sum_{v \in Y \setminus V} p_v)(R_i^d - P_i^d)$;
    $\mathsf{EU}_i^u \leftarrow (t_i + q_i \sum_{v \in Y \setminus V} p_v) P_i^d$;
    $P_{i,r} \leftarrow (t_O - t_i)! \left(\sum_{x=0}^{r-1} f(s, x, t_O - t_i)\right)$;
    $\mathsf{EU} \leftarrow \mathsf{EU} + P_{t_O} \binom{t_O}{t_i} q_i^{t_i} \cdot P_{i,r} \cdot EG_i$;
    $\mathsf{EU} \leftarrow \mathsf{EU} + P_{t_O} \binom{t_O}{t_i} q_i^{t_i} (1 - q_i^{t_i}) \mathsf{EU}_i^u$;
$\mathsf{DefEU}(U) \leftarrow \mathsf{EU}$;

Algorithm 7: Calculate $f(\cdot)$ given t_O,i,t_i.

$\{i_1, \ldots, i_{n-1}\} \leftarrow T \setminus \{i\}$;
$\mathsf{EG}_i = (t_i + q_i \sum_{v \in Y \setminus V} p_v)(R_i^d - P_i^d)$;
Initialize $f(s, x, y) \leftarrow 0$ for all s, x, y;
$f(0, 0, 0) \leftarrow 1$;
for $s \leftarrow 1$ *to* $n - 1$ **do**
  for $x \leftarrow 0$ *to* $\min(s, r)$ **do**
    for $y \leftarrow 0$ *to* $t_O - t_i$ **do**
      for $\tilde{y} \leftarrow 0$ *to* y **do**
        $\mathsf{EG}_{i_s} = (\tilde{y} + q_{i_s} \sum_{v \in Y \setminus V} p_v)(R_i^d - P_i^d)$;
        if $\mathsf{EG}_{i_s} > \mathsf{EG}_i$ **then**
          $f(s, x, y) \leftarrow f(s, x, y) + \frac{q_{i_s}^{\tilde{y}}}{\tilde{y}!} f(s - 1, x - 1, y - \tilde{y})$;
        else
          $f(s, x, y) \leftarrow f(s, x, y) + \frac{q_{i_s}^{\tilde{y}}}{\tilde{y}!} f(s - 1, x, y - \tilde{y})$;

10.7 Defending Against Level-∞ Attackers

As discussed in Section 10.4.1, a level-l attacker may continue adapting to the updated marginal strategy induced by their current behavioral level. In this section, we first establish in Theorem 10.4 that a fixed-point strategy exists for the attacker under our level-l response model, and we then use this fixed-point characterization to define level-∞ attackers. We then formulate the task of

Table 10.1 Complexity of Different Algorithms

Algorithm	Time Complexity
EDPA	$O(\|X\|^k 2^{\|Y\|} n^2 r \|Y\|^3)$
C-TRUNCATED	$O(\|X\|^k n^2 r \|Y\|^{C+3})$
M-SAMPLING	$O(\|X\|^k M n^2 r \|Y\|^3)$
ASISI	$O(\|X\|^k n^2 r \|Y\|^4)$
GSA	$O(2^k \|X\| n^2 r \|Y\|^3)$

computing the defender's optimal strategy in this setting as a mathematical program. However, this program can be prohibitively large to solve directly. To address this, we introduce a novel reduction technique that transforms the problem into a bi-level optimization formulation, where both levels are significantly more tractable.

Theorem 10.4. *Let* $\Delta_n = \{\mathbf{q} \mid \mathbf{q} \in [0,1]^n, \mathbf{1}^T\mathbf{q} \leq 1\}$. *Given defender's strategies* $\mathbf{x}_0$ *and* $\mathbf{x}(\mathbf{V})$, *there exists* $\mathbf{q}^* \in \Delta_n$ *such that* $\mathbf{q}^* = \mathsf{QR}(\mathsf{MS}(\mathbf{x}_0, \mathbf{x}, \mathbf{q}^*))$.

Definition 10.1 (level-∞ attacker). *Given the defender's strategies* $\mathbf{x}_0$ *and* $\mathbf{x}(\mathbf{V})$, *the strategy* $\mathbf{q}$ *of a level-*∞ *attacker satisfies* $\mathbf{q} = \mathsf{QR}(\mathsf{MS}(\mathbf{x}_0, \mathbf{x}, \mathbf{q}))$.

Remark 10.1. *Note that Definition 10.1 is not obtained by taking the limit of the level-*l *definition, since such a limit may not even exist. Consider an example where there is a single attacker and two targets with the following payoffs:*

$$R_1^a = 0.6, R_2^a = 0.8,$$
$$P_1^a = -0.8, P_2^a = -0.6.$$

In this case, there are only two possible tips: the attacker attacks target 1 ($\mathbf{V}_1$), *and the attacker attacks 2* ($\mathbf{V}_2$). *Assume that only 1 informant is recruited with report probability* $w = 0.5$. *The defender has only 1 defensive resource and uses the following strategy:*

$$\mathbf{x}_0 = (0.5, 0.5), \mathbf{x}(\mathbf{V}_1) = (1.0, 0.0), \mathbf{x}(\mathbf{V}_2) = (0.0, 1.0).$$

When the attacker has $\lambda = 2.9$, *the level-*l *response will converge to* $\mathbf{q} = (0.4283, 0.5717)$. *However, if* $\lambda = 3.0$, *then the process will eventually oscillate between* $\mathbf{q} = (0.2924, 0.7076)$ *and* $\mathbf{q}' = (0.5676, 0.4324)$ *iteratively.*

Remark 10.2. *Although the level-∞ attacker is defined through a fixed point argument, we still stick to the Stackelberg assumption: the defender leads and the attacker follows. Notice that in the equation $\mathbf{q} = \mathsf{QR}(\mathsf{MS}(\mathbf{x}_0, \mathbf{x}, \mathbf{q}))$, $\mathbf{q}$ will only be defined after the defender commits to strategies $\mathbf{x}_0$ and $\mathbf{x}$. However, it is different from the standard Strong Stackelberg Equilibrium [Korzhyk et al. 2011] in that the attacker is following a level-∞ response model, as defined by the fixed point equation.*

Also, as we will discuss in Section 10.9.1.3, when $r = n$, the defender's optimal strategy is not to use up all the available resources. This is clearly different from a Nash equilibrium, as the defender still has incentives to use more resources.

10.7.1 Convergence Condition for the Level-l Response Model

We focus on the single-attacker case, where there are only n different types of tips. We use $\mathbf{V}_i$ to denote the tips where the attacker is reported to attack target i. When the attacker is using strategy q, the probability of receiving $\mathbf{V}_i$ is $\Pr\{\mathbf{V}_i\} = wq_i$.

Theorem 10.5. *Let $\bar{x}_i = \max_j\{x_i(\mathbf{V}_j)\}$. In the single attacker case, if there exists constant $L \in [0, 1)$, such that $\bar{x}_i \leq \frac{L}{n\lambda(R_i^a - P_i^a)}, \forall i$, then level-$l$ agents converge to level-∞ agents as l approaches infinity.*

Corollaryrk 10.1. *If there is a single attacker, and there is a constant $L \in [0, 1)$, such that $\frac{L}{n\lambda(R_i^a - P_i^a)} > 1, \forall i$, then level-$l$ agents converge to level-∞ agents as l goes to infinity.*

10.7.2 A Bi-Level Optimization for Solving the Optimal Defender's Strategy

In this section, we continue to consider the single-attacker setting and assume the defender has $r \geq 1$ resources. It is clear that the optimal informant set consists of those with the highest information-sharing intensities. The remaining task is to compute the optimal strategies $\mathbf{x}_0$ and $\mathbf{x}(\mathbf{V})$. Given the optimal set of informants U^*, the probability of receiving a tip is $w = 1 - \prod_{u \in U^*}(1 - w_{u1})$. Let $\Pr\{\mathbf{V}\}$ be the probability of receiving tips $\mathbf{V}$, which depends $\mathbf{q}$ and $\mathbf{x}(\mathbf{V}) = (x_1(\mathbf{V}), \ldots, x_n(\mathbf{V}))$ be the defender strategy when receiving tips $\mathbf{V}$. Let $\mathbf{q} = (q_1, \ldots, q_n)$ be the strategy of the level-∞ attacker. Given $\mathbf{V}$ and the corresponding t_i's, the expected number of attackers that are going to attack target i is $d_i = t_i + (1 - \sum_j t_j)\tilde{p}_v(\emptyset)q_i$. Therefore, given $\hat{\mathbf{x}}$

we have the defender's expected utility $\mathsf{DefEU}(\mathbf{x}_0, \mathbf{x})$ as

$$\mathsf{DefEU}(\mathbf{x}_0, \mathbf{x}) = \textstyle\sum_{\mathbf{V},i} \Pr\{\mathbf{V}\} d_i \left[P_i^d + x_i(\mathbf{V}) \left(R_i^d - P_i^d\right)\right].$$

Then computation of the defender strategy becomes the following optimization problem:

$$\begin{aligned} \underset{\mathbf{x}_0, \mathbf{x}}{\text{maximize}} \quad & \mathsf{DefEU}(\mathbf{x}_0, \mathbf{x}) \\ \text{subject to} \quad & \mathbf{q} = \mathsf{QR}(\mathsf{MS}(\mathbf{x}_0, \mathbf{x}, \mathbf{q})). \end{aligned}$$

In the single-attacker case, we need n and n^2 variables to represent $\mathbf{x}_0$ and $\mathbf{x}$. We can use the QRI-MILP algorithm to find the solution. However, this approach needs to solve a mixed integer program and does not scale well.

To address this problem, we work with the defender's marginal strategy rather than the full strategy representation, and decompose the program into a bi-level optimization formulation.

Let $\hat{\mathbf{x}} = \mathsf{MS}(\mathbf{x}_0, \mathbf{x}, \mathbf{q}) = \sum_{\mathbf{V}} \Pr\{\mathbf{V}\}\mathbf{x}(\mathbf{V})$, where we slightly abuse notation and use $\mathbf{V} = \emptyset$ to denote the case of receiving no tip, $\mathbf{x}(\emptyset)$ to denote $\mathbf{x}_0$. The bi-level optimization method works as follows. At the inner level, we fix an arbitrary feasible $\hat{\mathbf{x}}$, and solve the following mathematical program:

$$\begin{aligned} \underset{\mathbf{x}(\mathbf{V})}{\text{maximize}} \quad & \mathsf{DefEU}(\hat{\mathbf{x}}) \\ \text{subject to} \quad & \sum_{\mathbf{V}} \Pr\{\mathbf{V}\}\mathbf{x}(\mathbf{V}) = \hat{\mathbf{x}}, \\ & \mathsf{QR}(\hat{\mathbf{x}}) = \mathbf{q}, \\ & \mathbf{1}^\top \mathbf{x}(\mathbf{V}) \le r, \qquad \forall \mathbf{V}, \\ & x_i(\mathbf{V}) \in [0, 1], \qquad \forall i. \end{aligned}$$

Since $\hat{\mathbf{x}}$ is fixed, $\mathbf{q}$ and $\Pr\{\mathbf{V}\}$ are also fixed. Thus, the program above becomes a linear program, with $\mathbf{x}(\mathbf{V})$ as variables. We can always find a feasible solution to it by simply setting $\mathbf{x}(\mathbf{V}) = \hat{\mathbf{x}}, \forall \mathbf{V}$. Solving this linear program gives us the optimal defender's utility $\mathsf{DefEU}(\hat{\mathbf{x}})$ for any possible $\hat{\mathbf{x}}$. To find the optimal defender strategy, we solve the outer-level optimization problem below:

$$\begin{aligned} \underset{\hat{\mathbf{x}}}{\text{maximize}} \quad & \mathsf{DefEU}(\hat{\mathbf{x}}) \\ \text{subject to} \quad & \mathbf{1}^\top \hat{\mathbf{x}} \le r, \end{aligned}$$

$$\hat{\mathbf{x}}_i \in [0,1], \quad \forall i.$$

Since the feasible region of $\hat{\mathbf{x}}$ is continuous, we can use any known algorithm (e.g., gradient descent) to solve the outer-level program.

The inner-level linear program still faces a scalability challenge. However, when multiple attackers are present, the optimal objective value can be well approximated by sampling a subset of possible $\mathbf{V}$'s or by considering only those $\mathbf{V}$ with the highest probabilities. For any $\mathbf{V}$ not included in this subset, we may simply assign the default strategy $\mathbf{x}_0$ to $\mathbf{x}(\mathbf{V})$.

10.8 Defending Against Informant-Aware Attackers

We now consider a variant of our model in which attackers account for the influence of informants when choosing which target to attack. Specifically, we assume attackers follow the QR model, but adjust their expected utility to include the probability of being discovered.[1] In this setting, the attackers' subjective belief $\mathbf{x}'$ about target coverage probabilities does not necessarily satisfy $\sum_i x'_i \leq r$. For example, consider a single attacker and a single informant with report intensity 1. Suppose the defender has $r = 1$ and always protects any reported target with probability 1. Then, regardless of which target the attacker chooses, that target will always be covered.

We focus on the single-attacker setting with $r \geq 1$. We begin by addressing the problem of computing the optimal defender strategy given a set of informants U and the resulting probability of receiving a tip $w = 1 - \prod_{u \in U}(1 - w_{u1})$. In the general multi-attacker case, the defender must specify a strategy for every possible combination of received tips. However, with only one attacker, the strategy can be described succinctly by the defender's default strategy without tips, $\mathbf{x}$, and by $\mathbf{z}$, the probability of defending a location after receiving a tip for that location. Under the QR adversary model, the probability q_i that the attacker targets location i is then given by:

$$q_i = \frac{\exp\left(\lambda\left\{[(1-w)x_i + wz_i]\,P_i^a + [1-(1-w)x_i - wz_i]\,R_i^a\right\}\right)}{\sum_{j \in \mathcal{T}} \exp\left(\lambda\left\{[(1-w)x_j + wz_j]\,P_j^a + [1-(1-w)x_j - wz_j]\,R_j^a\right\}\right)}.$$

This yields the following optimization problem, which we refer to as QRI, to compute the optimal defender strategy:

---

[1]Consider attackers who have accumulated experience against the defender. Over time, they may begin to reason about their realized expected utility, which is affected by informants.

$$\begin{aligned}
\underset{\mathbf{x},\mathbf{y},\mathbf{z}}{\text{maximize}} \quad & \frac{\sum_{i\in\mathcal{T}} \exp(\lambda R_i^a)\exp(-\lambda(R_i^a - P_i^a)y_i)\left[(R_i^d - P_i^d)y_i + P_i^d\right]}{\sum_{i\in\mathcal{T}} \exp(\lambda R_i^a)\exp\left(-\lambda(R_i^a - P_i^A)y_i\right)} \\
\text{subject to} \quad & y_i = (1-w)x_i + wz_i, \quad \forall i \in \mathcal{T}, && (10.3a) \\
& \sum_{i\in\mathcal{T}} x_i \le r, && (10.3b) \\
& x_i, z_i \in [0,1], \qquad \forall i \in \mathcal{T} && (10.3c)
\end{aligned}$$

We can compute the optimal defender strategy by adapting the approach used in the PASAQ algorithm [Yang et al. 2012]. Propositions 10.3 and 10.4 provide that the conditions for algorithm PASAQ hold in our setting.

Proposition 10.3. *The optimal objective of* QRI *is non-decreasing in* w.

Proposition 10.3 implies that when selecting informants, it is optimal to simply maximize w. Since $w = 1 - \prod_{u\in U}(1 - w_{u1})$, we can select informants greedily and choose the k informants with the largest information sharing intensity w_{u1}. We can then solve the optimization problem to find the optimal allocation of resources. Finally, we discuss how to find an approximate solution to QRI using a MILP approach.

We can compute the optimal defender strategy by adapting the approach used in the PASAQ algorithm [Yang et al. 2012]. Let $N(y), D(y)$ be the numerator and denominator of the objective in QRI. As with PASAQ, we binary search on the optimal value δ^*. We can check for feasibility of a given δ by rewriting the objective to $\min_{x,y,z} \delta D(y) - N(y)$ and checking if the optimal value is less than 0. To solve the new optimization problem, which still has a non-linear objective function, we adapt their approach of approximating the objective function with linear constraints and write a MILP.

First, let $\theta_i = \exp(\lambda R_i^a)$, $\beta_i = \lambda(R_i^a - P_i^a)$, and $\alpha_i = R_i^d - P_i^d$. We rewrite the objective as

$$\sum_{i\in\mathcal{T}} \theta_i(\delta - P_i^d)\exp(-\beta_i(y_i)) + \sum_{i\in\mathcal{T}} \theta_i\alpha_i y_i \exp(-\beta_i(y_i)).$$

We have two non-linear functions that need approximation $f_i^1(y) = \exp(-\beta_i y)$ and $f_i^2(y) = y \cdot \exp(-\beta_i y)$. Let γ_{ij} be the slope for the linear approximation of $f_i^1(y)$ from $(\frac{j}{K}, f_i^1(\frac{j}{K}))$ to $(\frac{j+1}{K}, f_i^1(\frac{j+1}{K}))$ and similarly with μ_{ij} for $f_i^2(y)$.

The key change in our MILP compared to PASAQ is that we replace the original defender resource constraint with constraints (10.4a) - (10.4d), which take into account the defender's ability to respond to tips. Our MILP (which we call QRI-MILP) is listed as follows:

$$\begin{aligned}
\underset{\mathbf{x},\mathbf{y},\mathbf{z},\mathbf{a}}{\text{minimize}} \quad & \sum_{i\in\mathcal{T}} \theta_i(\delta - P_i^d)\left(1 + \sum_{j=1}^{K} \gamma_{ij} y_{ij}\right) - \sum_{i\in\mathcal{T}} \theta_i \alpha_i \sum_{j=1}^{K} \mu_{ij} y_{ij} \\
\text{subject to} \quad & \sum_{j=1}^{K} y_{ij} = (1-w)x_i + w z_i, \quad \forall i, && (10.4a) \\
& \sum_{i\in\mathcal{T}} x_i \le r, && (10.4b) \\
& x_i \in [0,1], \qquad \forall i, && (10.4c) \\
& z_i \in [0,1], \qquad \forall i, && (10.4d) \\
& y_{ij} \in [0, \frac{1}{K}], \qquad \forall i, j = 1 \ldots K, && (10.4e) \\
& a_{ij}\frac{1}{K} \le y_{ij}, \qquad \forall i, j = 1 \ldots K-1, && (10.4f) \\
& y_{i(j+1)} \le a_{ij}, \qquad \forall i, j = 1 \ldots K-1, && (10.4g) \\
& a_{ij} \in \{0,1\}, \qquad \forall i, j = 1 \ldots K-1. && (10.4h)
\end{aligned}$$

Proposition 10.4. *The feasible region for* $\mathbf{y} = \langle y_i = \sum_{j=1}^{K} y_{ij}, i \in \mathcal{T}\rangle$ *of* QRI-MILP *is equivalent to that of* QRI.

As a consequence, we can find an ε-optimal solution for arbitrarily small ε [Yang et al. 2012].

10.9 Experiments

In this section, we evaluate the effectiveness of our proposed algorithms through extensive experiments. All reported results are averaged over 30 randomly generated game instances. To generate each instance of $G_S = (X, Y, E)$, we first fix the sets X and Y. For each $u \in X$, we sample its degree d_u uniformly from $[|Y|]$ and then select a uniformly random subset of Y of size d_u. For every $(u, v) \in E$, the value w_{uv} is drawn from $U[0, 0.2]$. For the attack probabilities p_v, in the general case each p_v is sampled from $U[0.4, 1]$. When imposing the constraint $\sum_{v\in Y} p_v \le C'$, we instead draw a vector $\mathbf{t} = (t_1, \ldots, t_{|Y|})$ from $U[0,1]^{|Y|}$ and set $p_v = \min\left\{1, C' \cdot \frac{t_v}{\|\mathbf{t}\|_1}\right\}$. For the payoff matrix, each R_i^d (R_i^a) is drawn from $U(0, Q]$ and each P_i^d (P_i^a) is drawn from $U[-Q, 0)$, with $Q = 2$. The precision parameter is set to $\lambda = 2$. The quantities DefEU_0 and the q_i values are computed via binary search combined with convex optimization as described in [Yang et al. 2012]. The number of samples used in M-SAMPLING is set to $T = 100$. In GSA, EDPA is used to compute $\mathsf{DefEU}(U)$.

In the QRI-MILP algorithm, the optimal defender strategy is computed using an approximation parameter of $K = 10$. The bi-level optimization procedure is implemented in MATLAB R2017a, where the lower-level linear program is solved using the linprog function and the upper-level optimization is handled by fmincon. Unless otherwise stated, all game instances used in our experiments are generated as described above.

10.9.1 Results

We compare the scalability and the solution quality of SELECT using EDPA, C-TRUNCATED, M-SAMPLING to obtain DefEU and GSA for different settings of the problems against level-0 attackers.

We first evaluate the scenario where $\sum_{v \in Y} p_v < 3$. We set $|X| = 6$, $k = 4$, $n = 8$, and $r = 3$, and vary $|Y|$ from 2 to 16. The results are shown in Figure 10.1. As a baseline, we include GREEDY, which always selects the informants that maximize the probability of receiving tips. We observe that M-SAMPLING achieves the best runtime but fails to deliver high-quality solutions. In contrast, although C-TRUNCATED is slower than M-SAMPLING, it yields the highest-quality results with zero error across all test cases.

When the constraint on $\sum_{v \in Y} p_v$ is removed, Figure 10.2 shows that C-TRUNCATED performs poorly, even worse than GREEDY for large $|Y|$. Meanwhile, M-SAMPLING performs substantially better, and GSA provides the strongest overall performance.

We further fix $|X| = 7$, $|Y| = 10$, $k = 3$, and $r = 5$, and vary the number of targets n from 5 to 25 under the condition $\sum_{v \in Y} p_v < 3$. The results are presented in Figure 10.3. GSA is the fastest method, though it produces solutions slightly inferior to those of C-TRUNCATED. The runtime of GREEDY remains below 0.3 seconds for all tested instances.

We next conduct a case study to examine the trade-off between the optimal number of defensive resources and the optimal number of informants to recruit under budget constraints when defending against level-0 attackers.

We set $|X| = |Y| = n = 6$ and generate a single game instance. The cost of deploying one defensive resource is $C_r = 3$, and the cost of hiring one informant is $C_i = 1$. Given a budget B, we can recruit k informants and allocate r resources when $k \cdot C_i + r \cdot C_r \leq B$. The trade-off between the optimal k and r is shown in Figure 10.4. Using the same instance, we also analyze how the defender's utility changes as the number of recruited informants increases while holding r fixed. With a fixed number of defensive resources, the defender should recruit as many informants as possible. We additionally observe that once the defender has access to sufficient resources, the marginal benefit of recruiting additional informants diminishes. These observations provide practical guidance for defenders, such as conservation agencies, on how to balance budget allocation between recruiting informants and deploying defensive resources.

10.9.1.1 Level-0 vs. Level-∞ attackers

We set $|X| = n = 6$, $|Y| = p_1 = 1$, and assume that G_S is fully connected. We consider $r \in 2, 4, 6$ and vary k between 1 and 6. We first fix the defender's strategy to the one optimized against level-0 attackers and compare the resulting defender utility when the opponent is a level-0 attacker versus a level-∞ attacker. Figure 10.5a shows how the defender's utility changes with the number of informants and defensive resources. On average, the defender's utility is lower when facing a level-∞ attacker than when facing a level-0 attacker. We also plot the defender's utility when using the strategy that is optimal specifically against a level-∞ attacker. In this case, we observe that the defender achieves noticeably higher utility compared to using the strategy designed for level-0 attackers.

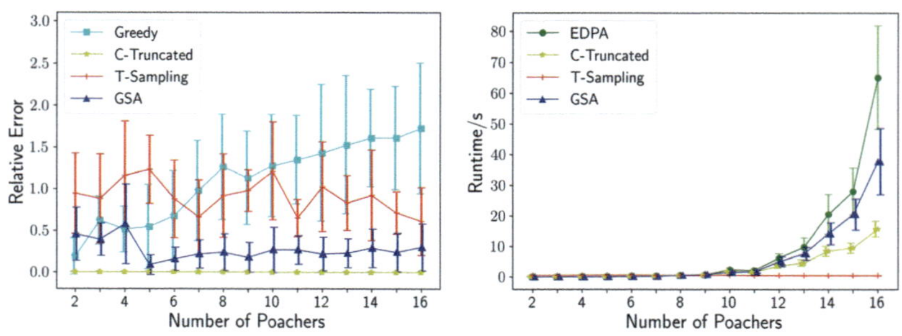

Figure 10.1 Runtime and solution quality with $\sum_{v \in Y} p_v < 3$.

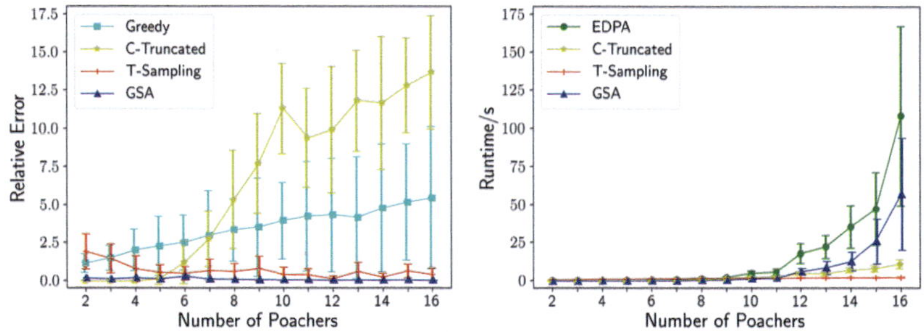

Figure 10.2 Runtime and solution quality for general cases.

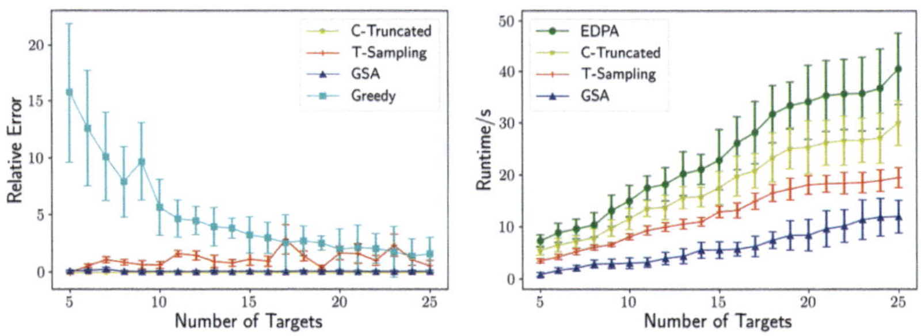

Figure 10.3 Runtime and solution quality increasing n with $\sum_{v \in Y} p_v < 3$.

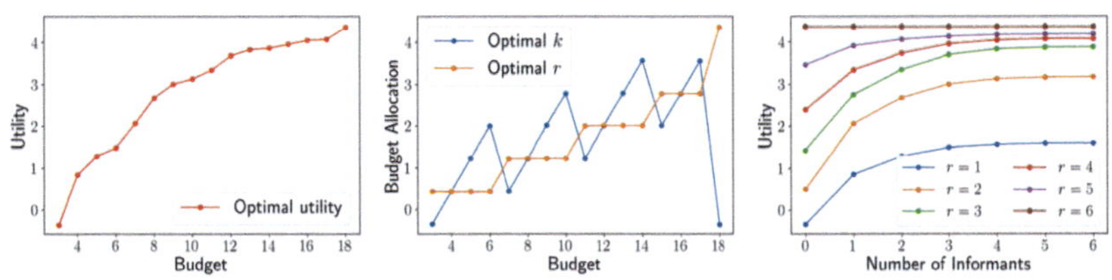

Figure 10.4 Trade-off between r and k, and increase of utility with fixed r ($|X| = 6$, $|Y| = 6$, $n = 6$).

10.9.1.2 Level-0 vs. informant-aware defenders

We set $|X| = n = 6$, $|Y| = p_1 = 1$, and assume that G_S is fully connected. We vary both r and k from 0 to 6. The defender is assumed to recruit the k informants with the highest information-sharing intensities w_{u1}. The optimal defender strategy for the informant-aware attacker is computed using QRI-MILP. The defender strategy for the level-0 attacker is obtained using

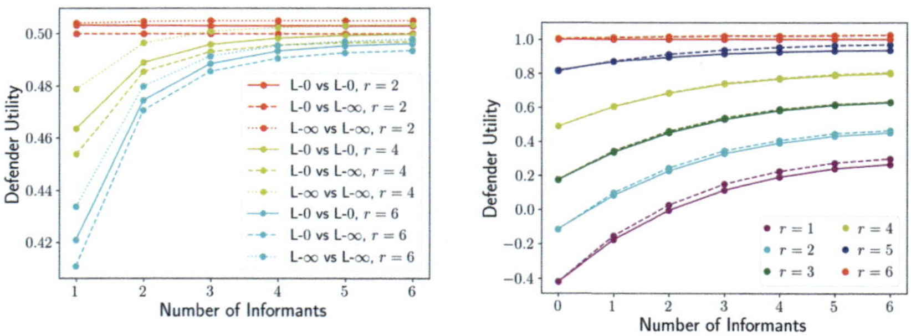

(a) Comparison between the defender utility against attackers of different levels, where "L-0 vs L-∞" means that the defender uses the optimal strategy against a level-0 attacker, while the actual attacker is of level-∞.

(b) Comparison between defender utility against informant-aware (solid lines) and level-0 (dashed lines) attackers, where the defender uses the corresponding optimal strategy respectively.

Figure 10.5 Defender's utility when faced with different attackers.

PASAQ [Yang et al. 2012]. The defender's utility against the level-0 attacker is then determined by first computing q_i and DefEU_0, and subsequently using these values to compute $\mathsf{DefEU}(U)$.

In Figure 10.5b, we show how the defender utility in the two cases varies with the number of informants and defensive resources. On average, we see that the defender utility is marginally higher against the level-0 attacker than against the informant-aware attacker, particularly when the defender has either very few or very many defensive resources.

We also conduct experiments for the SISI setting and perform a case study examining the estimation errors for all $U \subseteq X$ across two instances. In Figure 10.6, we compare the performance of the level-0 defender with that of the informant-aware defender when both face an informant-aware attacker. We observe that, although the level-0 defender's strategy is derived under the level-0 attacker assumption, its utility is only slightly lower than that of the informant-aware defender. For a fixed value of r, the utility gap increases as the defender recruits more informants and thus faces a higher probability of receiving a tip.

10.9.1.3 Comparison between the Bi-Level Algorithm and QRI-MILP

We empirically compare the bi-level optimization algorithm with QRI-MILP. We set $|X| = n = 6$, $|Y| = p_1 = 1$, and G_S to be fully connected. We vary r from 1 to 6 and k from 0 to 6.

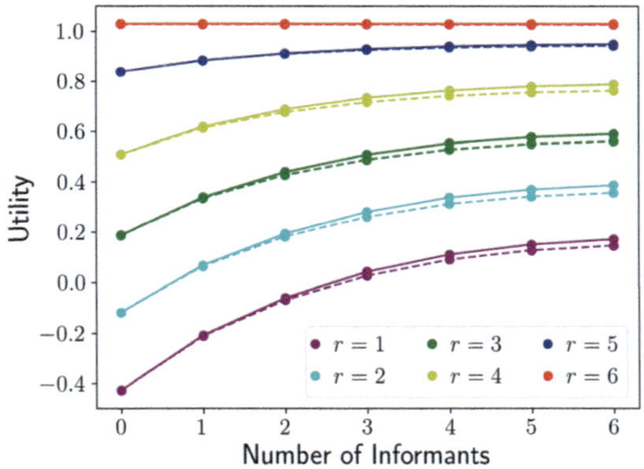

Figure 10.6 Utility comparison between the level-0 defender (dashed lines) and the informant-aware defender (solid lines) against an informant-aware attacker.

In both cases, we assume that the defender recruits the k informants with the highest information-sharing intensities w_{u1}. The results are presented in Figure 10.7. Overall, our bi-level algorithm achieves higher expected defender utilities than the QRI-MILP algorithm, except when $r = 1$. The results also indicate that increasing either the number of defensive resources or the number of recruited informants improves the defender's utility. However, as the number of resources r grows, the marginal utility gained from hiring additional informants gradually diminishes.

Intuitively, when the number of defensive resources equals the number of targets, the defender should always be able to cover every target. Interestingly, our experiments reveal that in such cases the optimal defender strategy does not always deploy all available resources. In a general-sum game, deliberately reducing the protection probability of a particular target can lure the attacker into choosing that target more often, thereby increasing the defender's expected utility. This type of strategic behavior has real-world analogs in wildlife protection, where patrollers may intentionally ignore certain tips to manipulate poacher behavior. This phenomenon is also reflected in our bi-level algorithm. If the defender always uses all available resources, then both the defender's and attacker's strategies become fixed, and hiring additional informants no longer improves the defender's expected utility. In contrast, if the defender sometimes withholds resources, recruiting more informants can indeed be beneficial—an effect visible in the $r = 6$ case in Figure 10.7.

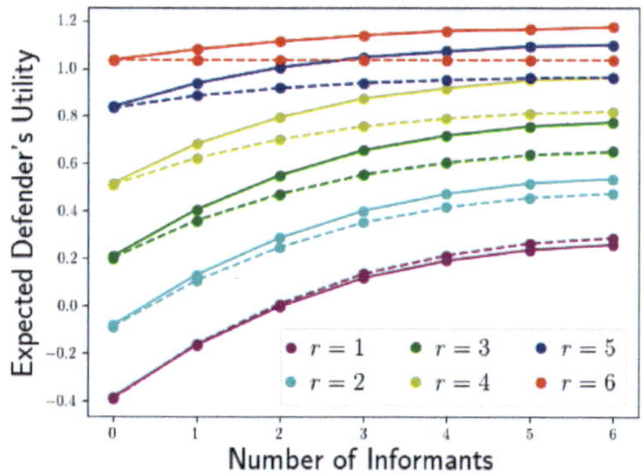

Figure 10.7 Comparison between the bi-level optimization algorithm (solid lines) and QRI-MILP (dashed lines).

10.10 Discussion

In this chapter, we introduced a new two-stage security game model along with a multi-level QR behavioral model that incorporates community engagement. We established complexity results, developed algorithms for identifying (sub-)optimal sets of informants to recruit against level-0 attackers, and evaluated these algorithms through extensive experiments. Our methods naturally extend to settings where informants have heterogeneous recruitment costs and to alternative attacker response models—such as the SUQR model [Nguyen et al. 2013]—by appropriately recalculating the attacker's response. In Section 10.7, we further defined a more sophisticated class of attackers capable of responding to the defender's marginal strategy, and we proposed a bi-level optimization algorithm for computing the optimal defender strategy in this advanced setting.

In the anti-poaching domain, conservation site managers often rely on "intelligence" operations that use informants from nearby villages to alert rangers when they learn of poachers' plans in advance. The effectiveness of these operations depends heavily on the site manager's knowledge of social connections within the surrounding communities. In practice, the edges and parameters of the bipartite graph in our model can be derived from local social media platforms or from historical information gathered by site managers. Because recruiting and training reliable informants is costly, managers can typically afford to hire only a limited number. Our model and solution techniques enable managers to efficiently select informants, make the best use of the tips they receive, and evaluate the trade-off between allocating budget to hiring rangers versus recruiting informants—all in a timely and data-driven manner.

In practice, rather than relying on a specific behavioral model, one could use historical data to learn attacker behavior across different domains. It would also be valuable to study scenarios in which informants provide imperfect or alternative types of tips—for example, indicating that some subset of targets may be attacked rather than identifying a single location. Another promising direction is to model informants as strategic agents. In real-world settings, informants may supply misleading information if doing so aligns with their own incentives. Designing mechanisms that reward informants for truthful reporting could help elicit accurate information and further improve the defender's utility.

Part II

Cross-Cutting Challenges

11

Cross-Cutting Challenges in Using AI for Societal Applications

Ayan Mukhopadhyay[1] and Yevgeniy Vorobeychik[2]

[1]College of William & Mary
[2]Washington University in St. Louis

Abstract

In the next section of the book, we turn our attention to cross-cutting challenges that arise in nearly every application of AI for social good, setting the stage for the following chapters. We begin by outlining the central technical and societal concerns that accompany AI deployment: protecting individual privacy, addressing fairness considerations, and securing systems against adversarial threats. We also raise broader questions of accountability when AI systems fail or cause harm, and how such risks can be anticipated and mitigated. By situating these technical and governance challenges together, we provide a unifying lens for thinking critically about the social implications of AI design and deployment.

11.1 Overview of Part II

As we have seen in the first section of the book, the increasing integration of Artificial Intelligence (AI) into societal applications has undeniably brought transformative benefits. Yet, it also presents significant challenges, particularly regarding interpretability, fairness, equity, privacy, security, and intended and unintended consequences of using AI for societal applications that inform public policy. We must consider two key questions in this context. First, as AI researchers, practitioners, and users, we must identify and quantify the potential harm that AI might cause. This concern is present across the different

DOI: 10.1201/9788743812074-13

application areas of AI, including public transportation, medicine, security, and others. The second issue lies at the core of designing and deploying *responsible AI systems*: who assumes the responsibility? AI researchers, practitioners, software developers, underlying corporate entities, users, and governments are all *entities* that participate in the development, deployment, and usage of AI. How can we determine what degree of responsibility is ascribed to each entity? Answering these questions is critical to responsibly developing, designing, and deploying AI.

We will begin this section by presenting three chapters that examine the first issue. As AI-based systems become more data-intensive, it is crucial to study how data-driven models can be learned and deployed to preserve the privacy of individuals and groups. In Chapter 12, Kantarcioglu explores different notions and definitions of privacy, their mathematical representations, and algorithmic approaches to preserving privacy. Second, Vorobeychik considers fairness in AI in Chapter 13, exploring the mathematical foundations of representing and quantifying fairness and discussing how we can achieve it in data-driven and learning-based applications. Next, in Chapter 14, Tong and Vorobeychik investigate how AI systems are vulnerable from a security perspective, emphasizing criteria for trustworthy AI. They discuss how AI systems (specifically, systems based on machine learning) can be vulnerable in adversarial settings, where attackers attempt to undermine their integrity. A key method for achieving this is through the use of a threat model, a systematic approach to identifying possible threats and weaknesses that may jeopardize the system's integrity. The chapter will discuss how to analyze potential risks and the adversaries that might exploit them.

Finally, the book's last chapter discusses the intersection of ethics and law in AI. In this chapter, Kim examines various approaches to ensuring AI development benefits society, focusing on ethics, law, and policy. While these are clearly interconnected, examining them separately reveals each approach's unique strengths and limitations, and Chapter 15 presents an analysis of AI through these three lenses.

12

Privacy-preserving Technologies for Artificial Intelligence

Murat Kantarcioglu

University of Texas at Dallas

Abstract

Privacy remains a significant barrier to unlocking the full potential of AI in sensitive domains such as healthcare. In this chapter, we survey methods for preserving privacy while enabling useful data analysis. We review anonymization approaches, including k-anonymity, differential privacy, and federated learning, and explain the strengths and weaknesses of each. The chapter emphasizes the trade-offs between utility, privacy, and computational cost, and illustrates how these trade-offs manifest in practical deployment. We also discuss real-world examples that demonstrate how privacy-preserving AI can facilitate innovation without compromising individual protections.

12.1 Introduction

In order to protect individual privacy, in many applications, unique identifiers such as social security numbers, names, and phone numbers are removed from a data set before public release. However, as Sweeney [2002] discusses, such measures may not be sufficient considering the vast amount of additional information that is publicly available (e.g., census rolls). While not unique identifiers by themselves, certain attributes called *quasi-identifier* attributes can be combined with public directories to identify individuals accurately. This notion is exemplified by Sweeney [2002], where an attack against William Weld, the governor of Massachusetts at that time, disclosed his medical records. In fact, Sweeney argues in this study that 87% of US citizens could possibly be uniquely identified using postal code (ZIP), sex and birth date attributes.

DOI: 10.1201/9788743812074-14

Anonymization is one popular solution against such attacks. By generalizing the values of quasi-identifying attributes (i.e., generalization) and/or removing certain records from the data set (i.e., suppression), anonymization methods try to satisfy certain definitions of anonymity. The most well-known of such definitions is k-anonymity [Sweeney 2002]. According to k-anonymity, every combination of quasi-identifier values (called an equivalence class) in the anonymized data set should appear at least k times, so that any individual cannot be distinguished within a group of size at least k. Alternatively, any query over the quasi-identifier attributes should not retrieve a result set of size less than k [LeFevre et al. 2006].

Privacy sensitive information related to individuals, such as medical data, is today collected, stored and processed in a large variety of application domains. Such data is typically used to provide better quality services to individuals and its availability is crucial in many contexts. In the case of healthcare, for example, the availability of such data helps prevent medical errors and enhance patient care. Privacy sensitive data may have many important legitimate uses serving distinct purposes outside the specific domain in which it has initially been collected. For example, drug companies and researchers may be interested in patient records for drug development. Such additional uses of data are important and should certainly be supported. Yet, privacy of the individuals to whom the data is related should be assured as well.

To address the conflicting requirements of assuring privacy while at the same time supporting legitimate use, several different techniques ranging from cryptographic methods [Kantarcıoğlu and Clifton 2004, Lindell and Pinkas 2002] to perturbation methods [Kargupta et al. 2003] have been proposed. Among those methods, anonymization techniques have emerged as one of the most important privacy preservation tools. Recently, several anonymization methods have been proposed based on different privacy definitions (e.g., k-anonymity [Sweeney 2002], l-diversity [Machanavajjhala et al. 2006], t-closeness [Li et al. 2007]), different algorithms, (e.g., DataFly [Sweeney 2002], Top-down specialization, Incognito [LeFevre et al. 2005], Mondarian multi-dimensional k-anonymity [LeFevre et al. 2006]), and different data assumptions (e.g., anonymizing data streams [Tan et al. 2008]). Anonymization techniques such as k-anonymization [Sweeney 2002] usually use privacy metrics that measure the amount of privacy protection and transform the original data in such a way that it will be hard to infer identities of the individuals when released for outside use.

For example, consider data set R in Table 12.1 that stores age and education information of certain individuals. Under the k-anonymity approach,

Table 12.1 Data set R and R's 3-anonymous generalization R'

R	A_1	A_2
r_1	Masters	35
r_2	Masters	36
r_3	Masters	36
r_4	11th	28
r_5	11th	22
r_6	12th	33

R'	A_1	A_2
r'_1	Masters	[35-37)
r'_2	Masters	[35-37)
r'_3	Masters	[35-37)
r'_4	Senior Sec.	[1-35)
r'_5	Senior Sec.	[1-35)
r'_6	Senior Sec.	[1-35)

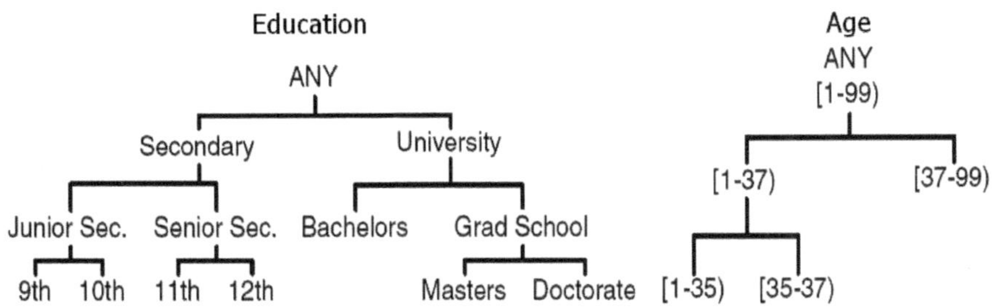

Figure 12.1 Value generalization hierarchies for Education and Age attributes

quasi-identifier fields age and education are generalized according to value generalization hierarchies (e.g., see Figure 12.1) such that there are at least k individuals that share the same quasi-identifying information. The data set R' in Table 12.1 is one the many 3-anonymous versions of R.

One important purpose for which anonymized data is used is represented by data mining. Data mining is an important form of knowledge extraction. Data mining harnesses huge amounts of data available in many application domains to extract knowledge crucial to the progress of research and other human activities. A key question is thus whether and how anonymized data can be effectively used for data mining and which anonymization methods and/or privacy definitions best support different data mining tasks.

For some data mining tasks, there are trivial and effective answers to this question. For example, if each attribute is anonymized to the same level in the data set and we want to build decision trees, we could directly build decision trees on the anonymized data by treating each generalization as a discrete attribute. Consider the anonymized table R' in Table 12.1. Attribute value "Senior Sec." can be considered a discrete value without even considering the fact that it actually represents either "11th" grade, or "12th" grade.

Obviously, given a data set, multiple possible k-anonymizations might exist. Meyerson and Williams [2004] prove that finding an optimal k-anonymization that minimally distorts the input data set is NP-hard. The reduction is from k-dimensional perfect matching. Still, various effective heuristic solutions to the problem exist [Fung et al. 2005, LeFevre et al. 2005, 2006, Sweeney 2002].

The concept of k-anonymity as a privacy definition has been challenged by many related works in the area. The first privacy definition to address the limitations of k-anonymity has been the ℓ-diversity privacy definition [Machanavajjhala et al. 2006], where adversaries with certain background knowledge are able to violate individual privacy. Two scenarios are discussed: the homogeneity attack and the background knowledge attack. In the first scenario, lack of diversity over a sensitive attribute (e.g., diagnosis) within equivalence classes allows the attacker to directly infer the value for an individual. The second scenario is rather complex but is also rooted in lack of diversity.

As a solution, ℓ-diversity definition requires each equivalence class to contain ℓ *well-represented* sensitive attribute values. Different instantiations of the privacy definition based on the concept of being well represented are provided in Machanavajjhala et al. [2006].

One simplified diversity formulation used in Xiao and Tao [2006] is to bound the fraction of records in an equivalence class that have the same sensitive attribute value. This condition is easy to enforce, as it amounts to checking that no value occurs with frequency larger than $1/\ell$.

A more complex condition is the recursive (c, ℓ)-diversity of Machanavajjhala et al. [2006]. Denote by f_i the number of occurrences of the ith sensitive attribute value in an equivalence class, and assume that these values are sorted in decreasing order according to occurrence frequency (i.e., f_1 is the highest value). Then (c, ℓ)-diversity is satisfied if for every equivalence class it holds that

$$f_1 < c(f_\ell + f_{\ell+1} + \ldots + f_m)$$

where m is the cardinality of the sensitive attribute domain.

t-closeness [Li et al. 2007] is another popular privacy definition along the same direction. Here, the privacy parameter t measures the distance between probability distributions over each equivalence class and the entire input data set through the Earth Mover's metric. ℓ-diversity and t-closeness privacy definitions can be satisfied by modifying any method originally devised for k-anonymity.

12.2 Differential Privacy

A statistical database answers aggregate queries such as $Count$ or Sum queries. In this study, we consider aggregate *range* queries, that can be expressed by d-dimensional hyper-rectangles in the attribute domain space $A_1 \times \ldots \times A_d$. A range query is represented as a Cartesian product $Q = [x_1^Q, y_1^Q] \times \ldots \times [x_d^Q, y_d^Q]$ where $[x_i^Q, y_i^Q]$ is the extent of Q on attribute A_i. For instance, the $Count$ query

$$\texttt{SELECT COUNT}(*)\ \texttt{FROM T WHERE}\ (40 \leq Age \leq 60);$$

has extent $[40, 60]$ on attribute Age.

Statistical databases are designed to let users retrieve coarse-grained aggregate information while protecting the privacy of individual records by disallowing queries that are too fine-grained. One common safeguard is to prohibit queries whose extents fall below certain thresholds, for example, age ranges smaller than 10 years or salary ranges narrower than $10K. However, such restrictions may still be insufficient. Consider a malicious user, Mallory, who knows that his colleague Alice is the only employee in the company who is 51 years old. Mallory could issue the following two queries:

$$\begin{aligned} \texttt{Q1}: &\ \texttt{SELECT COUNT}(*)\ \texttt{FROM T} \\ &\ \texttt{WHERE}\ (40 \leq Age \leq 50)\ \texttt{AND}\ (30k \leq Salary \leq 40k); \\ \texttt{Q2}: &\ \texttt{SELECT COUNT}(*)\ \texttt{FROM T} \\ &\ \texttt{WHERE}\ (40 \leq Age \leq 51)\ \texttt{AND}\ (30k \leq Salary \leq 40k). \end{aligned}$$

Suppose the response to Q_1 is 10, while the response to Q_2 is 11. From this, Mallory can conclude that Alice must be included in the result of Q_2, and therefore her salary must lie in the range $[30K, 40K]$. This attack succeeds because Mallory is able to access the query results for two views, T_1 and T_2, of the underlying table T that differ by exactly one record–Alice's.

Differential privacy aims to prevent this type of inference by adding random noise to each query result [Dwork et al. 2006]. The interaction between a user and the database is expressed as a *transcript*. Formally,

Definition 1 (Transcript). *Let $\mathcal{Q} = \{Q_1, \ldots, Q_q\}$ be a set of aggregate queries, and denote by $Q_i^T{}_{(1 \leq i \leq q)}$ the result of answering query Q_i on table T. A* transcript

$$\mathcal{TR}_{\mathcal{Q}}^T = \{(Q_1, a_1), \ldots, (Q_q, a_q)\}$$

is the response of a statistical database to the query set $\mathcal{Q}$ on database table T, where $a_i = Q_i^T$.

A statistical database satisfies ϵ-differential privacy if the ϵ-indistinguishability condition [Dwork et al. 2006] is fulfilled:

Definition 2 (ϵ-indistinguishability). *Consider a statistical database that produces the transcript $\mathcal{U}$ on the set of queries $\mathcal{Q} = \{Q_1, \ldots, Q_q\}$, and let $\epsilon > 0$ be an arbitrarily-small real constant. Transcript $\mathcal{U}$ satisfies* ϵ-indistinguishability *if for every pair of views T_1, T_2 such that $|T_1| = |T_2|$ and T_1, T_2 differ in only one record, it holds that*

$$\left| \ln \frac{Pr[\mathcal{TR}_{\mathcal{Q}}^{T_1} = \mathcal{U}]}{Pr[\mathcal{TR}_{\mathcal{Q}}^{T_2} = \mathcal{U}]} \right| \leq \epsilon \tag{12.1}$$

In other words, an attacker should not be able to determine whether the transcript was produced by answering the query set $\mathcal{Q}$ on view T_1 or on view T_2. To achieve ϵ-indistinguishability, a statistical database injects noise into each query result Q_i^T. The amount of noise required is proportional to the *sensitivity* of the query set $\mathcal{Q}$, defined as follows:

Definition 3 (L_1-sensitivity). *Over any two views T_1, T_2 such that $|T_1| = |T_2|$ and T_1, T_2 differ in only one record, the* L_1-sensitivity *of query set $\mathcal{Q} = \{Q_1, \ldots, Q_q\}$ is measured as*

$$S_{L_1}(\mathcal{Q}) = \max_{\forall T_1, T_2} \sum_{i=1}^{q} |Q_i^{T_1} - Q_i^{T_2}|$$

The following theorem from Dwork et al. [2006] gives a sufficient condition for a statistical database to satisfy ϵ-differential privacy:

Theorem 1. *Let $\mathcal{Q}$ be a set of queries answered by a statistical database, and denote by $S_{L_1}(\mathcal{Q})$ the L_1-sensitivity of $\mathcal{Q}$. Then, differential privacy with parameter ϵ can be achieved by adding to each query result random noise X, i.e., $Q_i^T \leftarrow Q_i^T + X$, where X is a random, i.i.d. variable drawn from a Laplace distribution with mean 0 and magnitude $\lambda \geq S_{L_1}(\mathcal{Q})/\epsilon$.*

An essential operation in enforcing differential privacy is determining the sensitivity $S_{L_1}(\mathcal{Q})$. Interestingly, it is shown by Dwork et al. [2006] that $S_{L_1}(\mathcal{Q})$ is independent of the data set T, and can be determined based on the query set $\mathcal{Q}$ alone. However, Xiao and Tao [2008] showed that computing sensitivity is NP-hard for arbitrary query sets.

Nevertheless, if certain restrictions are imposed on $\mathcal{Q}$, sensitivity (or its approximation) for sets of $Count$ queries can be efficiently computed. Specifically:

1. If all queries in $\mathcal{Q}$ have disjoint ranges, $S_{L_1}(\mathcal{Q}) = 2$.
2. If queries in $\mathcal{Q}$ have overlapping ranges, then a 2-approximation of $S_{L_1}(\mathcal{Q})$ is given by the maximum number of queries that overlap the same point in the data space. Formally, for any data space point $p \in A_1 \times \ldots \times A_d$, define

$$\mathcal{Q}^p = \{Q \in \mathcal{Q} | p \in Q\}$$

i.e., the set of queries that cover point p. Then, we have

$$S_{L_1}(\mathcal{Q}) \leq 2 \cdot \max_{p \in A_1 \times \ldots \times A_d} |\mathcal{Q}^p|.$$

12.2.1 Mean and Sum

Consider two databases, D_1 and D_2, with n records each. We refer to these as *sibling databases* (or just siblings) if they differ by exactly one record. Next we establish sensitivity of *mean* and *sum* queries given sample size n and d attributes.

Theorem 2. *Consider sibling databases, D_1 and D_2, with $n \geq 1$ records in each. Let $Q = \{Mean_1, ..., Mean_d\}$, where $d \geq 1$. Then, $S(Q) = d/n$.*

We can obtain an analogous result for the sum.

Theorem 3. *Consider sibling databases, D_1 and D_2, with $n \geq 1$ records in each. Let $Q = \{Sum_1, ..., Sum_d\}$, where $d \geq 1$. Then $S(Q) = d$.*

All the Theorems so far do not depend on the distribution of A_i over the interval $[0, 1]$. The sensitivity of $Q = \{Mean_1, ..., Mean_d\}$ improves linearly as the sample size n increases given a fixed d. On the other hand increasing the sample size n will not improve the sensitivity of $Q = \{Sum_1, ..., Sum_d\}$, which is determined solely by dimension d.

12.3 Secure Multi-Party Computation

Secure Multi-party Computation (SMC) protocols provide provably secure, cryptographic solutions to the more general problem of privacy preserving data analytics. As explained by Yao [1982] through the famous Yao's Millionaire problem, any function whose secret inputs are distributed across multiple parties can be computed securely revealing nothing but the result and what can be inferred from the result. In fact, such secure protocols can be generated automatically as a circuit of logic gates.

Substantial work has been devoted to secure multiparty computation (SMC). A key result is that a broad class of computations can be performed securely under reasonable assumptions. Below, we provide a brief overview of this line of work. For simplicity, we focus on the two-party setting; extending the definitions to the multi-party case is straightforward.

12.3.1 SMC in the Semi-Honest Model

A semi-honest party follows the protocol faithfully using its correct input, but may later attempt to exploit any information observed during the protocol's execution to compromise security. This model is often realistic in practice because parties who seek to collaboratively mine data for mutual benefit typically follow the protocol to obtain accurate results. In many situations, parties may care only about the final output rather than the underlying data. For example, a major credit card transaction-processing company was recently hacked, resulting in the theft of transaction data involving 40 million credit card numbers. The data had been stored solely for data-mining purposes; however, its exposure left the company vulnerable to potential lawsuits [Bray and Talcott 2005]. Similar situations can arise with healthcare data as well.

We now formalize the notion of secure two-party computation in the semi-honest model.

Definition 4 (Privacy w.r.t. semi-honest behavior). *Let* $f : \{0,1\}^* \times \{0,1\}^* \longmapsto \{0,1\}^* \times \{0,1\}^*$ *be a probabilistic, polynomial-time function, where* $f_1(x,y)$ *(resp.,* $f_2(x,y)$*) denotes the first (resp., second) element of* $f(x,y)$*) and let* Π *be a two-party protocol for computing* f*. Let the view of the first (resp., second) party during an execution of* Π *on* (x,y)*, denoted* $view_1^{\Pi}(x,y)$ *(resp.,* $view_2^{\Pi}(x,y)$*) is* $(x, r_1, m_1, \ldots, m_t)$ *(resp.,* $(y, r_2, m_1, \ldots, m_t)$*) where* r_1 *represents the outcome of the first (resp.,* r_2 *second) party's internal coin tosses, and* m_i *represents the* i^{th} *message it has received. The output of the first (resp., second) party during an execution of* Π *on* (x,y) *is denoted* $output_1^{\Pi}(x,y)$ *(resp.,* $output_2^{\Pi}(x,y)$*) and is implicit in the party's view of the execution.* Π *privately computes* f *if there exist probabilistic polynomial time algorithms, denoted* S_1, S_2 *such that*

$$\begin{aligned} &\{(S_1(x, f_1(x,y)), f_2(x,y))\}_{x,y\in\{0,1\}^*} \\ &\quad \equiv^C \left\{\left(view_1^{\Pi}(x,y), output_2^{\Pi}(x,y)\right)\right\}_{x,y\in\{0,1\}^*} \end{aligned} \tag{12.2}$$

$$\{(f_1(x,y), S_2(x, f_1(x,y)))\}_{x,y\in\{0,1\}^*}$$

$$\equiv^C \left\{\left(output_1^\Pi(x,y), view_2^\Pi(x,y)\right)\right\}_{x,y\in\{0,1\}^*} \qquad (12.3)$$

where $\equiv^C$ *denotes computational indistinguishability.*

The definition above states that a computation is secure if each party's view during the execution of the protocol can be effectively simulated using only that party's input and output. This is not identical to saying that all private information is protected. For example, suppose two parties use a secure protocol to mine distributed association rules. Even under a secure protocol, if a particular rule is not supported by one site but appears in the globally supported rule set, that site can infer that the other site must support the rule. This deduction arises solely from comparing the site's locally supported rules with the global results. However, the exact support count of any itemset cannot be inferred from the globally supported rules alone. When three or more parties participate, the fact that a rule is globally supported reveals only that at least one site supports it; no site can determine which other site (besides itself) provides the support. In summary, a secure multi-party protocol ensures that no party learns more information than what can already be inferred from its own input and the final output.

A key result from the SMC literature is the *composition theorem.* We state it for the semi-honest model. A detailed discussion of this theorem, as well as its proof, can be found in Goldreich [2004].

Theorem 4 (Composition theorem for the semi-honest model [Goldreich 2004]). *Suppose that g is privately reducible to f and that there exists a protocol for privately computing f. Then there exists a protocol for privately computing g.*

This allows us to use existing secure protocols as components in a black-box fashion.

12.3.2 Yao's General Two-Party Secure Function Evaluation

Yao's general secure two-party computation protocol is based on expressing the function $f(x,y)$ as a Boolean circuit and encrypting the gates to enable secure evaluation [Yao 1986]. This protocol allows any two-party function to be computed securely in the semi-honest model, provided the function has an efficiently evaluable (i.e., small) circuit representation. We omit the details of this generic technique here. In several of our protocols, we rely on this general result to determine whether $a \geq b$ for arbitrary integers a and b. For securely comparing two integers, Yao's generic method remains one of the most efficient known approaches, although other asymptotically equivalent but more practically efficient algorithms also exist [Ioannidis and Grama 2003].

Garbled circuits [Yao 1986] allow two parties to evaluate an arbitrary function represented as a Boolean circuit on private inputs from both parties, leaking nothing beyond the output of the function. A garbling scheme is a tuple of algorithms $\mathsf{GC} = (\mathsf{Garble}, \mathsf{Eval}, \mathsf{Decode})$. During Garble, the *garbler* party creates a "garbled" representation of a Boolean circuit in which each wire is associated with two cryptographic keys, called *labels*, one for 0 and one for 1. In the garbled representation, the gates of the circuit are tables of ciphertexts encrypted using the wire labels (e.g., via AES). The garbled circuit consisting of all garbled gates is sent to the *evaluator* party. Then, the garbler provides the input garbled values to the evaluator. For its own input bits, the garbler directly sends the corresponding garbled labels. For the evaluator's input bits, the two parties run *oblivious transfer (OT)* protocols, enabling the evaluator to obtain the garbled labels without revealing its inputs. During Eval, the evaluator evaluates the garbled circuit on the received garbled labels. Finally, the garbled output is decoded using the corresponding output wire labels in Decode.

Formally, the GC algorithms are:

- $\mathsf{Garble}(f, x) \rightarrow (\mathcal{C}, X, d)$: on input function f and input bits $x \in \{0,1\}^n$, output garbled representation $\mathcal{C}$, garbled input labels pairs $X = \{\mathsf{lab}_i^0, \mathsf{lab}_i^1\}_{i \in [n]}$, decoding map d.
- $\mathsf{Eval}(\mathcal{C}, \bar{X}) \rightarrow Y$: on input garbled representation $\mathcal{C}$ and a set of garbled input labels $\bar{X} = \{\mathsf{lab}_i^{x_i}\}_{i \in [n]}$ associated to input $x \in \{0,1\}^n$, output garbled output labels Y.
- $\mathsf{Decode}(d, Y) \rightarrow y$: on input decoding map d and garbled output labels Y, output the circuit's output y.

A garbling scheme is *correct* if Decode outputs $y = f(x)$ for the desired function f and input x. A garbling scheme is *private* if, given $\mathcal{C}$, the garbled input labels $\bar{X}$ of the circuit wires and the decoding map d, an adversary learns nothing apart from the number of inputs, the size of the circuit and y.

12.3.3 Leveled Homomorphic Encryption (HE)

A *leveled homomorphic encryption scheme* supports the encrypted evaluation of bounded-degree polynomials or bounded-depth arithmetic circuits. In HE schemes based on the Learning with Errors hardness problem, each operation evaluated on ciphertexts introduces some noise, which can cause incorrect decryption if it overflows. Multiplication introduces the most noise. Therefore, we wish to evaluate low-depth circuits, i.e., few sequential multiplications.

Plaintext and ciphertext can encode a vector of scalars; an operation applied on a ciphertext is applied component-wise on the encrypted vector. This allows us to perform component-wise *additions* and *multiplications* between ciphertext or between a plaintext and a ciphertext, and vector *rotations* (cyclic permutations of the encrypted vector).

Formally, a leveled homomorphic encryption scheme is a tuple of algorithms $\mathsf{LHE} = (\mathsf{KeyGen}, \mathsf{Enc}, \mathsf{Dec}, \mathsf{Eval})$:

- $\mathsf{KeyGen} \to (\mathsf{pk}, \mathsf{sk}, \mathsf{evk})$: outputs a public key pk, a secret key sk, and an evaluation key evk.
- $\mathsf{Enc}_{\mathsf{pk}}(m) \to c$: on input public key pk and a message m, output a ciphertext c.
- $\mathsf{Dec}_{\mathsf{sk}}(c) \to m$: on input secret key sk and a ciphertext c, output a message m.
- $\mathsf{Eval}_{\mathsf{evk}}(f, c_1, c_2, m_3) \to c$: on input evaluation key evk, ciphertexts c_1, c_2 encrypting messages m_1, m_2, a message m_3 and a depth-d arithmetic circuit f, output a new ciphertext c. The inputs c_2, m_3 are optional.

Briefly, LHE is *correct* if $\mathsf{Dec}_{sk}(\mathsf{Enc}_{\mathsf{pk}}(m)) = m$ and $\mathsf{Dec}_{\mathsf{sk}}(\mathsf{Eval}_{\mathsf{evk}}(f, \mathsf{Enc}_{\mathsf{pk}}(m), \mathsf{Enc}_{\mathsf{pk}}(m'))) = f(m, m')$. LHE is *IND-CPA secure* if the encryptions of any two messages are computationally indistinguishable, and *function private* if a ciphertext obtained from the homomorphic evaluation of a function, together with the private key, reveals only the result of the evaluation and nothing else about the function.

12.4 Secure Algebraic Calculations

Several of the privacy-preserving algorithms developed later rely on secure two-party computation protocols. We summarize them in this section.

12.4.1 Secure Sum

One building block frequently required is to securely calculate the sum of values from individual sites. Assuming three or more parties and no collusion, the following method from Kantarcıoğlu and Clifton [2002] securely computes such a sum.

Assume that the value $v = \sum_{i=1}^{k} v_i$ to be computed is known to lie in the range $[0..n-1]$. One site is designated the *master* site, numbered 1. The remaining sites are numbered $2..k$. Site 1 generates a random number R, uniformly chosen from $[0..n-1]$. Site 1 adds this to its local value v_1, and sends the sum $R + v_1 \bmod n$ to site 2. Since the value R is chosen uniformly from $[0..n-1]$, the number $R + v_1 \bmod n$ is also distributed uniformly across this region, so site 2 learns nothing about the actual value of v_1.

For the remaining sites $i = 2..k-1$, the algorithm is as follows. Site i receives

$$V = R + \sum_{j=1}^{i-1} v_j \bmod n.$$

Since this value is uniformly distributed across $[0..n-1]$, i learns nothing. Site i then computes

$$R + \sum_{j=1}^{i} v_i \bmod n = (v_i + V) \bmod n$$

and passes it to site $i+1$.

Site k performs the above step, and sends the result to site 1. Site 1, knowing R, can subtract R to get the actual result. Note that site 1 can also determine $\sum_{i=2}^{k} v_i$ by subtracting v_1. This is possible from the global result *regardless of how it is computed*, so site 1 has not learned anything from the computation.

This method encounters an obvious issue when sites collude. Sites $i-1$ and $i+1$ can compare the values they send and receive to deduce the exact value of v_i. The approach can be extended to operate securely under an honest majority. In this extension, each site splits v_i into multiple shares, and the sum of each share is computed separately. The communication path is permuted for each share so that no site has the same neighbor more than once. Consequently, to recover v_i, all of the neighbors of site i across the different iterations would need to collude. By adjusting the number of shares, one can control the number of dishonest (colluding) parties required to compromise security.

12.4.2 1-out-of-N Oblivious Transfer

The 1-out-of-N Oblivious Transfer protocol involves two parties, Alice and Bob. Alice has an input σ, $1 \leq \sigma \leq N$, while Bob has N inputs $X_1, \ldots, X_n$. At the end of the protocol, Alice learns only X_σ and nothing else while Bob learns nothing at all. The 1-out-of-2 Oblivious Transfer (OT_1^2) was suggested by Even et al. [1985] as a generalization of Rabin's "oblivious transfer" [Rabin 1981]. Naor and Pinkas [2001] provide efficient protocols for 1-out-of-N Oblivious Transfer. For completeness, we now describe a very simple (though inefficient) method for doing Oblivious Transfer for semi-honest parties.

Bob generates N public key pairs $E_1, D_1, \ldots, E_N, D_N$.
Bob sends $E_1, \ldots, E_N$ to Alice.
Alice generates an asymmetric key K.
Alice forms the vector $\vec{V}$: if $i = \sigma$, $V_i = E_i(K)$; otherwise $V_i =$ (a random) R_j.
Alice sends the N-dimensional vector $\vec{V}$ to Bob.
Bob decrypts $\vec{V}$ to form the vector $\vec{K}$ where $K_i = D_i(V_i)$.
Bob encrypts his data items with the keys in $\vec{K}$ and sends them to Alice (i.e. Bob sends $K_i(X_i), i = 1 \ldots N$ to Alice)
Since $K_\sigma = D_\sigma(E_\sigma(K)) = K$, Alice decrypts the σ row with K to get X_σ.

Clearly, this protocol reveals nothing to Bob [Goldreich 2004]. In the semi-honest model, as long as Alice follows the protocol exactly, she also learns nothing, since all other values are encrypted with random keys unknown to her. Although this protocol can be easily broken if parties are allowed to behave maliciously, more secure and efficient alternatives are available in the literature.

12.5 Federated Learning (FL)

At a high level, federated learning (FL) is a multi-round protocol between an aggregation server and a collection of agents who jointly train a model. Formally, the participating agents seek to minimize the average of their loss functions,

$$\text{argmin}_{w \in R^d} f(w) = \frac{1}{K} \sum_{k=1}^{K} f_k(w),$$

where f_k is the loss function of kth agent. For example, for neural networks, f_k is typically empirical risk minimization under a loss function L such as cross-entropy:

$$f_k(w) = \frac{1}{n_k} \sum_{j=1}^{n_k} L(x_j, y_j; w),$$

with n_k being the total number of samples in agent's dataset and (x_j, y_j) being the jth sample.

Concretely, the FL protocol proceeds as follows: in round t, the server samples a subset of agents S_t and sends them the current model weights w_t. Upon receiving w_t, the kth agent initializes its local model with these weights, trains for several iterations (e.g., via stochastic gradient descent), and obtains updated weights w_t^k. The agent then computes its update as $\Delta_t^k = w_t^k - w_t$ and sends this update back to the server. After receiving updates from all agents in S_t, the server computes the next-round model by aggregating the updates using an aggregation function $\mathbf{g}\colon \mathbb{R}^{|S_t| \times d} \rightarrow \mathbb{R}^d$ and adding the result to w_t. Formally, $w_{t+1} = w_t + \eta \cdot g(\{\Delta_t\})$ where $\{\Delta_t\} = \cup_{k \in S_t} \Delta_t^k$, and η is the server's learning rate. For example, McMahan et al. [2016] and many subsequent works on FL use weighted averaging to aggregate updates [Bagdasaryan et al. 2020, Bhagoji et al. 2019, Bonawitz et al. 2017, Geyer et al. 2017, Sun et al. 2019]. This aggregation is referred as Federated Averaging (FedAvg), and yields the following update rule:

$$w_{t+1} = w_t + \eta \frac{\sum_{k \in S_t} n_k \cdot \Delta_t^k}{\sum_{k \in S_t} n_k}.$$

In practice, training rounds may continue indefinitely, as new agents can join the protocol at any time, or they may stop once the model satisfies a desired performance criterion on a validation dataset maintained by the server. Prior work has shown that models trained via FL can outperform locally trained models in a variety of settings [Hard et al. 2018, McMahan et al. 2016].

13

Fairness in AI

Yevgeniy Vorobeychik

Washington University in St. Louis

Abstract

Fairness is a fundamental consideration in the design and deployment of AI systems. This chapter reviews the formal definitions of algorithmic fairness, including both individual- and group-based criteria, and highlights the trade-offs that naturally arise between them. We examine practical approaches for incorporating fairness into machine learning, ranging from pre-processing and in-processing techniques to post-processing adjustments. We also explore how striving for fairness often requires balancing it against accuracy and efficiency, which can lead to difficult design and policy choices. We conclude with open questions about how fairness should be prioritized relative to other objectives and how it can be embedded into broader governance and accountability frameworks.

13.1 Introduction

In May, 2016, ProPublica published an article, "Machine Bias" with a provocative subtitle: "*There's software used across the country to predict future criminals. And it's biased against blacks.*" [Angwin et al. 2016]. At issue was a tool, *Correctional Offender Management Profiling for Alternative Sanctions (COMPAS)*, that assesses (for our purposes, predicts) recidivism risk, which we can interpret as the probability that an individual charged with a crime will reoffend in the future. The article had observed that while accuracy of the tool was similar for African American and White defendants, the former had a much higher chance of being labeled as high-risk despite not going on to

DOI: 10.1201/9788743812074-15

commit a crime than the latter. In response to this, Northpointe, the company which developed the COMPAS tool, argued that its recidivism risk scores were roughly *equally well-calibrated* for both White and African American defendants [Dieterich et al. 2016], that is, for each discretized risk score, similar fractions of both groups have reoffended. Moreover, these fractions predictably increased with risk scores for both groups.

Who is right? The short answer is, both; evidently, it depends on *how one measures the efficacy of prediction*. Moreover, it is not necessarily self-evident how, in an objective sense, we *should* measure efficacy, particularly if we wish to compare performance across groups. The goal of this chapter is to explore this issue, which has given rise to a research subfield of *algorithmic fairness*, in greater depth.

13.2 Measuring Efficacy and Fairness

We begin by introducing some notation, as well as several measures of machine learning efficacy that have played an important role in assessing algorithmic fairness. Let x be a vector of attributes or *features* associated with an individual and y denote the *label*, or *output*, which we take to be the ground truth. For example, in the context of predicting recidivism, y would correspond to whether or not the individual with features x *actually reoffended* within a predefined time range. Note that the measurement of recidivism must of necessity be retrospective: first, we would consider those who have initially committed a crime, and subsequently after a time period T, evaluate whether they have done so again. The prediction or risk assessment, on the other hand, would be prospective, upon only observing the first crime. Throughout this chapter, we will keep things simple by focusing on binary outcomes $y \in \{0, 1\}$. Furthermore, it will be useful to view $y = 1$ as a desirable outcome. For example, $y = 1$ would indicate that the individual is, in fact, qualified for the job, did *not* reoffend, and so on.

We let $\hat{f}(x)$ represent a model which predicts outcomes (labels) given an input feature vector x, and suppose that there is, additionally, the *true* prediction $p(x)$. The nature of this true $p(x)$ will be quite consequential conceptually. Further, let $\mathcal{X}$ denote the entire input (feature vector) space. Our core consideration will involve efficacy comparisons across groups. Often, these are going to be defined in terms of particular demographic characteristics, but for our purposes here, we can define them abstractly and very generically as a set $\mathcal{G}$ of groups under consideration, with $g \in \mathcal{G}$ a particular group to which an individual belongs.

Fairness is typically assessed with respect to efficacy measures, which are metrics that quantify how well a model $\hat{f}$ performs on a given dataset. When a model $\hat{f}$ is trained using machine learning methods, such assessment entails splitting up a training and validation (or test) datasets, using the former to train $\hat{f}$ while efficacy is evaluated on the latter. Let us denote the overall dataset by $D = \{(x_i, y_i)\}$, with $D = D_{train} \cup D_{val}$, i.e., splitting D into train and validation subsets.

The most natural efficacy measure for binary prediction is *accuracy*, defined theoretically as:

$$\mathcal{M}_{acc}(\hat{f}) = \Pr[\hat{f}(X) = Y], \tag{13.1}$$

where (X, Y) are random variables corresponding to inputs (feature vectors) and labels x and y, respectively. In practice, we can evaluate it on a finite dataset as

$$\mathcal{M}_{acc}(\hat{f}, D) = \frac{1}{|D|} \sum_{(x,y)\in D} \mathbf{1}(\hat{f}(x) = y), \tag{13.2}$$

$\mathbf{1}(\cdot)$ is an indicator function which is 1 whenever its argument is true and 0 otherwise. Henceforth, we will define efficacy measures using expectations, with the understanding that there are analogous ways to approximate these on finite validation datasets.

To assess algorithmic fairness, we need to specialize accuracy to a particular group g. The resulting group-conditional accuracy measure is then

$$\mathcal{M}_{acc}(\hat{f}, g) = \Pr[\hat{f}(X) = Y | G = g], \tag{13.3}$$

where G is a random variable corresponding to groups. On finite data, this would just be the accuracy restricted to only individuals in group g, that is, using dataset D_g restricted to individuals in g. Now, if we have just two groups, 0 and 1, we would say that $\hat{f}$ is fair in terms of accuracy when $\mathcal{M}_{acc}(\hat{f}, 0) = \mathcal{M}_{acc}(\hat{f}, 1)$. This is straightforward to generalize to an arbitrary number of groups, but perfect fairness is unlikely, particularly on finite datasets. Consequently, a better general definition has the form

$$\Delta_{acc}(\hat{f}) = \max_{g \in \mathcal{G}} |\mathcal{M}_{acc}(\hat{f}, g) - \mathcal{M}_{acc}(\hat{f})|.$$

Interestingly, the ProPublica investigation that we opened this chapter with did not find any disparity in regards to accuracy. Rather, they found a rather different issue: far more African American defendants who did not reoffend were flagged as high-risk compared to White defendants. We now translate this into a common *true positive rate (TPR)* performance measure. Before doing so, let us first offer an alternative account to motivate it, one that comes from employment. Suppose that the label $y \in \{0, 1\}$ indicates whether the individual is qualified for the job ($y = 1$) or not ($y = 0$). It would intuitively seem grossly unfair if *qualified* individuals from one group (for example, African American applicants) were less likely, on average, to be *predicted* as qualified (e.g., invited for an interview) compared to other groups (for example, White applicants). This, too, amounts to measuring inequality between the groups in terms of TPR.

Formally, TPR is defined as follows:

$$\mathcal{M}_{TPR}(\hat{f}) = \Pr[\hat{f}(X) = 1 | Y = 1], \tag{13.4}$$

and its group-conditional variant is

$$\mathcal{M}_{TPR}(\hat{f}, g) = \Pr[\hat{f}(X) = 1 | Y = 1, G = g]. \tag{13.5}$$

In the ProPublica analysis, if we define $Y = 1$ to mean that the individual *did not reoffend*, the concern is that COMPAS fails the condition that $\mathcal{M}_{TPR}(\hat{f}, 0) \approx \mathcal{M}_{TPR}(\hat{f}, 1)$, where 0 and 1 are (in their analysis) African American and White defendants, even though it is the case that $\mathcal{M}_{acc}(\hat{f}, 0) \approx \mathcal{M}_{acc}(\hat{f}, 1)$. This form of TPR-based equality is commonly called *equal opportunity (EO)* [Hardt et al. 2016]. Its more general variant has the form:

$$\Delta_{TPR}(\hat{f}) = \max_{g \in \mathcal{G}} |\mathcal{M}_{TPR}(\hat{f}, g) - \mathcal{M}_{TPR}(\hat{f})|.$$

We can similarly define fairness in terms of true negative rate (TNR),

$$\Delta_{TNR}(\hat{f}) = \max_{g \in \mathcal{G}} |\mathcal{M}_{TNR}(\hat{f}, g) - \mathcal{M}_{TNR}(\hat{f})|.$$

where

$$\mathcal{M}_{TNR}(\hat{f}) = \Pr[\hat{f}(X) = 0 | Y = 0] \quad \text{and}$$
$$\mathcal{M}_{TNR}(\hat{f}, g) = \Pr[\hat{f}(X) = 0 | Y = 0, G = g].$$

There is a related measure of algorithmic fairness to EO, which is motivated by the guidelines in anti-discrimination law [Barocas et al. 2023]: inequality in outcomes. In formal terms, the group-conditional version of this measure is

$$\mathcal{M}_o(\hat{f}, g) = \Pr[\hat{f}(X) = 1 | G = g].$$

The problem with this as a measure of inequality is that "base rates" (for example, qualification rates) may differ across groups. For example, ProPublica documents this to be the case for the likelihood of reoffense. Consequently, *even a perfect predictor will fail such a test.*

The Northpointe counter to the ProPublica article did not disagree with their assessment. Rather, they argued that on a different metric—*calibration*—COMPAS performed admirably both in terms of efficacy and fairness. What is calibration? To get some intuition, consider the task of predicting coin flips, and suppose that the coin is unbiased (that is, $p(x) = 0.5$, using our notation above). Suppose that our prediction is $\hat{f}(x) = 0.51$ (that is, the predicted "score" or probability of heads is 0.51). Is this a good prediction? If we just use accuracy as a measure, we would typically have to superimpose a threshold on $\hat{f}$, say, 0.5, and our prediction accuracy will only be 50% (the best you can possibly do), but that seems clearly wrong. It is, indeed, intuitive that our $\hat{f}$ is actually making very good *probabilistic* predictions—which is what risk scoring is generally supposed to do. What we'd like to check is that the *predicted distribution* over outcomes is similar to the *true distribution* (often measured using the empirical distribution), which is the case for our fictitious coin flip prediction. This is where calibration comes in. In the example above, calibration would say that the empirical probability of heads is roughly the same as the true probability.

More generally, suppose that we discretize our predicted scores to be in a set S (for example, probability values in the set $\{0, 0.1, 0.2, \ldots, 1\}$), and let $\hat{f}(x)$ map inputs x to an element in S (a score). Calibration is then defined as

$$\Pr[Y = 0|\hat{f}(X) = s] \approx s \quad \forall s \in S. \tag{13.6}$$

Our choice of $Y = 0$ in this definition is arbitrary, but allows us to be consistent with $Y = 1$ indicating that an individual does not reoffend in the ProPublica example. Thus, a well-calibrated risk scoring model $\hat{f}$ that predicts a risk level of s will, on average, result in an *actual risk* (probability that an individual reoffends, which is indicated by $Y = 0$) of s.

What is conceptually crucial in assessing the difference between accuracy and TPR on the one hand, and calibration on the other, as efficacy metrics is how we model the environment itself. If we suppose that $p(x) \in \{0, 1\}$—there is an essentially deterministic underlying reality that we wish to predict—then binary prediction and associated metrics (accuracy and TPR) are well-suited to the task. Thus, for example, if qualification is a binary deterministic criterion that we wish to predict (an individual is either qualified or not), the intuition that TPR disparities are inherently unjust seems well-founded in the notion of equal opportunity. On the other hand, if we suppose an alternative reality in which $p(x)$ is non-binary—a reality that is incommensurate with the one above—while all that we observe are the *samples* from this distribution, binary prediction efficacy may no longer be appropriate. For example, if we take reoffense to be a *random* outcome of an underlying and unknown *risk of reoffense*, a connection of TPR to equal opportunity is less evident (since it is no longer clear whether an observation whether someone reoffended is indicative of their underlying recidivism risk, or due to noise), and calibration may well be a more appropriate measure of efficacy.

Returning to the formalization of calibration, we can its measure (for the purposes of comparisons) as

$$\mathcal{M}_{cal}(\hat{f}, s) = \Pr[Y = 0|\hat{f}(X) = s]$$

while its group-conditional variant is

$$\mathcal{M}_{cal}(\hat{f}, g, s) = \Pr[Y = 0|\hat{f}(X) = s, G = g].$$

The resulting fairness metric is then

$$\Delta_{cal}(\hat{f}) = \max_{g \in G, s \in S} |\mathcal{M}_{cal}(\hat{f}, g, s) - \mathcal{M}_{cal}(\hat{f}, s)|.$$

An alternative way of consideration fairness in terms of calibration that is stronger is to aim for group-conditional calibration measures be approximately well-calibrated for each group, that is,

$$\Delta_{cal}(\hat{f}) = \max_{g \in G, s \in S} |\mathcal{M}_{cal}(\hat{f}, g, s) - s|.$$

A useful and commonly referenced special case of calibration is *positive predictive value (PPV)*. In this case, suppose that we are back in the world of binary outcomes to be predicted, and thus discretize the set of scores as $S = \{0, 1\}$. Then the calibration measures are equivalent to

$$\Pr[Y = 1|\hat{f}(X) = 1] \quad \text{and} \quad \Pr[Y = 1|\hat{f}(X) = 0].$$

The first of these is PPV, whereas the latter is false omission rate, or FOR. The associated group-conditional variations and fairness metric can then be obtained as above.

13.3 Fundamental Tradeoffs in Algorithmic Fairness

We have defined a number of distinct measures by which one can evaluate fairness (or equality) of algorithms in terms of their prediction quality. Can they all be satisfied simultaneously? Kleinberg et al. [2017] provide a decisively negative answer to this question, at least in regards to achieving equality in terms of both TPR and calibration, even between only two groups.

The actual result of Kleinberg et al. [2017] provides for models $\hat{f}$ that predict scores rather than binary outcomes, representing the "second" world discussed in Section 13.2 in which we suppose that the underlying $p(x)$ is non-binary. Consequently, they use a generalization of TPR and TNR that they refer to as *balance for positive and negative class*, respectively (we refer to these as BPC and BNC). In particular, BPC is, roughly,

$$\mathbb{E}[\hat{f}(X)|Y = 1, G = g] \approx \mathbb{E}[\hat{f}(X)|Y = 1, G = g']$$

for two groups, g and g', and BNC is defined analogously, but replacing $Y = 1$ with $Y = 0$. Thus, if $\hat{f}$ produces binary predictions, we recover TPR in the case of BPC and TNR as the special case of BNC. Their main result is

Theorem 13.1 (informal). *Achieving approximate fairness in calibration, BPC, and BNC simultaneusly implies that either a) $p(x) \in \{0, 1\}$ and predictions are nearly perfect or b) base rates are approximately the same for g and g', i.e.,* $\Pr[Y = 1|G = g] \approx \Pr[Y = 1|G = g']$.

In other words, it is impossible to achieve, say, TPR and PPV together, except in the highly restricted special case that the base rates are essentially the same, barring, of course, an unlikely ability to make perfect predictions.

The impossibility of achieving the best of all worlds is perhaps not surprising, given the inherently incommensurate world models involved when we consider TPR and BPC on the one hand (or, analogously, TNR and BNC), and calibration on the other. Practically, what this (and a number of other, related, impossibility results that have emerged) demonstrates is that achieving algorithmic fairness inherently entails tradeoffs. But how then should we choose which to prioritize? A natural approach is to consider the more plausible assumptions about the underlying "world" in the situation being confronted. In particular, is it the case that the outcomes we observe correspond to an underlying determinism in the world (i.e., $p(x) \in \{0, 1\}$), or are they samples from an unknown (and, perhaps, unknowable) distribution $p(x)$? An answer to this question can provide useful guidance about which efficacy and fairness measure may be most appropriate.

Another fundamental tradeoff is between fairness and accuracy. Indeed, what we will now illustrate is that if we require fairness to hold in terms of accuracy, we may need to sacrifice accuracy for one of the groups *without any accuracy gain for the other*. In particular, consider the example illustrated in Figure 13.1. In this figure, we suppose that predictions are 0 or 1 (the positive

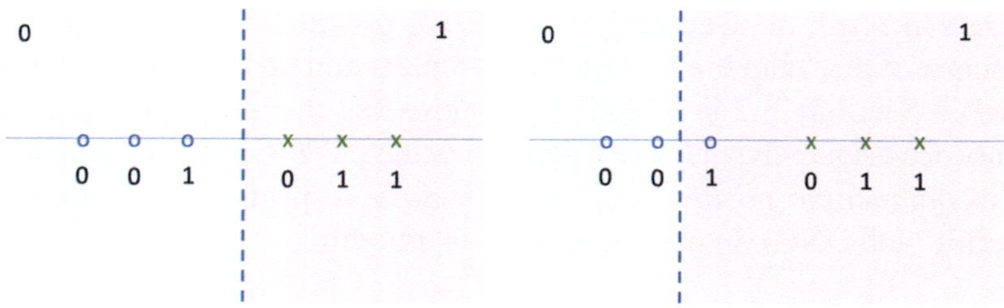

Figure 13.1 Illustration of an inherent tradeoff between fairness (left) and accuracy and Pareto optimality in terms of group-level accuracy (right).

class), while two groups are represented by "o"s and "x"s, and the horizontal line represents the scalar feature values x (i.e., this is a one-dimensional classification problem). Consider the figure on the left, which shows the fair classifier in terms of accuracy for both groups. Indeed, all accuracy-fair classifiers in this example will draw the vertical line (threshold) somewhere between the rightmost o and the leftmost x. The resulting "fair" accuracy for each group is then 2/3. Considering next the right figure, we shifted the vertical line to the left. This doesn't change accuracy for the "x"s, which remains at 1/3, but the accuracy for the "o"s is now 100%. Of course, overall accuracy also improves as a consequence!

What we have shown, in fact, is that fair classifiers can produce results that are *Pareto suboptimal*, to use the language from Economics. To explain, we start by defining what it means to be Pareto optimal, in general. Let us suppose that we have a collection of agents $\mathcal{A}$ and a set of possible outcomes $\mathcal{O}$. Each agent $a \in \mathcal{A}$ has a utility function $u_a(o)$ over outcomes $o \in \mathcal{O}$. We say that an outcome o is *Pareto optimal* (or Pareto efficient) if there does not exist any other outcome $o' \in \mathcal{O}$ with the property that (a) for each agent a, $u_a(o') \geq u_a(o)$, and (b) there is *some* agent with $u_a(o') > u_a(o)$. If an outcome o does not satisfy this property, we call it *Pareto suboptimal*. Now, returning to our setting, let us identify groups as agents, whereas outcomes are classification results. In the example in Figure 13.1, then, we see that fair classifiers are Pareto suboptimal since one group (the "o"s) benefits (obtains *strictly* higher utility while the other group (the "x"s) is not harmed.

A clever reader may notice something odd about the example, however: if we are only to randomize the decision boundary, we can, in fact, achieve both Pareto optimality and fairness *on average* (draw the decision boundary as in the right plot half the time, and symmetrically to that the other half the time)! However, this requires randomization. In practice, that is often a tall order. Imagine, for example, how it would look if judges made bail decisions by flipping a coin. In many situations, intuition and social norms will preclude effective use of randomized decision making, partly because the expectations are that every decision is, or should be, principled (whether or not that aligns with reality), and randomization may come across as unprincipled (and, ex post, unjust).[1]

13.4 Achieving Fairness in Machine Learning

So far, we have discussed the problem of assessing fairness of predictive models, as well as some fundamental limitations in algorithmic fairness. Next, we discuss some of the approaches that one can adopt to obtain models that are fair in terms of (at least) one of the efficacy and fairness measures.

13.4.1 Training Fair Classifiers

Say we have a dataset D and wish to train on it a *fair* classifier. How shall we go about this task? In conventional machine learning, we would simply solve the *empirical risk minimization (ERM)* problem:

$$\min_{\theta} \sum_i \ell(\hat{f}_\theta(x_i), y_i), \tag{13.7}$$

where θ represents the parameters of a classification (prediction) model $\hat{f}$. We can extend this problem to training a fair classifier by adding fairness as an explicit set of constraints. For two groups $g \in \{0, 1\}$, the resulting constrained optimization problem would take the following form:

$$\begin{aligned} \min_{\theta} \quad & \sum_i \ell(\hat{f}_\theta(x_i), y_i) \\ \text{s.t.}: \quad & \mathcal{M}(\hat{f}_\theta, 0) = \mathcal{M}(\hat{f}_\theta, 1) \end{aligned}$$

for any efficacy measure $\mathcal{M}$ of our choosing. If we wish to relax this constraint to only hold approximately—with approximation measured by some $\epsilon > 0$, we could use instead a constraint $|\mathcal{M}(\hat{f}_\theta, 0) - \mathcal{M}(\hat{f}_\theta, 1)| \leq \epsilon$. Indeed, a more

[1] See also Barocas et al. [2023] for a discussion of randomization and fairness.

general version of the constraint can take the form $\Delta(\hat{f}_\theta) \leq \epsilon$, using any of the fairness measures we discussed in Section 13.2, for example.

However, such variants of fairness-constrained ERM induce a rather challenging optimization problem to solve, particularly when model architectures are themselves complex and non-linear, such as neural networks. This is especially the case because while typical algorithms make use of convex and (piecewise) smooth loss functions $\ell()$, arbitrary measures $\mathcal{M}(\hat{f}_\theta, g)$ that we include in the constraints may well not even be convex or even piecewise differentiable. A pragmatic remedy is two-fold: combining Lagrangian relaxation with differentiable proxies $\bar{\Delta}(\hat{f}_\theta)$ as fairness measures. As a result, we would end up with an unconstrained problem of the form

$$\min_\theta \quad \sum_i \ell(\hat{f}_\theta(x_i), y_i) + \lambda\bar{\Delta}(\hat{f}_\theta)$$

with the fairness measure itself now evaluated on training data, and serving as a form of regularization in learning.

To illustrate, suppose that we are concerned with equalizing accuracy between two groups, 0 and 1. We partition the dataset D into subsets corresponding to the groups: $D = D_0 \cup D_1$. The resulting problem is then

$$\min_\theta \quad \sum_i \ell(\hat{f}_\theta(x_i), y_i) + \lambda\Delta_{acc}(\hat{f}_\theta).$$

This entails computing $\mathcal{M}_{acc}(\hat{f}, D_g)$ for $g \in \{0, 1\}$, but recall that this calculation involves an indicator function which represents a binary loss (either we make a mistake or not). Fortunately, we can directly replace such a non-differentiable loss with a convex differentiable proxy as we would in conventional machine learning approaches. The resulting proxy accuracy measures will, in turn, produce a proxy fairness measure $\bar{\Delta}_{acc}$ which is differentiable in θ. Thus, we can apply the common gradient-based algorithms to this modified objective.

Another way of thinking about algorithmic fairness is through the lens of *distributional robustness* [Chen et al. 2020]. Let $\mathcal{P}(G)$ be the space of all distributions over groups in G. We can write a distributionally-robust variant of ERM as

$$\min_\theta \max_{\sigma \in \mathcal{P}(G)} \sum_{g \in G} \frac{\sigma_g}{|D_g|} \sum_{(x_i, y_i) \in D_g} \ell(\hat{f}_\theta(x_i), y_i),$$

with σ_g the probability of g under distribution σ and D_g the subset of the training data restricted to individuals in group g. Note that the inner maximum is actually easy to compute, since it will always select the most disadvantaged group in terms of average loss. Consequently, we can solve it using gradient-based methods by simply alternating the gradient updates with respect to θ with solutions to the inner maximization problem that effectively determine which group will guide the gradient learning.

13.4.2 Post-Processing Predictions to Achieve Fairness

Suppose that we have trained a binary classifier $\hat{f}$, but found that it fails to yield approximately similar performance between two groups, 0 and 1, in terms of TPR and TNR—a violation of a condition sometimes referred to as *equalized odds* [Hardt et al. 2016]. One option is to retrain the classifier to achieve fairness, but that can be quite expensive both in terms of time and compute, particularly on large datasets. An alternative is to derive a new classifier, $\tilde{f}$, which satisfies the fairness constraint while also maximizing accuracy (or minimizing loss). The key insight is that randomization as well as an ability to condition it on the protected category allows us to usefully trade off TPR and TNR to facilitate fairness.

More precisely, the classifier $\tilde{f}$ takes as input 1) the prediction $\hat{y} = \hat{f}(x)$ and 2) the group $g \in \{0, 1\}$, and returns the probability of predicting $\tilde{y} = 1$. Note that if group g and predictions $\hat{f}$ are binary, the randomized classifier $\tilde{f}$ can thus be represented using four probabilities:

$$\begin{aligned}
p_{0,0} &\equiv \Pr[\tilde{Y} = 1 | \hat{Y} = 0, g = 0] \\
p_{0,1} &\equiv \Pr[\tilde{Y} = 1 | \hat{Y} = 0, g = 1] \\
p_{1,0} &\equiv \Pr[\tilde{Y} = 1 | \hat{Y} = 1, g = 0] \\
p_{1,1} &\equiv \Pr[\tilde{Y} = 1 | \hat{Y} = 1, g = 1],
\end{aligned}$$

where $\hat{Y} = \hat{f}(X)$. Moreover, we can express TPR and TNR as convex combinations of these. For example, TPR for group g is

$$\begin{aligned}
\Pr[\tilde{Y} = 1 | g, Y = 1] = \Pr[\tilde{Y} = 1 | \hat{Y} = 0, g] \Pr[\hat{Y} = 0 | g, Y = 1] + \\
\Pr[\tilde{Y} = 1 | \hat{Y} = 1, g] \Pr[\hat{Y} = 1 | g, Y = 1] = \\
= (1 - \mathcal{M}_{TPR}(\hat{f}, g)) p_{0,g} + \mathcal{M}_{TPR}(\hat{f}, g) p_{1,g}.
\end{aligned}$$

Further, let $\ell(\hat{y}, y)$ be the loss function. We can compute optimal values of $p_{\tilde{y},g}$ for all $\tilde{y}$ and g using a simple linear program to equalize TPR:

$$\min_p \quad \sum_i p_{\hat{f}(x_i), g_i} \ell(\hat{f}(x_i), y_i) + p_{1-\hat{f}(x_i), g_i} \ell(1 - \hat{f}(x_i), y_i)$$

$$\text{s.t. :} \qquad \Pr[\tilde{Y} = 1|0, Y = 1] = \Pr[\tilde{Y} = 1|1, Y = 1] \quad p_{\tilde{y},g} \in [0, 1] \, \forall \, \tilde{y}, g,$$

noting that the objective, as well as the constraint equalizing TPR across the two groups are linear in p, while $\mathcal{M}_{TPR}(\hat{f}, g)$ can be precomputed (estimated) on training data.

13.5 Individual Fairness

The notions of fairness we defined above have been tied to inter-group comparisons. There is, however, an entirely different notion that has been proposed that is not about groups at all. Rather, it involves comparisons *between individuals*. At the high level, individual fairness requires that decisions should be similar for similar individuals—with similarity measured with respect to the feature vectors x representing them (as inputs into the model $\hat{f}(x)$) [Dwork et al. 2012].

One point is immediate: if two individuals have identical features, the prediction for them *must* be identical (in the case when $\hat{f}$ is randomized, the distribution must be identical), since $\hat{f}$ is a function (i.e., any fixed input maps to exactly one output). But what about when we have two individuals, x and x' that are "similar"? The first question to answer is: what does similar mean? For example, if two individuals are identical, except that one of them murdered someone, then perhaps they are not very similar at all. The individual fairness framework does not answer this question directly. Instead, we suppose that we are given a similarity metric $d(x, x')$ which is smaller whenever x and x' are more similar.

Next, what does it mean for decisions to be similar? If $\hat{f}$ is a deterministic binary classifier, similar must mean *identical*, which is not particularly useful since similarity may not be transitive. For example, suppose features are scalar, and similarity is defined by $|x - x'| \leq \epsilon$ for some $\epsilon > 0$. If $x = 0$ and $x' = \epsilon$, x and x' are similar. But now, take $x'' = 2\epsilon$. Clearly, x' and x'' are similar, but x and x'' are not. Thus, if we are to use this notion of fairness, the only way to guarantee it would be to make $\hat{f}$ a constant.

Fortunately, randomization comes to the rescue. In particular, if we allow $\hat{f}$ to be randomized, we no longer have this issue; rather, we require that if x and x' are similar, so are the *distributions* over the classification decisions. We can formalize this as follows. Let $\Delta(P, P')$ be a measure of distance between two distributions, P and P'—for example, Kullback-Leibler divergence. Then we can define individual fairness as the following condition:

$$\Delta(\hat{f}(x), \hat{f}(x')) \leq d(x, x'), \tag{13.8}$$

which is just a mathematical formalization of the intuition that whenever x and x' are close, so must be the distributions over outcomes induced by $\hat{f}(x)$ and $\hat{f}(x')$, respectively. If we restrict attention to binary classification, distributional distance can just be measured as the absolute difference between the predicted positive probabilities, i.e.,

$$|\hat{f}(x) - \hat{f}(x')| \leq d(x, x'). \tag{13.9}$$

Note, also, that at least conceptually, we can use the same definition if we wish to obtain $\hat{f}$ which is deterministic but predicts scores rather than discrete categories (e.g., for risk assessment).

An important practical challenge in using the individual fairness notion is that classifiers satisfying it are difficult to train. For example, if we take it as an explicit constraint, the resulting constraint ERM problem has the form

$$\begin{aligned} \min_{\theta} \quad & \sum_i \ell(\hat{f}_\theta(x_i), y_i) \\ \text{s.t.}: \quad & |\hat{f}_\theta(x) - \hat{f}_\theta(x')| \leq d(x, x') \quad \forall\, x, x' \in D. \end{aligned}$$

If $\hat{f}_\theta$ is non-linear, even finding a feasible solution is challenging. A possible solution is to approximate this with an unconstrained version such as

$$\min_{\theta} \quad \sum_i \ell(\hat{f}_\theta(x_i), y_i) + \lambda \frac{|\hat{f}_\theta(x) - \hat{f}_\theta(x')|}{d(x, x')}.$$

A second practical challenge in applying individual fairness is specifying the similarity metric $d(x, x')$. Several solutions have been proposed that involve inferring it from opinions elicited from people [Ilvento 2020]. However, this idea has its own limitations, for example, a concern that people may disagree with such judgments, or that these may be very sensitive to context.

13.6 Discussion

This chapter provides but a brief introduction to what has come to be an extensive literature on algorithmic fairness. A number of other notions of fairness have been entertained [Buolamwini and Gebru 2018b, Kilbertus et al. 2017, Mitchell et al. 2021], and algorithmic approaches for achieving both individual measures and combinations thereof abound [Agarwal et al. 2018, Corbett-Davies et al. 2017, Kearns et al. 2018]. Moreover, a recent book offers a considerably more extensive treatment of the subject [Barocas et al.

2023]. Additionally, this has now received extensive consideration in the legal literature (see Chapter 15).

However, most of the literature on algorithmic fairness has analyzed the problem in terms of *outcomes*—the distribution of predictions made—while approaches for training fair classifiers have commonly taken the dataset used as a given, although several approaches have considered the problem from an active learning perspective (see, e.g., Pang et al. [2024]). We now briefly mention two alternative perspectives on the problem: procedural fairness and representative dataset construction.

Procedural fairness takes the perspective that human perceptions of fairness are influenced at least as much by their experience with procedures involved as with final outcomes [Fodchuk and Sidebotham 2005, Houlden et al. 1978, Lemons and Jones 2001, Sunshine and Tyler 2003, Thibaut and Walker 1975, Tyler 2003, 2006, Tyler and Huo 2002]. For example, in the two settings most commonly studied within this framework, promotion and criminal justice, people are more likely to be satisfied with their experience if their perception is that the judgment was neutral, transparent, and based on trustworthy motives, and they have been treated with respect and given a voice [Tyler 2006], than if these factors were not present. Several efforts explored the issue of procedural fairness within the context of algorithmic decision making [Binns et al. 2018, Lee et al. 2019, Vaccaro et al. 2019, Wang et al. 2020, Woodruff et al. 2018], with some of them focusing in particular on the fairness of *features* used in the decisions [Albach and Wright 2021, Grgic-Hlaca et al. 2018, Grgić-Hlača et al. 2018]. One approach suggests using human assessments of feature fairness in determining what information to use [Grgic-Hlaca et al. 2018]. However, there is evidence that many people view the accuracy of algorithms themselves as an important indicator of fairness, although this perspective is strongly influenced by the role they play (e.g., employer vs. employee) [Estornell et al. 2024]. Additionally, volitionality and relevance of features plays an important role in fairness judgments [Estornell et al. 2024].

The problem of dataset construction arises because commonly the assumption of a fixed dataset is quite limiting, and many programs—such as clinical research—actively engage in constructing datasets. In this context, *representativeness* can play an important role. While in principle, one can use stratified sampling to achieve representativeness, this is often impractical. For example, clinical studies may involve multiple geographically diverse centers, and the choice space commonly involves budget allocation across these, rather than hand picking individuals, with each center, in turn, inducing a particular distribution over demographics of the population it serves. This problem has been studied algorithmically from the perspective of *multi-armed bandits*, in which centers (or locations, which correspond to distinct distributions over demographics, clinical outcomes, etc) are arms (or choices), and the goal is to dynamically allocate a fixed budget so as to achieve given representativeness targets [Borza et al. 2022, 2025, Nargesian et al. 2021].

14

Security of AI Systems

Liang Tong[1] and Yevgeniy Vorobeychik[2]

[1]Stellar Cyber
[2]Washington University in St. Louis

Abstract

AI systems are not only tools for improving security–they are also targets of attack. In this chapter, we explore the vulnerabilities of machine learning systems to adversarial manipulation, ranging from imperceptible feature-space perturbations to realizable attacks on sensors and inputs. We review key attack strategies, including adversarial examples, poisoning, and evasion, and we survey defenses such as robust training, detection mechanisms, and certified defenses. To illustrate the stakes of these challenges, we present a detailed case study on adversarial robustness in face recognition systems. We emphasize that adversarial robustness is not merely a technical hurdle but a prerequisite for building trust in AI systems deployed in safety-critical domains. We close by identifying open challenges and calling for multidisciplinary research to develop AI systems that remain resilient in the face of evolving threats.

14.1 Introduction

In previous chapters, we covered the general privacy and security concerns associated with AI systems and the game-theoretic perspective on these issues. Here, we discuss AI system (particularly machine learning system) vulnerabilities from a security perspective, emphasizing *integrity*. Integrity is a necessary criterion for trustworthy AI—an AI system that demonstrates integrity operates correctly as defined by its designer and can therefore be trusted. Our objective is to understand how AI systems can fail in adversarial environments where an

DOI: 10.1201/9788743812074-16

attacker seeks to compromise its integrity. An important tool in achieving this objective is a *threat model*. For a machine learning (ML) system, a threat model is a structured and systematic approach for identifying potential threats and vulnerabilities that may compromise its integrity. It involves a comprehensive analysis and assessment of potential risks and the adversaries that may exploit them. Specifically, the construction of a threat model typically involves several key aspects.

- The *adversary's knowledge* about the targeted ML system, such as its access to training data and machine learning model.
- The *adversary's capabilities* such as its budget for executing attacks.
- The *adversary's goal*, such as avoiding being detected, or being misclassified as a targeted label.

Once a threat model has been constructed, it can be utilized to identify ML system vulnerabilities and countermeasures.

In this chapter, we limit the scope of our consideration of vulnerability to *decision-time attacks*, in which an adversary manipulates the input to a deployed ML system to affect its prediction. We then use two domains as concrete case studies: *PDF malware detection* and *face recognition*.

14.2 Decision-Time Attacks

In the (supervised) machine learning literature, it is common to abstract the problem as follows. We are given a training dataset $\mathsf{D} = \{(\boldsymbol{x}_i, y_i)\}$, where $\boldsymbol{x}_i \in \mathsf{X} \subseteq \mathbb{R}^n$ are numeric feature vectors in some feature space X, and $y_i \in \mathsf{L}$ are labels in a label space L. Each data point (or example) in the dataset D is assumed to be generated in an independent and identically distributed (i.i.d.) manner according to an unknown distribution P. In addition, we are given a hypothesis (model) space, H. Our objective is to identify (*learn*) a good model $h_{\boldsymbol{\theta}} \in \mathsf{H}$ parameterized by $\boldsymbol{\theta}$ in the sense that it yields a minimal error on new examples drawn from P. Since P is unknown in practice, one typically aims to find $h_{\boldsymbol{\theta}} \in \mathsf{H}$ which (approximately) minimizes empirical error on the training data D.

To undermine the integrity of an ML model, a decision-time attack is usually employed by an adversary to induce predicting mistakes after the model has been deployed. To achieve this goal, the adversary manipulates an adversarial example by transforming $\boldsymbol{x}$ to $\boldsymbol{x}'$ such that $\boldsymbol{x}'$ is similar to $\boldsymbol{x}$ but the model makes an incorrect prediction on $\boldsymbol{x}'$ (while making a correct prediction on the original input $\boldsymbol{x}$). A key distinction we make in this chapter is between two types of threat models. The first type, *feature-space attacks*, modify features directly. The second, *realizable attacks*, account for practical domain constraints that limit what kinds of attacks can be executed, and impact attack efficacy.

14.2.1 Feature-Space Attacks

As the name implies, feature-space attacks work directly in the *feature space*, as is typical in the machine learning literature [Athalye et al. 2018, Biggio et al. 2013, Carlini and Wagner 2017, Dalvi et al. 2004, Goodfellow et al. 2015, Lowd and Meek 2005, Zhang et al. 2015], including the application of machine learning (especially, deep neural networks) in computer vision tasks [Carlini and Wagner 2017, Goodfellow et al. 2015, Moosavi-Dezfooli et al. 2016, Papernot et al. 2016, Szegedy et al. 2014].

In feature-space attacks, the attacker is *modeled* as starting with a malicious feature vector $\boldsymbol{x}$ and *directly modifying the features* to produce another feature vector $\boldsymbol{x}' \in \mathsf{X}$, to yield erroneous predictions, i.e., $y' = h_{\boldsymbol{\theta}}(\boldsymbol{x}')$ (for example, being mislabeled as benign). Crucially, because feature vectors are an abstract representation of the underlying problem instances (such as scenes being photographed in computer vision, or files in the context of malware detection), we must abstract the notion of preserving (malicious) functionality. This is accomplished through the use of a cost function, $c(\boldsymbol{x}, \boldsymbol{x}')$, whereby the attacker is penalized for greater modifications to the given feature vector $\boldsymbol{x}$, typically measured using an ℓ_p norm difference between the original malicious instance and the modified feature vector [Biggio et al. 2013, Li and Vorobeychik 2018]. Within computer vision, a common motivation of the use of ℓ_p norm is that when the norm of the adversarial perturbation is small, it is imperceptible to a human. We term these the *feature-space attacks*.

The construction of an adversarial example in feature space for $\boldsymbol{x}$ can be represented by the following optimization problem (or its variants):

$$\max_{\boldsymbol{\delta} \in \Delta(\epsilon)} \mathcal{L}\left(h_{\boldsymbol{\theta}}(\boldsymbol{x} + \boldsymbol{\delta}), y\right), \tag{14.1}$$

where $\boldsymbol{\delta}$ is the adversarial perturbations to be added on $\boldsymbol{x}$. $\mathcal{L}(\cdot)$ is the loss function used to train the classifier $h_{\boldsymbol{\theta}}$. $\Delta(\epsilon)$ is the feasible perturbation space which is commonly represented as a ℓ_p ball: $\Delta(\epsilon) = \{\boldsymbol{\delta} : \|\boldsymbol{\delta}\|_p \leq \epsilon\}$. Many solutions have been proposed to solve the aforementioned optimization problem. Next, we present several prominent examples.

FGSM. The *Fast Gradient Sign Method (FGSM)* [Goodfellow et al. 2015] is one of the earliest paradigms for constructing adversarial examples in

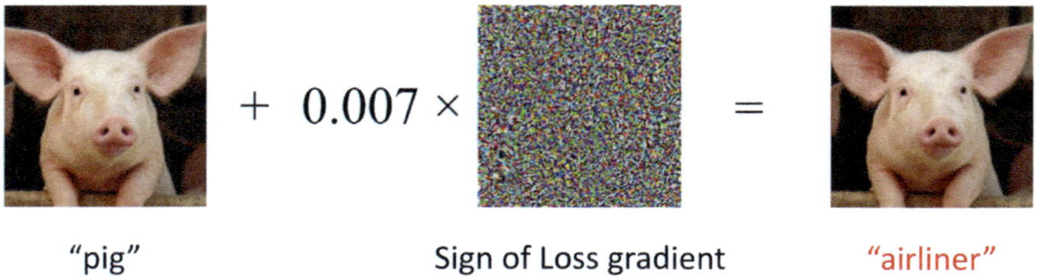

Figure 14.1 An illustration of the FGSM attack [Goodfellow et al. 2015]. The original image is correctly classified as a pig. After adding the imperceptible FGSM perturbation, the image is misclassified as an airliner. The perturbation is magnified for better visualization.

the feature space, illustrated in Figure 14.1. FGSM assumes that constraints on adversarial perturbations $\boldsymbol{\delta}$ are imposed in terms of the ℓ_∞ norm, i.e., $\Delta(\epsilon) = \{\boldsymbol{\delta} : \|\boldsymbol{\delta}\|_\infty \leq \epsilon\}$, and uses a linear approximation to compute the perturbations in closed form as

$$\boldsymbol{\delta}^* = \epsilon \cdot \text{sign}(\nabla_{\boldsymbol{\delta}} \mathcal{L}\left(h_{\boldsymbol{\theta}}(\boldsymbol{x} + \boldsymbol{\delta}), y\right)). \tag{14.2}$$

While FGSM was shown to be quite effective initially, it ultimately proved to be a relatively weak approach for generating adversarial perturbations. Next, we describe three considerably stronger approaches: PGD, DeepFool, and CW.

PGD. The key limitation of FGSM is that it effectively takes only a single gradient step. A natural generalization is to perform FGSM iteratively, each time projecting the gradient step to the feasible region (in terms of both the feature space and magnitude of the perturbation. This approach has come to be known simply as *Projected Gradient Descent (PGD)* [Madry et al. 2018] (even though it typically performs gradient ascent, as in the case of the objective represented in Problem (14.1). Specifically, each PGD iteration performs the following gradient update, followed by a projection step:

$$\boldsymbol{\delta}_{t+1} = \boldsymbol{\delta}_t + \alpha \cdot \epsilon \cdot \text{sign}(\nabla_{\boldsymbol{\delta}_t} \mathcal{L}\left(h_{\boldsymbol{\theta}}(\boldsymbol{x} + \boldsymbol{\delta}_t), y\right)), \tag{14.3}$$

where α is the step size. We can initialize $\boldsymbol{\delta}_0 = \mathbf{0}$, although a more effective variant also considers random starts with $\boldsymbol{\delta}_0$ initialized to a small random vector. PGD has proved to be one of the most powerful attacks in practice, particularly if we use a sufficient number of iterations and random starts, and remains one of the main ways to empirically evaluate robustness of models to adversarial perturbations with ℓ_p-norm constraints.

CW. Another powerful class of attacks was designed by Carlini and Wagner [2017]; we refer to these simply as CW. The most basic variant of CW attacks assumes that adversarial perturbation constraints are in terms of the ℓ_2-norm bounds. CW formulates the optimization problem for identifying adversarial perturbations as follows:

$$\min ||\boldsymbol{\delta}||_2 + c \cdot f(\boldsymbol{x} + \boldsymbol{\delta}), \tag{14.4}$$

f is a function such that $h_{\boldsymbol{\theta}}(\boldsymbol{x} + \boldsymbol{\delta}) = t$ only if $f(\boldsymbol{x} + \boldsymbol{\delta}) \leq 0$ for a target prediction t. There are many possible choices for f, with the one that yields the best performance being

$$f(\boldsymbol{x}') = \max(\max_{i \neq t} Z(\boldsymbol{x}')_i - Z(\boldsymbol{x}')_t, 0), \tag{14.5}$$

where Z returns the logits of the last layer of $h_{\boldsymbol{\theta}}$. Then, the optimization problem in Eq.(14.4) can be solved by any gradient-based method.

Coordinate Greedy. When the features are binary, the optimization problem in Eq. (14.1) can be solved by using *Coordinate Greedy* (also known as an iterative improvement) [Li and Vorobeychik 2018], which optimizes one randomly chosen coordinate of the feature vector at a time, until a local optimum is reached. In order to improve the quality of the resulting solution (given that $\mathcal{L}(\cdot)$ is typically non-concave), the above process can be repeated from multiple random starting points [Li and Vorobeychik 2018, Madry et al. 2018], just as described above for PGD attacks.

14.2.2 Realizable Attacks

Feature-space attacks are clearly an abstraction. But an abstraction of what? In reality, the machine learning pipeline does not begin with features—it begins with *entities*. In the context of malware detection, entities are typically executable files. One prepares datasets for training malware detectors by first defining feature extraction functions, which then map each file to an associated feature vector. In the context of computer vision, on the other hand, entities are scenes, which are translated into features when a camera photographs the scene. We can formalize this by letting e denote the actual entity, with $\boldsymbol{x}(e)$ the feature vector extracted from it. A *realizable attack* is an attack directly on the entity e, which indirectly (through a feature extractor, such as a camera taking the photograph) impacts its feature vector $\boldsymbol{x}$. Realizable attacks must abide by practical constraints imposed by the fact that an actual entity is modified, rather then feature values. For example, when a scene is modified, it is not

Figure 14.2 An illustration of realizable attacks on face recognition [Sharif et al. 2016b]. A person's face image is misidentified as that of another when he employs an adversarial eyeglass frame.

meaningful to talk about perturbations to pixels; rather, modifications are, for example, to objects in the scene.

In the context of cybersecurity, an early realizable attack on machine learning was devised by Fogla et al. [2006] who attack an anomaly-based intrusion detection systems. Šrndic and Laskov [2014] present a case study of an evasion attack against PDFRate [Smutz and Stavrou 2012], a state-of-the-art PDF malware classifier, while [Xu et al. 2016a] propose EvadeML, a fully realizable attack on PDF malware classifiers that generates evasion instances by directly modifying PDF source using genetic programming and a sandbox to ensure malicious functionality.

In computer vision, two noteworthy examples of realizable (or physical) attacks involve adversarial occlusions placed on objects in the scene. Sharif et al. [2016a] design printable eyeglass frames with adversarial noise inside them, as illustated in Figure 14.2, with the goal of face images being misclassified as a different person than actually photographed. Eykholt et al. [2018], on the other hand, design adversarial stickers that can be printed and placed on road signs (notably, a stop sign) with the goal of these being misclassified (e.g., a stop sign incorrectly classified as a speed limit sign).

Next, we discuss the design of decision-time attacks on face recognition to illustrate these concepts.

14.3 Illustration: Face Recognition

14.3.1 Face Recognition Systems

In computer vision tasks such as face recognition, the raw feature extractor is often a camera that captures real-world entities and converts them into pixel-based images in the digital domain. These images are then passed to deep neural networks, which compute higher-level representations such as shapes and edges.

In general, deep face recognition systems aim to address two tasks: 1) *Face identification*, which outputs the predicted identity of a given test face image, and 2) *Face verification*, which determines whether a test (or probe) face image and a gallery face image correspond to the same individual. Depending on whether all test identities appear in the training set, face recognition systems can be further categorized into *closed-set systems* and *open-set systems* [Liu et al. 2017], as illustrated in Fig. 14.3.

In closed-set face recognition tasks, all identities appearing in the test samples are already included in the training set. Specifically, face identification can be formulated as a *multi-class classification* problem [Sun et al. 2014a,b, Taigman et al. 2014]. Face verification naturally extends this setup by performing the classification twice—once for the test image and once for the gallery image—and then comparing the predicted identities.

In contrast, for open-set tasks, there is typically no overlap between identities in the training set and those in the test set. Under this setting, face verification becomes a *metric learning* problem, whose objective is to minimize *intra-class distance* and maximize *inter-class distance* within a

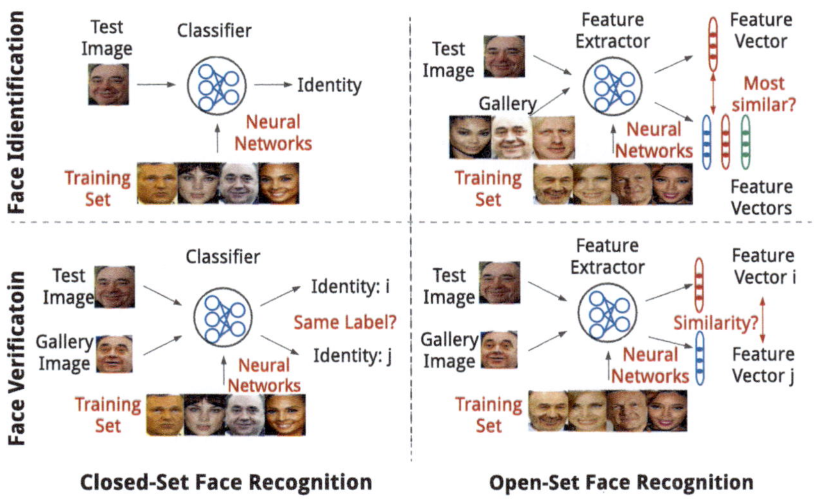

Figure 14.3 Closed-set and open-set face recognition systems.

chosen metric space [Deng et al. 2019, Liu et al. 2016, 2017, Parkhi et al. 2015, Schroff et al. 2015, Wen et al. 2016]. This process generally involves two steps. First, a feature extractor is trained to map each face image into a discriminative feature space using an appropriately designed loss function. Second, the distance between the feature vectors of the test and gallery images is computed and compared against a verification threshold.

As an extension of face verification, face identification additionally evaluates the distances between the test image's feature vector and each gallery feature vector, selecting the identity associated with the smallest distance. In this work, we focus on face identification for closed-set systems, as the threat models for face verification and open-set systems are direct extensions of this setting.

14.3.2 Threat Models for Face Recognition

We focus on the vulnerability of face recognition systems to both feature-space attacks and *the digital representation of physically realizable attacks* (henceforth referred to simply as *physically realizable attacks*). These attacks generate adversarial perturbations that are visually unobtrusive in the digital domain and can subsequently be reproduced in the physical world through techniques such as 3D printing (*e.g.*, Fig. 14.4 shows an example of such an attack). Compared with attacks implemented directly in real-world scenes, physically realizable attacks enable more efficient evaluation of system robustness. On the one hand, they allow iterative modification of digital images, which is substantially faster than repeatedly altering physical objects and re-photographing them. On the other hand, robustness to physically realizable attacks provides a lower bound on robustness to analogous physical-world attacks, since the digital setting imposes fewer constraints and admits a larger solution space.

Formally, both feature-space and physically realizable attacks can be performed by solving the following general form of an optimization problem (*e.g.*, for closed-set identification task):

$$\text{argmax}_{\boldsymbol{\delta}}\, \mathcal{L}(S(\boldsymbol{x} + M\boldsymbol{\delta}), y) \qquad s.t.\ \boldsymbol{\delta} \in \Delta, \tag{14.6}$$

where S is the target face recognition model, $\mathcal{L}$ is the adversary's utility function (*e.g.*, the loss function used to train S), $\boldsymbol{x}$ is the original input face image, y is the associated identity, $\boldsymbol{\delta}$ is the adversarial perturbation, and Δ is the feasible space of the perturbation. Here, M denotes the mask matrix that

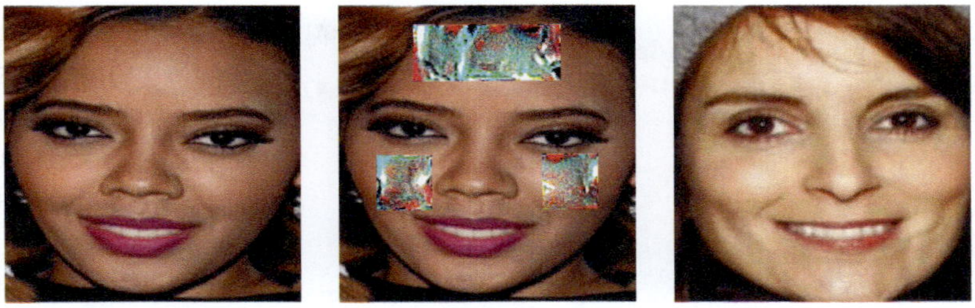

Figure 14.4 Sticker attack: an example of a physically realizable attack on face recognition systems. Left: the original input image. Middle: the face with an adversarial sticker applied. Right: the resulting predicted identity. In practice, such adversarial stickers can be printed and placed directly on a person's face.

constrains the area of perturbation; it has the same dimension as δ and contains 1s where the perturbation is allowed and 0s where there is no perturbation.

Next, we present several threat models for face recognition systems, categorized along the following dimensions:

- *Perturbation type*, such as perturbations produced by pixel-level feature-space attacks and physically realizable attacks.
- *The adversary's knowledge of the target system*, *i.e.*, the information about which sub-components of S are leaked to the adversary.
- *The adversary's goal*, such as the circumvention of detection (dodging) and the misrecognition as a target identity (impersonation).
- *The adversary's capability*. For example, an attacker can either individually perturb each input face image, or produce universal perturbations for images batch-wise.

14.3.2.1 Perturbation Type

In general, there are three categories of threat models using different perturbation types: *digital attack*, *pixel-level physically realizable attack*, and *grid-level physically realizable attack*, as shown in Figure 14.5.

- *Feature-Space Attacks*. Feature-space attacks produce small perturbations on the entire input face image, such as the PGD attack [Madry et al. 2018] that uses the ℓ_∞-norm, and the CW attack [Carlini and Wagner 2017] which is an ℓ_2 attack, described in Section 14.2.1.
- *Pixel-level Physically Realizable Attacks*. This category of attacks features pixel-level perturbations that can be realized in the physical world (*e.g.*, by printing them on glossy photo papers). In this case, the attacker

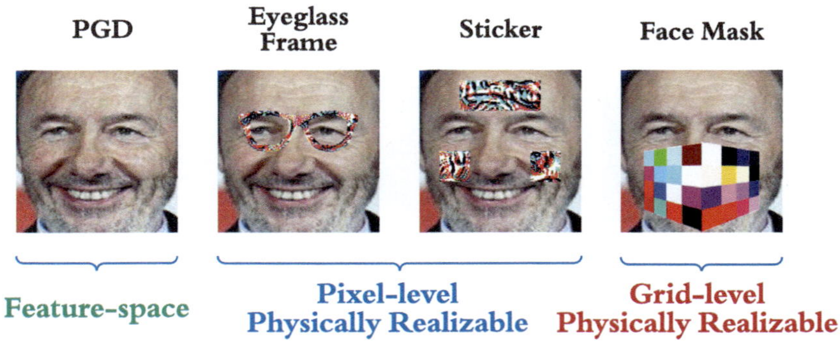

Figure 14.5 Threat models by perturbation types.

adds large pixel-level perturbations to a small area of the input image (*e.g.*, face accessories such as an eyeglass frame or face stickers). Such attacks have been demonstrated to successfully fool VGG-based face recognition systems [Sharif et al. 2016b].

- *Grid-level Physically Realizable Attacks*. In practice, pixel-level perturbations cannot be faithfully reproduced on face accessories made from *coarse* materials, such as cloth or non-woven fabric masks. To overcome this limitation, grid-level physically realizable face mask attacks introduce a colored grid pattern onto the mask surface, as illustrated in Figure 14.5.

14.3.2.2 Adversary's System Knowledge

The key components of a face recognition system S are the training set D and neural architecture h. It is natural to categorize threat models based on the adversary's knowledge of these two components. From the attackers' perspective, threat models can be classified into the following scenarios:

- *Zero Knowledge*. Both D and h are invisible to the adversary. This is the weakest adversarial setting, as no critical information of S is leaked. Thus, it provides a lower bound for the vulnerability of S. In this scenario, the attacks are referred to as *black-box attacks*, where the adversary needs no internal details of S to compromise it.
- *Training Set*. This scenario enables the assessment of the robustness of the training set of S in adversarial settings. Here, only the training set D is visible to the adversary. Without knowing h, an adversary constructs a surrogate system S' by training a surrogate neural architecture h' on

Table 14.1 Attack success rate of dodging attacks on closed-set face recognition systems by the attacker's system knowledge [Tong et al. 2021]. Z represents zero knowledge, T is training set, A is neural architecture, and F represents full knowledge.

Target System	Attack Type	Attacker's System Knowledge			
		Z	T	A	F
VGGFace [Parkhi et al. 2015]	PGD	0.40	0.51	0.93	0.94
	Eyeglass Frame	0.23	0.28	0.70	0.99
	Sticker	0.05	0.06	0.47	0.98
	Face Mask	0.26	0.32	0.63	1.00
FaceNet [Schroff et al. 2015]	PGD	0.83	0.83	1.00	1.00
	Eyeglass Frame	0.13	0.16	0.90	1.00
	Sticker	0.01	0.01	0.92	1.00
	Face Mask	0.30	0.42	0.83	1.00
ArcFace18 [Deng et al. 2019]	PGD	0.87	0.92	0.97	1.00
	Eyeglass Frame	0.06	0.06	0.44	1.00
	Sticker	0.01	0.01	0.37	1.00
	Face Mask	0.27	0.33	0.71	1.00
ArcFace50 [Deng et al. 2019]	PGD	0.87	0.90	0.81	0.99
	Eyeglass Frame	0.09	0.12	0.44	0.99
	Sticker	0.00	0.01	0.14	0.94
	Face Mask	0.29	0.36	0.67	0.99
ArcFace101 [Deng et al. 2019]	PGD	0.81	0.78	0.86	0.96
	Eyeglass Frame	0.03	0.03	0.26	0.98
	Sticker	0.04	0.04	0.08	0.95
	Face Mask	0.26	0.36	0.54	0.99

D, *i.e.*, $S' = f(h'; D)$. Then, the adversary performs the aforementioned transfer-based attack on S' and evaluates S using the transferred adversarial examples.

- *Neural Architecture*. The adversary only knows the neural architecture h of S but has no access to the training set D., This enables the evaluation of the vulnerability of the neural architecture h of S. Without knowing D, the attacker can build its surrogate system $S' = f(h; D')$ for some surrogate dataset D', and conduct a transfer attack to evaluate S.
- *Full knowledge*. In the worst case, the adversary can have an accurate knowledge of both the training set D and neural architecture h. Thus, it provides an upper bound for vulnerability evaluation on S. In this scenario, the attacker can fully reproduce S offline and then perform *white-box attacks* on S.

Recently, we analyzed and quantified the vulnerability of various components in open-source face recognition systems when subjected to decision-time attacks, considering different perturbation types and varying levels of adversarial knowledge [Tong et al. 2021]. The results are summarized in Table 14.1. A key observation is that *the neural architecture is substantially more fragile than the training set across most adversarial scenarios*. For instance, when the attacker has access only to the neural architecture, the sticker attack achieves a high success rate of 0.92 on FaceNet. In contrast, if the attacker knows only the training set, the success rate drops sharply to 0.01. Furthermore, comparing rows corresponding to the same target system in Table 14.1 reveals that *feature-space (PGD) attacks are markedly more powerful than physically realizable attacks in closed-set settings*. Among the physically realizable attacks, grid-level perturbations applied to face masks exhibit considerably higher effectiveness than pixel-level perturbations such as the eyeglass-frame and sticker attacks.

14.3.2.3 Adversary's Goal

In addition to the adversary's knowledge about the target face recognition system, threat models can differ in specific goals detailed below.

- *Dodging (Untargeted)*. In a dodging attack, an adversary aims to have his/her face misidentified as another arbitrary face. For example, the adversary can be a terrorist who wants to bypass a face recognition system for biometric security checking. As the dodging attack has no specific target identity, it is also called the *untargeted attack*.
- *Impersonation (Targeted)*. In an impersonation, or targeted, attack, an adversary seeks to produce an adversarial example that cases the face to be incorrectly recognized as a target identity. For example, the adversary may try to camouflage his/her face to be identified as an authorized user of a laptop that uses face recognition for authentication.

We observed that *while both attacks are highly effective in compromising different face recognition systems (with nearly 100% attack success rate), dodging attacks exhibit stronger transferability in black-box attacks than impersonation attacks* [Tong et al. 2021].

14.3.2.4 Adversary's Capability

In practice, even when the adversaries share the same system knowledge and goal, their capabilities can still differ due to time and/or budget constraints, such as the budget for printing adversarial eyeglass frames [Sharif et al. 2016b]. We can consider two categories of attacker capabilities: *individual attack* and *universal attack*.

- *Individual attack.* The adversary has sufficient time and budget to produce a specific perturbation for each input face image.
- *Universal attack.* The adversary has a time/budget constraint such that he/she can only generate a *universal (face-agnostic)* perturbation that fools a face recognition system for a batch of face images rather than for every input.

In a universal attack, the adversary can explicitly control the universality of the perturbation by setting different values of N, the number of face images that share the same physically realizable perturbation. In general, a larger N corresponds to a lower budget because more images share the perturbation, thereby imposing more constraints on the attack and decreasing its success rate. We showed that *most face recognition systems are susceptible to universal attacks even when N is as large as 20* [Tong et al. 2021],. Under these conditions, a universal attack can still obtain a success rate above 50%.

14.4 Robust Learning: Approaches and Efficacy

There have been numerous defense approaches to make ML robust. Here, we present two classes of methods to learn robust models that have proved both sufficiently scalable and effective even against adaptive attacks: *adversarial training* [Cohen et al. 2019, Goodfellow et al. 2015, Madry et al. 2018, Szegedy et al. 2014] and *randomized smoothing* [Cohen et al. 2019, Lecuyer et al. 2019].

Adversarial Training. The fundamental idea of adversarial training is to solve the following robust optimization problem:

$$\min_{\boldsymbol{\theta}} \frac{1}{|D|} \sum_{\boldsymbol{x},y \in D} \max_{\|\boldsymbol{\delta}\|_p \leq \epsilon} \mathcal{L}\left(h_{\boldsymbol{\theta}}(\boldsymbol{x}+\boldsymbol{\delta}), y\right), \tag{14.7}$$

where D is the training dataset. In practice, this problem is commonly solved by iteratively using the following two steps: 1) compute or approximate the solution to the inner maximization problem, and 2) use this solution to update the model parameters $\boldsymbol{\theta}$.

In most settings, the inner optimization problem is non-convex, and quite challenging to solve to optimality. There are two training paradigms that address this challenge. The first is to compute heuristic solutions as lower bounds to

$$\max_{\|\boldsymbol{\delta}\|_p \leq \epsilon} \mathcal{L}\left(h_{\boldsymbol{\theta}}(\boldsymbol{x}+\boldsymbol{\delta}), y\right). \tag{14.8}$$

Commonly, one would simply use one of the methods for generating adversarial perturbations—typically, feature-space attacks. For example, PGD has been shown to be an effective technique for generating heuristic solutions. More recently, a variant of FGSM in which we initialize $\boldsymbol{\delta}$ to a random start, rather than 0, has been shown to be highly effective as well, and considerably less expensive than PGD [Wong et al. 2020].

An alternative paradigm is to make use of provably upper bounds on the solution to Problem (14.8). These are often intimately tied to the goal of *certifying*, or proving, robustness of the model at decision time. For example, if the model $h_{\boldsymbol{\theta}}(\boldsymbol{x})$ is a neural network with ReLU activations, the problem of verifying robustness can be formulated as a mixed-integer linear program, and one can further make use of convex relaxations of the ReLU neurons to obtain a linear program. Moreover, [Wong and Kolter 2018] show that one can make use of a dual of this linear program, along with weak duality, to obtain a differentiable upper bound on the inner optimization problem. This upper bound can thus be used directly as a part of the stochastic gradient descent procedure of learning the model parameters.

Randomized Smoothing. The second class of methods for robust learning considers adding random perturbations to inputs at both training and test time. The basic idea is to construct a new smoothed classifier $g_{\boldsymbol{\theta}}(\cdot)$ from a base classifier $h_{\boldsymbol{\theta}}(\cdot)$ as follows: first, the base classifier $h_{\boldsymbol{\theta}}(\cdot)$ is trained with *Gaussian data augmentation* with variance $\boldsymbol{\sigma}^2$; then, for any input $\boldsymbol{x}$ at test time, the smoothed classifier $g_{\boldsymbol{\theta}}(\cdot)$ returns the class that has the highest probability measure for the base classifier $h_{\boldsymbol{\theta}}(\cdot)$ when inputs are perturbed with isotropic Gaussian noise:

$$\begin{aligned} g_{\boldsymbol{\theta}}(\boldsymbol{x}) &= \arg\max_{c} P(h_{\boldsymbol{\theta}}(\boldsymbol{x}+\boldsymbol{\eta}) = c) \\ \text{where } \boldsymbol{\eta} &\sim N\left(\mathbf{0}, \sigma^2 \boldsymbol{I}\right) \end{aligned} . \tag{14.9}$$

Indeed, the approaches for robust machine learning have generally proved quite effective in boosting both empirical and provable robustness under the ℓ_p-norm attacks [Cohen et al. 2019, Madry et al. 2018, Wong and Kolter 2018]. However, their efficacy is less evident in the context of robustness to realizable attacks.

In particular, we have investigated robustness of adversarial training that makes use of PGD to approximate the inner optimization problem (14.8) in yielding robustness to realizable attacks on PDF malware detection [Tong et al. 2019], demonstrating that their efficacy out of the box can vary. Moreover, our exploration of this issue in the context of image classification has shown

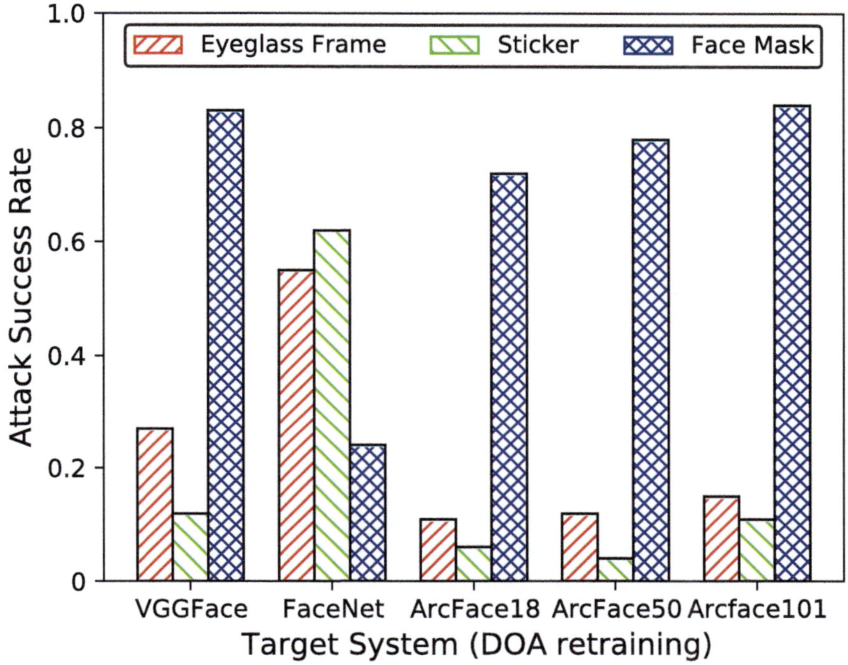

Figure 14.6 Attack success rate of dodging physically realizable attacks on closed-set systems with DOA retraining.

such approaches, as well as randomized smoothing techniques, to yield poor robustness to attacks involving physical occlusions [Wu et al. 2020]. Both [Tong et al. 2019] and [Wu et al. 2020] propose approaches that make use of the general adversarial training paradigm, but with modified adversarial models (i.e., versions of the inner problem), which significantly boost the ability to learn classifiers that are robust to realizable attacks.

Additionally, we recently explored this issue in the context of face recognition [Tong et al. 2021], further investigating the *defense against occlusion attacks (DOA)* approach proposed by [Wu et al. 2020]. Figure 14.6 presents the vulnerability of DOA-trained face recognition systems with different neural architectures in the face of different realizable attacks. It is evident that *DOA fails to defend against grid-level perturbations on face masks for most neural architectures*. In particular, face mask attacks achieve success rates exceeding 0.7 on four of the five DOA-refined face recognition systems. Moreover, we observe that *adversarial robustness to one perturbation type does not generalize to others*. For example, although VGGface-DOA maintains relatively strong robustness (over 70% accuracy) against pixel-level perturbations (*i.e.*, stickers and eyeglass frames), it remains highly susceptible to grid-level perturbations (*i.e.*, face masks). Conversely, applying DOA to FaceNet substantially improves its robustness to face mask attacks–the attack success rate drops from 1.0 to 0.24—yet it is far less effective against eyeglass-frame and sticker attacks. Overall, these findings suggest that it is extremely challenging to develop a universal "silver bullet" defense that remains effective across domains, architectures, and attack modalities.

14.5 Summary

This chapter focuses on AI/ML system vulnerabilities from a security perspective. Starting with general threat models, we introduced two representative attacks that can effectively compromise the integrity of ML systems: the feature-space attack and the realizable attack. We then elucidate these threat models in the context of face recognition, which has been shown to be vulnerable to a variety of attacks and for which numerous paradigms for robust ML systems have been proposed. We demonstrate that those robust ML systems are still susceptible to a variety of realizable attacks, and that robustness against one type of attack cannot be extrapolated to other types of attacks or systems with distinct neural architectures. Building ML systems that are resilient to a variety of threat models is therefore still an unresolved problem.

One future research direction can be identifying robust features for ML systems. Recent research such as [Tong et al. 2019] has shown that the collection of conserved features – those that cannot be modified unilaterally without compromising malicious functionality – is the key to ML robustness against realizable attacks. On the other hand, the vulnerability of ML systems to adversarial examples can be directly ascribed to the presence of *non-robust features* [Ilyas et al. 2019]. Several unresolved issues can be explored, including how to automatically identify robust features and whether robust features can be constructed from non-robust features, such as via non-linear combination.

15

AI Ethics, Law, and Policy

Pauline T. Kim

Washington University in St. Louis

Abstract

In this concluding chapter, we examine the governance frameworks that shape how AI is developed and deployed, focusing on ethics, law, and policy. We analyze the strengths and limitations of each: ethical guidelines provide aspirational principles but lack enforcement, legal frameworks create binding rules yet often lag behind technological change, and policies offer flexibility but may vary across jurisdictions. Using examples from privacy, discrimination, and criminal justice, we show how each framework contributes differently to ensuring AI systems are beneficial and trustworthy. We argue that no single approach is sufficient on its own, and we make the case for a hybrid governance model that blends ethical reflection, legal enforcement, and policy experimentation. Our aim is to provide a roadmap for decision-makers who must balance the drive for innovation with the responsibility to protect society as AI continues to evolve.

15.1 Introduction

Advances in artificial intelligence (AI) offer the potential for enormous societal benefit, but also raise risks of significant physical, economic and societal harms. As a result, these technologies pose a challenge: how to channel their development to benefit society as a whole, while avoiding their harmful consequences. As AI is more widely incorporated into everyday systems, it poses increasing risks, including misinformation, unfair or discriminatory treatment and threats to human health and safety. Growing awareness of these risks has in turn generated myriad efforts by private industry, academia,

DOI: 10.1201/9788743812074-17

government agencies, legislators, and civil society groups to identify and mitigate potential harms of AI.

This chapter explores the different governance tools that have been considered for guiding developments in AI in socially beneficial ways, examining the relevance of ethics, law, and policy. Ethics focus on articulating important values and principles and are intended to guide behavior. Initiatives in this area identify principles to govern the development and use of AI tools, but typically lack any formal enforcement mechanism. Laws are enacted through some kind of public process and have binding effect. Actors who violate legal standards or requirements can face liability resulting in payment of damages or other penalties. Policy-making sometimes results in the passage of laws, but often has a broader, more exploratory emphasis, incorporating research, planning, and experimentation in an effort to identify solutions. The categories of ethics, law, and policy overlap and interrelate in important ways, but analyzing them as distinct categories helps to highlight the differences between them, as well as the advantages and limitations of each approach.

Efforts to ensure that AI works for societal benefit face several fundamental challenges. First, AI is notoriously difficult to define. Systems that autonomously replicate some form of human behavior are everywhere. They may involve trivial processing that follows steps clearly defined by humans in advance, or complex decision-making algorithms developed through supervised machine learning processes. More recently, generative AI systems that can produce unstructured text, images, or code in response to natural language prompts have grown in prominence. Given the immense variety of technologies and possible applications, the scope of the inquiry is ambiguous, making it hard to definitively enumerate all the potential challenges raised by AI.

Second, even if a definitive taxonomy of risk and harms could be developed, it would only be a first step. What is ultimately required is the creation of systems, structures, and laws that can effectively channel the development of AI to promote socially beneficial uses and mitigate the risks of harm, or determine which AI systems should not be developed at all.

A third challenge, closely related to the first two, is finding the appropriate level of generality for action given that AI refers to many different technologies and is used in many different contexts. A broad approach has the advantage of addressing the issues wholesale, but risks being either so vague as to be meaningless or so specific that it produces unintended consequences in atypical situations. An alternative strategy would create rules or guidelines for each specific context. While this approach is more precisely tailored, it is slower and more cumbersome to develop and could leave significant gaps in coverage. The dilemma echoes a longstanding debate in the privacy literature regarding whether omnibus legislation or sector-specific regulation is preferable [Richards et al. 2022, Solove 2015].

These challenges are compounded by the industry's push to create artificial general intelligence (AGI)–AI that would exceed human intelligence and can learn and act autonomously. While there are ongoing debates about whether or when AGI is achievable and whether it poses an existential threat to humanity, we do not address those questions in this chapter. We focus on the risks and harms posed by existing technologies, analyzing the types of tools available to address them.

There is no single solution for guiding the development of AI. Instead, harnessing the benefits and avoiding the harms of AI will require a mix of approaches. This chapter explores the advantages and limitations of relying on ethical principles, legal rules, and policy-making to achieve these goals. To ground the discussion, it relies on a handful of commonly mentioned areas of concern as examples–namely, consumer privacy, bias and discrimination, and fairness in criminal law enforcement. Other concerns surrounding AI, such as environmental degradation, security breaches, misinformation and disinformation, health and safety concerns, and threats to democratic institutions, are also salient, and efforts to mitigate these harms could be subject to similar analyses of the interplay between ethics, law, and policy.

15.2 Ethical Principles

As awareness has grown that AI can cause harm, efforts to identify the ethical principles that should govern development of these systems have proliferated. Private firms, industry groups, government entities, intergovernmental organizations, and civil society groups have all undertaken initiatives in this area. In 2020, Fjeld et al. collected 36 prominent statements of ethical AI principles [Fjeld et al. 2020]. Similarly, Jobin et al. conducted a global survey and identified 84 such documents [Jobin et al. 2019], while Schiff et al. evaluated 112 statements [Schiff et al. 2021]. A crowdsourced list on AlgorithmWatch listed over 160 as of September 2022 [Kim and Durrie 2025].

Several studies have conducted meta-analyses of ethical AI principles to identify themes and look for areas of convergence or consensus [Cath et al. 2018, Hagendorff 2020, Zeng et al. 2018]. Fjeld et al. [Fjeld et al. 2020] found eight prominent themes: privacy, accountability, safety and security, transparency and explainability, fairness and nondiscrimination, human control, professional responsibility, and promotion of human values. These themes are mentioned in nearly all of the documents they examined, and each in turn encompasses a number of subsidiary principles, resulting in a total of forty-seven identified principles. Jobin et al. [2019] undertook a similar type of analysis on a larger sample of documents and concluded that there is an emerging global convergence around five core principles: transparency, justice and fairness, non-malfeasance, responsibility, and privacy. Schiff et al. [2021] identified 25 topics, with the most prominent being social responsibility, transparency, bias and fairness, privacy, and safety and reliability.

AI principles are typically stated at a high level of generality. For example, protection of privacy appears in a majority of statements, but what exactly that entails is rarely explained. The Asilomar Principles of AI [Future of Life Institute. 2017] address privacy in two sentences: "People should have the right to access, manage and control the data they generate" and "The application of AI to personal data must not unreasonably curtail people's real or perceived liberty." The OECD's discussion of privacy [Organisation for Economic Cooperation and Development 2022] is even briefer, including "privacy and data protection" in a list of human rights and democratic values that should be respected. Guidelines by the High-Level Expert Group on Artificial Intelligence (HLEG Guidelines) set up by the European Commission [European Commission High-Level Expert Group on Artificial Intelligence 2019] say a bit more, explaining that protecting privacy "necessitates adequate data governance that covers the quality and integrity of data used, its relevance in light of the domain in which the AI systems will be deployed, its access protocols and the capability to process data in a manner that protects privacy." While this added detail directs attention to aspects of the development process, it remains unclear how to operationalize the principle in a concrete setting.

Ethical principles that address risks of bias and discrimination are similarly vague. The OECD calls for "reducing economic, social, gender and other inequalities" and respecting democratic values including "non-discrimination and equality, diversity, fairness, [and] social justice" [Organisation for Economic Cooperation and Development 2022]. The HLEG Guidelines state that AI systems should ensure "equal access through inclusive design processes, as well as equal treatment," that "identifiable and discriminatory bias should be removed" when collecting data, and that "oversight processes" should be put in place [European Commission High-Level Expert Group on Artificial Intelligence 2019]. Other statements more vaguely refer to cultural diversity and human dignity, rights, and freedoms as important values [Future of Life Institute. 2017, Information Technology Industry Council 2021].

The articulation of ethical principles for AI is an important first step in moving away from technological determinism. These efforts entail recognition that AI systems are not technical artifacts with independent existence, but instead are part of sociotechnical systems [Van de Poel 2020]. The types of AI that are developed and the uses to which they are put are not inevitable; rather, their creation and deployment result from and reflect social processes, and their use will have profound societal consequences. AI principles can serve as a crucial acknowledgement and a reminder of these facts.

At the same time, ethical principles will likely have limited practical impact. They are inherently vague because they aim to guide behavior in a wide range of situations. Their generality offers the advantage of being broadly applicable, as well as increasing the likelihood that they will be widely endorsed. The downside to this breadth is that these principles often amount to little more than platitudes that do not grapple seriously with difficult ethical questions. No one would disagree that "justice and fairness" are desirable goals, but what does that mean when designing a system that will influence or determine who is released from jail or gets a job? Precisely because there is widespread disagreement about what justice requires in concrete settings, general principles will rarely help with difficult choices in the design or deployment of AI tools.

Consider the ethical principle of protecting personal privacy. What constraints does that principle put on the collection and analysis of information about individual people? AI systems that are used to screen and select people for employment, housing or credit rely on large amounts of personal data. Does protecting privacy entail limits on the types of personal information that can be collected? Or is it sufficient that individuals have consented to the collection of that information? Can their consent be presumed because they failed to opt out of a default setting? Does it matter whether they were told what information would be collected, how it would be used and what the potential social, financial, and reputational risks might be? In other words, do the conditions under which that consent was obtained matter? And once data has been collected, can it be used for any purpose, including making inferences about people? What if those inferences might reveal sensitive information such as a person's medical conditions, religious practices, or sexual preferences? These issues have been widely debated, but generalized statements about respecting individual privacy provide no clear answers, leaving practitioners free to interpret and apply the principles for themselves.

General statements of ethics may also mask significant underlying disagreements about the meaning of the articulated values. AI principles almost always include fairness and nondiscrimination, and yet the meaning of those terms is deeply contested. Invidious prejudice is easy to condemn, but beyond that baseline, the consensus around what is wrongful discrimination breaks down. On one view, unfair discrimination occurs only when a negative decision, such as refusing someone a job or denying them a loan, is based on a protected characteristic. So long as race or gender was not part of the decision, the demands of fairness are satisfied. Alternative views condemn decisions that systematically disadvantage groups that have been historically subordinated, such as people of color and women, regardless of whether it can be proven that the effects are intentional. Fairness would thus require more than avoiding intentional discrimination; it would also encompass a duty to avoid or dismantle systems that reinforce systemic inequality.

These debates mean that ethical principles of nondiscrimination are indeterminate when applied to AI systems. Fairness might turn on the inputs to a system, such that a model that does not include features like race or gender (and perhaps proxies for those characteristics as well) would be considered fair. Alternatively, fairness might require scrutiny of the outputs–specifically, whether the predictions of an AI system are fair across groups. Examining outputs leads to further questions about how to measure fairness–whether by requiring equal accuracy rates, equal false positive or false negative rates, equal outcomes, or something else [Kleinberg et al. 2016]. Multiple formal measures of group fairness have been proposed in the computer science literature and it will often be impossible to satisfy them all [Kleinberg et al. 2016]. Because statements of ethical AI do not resolve these debates, they cannot meaningfully constrain how the technology will be developed and deployed.

Ethical guidelines can also obscure ways in which high-level principles may conflict with one another and thereby avoid resolving those tensions. These guidelines often identify both protecting privacy and freedom from discrimination as important governing principles, but with little acknowledgement that the two values are sometimes in tension. One of the reasons predictive AI may exhibit bias is a lack of sufficient data for certain subgroups. As a result, efforts to reduce that bias will often motivate increased data gathering, which can in turn incentivize increased surveillance of disadvantaged and marginalized groups. And, depending upon the uses to which the technology is put, more accurate, less biased forms of AI could cause disproportionate harm to those communities [Greene et al. 2019].

A case in point is facial recognition systems. After researchers documented that several commercially available facial recognition systems made more errors on faces with darker skin tone [Buolamwini and Gebru 2018a], Microsoft responded by expanding the training and benchmark datasets and "launched new data collection efforts" in order to increase the accuracy of its tool "across all skin tones" [Roach 2018]. In other words, it increased collection of images from communities of color. While Microsoft viewed these steps as positive efforts to reduce unequal accuracy rates, the impact on those communities is more ambiguous. Efforts to reduce bias and improving accuracy of facial recognition technologies stand in considerable tension with protecting personal privacy. If those technologies are then deployed disproportionately in communities of color by law enforcement, then the push to reduce bias also conflicts with their interests in reducing discriminatory policing.

Critics have argued that ethical guidelines are likely to have little actual effect. In one study [McNamara et al. 2018], researchers instructed some software developers and students about ethical guidelines, then examined their responses to scenarios presenting ethical dilemmas. They found no differences in the responses of those who had received information about the ethical guidelines and those who had not [Roach 2018]. In real world settings, where professionals face competitive pressures to create products and scale them quickly, it is even less likely that unenforceable guidelines will meaningful shape behavior, especially when ethical consideration conflict with immediate professional gains.

Observers have expressed particular skepticism about AI principles published by companies that build and profit from these technologies [Cath et al. 2018, Hagendorff 2020]. They argue that these statements are self-serving, encouraging the public to trust their AI, while providing no transparency as to how these systems work and little accountability for their consequences. By prominently announcing their commitment to ethics, these companies may be engaging in a form of "ethics-washing." These statements may signal concern about ethics in order to deflect public or government scrutiny and to forestall meaningful legal regulation while providing no real protection to the public. Consistent with these concerns, Schiff et al. [2021] found that ethical statements from the private sector have less breadth and depth, and less engagement with law and regulation than statements from the public sector or non-governmental organizations.

A further criticism of ethical AI principles is that they tend to assume that the solutions are purely technical in nature rather than examining the broader social context. Statements by private entities are particularly prone to emphasize technical fixes to ethical challenges [Schiff et al. 2021]. Greene et al. argue that many of these statements "co-opt the language of ... critics, folding them into a limited, technologically deterministic, expert-driven view of what ethical AI/ML means" [Greene et al. 2019]. For example, ITI's Global AI Policy Recommendation emphasizes the use of techniques such as anonymization, pseudonymization, de-identification, and other privacy enhancing techniques "to ensure data can be used to train algorithms and perform AI tasks without breaching privacy" [Information Technology Industry Council 2021]. This recommendation emphasizes expert-driven responses to what are in fact contested social and political questions. It assumes individual privacy interests are only about non-disclosure, thereby narrowing the ethical inquiry to technologically-achievable solutions, rather than engaging a broader conversation about whether businesses and government should be permitted to collect all manner of personal data and what limits should be placed on how they use the data they do collect.

On the other hand, guidelines and principles can serve as useful tools for internal governance, shaping an organization's culture and values and channeling behavior of its agents toward socially appropriate goals. Their effectiveness, however, depends largely upon how they are implemented and whether the organization backs its broad principles with oversight and accountability mechanisms. Because ethical statements by private firms are typically intended to shape their internal culture or to communicate their values to the public, readers should understand them in light of those limited purposes. Private ethical statements are not universal principles identifying all relevant ethical concerns, nor should they be understood to delimit the appropriate sphere of regulation or public policy.

Standing alone, then, ethical principles will have quite limited impact. Not only are they vague and therefore difficult to operationalize, but the guidance they offer is not enforceable. They serve as aspirational goals rather than rules with binding effect.

15.3 Law

Unlike statements of ethical principles, legal rules have binding force. Laws are enacted through some type of public process, and they are backed by the power of the state or other governing entity. And while ethical principles are stated in aspirational terms–for example, the statement that AI applications should be "fair, transparent and accountable" [Partnership on AI]–legal rules are typically framed in terms of prohibitions. Laws prohibit employers or lenders from discriminating, forbid police from conducting certain searches without probable cause, bar health care providers from revealing personal medical information, and so on. These prohibitions are backed by sanctions of various sorts. An entity that violates a legal rule may face a lawsuit or an investigation by a regulatory agency. If a violation is found, it may be required to compensate another party for the harm, pay a penalty, or face a court order requiring compliance.

While the law operates with greater force than ethical principles, it also has significant limitations in shaping the development of socially beneficial AI. To start, a significant gap exists between what is lawful and what is ethical and socially responsible. Activities that produce significant harms and are socially undesirable may nevertheless be legally permissible. Thus, the fact that a firm is fully in compliance with existing law does not answer the question whether its activities are ethical and offers no guarantee that the technology it develops is socially beneficial.

A gap between law and ethics can occur for a number of reasons, but it is often due to lags in regulation. New technologies and practices are constantly introduced, but the risks and harms they pose are not immediately apparent. Once problems are identified, it takes time to sort out how existing laws apply and whether they are sufficient to address those harms. Where existing law does not adequately address the risks of harm, new legislation may be needed to fill the gaps. Drafting new laws, however, can be challenging. With complex and evolving technologies, it is difficult to craft clear legal rules delineating what is permissible and what is not. Moreover, legislators often lack technical expertise and may be highly influenced by industry lobbyists seeking to avoid regulation. As a result, lawmakers may fail to adequately take into account the interests of a diffuse, unorganized public, or marginalized groups like criminal defendants or low-income workers who may be negatively impacted by AI applications.

Concerns about the potential for discrimination and invasions of privacy illustrate these challenges. Existing laws that prohibit discrimination can be applied to automated decision systems, offering a legal framework for challenging discriminatory AI; however, some gaps and uncertainties remain because the laws were enacted with human decision-makers in mind. In the case of threats to privacy, technological developments have largely outstripped prior legal approaches, leaving significant gaps in protection, particularly under U.S. laws. And while a few states have taken steps to regulate AI, these laws do not apply nationally, and offer quite limited protection against discrimination and privacy harms.

Regarding discrimination, traditional legal doctrine recognizes two distinct theories of discrimination: disparate treatment and disparate impact. Disparate treatment involves adverse treatment of an individual because of a protected characteristic like race, sex, or disability. When dealing with human decision-makers, courts typically frame that causal inquiry as a question of intentional discrimination—i.e. was the decision-maker motivated by the protected characteristic [U.S. Supreme Court 1973]. Disparate impact cases do not require proof of intent, but instead focus on discriminatory effects [U.S. Supreme Court 1971]. Liability for disparate impact discrimination arises when a facially neutral procedure or practice disproportionately harms a protected group and no legitimate business reason justifies that practice.

The most common use of the disparate impact theory has been to challenge employment tests and requirements. The Supreme Court case that first recognized the theory is Griggs v. Duke Power Co [U.S. Supreme Court 1971]. A group of black workers sued Duke Power Company, challenging its policy that a high school diploma and minimum scores on a standardized test were required for certain skilled positions. These requirements had the effect of barring far more black than white workers from the higher-paying jobs because a long history of segregated schools in the region had deprived them of equal educational opportunities. Because the requirements bore no relationship to the skills needed to successfully perform the jobs at issue, the Court found that imposing these requirements was discriminatory and violated federal anti-discrimination law. Subsequent cases have involved challenges to other written tests, or requirements like minimum height and weight requirements that disproportionately screen out female applicants [U.S. Supreme Court 1975, 1977].

How do these legal theories of discrimination apply to AI tools? Consider first the theory of disparate treatment. If the creator of an AI tool deliberately designs it with the purpose of screening out members of a historically disadvantaged group, that effort would clearly amount to disparate treatment discrimination. Proof of motive might be challenging, but this scenario presents no particular conceptual difficulty. On the other hand, the mere fact that the creators of a predictive tool did not intend to discriminate is not decisive of the legal question. In complex machine learning models, close proxies often exist for characteristics like race and sex, and predictive models can incorporate human biases or reproduce existing patterns of disadvantage or exclusion [Barocas and Selbst 2016]. When this happens, an AI tool may systematically disadvantage historically subordinated groups, such as racial minorities or women [Kim 2016].

In situations like these, disparate impact theory will prohibit practices that have unjustified discriminatory effects. However, ambiguity exists as to how existing doctrine should be applied to predictive AI tools. For example, it is uncertain what statistical test should be used to determine whether an automated decision system has a disparate impact [Raghavan and Kim 2024]. If a discriminatory impact is shown, the employer can defend its practice as "job related for the position in question and consistent with business necessity" [Civil Rights Act 1964]. With a traditional employment test, an employer does so by demonstrating its validity–i.e. by showing that the test or requirement actually measures job-relevant skills or attributes [Equal Employment Opportunity Commission 1978]. This concept of job validation is rooted in the industrial psychology literature and focuses on measuring individual skills and capacities.

AI tools, however, typically do not start with an analysis of the skills needed to do a job, but instead extract patterns from the available data to predict candidates' future performance. The data used to train the model may contain features that are strongly predictive of the target variable, yet have no clear connection to job performance. Given the complexity and opacity of some ML models, an employer may not be able to explain how a decision to hire or reject a specific candidate was reached, and may argue that the existence of a statistical correlation with the outcome of interest is sufficient to justify its practice.

This argument fails to recognize that statistical correlations may mask reliance on factors that are wholly arbitrary or implicitly discriminatory. Data mining often uncovers unexpected or even inexplicable correlations, not all of which are fair to rely on. One study found that liking curly fries on Facebook was correlated with higher intelligence [Kosinski et al. 2013]. Clearly, the relationship is not causal, nor is there any direct or necessary relationship between the two variables, apart from their coincidence in the particular dataset studied. But suppose an employer relied on a strong correlation between liking something on Facebook and positive job performance to justify a selection tool that had a discriminatory effect. No court would accept this justification, because such a tool would create "'built-in headwinds' for minority groups" and be "unrelated to measuring job capability," which is exactly the type of practice condemned by the Supreme Court in the Griggs case [U.S. Supreme Court 1971].

Alternatively, an algorithm might capture real differences between groups, but in ways that leverage proxies for protected characteristics. For example, a hiring algorithm that aims to predict longevity on the job may systematically screen out or disfavor women of childbearing age and individuals with disabilities because they are statistically more likely to take breaks from employment. If an employer explicitly relied on childbearing capacity or disability to screen applicants, it would violate the law. The legal outcome should not be different when an opaque model produces the same effects.

Because relying on statistical correlations alone could deprive people of opportunities based on proxies for protected characteristics or wholly arbitrary features, an employer should be legally required to demonstrate the substantive validity of its selection tools. It should bear the burden of showing that the model was built using accurate, representative, and unbiased data, and that it actually measures job-relevant skills and abilities [Kim 2016]. A coalition of prominent civil rights organizations endorsed such an approach, stating that "organizations should do the necessary work of studying and understanding the knowledge, skills, and abilities required by a particular job," and that "mere correlations between traits and purported job performance should not be sufficient to justify adverse impact" [The Leadership Conference on Civil and Human Rights 2020].

The phenomenon of model multiplicity also creates challenges and opportunities for legal doctrine. In sufficiently complex systems, alternative models exist that will be substantially equivalent in performance but may have less discriminatory effects. Given the availability of equally performant but less discriminatory models, disparate impact law could be interpreted to require a reasonable search for these alternatives before deploying a model that has a discriminatory impact [Black et al. 2024].

Because predictive models can produce discriminatory effects, government agencies, employers, banks, and other entities that use these tools should regularly audit their performance. If they find unwarranted discriminatory effects, they have a legal responsibility to correct the problem or stop using the tool. However, efforts to correct a discriminatory algorithm may raise further legal questions. Some researchers have asked whether efforts to remove discriminatory effects might themselves run afoul of anti-discrimination law by taking account of race, sex, or other protected characteristics [Kim 2022]. In other words, they question whether considering sensitive characteristics in an effort to debias algorithms amounts to disparate treatment discrimination.

Although the courts have not addressed this issue in the context of AI tools, several legal principles emerge from past cases. First, employers and other entities are permitted to prospectively change practices that they discover have an unjustified disparate impact. Apart from the rare circumstance in which applicants have relied to their detriment on a previously announced policy, by, for example, expending time and money to study for a specific test [U.S. Supreme Court 2009], an employer is free to adjust its selection procedures going forward [U.S. District Court 2010, U.S. Second Circuit Court of Appeals 2013]. In fact, the Supreme Court has repeatedly emphasized the importance of voluntary employer efforts to remove discriminatory practices, stating that voluntary compliance is the "preferred means" and "essential" to achieving the objectives of anti-discrimination law [U.S. Supreme Court 1986a,b].

Past cases have allowed consideration of discriminatory effects when designing policies to ensure equal access to opportunities. For example, courts have permitted employers to take affirmative steps to build a broad and diverse applicant pool that includes more women and racial minorities [U.S. Eighth Circuit Court of Appeals 1997, U.S. Seventh Circuit Court of Appeals 2005, 2006] Courts have also viewed with favor efforts to obtain data from underrepresented groups to avoid inadvertently creating biased tests [U.S. Supreme Court 2009]. These opinions suggest that efforts made when building a model to prevent discriminatory outcomes pose no particular legal problems [Kim 2022]. Designers can examine proposed target variables for implicit bias and select a target that avoids that problem. They can scrutinize the representativeness and accuracy of training data, oversample underrepresented groups, or remove features that encode human bias, such as subjectively coded attributes. These types of strategies pay attention to race or other sensitive characteristics in order to build selection processes that are fair to all, but, unlike the college admissions policies struck down by the Supreme Court [U.S. Supreme Court 2023], they do not make decisions about individuals turn on those characteristics [Black et al. 2024, Kim 2022].

Although some areas of ambiguity exist, current anti-discrimination law offers a useful conceptual framework for analyzing and challenging biased AI tools. However, practical obstacles also make addressing discriminatory harms difficult. Anti-discrimination laws are primarily enforced when individuals bring lawsuits alleging they have suffered harm from a discriminatory decision.[1] This enforcement mechanism is less effective in a world in which decisions are rendered on a mass scale by complex algorithms operating behind the scenes. Individuals cannot easily detect when and how they have been affected by potentially discriminatory decisions. For that reason, many

[1] Anti-discrimination law can also be enforced by government agencies, but those cases today represent only a very small fraction of discrimination lawsuits.

researchers have called for entities to give clear notice when relying on automated decision systems and to provide greater transparency about how those systems operate [Citron and Pasquale 2014].

Those calls have in turn generated debate over what meaningful notice and transparency require [Edwards and Veale 2017, Huq 2020, Kaminski 2021, Urban and Kaminski 2019, Wachter et al. 2017]. Some have asserted that individuals subject to AI screening tools should have a right to an explanation for an adverse decision, a right to contest the decision, or a right to human review. Even with these rights, however, it will be difficult for an individual to challenge a systemically biased model. Doing so will require data showing how the system as a whole operates, not just in the individual case. It will also require significant resources and a high level of technical expertise unlikely to be available to an individual litigant. These practical obstacles to enforcing legal liability rules have led many to consider broader regulatory and policy approaches to prevent discrimination, as discussed in part 4 below.

In contrast to anti-discrimination law, which offers some leverage for challenging AI tools, privacy law in the U.S. has been outstripped by technological developments. Two aspects in particular make it unsuited to protecting personal information in an era of big data and artificial intelligence. First, U.S. law has taken a sectoral approach, focusing on certain types of highly sensitive information, leaving gaps in coverage as data collection and use has expanded [Richards et al. 2022]. Second, the law relies heavily on notice and consent to govern data privacy, which has permitted businesses and governments to amass enormous amounts of personal information [Solove 2013].

Unlike Europe, which takes an omnibus approach to data protection [European Union 2016], U.S. law is fractured depending upon the type of information at issue. For example, certain federal laws restrict who can gather medical and genetic information about specific individuals [U.S. Congress 1996, 2008]. Another law prohibits disclosure of educational records [U.S. Congress 1974], and yet another regulates consumer records [U.S. Congress 1970]. The common law tort of invasion of privacy, which appears to apply broadly, is also limited in scope. Because the privacy tort aims to redress intrusions that are "highly offensive to a reasonable person," [U.S. Congress 1970]. it focuses on inquiries or exposures that are embarrassing or humiliating, for example, involving medical conditions or sexual practices. The assumption underlying much existing legal protections for privacy in the U.S. is that certain types of information are particularly sensitive and warrant special protection.

Other information that is viewed as non-sensitive or trivial can be collected with few restrictions.

At the same time, U.S. law has viewed privacy primarily as a matter of personal control over information and therefore has leaned heavily on a regime of notice and consent [Solove 2013]. Laws give people rights to know about and review information collected about them, and rights to agree to or refuse collection of their personal information. With this set of tools, they are expected to engage in "privacy self-management"–i.e., to protect their own interests by exercising their rights to access their data records or to withhold consent to their collection in the first place [Solove 2013]. This emphasis on consent has legitimated the collection and use of all manner of personal data, on the assumption that people are capable of protecting their own interests.

The growth of AI technologies has put increasing strain on this framework, rendering it largely ineffective in protecting personal information. To start, the need for large datasets to train AI tools has created enormous demand for increasingly comprehensive information about more people. At the same time, the explosion of available data and rapid advances in computing power have rendered the assumptions underlying traditional privacy protections increasingly obsolete. The distinction between "sensitive" and "non-sensitive" personal information is becoming meaningless. Small bits of information about individuals, such as their consumer purchases, may seem quite trivial when viewed in isolation, and therefore, not to warrant protection. However, AI can aggregate those data points across time and populations, then mine them for new insights, revealing highly sensitive information, such as sexual orientation, medical risks or conditions, or whether someone is pregnant. Because entities with large amounts of data can "derive the intimate from the available," [Calo 2017] prohibiting them from collecting "sensitive" data will not prevent them from inferring that same information. As a result, regulation solely at the sectoral level leaves large gaps in coverage.

For similar reasons, relying on consent to protect personal information is increasingly problematic in a world of big data and machine learning [Richards and Hartzog 2018, Solove 2013]. Privacy disclosures are notoriously long, complex, and difficult to understand. No one has the time or cognitive bandwidth to read and comprehend all of the privacy policies encountered in daily life in order to exercise meaningful choice about what information to share. Even if it were possible, many policies are non-negotiable, and people cannot realistically refuse the collection and use of their personal information when doing so is a condition of accessing essential services.

AI tools put pressure on the notice and consent regime in another way as well. Because AI can produce novel insights from existing data, or leverage information in wholly unanticipated ways, it is impossible for people to rationally weigh the costs and benefits of sharing their personal data. The downstream uses of that information and the potential impact on their interests are unknowable at the time they are asked to consent to its collection. The solution is not simply to provide better notice in the form of more information. The entity collecting the information cannot anticipate all possible future uses, especially if the data may be shared or combined with other datasets. And adding more detailed, technical, and contingent information to privacy disclosures would only increase information overload and further vitiate meaningful consent.

Insights derived from AI may render consent altogether irrelevant in some contexts. As computational tools have become more powerful, it is no longer necessary to collect information from a particular person in order to learn about that individual. Data collected from other people can reveal startling insights, as demonstrated by the use of genetic databases to identify murder suspects, even though the suspects themselves had never shared their genetic data. Thus, advances in AI have largely rendered obsolete the traditional US approach of relying on sectoral regulation, and notice and consent, to protect personal information.

The European Union has taken a different approach. The General Data Protection Regulation (GDPR) [European Union 2016], which became effective in 2018, takes an omnibus approach, applying to all entities that process personally identifiable data, rather than limiting its focus to particular sectors or types of entities. In addition, the GDPR imposes a more robust requirement of consent, rendering consent ineffective "where there is a clear imbalance between the data subject and the [data] controller" [European Union 2016]. In those situations, an entity may not rely on a thin conception of consent but must instead justify its processing of personal data by some other means, such as by demonstrating that doing so is necessary to meet legitimate needs.

Recently, jurisdictions in the U.S. have begun to explore omnibus approaches to protecting personal data. Most notably, California enacted the first comprehensive state-level consumer privacy law and was soon followed by numerous other states [State of California 2018, 2020, State of Colorado 2021, State of Utah 2022, State of Virginia 2022, U.S. State Privacy Legislation Tracker 2025]. These laws have largely built on traditional data protection principles, emphasizing protections such as consumers' rights to know what data is collected, and to correct or request deletion of their personal information.

While an omnibus approach to data privacy offers more comprehensive coverage for individuals' data privacy, the very breadth and generality of these statutes, and the need to provide for numerous exceptions, can undermine their efficacy in protecting personal information.

This brief review of anti-discrimination and data privacy laws illustrates how existing laws can address specific risks of AI as well as the limitations of these approaches. Lawmakers are also beginning to regulate AI directly. In addition to addressing the collection of personal data, the GDPR places requirements on entities that use automated processing systems when they produce legal or similarly significant effects on a person. [art. 22(1)] [European Union 2016]. Such entities must provide "meaningful information about the logic involved" [art. 14(2)(g)] and give individuals subject to those decisions the right "to obtain human intervention . . . and to contest the decision." [art. 22(3)] [European Union 2016]. Many U.S. state data protection laws take a similar approach, giving data subjects the right to opt-out of automated decisions. These types of protections are more procedural in nature, rather than attempting to directly regulate harmful uses of automated decision systems.

Although no laws specifically directed at AI have been passed in the U.S. at the national level, several states have enacted such laws, reaching beyond data privacy to directly address AI, especially generative AI; many other such laws have been proposed. These bills generally emphasize disclosure requirements for certain AI-generated content and assessment of risks, rather than substantive regulation of AI applications [US State AI Governance Legislation Tracker]. The EU's AI Act goes a step further and bans altogether some AI uses that pose an unacceptable risk of harm. This category of uses appears to be quite narrow, however, and for most uses of AI, including those that are "high risk", the regulation takes a softer regulatory approach as discussed in part 4.

In sum, traditional forms of legal regulation offer both advantages and disadvantages for shaping the development of AI. Unlike ethical principles, legal rules are more likely to be concrete, specific, and enforceable. At the same time, however, law often lags significantly behind social and technological developments.

The difficulties with relying on legal regulation, however, do not stem merely from time lags. Lawmaking requires clearly delineating what activities are permitted and which are forbidden, a daunting task given the complexity and rapidly evolving nature of AI. This challenge is heightened because the use cases for AI are pervasive throughout society and widely varied in application. What risks are tolerable, and how they should be weighed against potential benefits, will differ depending upon the context and the gravity of the harm threatened. Because of the limitations inherent in traditional forms of direct regulation, researchers and policymakers are increasingly turning to a broader array of policy tools to govern the development of AI.

15.4 Policy

Policy has a broader focus than traditional lawmaking, as it seeks to promote socially beneficial outcomes rather than redressing harms suffered by particular individuals. Legal liability regimes are typically backward looking, coming into play after harm has occurred and focusing on questions of causation, culpability, and compensation. In contrast, policy approaches are forward looking, emphasizing strategies to achieve broad societal goals such as preventing environmental degradation or improving population health outcomes. Policy is softer than law, leveraging a variety of tools in an effort to influence behavior toward the desired ends.

Law and policy are not mutually exclusive. Laws that impose liability for causing harm can be part of an overall policy strategy to discourage socially negative behavior. Conversely, many policy levers require legal action–for example, to provide public funds for research, to create incentives to pursue certain activities, or to establish government agencies with oversight powers. Despite the overlap between law and policy, it is useful to consider policy approaches as distinct from the traditional legal focus on retrospective liability.

Some of the reasons for turning to policy tools for governing the development of AI were suggested in the previous section. AI tools are technologically complex, and their inner workings are often opaque. Their complexity and the need for deep technical expertise to understand the risks and tradeoffs make it difficult for lawmakers to articulate clear rules delineating in advance precisely which uses are permissible and which are not. In addition, the black box nature of many AI systems makes questions of causation and responsibility, which are central to retrospective liability schemes, very difficult to resolve. Individuals who are harmed by AI technologies may lack access to the resources or the expert knowledge needed to effectively litigate these issues.

A further reason for turning to policy solutions is that an individual rights-based approach is inadequate for recognizing and addressing broad societal harms. Legal liability focuses on the impact of a particular activity on identifiable people, but some of the most troubling effects of AI are systemic in nature. For example, an individual discrimination lawsuit would turn on the specific reasons that a particular person was not hired or was denied a loan, overlooking problems that only appear in the aggregate. If predictive algorithms systematically and unjustifiably disadvantage certain demographic groups when distributing benefits or opportunities, those effects are unlikely to be visible from the perspective of an individual lawsuit. Similarly, privacy rights that focus on an individual's choice to share information miss the larger context in which the actions of countless other people and entities determine what is known about that person.

Because of the limitations of legal liability as a solution, attention has increasingly turned to other forms of governance. The European Union's GDPR takes steps in this direction in addition to the individual rights mentioned in part 3 above, by, for example, requiring entities that process personal data to comply with record-keeping requirements [art. 30] and to conduct impact assessments [art. 35] [European Union 2016]. The Regulation also empowers public agencies to order disclosure of certain information about automated decision systems and to conduct audits [art. 58(1)] [European Union 2016]. The EU's Artificial Intelligence Act goes further in this direction, requiring "high-risk" AI systems (systems that pose high risk to the health and safety or fundamental rights of natural persons) to undergo pre-market registration and assessment, as well as an ongoing, iterative process of identifying, evaluating, reporting, and managing risks once deployed [European Parliament 2024].

In the U.S., the National Institute of Standards and Technology has issued risk management frameworks to provide guidance that organizations developing AI can voluntarily follow [National Institute of Standards and Technology 2023, 2024, Schwartz et al. 2022]. President Biden issued an Executive Order seeking to develop policies to ensure the "safe, secure, and trustworthy" development of AI [The White House 2023] and his administration published a "Blueprint" intended to guide the design and deployment of AI in ways that protect civil rights and privacy [The White House 2022]. Those initiatives were revoked by President Trump, who issued his own executive order on AI that prioritized rapid development of the technology, the US's global dominance in AI, and the removal of regulations and guidelines that might slow the development of the technology [The White House 2025]. Thus, policy levers–depending upon who is wielding them–can work to reduce risks of societal harms, or to marginalize concerns about those risks.

Scholars and policymakers concerned about the risks of AI promote a wide array of strategies for governing the development of AI to ensure its safety and adherence to fundamental values. Their proposals include requiring that AI tools be licensed, subject to design standards, or undergo pre-market testing and certification, either by a government agency or trusted third party. Alternatively, particularly with highly regulated applications, government agencies could create regulatory sandboxes which permit companies to experiment with new technologies in a supervised and controlled environment. Other approaches emphasize the importance of self-assessment, imposing a duty on entities to consider the societal impacts of automated decision-making, and to take into account their effects on health and safety, the environment, or fundamental human rights. Once a system has been deployed, companies might be required to audit its real-world effects or to comply with mandated forms of public disclosure or reporting.

It is beyond the scope of this chapter to fully explore and evaluate these various policy tools for governing the development of AI. More generally, though, policy approaches offer distinct advantages and disadvantages as compared with traditional legal liability regimes. On the plus side, policy tools can be more open-ended and experimental in nature, allowing for flexibility and nimbleness in responding to evolving technology. Government agencies can undertake research about the variety of uses of AI, the likely future development of these technologies, and the possible outcomes they will produce. In doing so, they might involve technical experts as well as affected members of the public and thereby expand the range of stakeholders participating in developing policy beyond what is typical in the legislative process.

Policy levers can also be used to influence the development of AI ex ante–for example, by assuring conformity with technical standards or design principles for privacy and fairness. These strategies may be more effective than ex post efforts at regulation because it will be increasingly difficult to identify and remove problems after significant investments have been made in building complex systems. Finally, policy approaches offer the opportunity to widen the lens and view technological challenges in a broader social context. Doing so will expand the choice set of possible actions beyond narrowly technical solutions. For example, to the extent that AI substitutes for human labor, observers have raised alarms that it will cause massive unemployment. If these concerns are considered solely from a technical perspective, the alternatives seem quite stark–either ban or strictly restrict the development of AI, or accept massive unemployment and the resulting social dislocation it will likely cause. A broader policy perspective brings into view numerous related social policies, such as the level of investment in education and training, public provision of essential needs like health care and retirement income which are currently linked to employment, and other policies that shape how economic gains and wealth are distributed across the economy.

Policy tools have weaknesses as well, and relying on them will not guarantee that AI is developed in socially beneficial ways. To a large extent, the effectiveness of policy initiatives will depend upon which strategies are chosen, and the details of how they are implemented. If the policy levers chosen rely too heavily on procedural requirements, such as conducting assessments and filing reports, they may incentivize empty compliance gestures at the expense of taking concrete steps to prevent harm. Similarly, a system premised on self-regulation by affected firms runs the risk of being toothless without clear standards by which to measure compliance and meaningful enforcement mechanisms. Giving government agencies power to promulgate and enforce appropriate regulations may be more effective; however, there remains a risk of regulatory capture, where actors from the regulated industry influence or even dominate the government agencies that are tasked with overseeing them.

Many current and proposed strategies for governing the development of AI rest on a model of risk regulation. That approach makes some sense given the reasons that AI systems pose risks: they are technologically complex, difficult to understand, and likely to fail, but in ways that are difficult to predict. On the other hand, a risk regulation model has inherent limitations when applied to AI [Kaminski 2023]. Some of the harms threatened by AI, such as privacy intrusions and discrimination, do not fit easily into traditional risk models because they are difficult to measure or quantify, and their very meaning is contested. They are not purely technical challenges but rather pose "hybrid technical-policy problems" that should be solved through public consideration and debate rather than by technical experts [Kaminski 2023]. And while risk regulation tools can be useful in mitigating future harms, another significant limitation is that they typically lack a mechanism for compensating people who actually suffer harm.

15.5 Conclusion

AI technologies promise many benefits, but they can also have significant negative impacts on human health, safety, well-being, and fundamental rights. Ethical, legal, and policy approaches offer tools to address these concerns; however, each has limitations, and none provides a complete solution in itself. Statements of ethical principles can articulate high-level values and goals to guide behavior, but are usually quite vague and difficult to operationalize. They also lack any enforcement mechanism. In contrast, legal rules are enforceable through court action and offer a way to compensate those suffering actual harms. However, the complexity and opacity of AI poses challenges to legal liability regimes by making it difficult to parse questions of causation and culpability. In addition, legal rules may not keep up with the rapid evolution of AI technologies. Policy tools are more flexible and forward-looking, and can help to anticipate and prevent harms, but may be ineffective if they lack robust standards or fail to require meaningful accountability from those who develop and deploy AI tools. Because each strategy has strengths and limitations, preventing social harms from the application of AI will require leveraging all three types of tools in complementary ways.

Bibliography

A. E. Abbas, M. Tambe, and D. Von Winterfeldt. 2017. *Improving Homeland Security Decisions*. Cambridge University Press.

M. Abdel-Aty, A. Pande, A. Das, and W. J. Knibbe. 2008. Assessing safety on Dutch freeways with data from infrastructure-based intelligent transportation systems. *Transportation Research Record*, 2083(1): 153–161. ISSN 0361-1981.

H. T. Abdelwahab and M. A. Abdel-Aty. 2002. Artificial neural networks and logit models for traffic safety analysis of toll plazas. *Transportation Research Record*, 1784(1): 115–125. ISSN 0361-1981. .

A. Abdulkadiroğlu and T. Sönmez. 2003. School choice: A mechanism design approach. *American economic review*, 93(3): 729–747.

A. Abdulkadiroğlu, P. Pathak, A. Roth, and T. Sönmez. May 2005a. The boston public school match. *American Economic Review*, 95(2): 368–371.

A. Abdulkadiroğlu, P. A. Pathak, and A. E. Roth. 2005b. The new york city high school match. *American Economic Review*, 95(2): pp. 364–367. ISSN 00028282. http://www.jstor.org/stable/4132848.

Civil Rights Act. 1964. Title VII of the Civil Rights Act of 1964. *Retrieved October*, 21: 2005.

A. Agarwal, A. Beygelzimer, M. Dudík, J. Langford, and H. Wallach. 2018. A reductions approach to fair classification. In *International Conference on Machine Learning*, pp. 60–69.

D. Ahn. 2006. The stages of event extraction. In *Workshop on Annotating and Reasoning About Time and Events*, pp. 1–8.

M. Akbarpour, S. Malladi, and A. Saberi. 2018. Diffusion, seeding, and the value of network information. In *Proceedings of the 2018 ACM Conference on Economics and Computation*, pp. 641–641.

M. M. Al Rahhal, Y. Bazi, H. AlHichri, N. Alajlan, F. Melgani, and R. R. Yager. 2016. Deep learning approach for active classification of electrocardiogram signals. *Information Sciences*, 345: 340–354.

M. Albach and J. R. Wright. 2021. The role of accuracy in algorithmic process fairness across multiple domains. In *ACM Conference on Economics and Computation*, pp. 29–49.

A. Aliamiri and Y. Shen. 2018. Deep learning based atrial fibrillation detection using wearable photoplethysmography sensor. In *Biomedical & Health Informatics (BHI), 2018 IEEE EMBS International Conference on*, pp. 442–445. IEEE.

J. Alonso-Mora, S. Samaranayake, A. Wallar, E. Frazzoli, and D. Rus. 2017. On-demand high-capacity ride-sharing via dynamic trip-vehicle assignment. *Proceedings of the National Academy of Sciences*, 114(3): 462–467.

B. An, J. Pita, E. Shieh, M. Tambe, C. Kiekintveld, and J. Marecki. March 2011. Guards and protect: Next generation applications of security games. In *SIGECOM*, volume 10, pp. 31–34.

J. Angwin, J. Larson, S. Mattu, and L. Kirchner. 2016. Machine bias. *ProPublica*.

A. H. Anwar and C. A. Kamhoua. 2022. Cyber deception using honeypot allocation and diversity: A game theoretic approach. In *Annual Consumer Communications & Networking Conference*, pp. 543–549.

K. Arulkumaran, M. P. Deisenroth, M. Brundage, and A. A. Bharath. 2017. Deep reinforcement learning: A brief survey. *IEEE Signal Processing Magazine*, 34(6): 26–38.

A. Athalye, N. Carlini, and D. Wagner. 2018. Obfuscated gradients give a false sense of security: Circumventing defenses to adversarial examples. In *International Conference on Machine Learning*, pp. 274–283.

B. Aydin, V. Akkineni, and R. A. Angryk. 2016. Modeling and indexing spatiotemporal trajectory data in non-relational databases. In *Managing Big Data in Cloud Computing Environments*, pp. 133–162. IGI Global.

A. Ayman, M. Wilbur, A. Sivagnanam, P. Pugliese, A. Dubey, and A. Laszka. September 2020. Data-driven prediction of route-level energy use for mixed-vehicle transit fleets. In *6th IEEE International Conference on Smart Computing (SMARTCOMP)*, pp. 41–48.

A. Ayman, A. Sivagnanam, M. Wilbur, P. Pugliese, A. Dubey, and A. Laszka. February 2022. Data-driven prediction and optimization of energy use for transit fleets of electric and ice vehicles. *ACM Transactions on Internet Technology*, 22(1): 7:1–7:29.

E. Bagdasaryan, A. Veit, Y. Hua, D. Estrin, and V. Shmatikov. 2020. How to backdoor federated learning. In *International Conference on Artificial Intelligence and Statistics*, pp. 2938–2948.

A. Banerjee, A. G. Chandrasekhar, E. Duflo, and M. O. Jackson. 2013. The diffusion of microfinance. *Science*, 341(6144).

A. Banerjee, A. G. Chandrasekhar, E. Duflo, and M. O. Jackson. 2019. Using gossips to spread information: Theory and evidence from two randomized controlled trials. *The Review of Economic Studies*, 86(6): 2453–2490.

J. Bao, P. Liu, and S. V. Ukkusuri. 2019. A spatiotemporal deep learning approach for citywide short-term crash risk prediction with multi-source data. *Accident Analysis & Prevention*, 122: 239–254. ISSN 0001-4575. .

S. Barocas and A. D. Selbst. 2016. Big data's disparate impact. *Calif. L. Rev.*, 104: 671.

S. Barocas, M. Hardt, and A. Narayanan. 2023. *Fairness and machine learning: Limitations and opportunities*. MIT Press.

A. Barragán-Montero, U. Javaid, G. Valdés, D. Nguyen, P. Desbordes, B. Macq, S. Willems, L. Vandewinckele, M. Holmström, F. Löfman, et al. 2021. Artificial intelligence and machine learning for medical imaging: A technology review. *Physica Medica*, 83: 242–256.

N. Basilico, A. Celli, G. De Nittis, and N. Gatti. 2017. Coordinating multiple defensive resources in patrolling games with alarm systems. In *AAMAS'17*, pp. 678–686.

H. Bastani, K. Drakopoulos, and V. Gupta. 2021. Efficient and targeted COVID-19 border testing via reinforcement learning. Nature, 599: 108–113.

A. Benton, M. Mitchell, and D. Hovy. 2017. Multi-task learning for mental health using social media text. In *Proceedings of EACL*.

D. Bertsimas and J. N. Tsitsiklis. 1997. *Introduction to Linear Optimization*. Athena Scientific.

E. Beyazit. 2011. Evaluating social justice in transport: lessons to be learned from the capability approach. *Transport Reviews*, 31(1): 117–134.

A. N. Bhagoji, S. Chakraborty, P. Mittal, and S. Calo. 2019. Analyzing federated learning through an adversarial lens. In *International Conference on Machine Learning*, pp. 634–643.

B. Biggio, I. Corona, D. Maiorca, B. Nelson, N. Srndic, P. Laskov, G. Giacinto, and F. Roli. 2013. Evasion attacks against machine learning at test time. In *European Conference on Machine Learning and Knowledge Discovery in Databases*, pp. 387–402.

R. Binns, M. Van Kleek, M. Veale, U. Lyngs, J. Zhao, and N. Shadbolt. 2018. 'it's reducing a human being to a percentage' perceptions of justice in algorithmic decisions. In *CHI Conference on Human Factors in Computing Systems*, pp. 1–14.

E. Black, J. L. Koepke, P. T. Kim, S. Barocas, and M. Hsu. 2024. Less discriminatory algorithms. *Geo. LJ*, 113: 53.

K. Bonawitz, V. Ivanov, B. Kreuter, A. Marcedone, H. B. McMahan, S. Patel, D. Ramage, A. Segal, and K. Seth. 2017. Practical secure aggregation for privacy-preserving machine learning. In *Proceedings of the 2017 ACM SIGSAC Conference on Computer and Communications Security*, pp. 1175–1191.

J. A. Bonneson and P. T. McCoy. 1993. Estimation of safety at two-way stop-controlled intersections on rural highways. *Transportation Research Record*, (1401): 83–89.

C. Borgs, M. Brautbar, J. Chayes, and B. Lucier. 2014. Maximizing social influence in nearly optimal time. In *Proceedings of the twenty-fifth annual ACM-SIAM Symposium on Discrete Algorithms*, pp. 946–957. SIAM.

V. A. Borza, E. W. Clayton, M. Kantarcioglu, Y. Vorobeychik, and B. A. Malin. 2022. A representativeness-informed model for research record selection from electronic medical record systems. In *AMIA Annual Symposium Proceedings*, p. 259.

V. A. Borza, A. Estornell, E. W. Clayton, C.-J. Ho, R. L. Rothman, Y. Vorobeychik, and B. A. Malin. 2025. Adaptive recruitment resource allocation to improve cohort representativeness in participatory biomedical datasets. In *AMIA Annual Symposium Proceedings*, p. 192.

H. Bray and S. Talcott. June 18 2005. Firm says up to 40m credit card files stolen. *Boston Globe*.

C. B. Browne, E. Powley, D. Whitehouse, S. M. Lucas, P. I. Cowling, P. Rohlfshagen, S. Tavener, D. Perez, S. Samothrakis, and S. Colton. 2012. A survey of monte carlo tree search methods. *IEEE Transactions on Computational Intelligence and AI in Games*, 4(1): 1–43.

J. Bruna, W. Zaremba, A. Szlam, and Y. Lecun. 2013. Spectral networks and locally connected networks on graphs. *arXiv: Learning*.

J. Buolamwini and T. Gebru. 2018a. Gender shades: Intersectional accuracy disparities in commercial gender classification. In *Conference on fairness, accountability and transparency*, pp. 77–91. PMLR.

J. Buolamwini and T. Gebru. 2018b. Gender shades: Intersectional accuracy disparities in commercial gender classification. In *Conference on fairness, accountability and transparency*, pp. 77–91.

T. U. S. C. Bureau, 2023. Longitudinal employer-household dynamics. https://lehd.ces.census.gov/data/.

J. Cai, A. De Janvry, and E. Sadoulet. 2015. Social networks and the decision to insure. *American Economic Journal: Applied Economics*, 7(2): 81–108.

R. Calo. 2017. Artificial intelligence policy: a primer and roadmap. *UCDL Rev.*, 51: 399.

N. Carlini and D. A. Wagner. 2017. Towards evaluating the robustness of neural networks. *IEEE Symposium on Security and Privacy*, pp. 39–57.

G. M. Carter, J. M. Chaiken, and E. Ignall. 1972. Response areas for two emergency units. *Operations Research*, 20(3): 571–594.

C. Cath, S. Wachter, B. Mittelstadt, M. Taddeo, and L. Floridi. 2018. Artificial intelligence and the 'good society': the us, eu, and uk approach. *Science and engineering ethics*, 24(2): 505–528.

Center of Disease Control and Prevention, 2019. Road traffic injuries and deaths – a global problem. https://www.cdc.gov/injury/features/global-road-safety/index.html.

G. Chamberlain. 1982. Multivariate regression models for panel data. *Journal of econometrics*, 18(1): 5–46.

C. P. Chambers and M. B. Yenmez. August 2017. Choice and matching. *American Economic Journal: Microeconomics*, 9(3): 126–47.

L. Y. Chang. 2005. Analysis of freeway accident frequencies: negative binomial regression versus artificial neural network. *Safety Science*, 43(8): 541–557. ISSN 0925-7535.

X. Chang, Z. Ma, Y. Yang, Z. Zeng, and A. G. Hauptmann. 2016. Bi-level semantic representation analysis for multimedia event detection. *IEEE Transactions on Cybernetics*, 47(5): 1180–1197.

K. Chaudhary, O. B. Poirion, L. Lu, and L. Garmire. 2017. Deep learning based multi-omics integration robustly predicts survival in liver cancer. *bioRxiv*, p. 114892.

Z. Che, S. Purushotham, R. Khemani, and Y. Liu. 2015. Distilling knowledge from deep networks with applications to healthcare domain. *arXiv preprint arXiv:1512.03542*.

R. Chen, I. C. Paschalidis, et al. 2020. Distributionally robust learning. *Foundations and Trends® in Optimization*, 4(1-2): 1–243.

S. Chen, Y. Ji, and L. Tong. 2012. Deadline scheduling for large scale charging of electric vehicles with renewable energy. In *2012 IEEE 7th Sensor Array and Multichannel Signal Processing Workshop (SAM)*, pp. 13–16. IEEE.

W. Chen, Y. Wang, and S. Yang. 2009. Efficient influence maximization in social networks. In *Proceedings of the 15th ACM SIGKDD international conference on Knowledge discovery and data mining*, pp. 199–208.

W. Chen, C. Wang, and Y. Wang. 2010. Scalable influence maximization for prevalent viral marketing in large-scale social networks. In *Proceedings of the 16th ACM SIGKDD International Conference on Knowledge discovery and Data Mining*, pp. 1029–1038.

W. Chen, Y. Wang, and Y. Yuan. 2013. Combinatorial multi-armed bandit: General framework and applications. In *International Conference on Machine Learning*, pp. 151–159.

W. Chen, J. Wilson, S. Tyree, K. Weinberger, and Y. Chen. 2015a. Compressing neural networks with the hashing trick. In *International Conference on Machine Learning*, pp. 2285–2294.

W. Chen, T. Lin, Z. Tan, M. Zhao, and X. Zhou. 2016a. Robust influence maximization. In *Proceedings of the 22nd ACM SIGKDD International Conference on Knowledge Discovery and Data Mining*, pp. 795–804.

Y. Chen, L. Xu, K. Liu, D. Zeng, and J. Zhao. 2015b. Event extraction via dynamic multi-pooling convolutional neural networks. In *International Joint Conference on Natural Language Processing*, pp. 167–176.

Y. Chen, T. Chen, Z. Xu, N. Sun, and O. Temam. 2016b. Diannao family: energy-efficient hardware accelerators for machine learning. *Communications of the ACM*, 59(11): 105–112.

Y. Chen, G. Wu, R. Sun, A. Dubey, A. Laszka, and P. Pugliese. March 2021. A review and outlook on energy consumption estimation models for electric vehicles. *SAE International Journal of Sustainable Transportation, Energy, Environment, & Policy*, 2(1): 79–96.

Y. Cheng, F. Wang, P. Zhang, and J. Hu. 2016. Risk prediction with electronic health records: A deep learning approach. In *Proceedings of the 2016 SIAM International Conference on Data Mining*, pp. 432–440. SIAM.

M. Cheung and J. M. Moura. 2020. Graph neural networks for covid-19 drug discovery. In *2020 IEEE International Conference on Big Data (Big Data)*, pp. 5646–5648. IEEE.

A. Chin, D. Eckles, and J. Ugander. 2018. Evaluating stochastic seeding strategies in networks. *arXiv preprint arXiv:1809.09561*.

E. Choi, Z. Xu, Y. Li, M. Dusenberry, G. Flores, E. Xue, and A. Dai. 2020. Learning the graphical structure of electronic health records with graph convolutional transformer. In *Proceedings of the AAAI conference on artificial intelligence*, volume 34, pp. 606–613.

F. Chollet et al., 2015. Keras. https://keras.io.

J. Chung, C. Gulcehre, K. Cho, and Y. Bengio. 2014. Empirical evaluation of gated recurrent neural networks on sequence modeling. *arXiv preprint arXiv:1412.3555*.

R. Church and C. ReVelle. 1974. The maximal covering location problem. volume 32, pp. 101–118.

D. K. Citron and F. Pasquale. 2014. The scored society: Due process for automated predictions. *Wash. L. Rev.*, 89: 1.

C. Clifton, M. Kantarcıoğlu, X. Lin, J. Vaidya, and M. Zhu. Jan. 2003. Tools for privacy preserving distributed data mining. *SIGKDD Explorations*, 4(2): 28–34.

J. M. Cohen, E. Rosenfeld, and J. Z. Kolter. 2019. Certified adversarial robustness via randomized smoothing. In *International Conference on Machine Learning*.

S. Corbett-Davies, E. Pierson, A. Feller, S. Goel, and A. Huq. 2017. Algorithmic decision making and the cost of fairness. In *ACM SIGKDD International Conference on Knowledge Discovery and Data Mining*, pp. 797–806.

K. J. Cormican, D. P. Morton, and R. K. Wood. 1998. Stochastic network interdiction. *Operations Research*, 46(2): 184–197.

Crisis Response. How waze crowdsourcing navigation app can help emergency services. https://www.crisis-response.com/Articles/594337/How_Waze_crowdsourcing.aspx.

N. Dalvi, P. Domingos, Mausam, S. Sanghai, and D. Verma. 2004. Adversarial classification. In *SIGKDD International Conference on Knowledge Discovery and Data Mining*, pp. 99–108.

P. Danaee, R. Ghaeini, and D. A. Hendrix. 2016. A deep learning approach for cancer detection and relevant gene identification. In *Pacific Symposium on Biocomputing*, volume 22, p. 219. NIH Public Access.

M. S. Daskin. 1983. A maximum expected covering location model: Formulation, properties and heuristic solution. *Transportation Science*, 17(1): 48–70.

C. De Cauwer, W. Verbeke, T. Coosemans, S. Faid, and J. Van Mierlo. 2017. A data-driven method for energy consumption prediction and energy-efficient routing of electric vehicles in real-world conditions. *Energies*, 10(5): 608.

J. A. Deacon, C. V. Zegeer, and R. C. Deen. 1974. Identification of hazardous rural highway locations. *Transportation Research Record*, 543.

J. Deng, J. Guo, N. Xue, and S. Zafeiriou. 2019. Arcface: Additive angular margin loss for deep face recognition. In *Proceedings of the IEEE Conference on Computer Vision and Pattern Recognition*, pp. 4690–4699.

U. Department of Homeland Security, 2019. Phases of Emergency Management.

F. Dernoncourt, J. Y. Lee, O. Uzuner, and P. Szolovits. 2017. De-identification of patient notes with recurrent neural networks. *Journal of the American Medical Informatics Association*, 24(3): 596–606.

W. Dieterich, C. Mendoza, and T. Brennan. 2016. Compas risk scales: Demonstrating accuracy equity and predictive parity. *Northpointe Inc*, 7(4): 1–36.

G. Dong, M. Tang, L. Cai, L. E. Barnes, and M. Boukhechba. 2021. Semi-supervised graph instance transformer for mental health inference. In *2021 20th IEEE International Conference on Machine Learning and Applications (ICMLA)*, pp. 1221–1228. IEEE.

N. Du, Y. Liang, M. Balcan, and L. Song. 2014. Influence function learning in information diffusion networks. In *International Conference on Machine Learning*, pp. 2016–2024.

R. Duffy, F. A. St John, B. Büscher, and D. Brockington. 2015. The militarization of anti-poaching: undermining long term goals? *Environmental Conservation*, 42(4): 345–348.

C. Dwork, F. McSherry, K. Nissim, and A. Smith. 2006. Calibrating noise to sensitivity in private data analysis. In *TCC*, pp. 265–284. Springer.

C. Dwork, M. Hardt, T. Pitassi, O. Reingold, and R. Zemel. 2012. Fairness through awareness. In *Innovations in Theoretical Computer Science Conference*, pp. 214–226.

F. Echenique and M. B. Yenmez. August 2015. How to control controlled school choice. *American Economic Review*, 105(8): 2679–2694.

L. Edwards and M. Veale. 2017. Slave to the algorithm? why a'right to an explanation'is probably not the remedy you are looking for. *Duke L. & Tech. Rev.*, 16: 18.

L. Ehlers and T. Morrill. 2020. (il) legal assignments in school choice. *The Review of Economic Studies*, 87(4): 1837–1875.

L. Ehlers, I. E. Hafalir, M. B. Yenmez, and M. A. Yildirim. 2014. School choice with controlled choice constraints: Hard bounds versus soft bounds. *Journal of Economic Theory*, 153: 648–683.

EIA, 2018. U.S. Energy Information Administration: Use of energy explained – energy use for transportation (2018). https://www.eia.gov/energyexplained/use-of-energy/transportation.php, Accessed: May 31st, 2020.

EPA, 2020. U.S. Transportation Sector Greenhouse Gas Emissions. https://nepis.epa.gov/Exe/ZyPDF.cgi?Dockey=P100ZK4P.pdf, Accessed: September 9th, 2020.

E. Erkut, A. Ingolfsson, and G. ErdoÄ§an. 2008. Ambulance location for maximum survival. *Naval Research Logistics*, 55(1): 42–58.

A. Estornell, T. Zhang, S. Das, C.-J. Ho, B. Juba, and Y. Vorobeychik. 2024. The impact of features used by algorithms on perceptions of fairness. In *International Joint Conference on Artificial Intelligence*, pp. 376–384.

European Commission High-Level Expert Group on Artificial Intelligence, 2019. Ethics Guidelines for Trustworthy Artificial Intelligence. https://digital-strategy.ec.europa.eu/en/library/ethics-guidelines-trustworthy-ai.

European Emergency Number Association, 2018. Exploring the use of waze for emergency response: A pilot project by waze and eena. https://eena.org/knowledge-hub/documents/waze-project-final-report/.

European Parliament, 2024. Laying down harmonised rules on artificial intelligence (Artificial Intelligence Act).

European Union, 2016. Regulation (eu) 2016/679 of the european parliament and of the council. *Regulation (eu)*, 679(2016): 10–13.

S. Even, O. Goldreich, and A. Lempel. 1985. A randomized protocol for signing contracts. *Communications of the ACM*, 28(6): 637–647.

K. Eykholt, I. Evtimov, E. Fernandes, B. Li, A. Rahmati, C. Xiao, A. Prakash, T. Kohno, and D. Song. 2018. Robust physical-world attacks on deep learning visual classification. In *Computer Vision and Pattern Recognition*.

F. Fang, T. Nguyen, B. Ford, N. Sintov, and M. Tambe. 2015. Introduction to green security games. In *International Joint Conference on Artificial Intelligence*.

F. Fang, T. H. Nguyen, R. Pickles, W. Y. Lam, G. R. Clements, B. An, A. Singh, B. C. Schwedock, M. Tambe, and A. Lemieux. 2017. PAWS - A deployed game-theoretic application to combat poaching. *AI Magazine*. http://www.aaai.org/ojs/index.php/aimagazine/article/view/2710.

S. S. Fatima, M. Wooldridge, and N. R. Jennings. 2006. Multi-issue negotiation with deadlines. *Journal of Artificial Intelligence Research*, 27: 381–417.

Federal Highway Administration, 2003. Status of the nation's highways, bridges, and transit: 2002 conditions and performance report.

S. L. Feld. 1991. Why your friends have more friends than you do. *American Journal of Sociology*, 96(6): 1464–1477.

J. Filar and K. Vrieze. 1997. *Competitive Markov Decision Processes*. Springer-Verlag.

J. Fjeld, N. Achten, H. Hilligoss, A. Nagy, and M. Srikumar. 2020. Principled artificial intelligence: Mapping consensus in ethical and rights-based approaches to principles for ai. *Berkman Klein Center Research Publication*, (2020-1).

L. Floridi, J. Cowls, T. C. King, and M. Taddeo. 2020. How to design AI for social good: Seven essential factors. *Sci Eng Ethics*.

K. M. Fodchuk and E. J. Sidebotham. 2005. Procedural justice in the selection process: a review of research and suggestions for practical applications. *The Psychologist-Manager Journal*, 8(2): 105–120.

P. Fogla, M. Sharif, R. Perdisci, O. Kolesnikov, and W. Lee. 2006. Polymorphic blending attacks. In *USENIX Security Symposium.*

J. Frantzeskakis, V. Assimakopoulos, and G. Kindinis. 1994. Interurban accident prediction by administrative area application in greece. *Institution of Transportation Engineers Journal*, 64(1): 35–42.

B. C. M. Fung, K. Wang, and P. S. Yu. 2005. Top-down specialization for information and privacy preservation. In *ICDE '05*, pp. 205–216. Washington, DC, USA.

Future of Life Institute., 2017. Asilomar AI Principles. https://futureoflife.org/2017/08/11/ai-principles/.

C. Gan, N. Wang, Y. Yang, D.-Y. Yeung, and A. G. Hauptmann. 2015. Devnet: A deep event network for multimedia event detection and evidence recounting. In *Conference on Computer Vision and Pattern Recognition*, pp. 2568–2577.

Y. Gao, S. Guo, J. Ren, Z. Zhao, A. Ehsan, and Y. Zheng. 2018. An electric bus power consumption model and optimization of charging scheduling concerning multi-external factors. *Energies*, 11(8): 2060.

N. Garg and D. Grosu. 2007. Deception in honeynets: A game-theoretic analysis. In *IEEE SMC Information Assurance and Security Workshop*, pp. 107–113.

A. Gelman. 2006. Multilevel (hierarchical) modeling: what it can and cannot do. *Technometrics*, 48(3): 432–435.

M. Gendreau, G. Laporte, and F. Semet. 1997. Solving an ambulance location model by tabu search. *Location Science*, 5(2): 75–88.

R. C. Geyer, T. Klein, and M. Nabi. 2017. Differentially private federated learning: A client level perspective. *arXiv preprint arXiv:1712.07557.*

C. Gill, D. Weisburd, C. W. Telep, and T. Bennett. 2014. Community-oriented policing to reduce crime, disorder and fear and increase satisfaction and legitimacy among citizens: A systematic review. *Journal of Experimental Criminology.*

O. Goldreich. 2004. *The Foundations of Cryptography*, volume 2, chapter General Cryptographic Protocols. Cambridge University Press. http://www.wisdom.weizmann.ac.il/~oded/PSBookFrag/prot.ps.

I. Goodfellow, J. Pouget-Abadie, M. Mirza, B. Xu, D. Warde-Farley, S. Ozair, A. Courville, and Y. Bengio. 2014. Generative adversarial nets. *Advances in neural information processing systems*, 27.

I. Goodfellow, J. Shlens, and C. Szegedy. 2015. Explaining and harnessing adversarial examples. In *International Conference on Learning Representations.*

Google, 2022a. General transit feed specification (GTFS) real-time overview. https://developers.google.com/transit/gtfs-realtime/,.

Google, 2022b. General transit feed specification (GTFS) static overview. https://developers.google.com/transit/gtfs/.

A. Goyal, W. Lu, and L. V. Lakshmanan. 2011. Celf++ optimizing the greedy algorithm for influence maximization in social networks. In *Proceedings of the 20th International Conference Companion on World Wide Web*, pp. 47–48.

H. D. Green Jr, K. de la Haye, J. S. Tucker, and D. Golinelli. 2013. Shared risk: who engages in substance use with American homeless youth? *Addiction*, 108(9): 1618–1624.

D. Greene, A. L. Hoffmann, and L. Stark. 2019. Better, nicer, clearer, fairer: A critical assessment of the movement for ethical artificial intelligence and machine learning.

H. Greenspan, B. van Ginneken, and R. M. Summers. 2016. Guest editorial deep learning in medical imaging: Overview and future promise of an exciting new technique. *IEEE Transactions on Medical Imaging*, 35(5): 1153–1159.

N. Grgic-Hlaca, E. M. Redmiles, K. P. Gummadi, and A. Weller. 2018. Human perceptions of fairness in algorithmic decision making: A case study of criminal risk prediction. In *World Wide Web Conference*, pp. 903–912.

N. Grgić-Hlača, M. B. Zafar, K. P. Gummadi, and A. Weller. 2018. Beyond distributive fairness in algorithmic decision making: Feature selection for procedurally fair learning. In *AAAI Conference on Artificial Intelligence*.

R. Grishman, D. Westbrook, and A. Meyers. 2005. Nyu's english ace 2005 system description. In *ACE 2005 Evaluation Workshop*.

N. R. Group et al. 2010. Results of the NIMH collaborative HIV/sexually transmitted disease prevention trial of a community popular opinion leader intervention. *Journal of Acquired Immune Deficiency Syndromes*, 54(2): 204–214.

Q. Guo, B. An, B. Bosansky, and C. Kiekintveld. 2017. Comparing strategic secrecy and stackelberg commitment in security games. In *IJCAI-17*.

I. E. Hafalir, M. B. Yenmez, and M. A. Yildirim. May 2013. Effective affirmative action in school choice. *Theoretical Economics*, 8(2): 325–363.

T. Hagendorff. 2020. The ethics of ai ethics: An evaluation of guidelines. *Minds and machines*, 30(1): 99–120.

M. Haklay and P. Weber. 2008. OpenStreetMap: User-generated street maps. *IEEE Pervasive Computing*, 7(4): 12–18.

W. L. Hamilton, Z. Ying, and J. Leskovec. 2017. Inductive representation learning on large graphs. pp. 1024–1034.

A. Hard, C. M. Kiddon, D. Ramage, F. Beaufays, H. Eichner, K. Rao, R. Mathews, and S. Augenstein, 2018. Federated learning for mobile keyboard prediction. https://arxiv.org/abs/1811.03604.

M. Hardt, E. Price, and N. Srebro. 2016. Equality of opportunity in supervised learning. In *Neural Information Processing Systems*.

E. Harris and F. Fessenden. 2017. The broken promises of choice in new york city schools. *New York Times, May*, 5.

D. Harvey. 2010. *Social justice and the city*, volume 1. University of Georgia press.

S. Hassold and A. Ceder. 2014. Improving energy efficiency of public transport bus services by using multiple vehicle types. *Transportation Research Record*, 2415(1): 65–71.

J. W. Hatfield and P. R. Milgrom. September 2005. Matching with contracts. *American Economic Review*, 95(4): 913–935.

S. H. Hattis. 2015. *Crime in the United States*. Lanham Bernan Press.

X. He and D. Kempe. 2018. Stability and robustness in influence maximization. *ACM Transactions on Knowledge Discovery from Data (TKDD)*, 12(6): 1–34.

X. He, K. Xu, D. Kempe, and Y. Liu. 2016. Learning influence functions from incomplete observations. In *Advances in Neural Information Processing Systems*, pp. 2073–2081.

G. Hinton, L. Deng, D. Yu, G. E. Dahl, A.-r. Mohamed, N. Jaitly, A. Senior, V. Vanhoucke, P. Nguyen, T. N. Sainath, et al. 2012. Deep neural networks for acoustic modeling in speech recognition: The shared views of four research groups. *IEEE Signal Processing Magazine*, 29(6): 82–97.

G. E. Hinton and T. J. Sejnowski. 1986. Learning and relearning in boltzmann machines. *Parallel Distributed Processing*, 1.

G. E. Hinton, S. Osindero, and Y.-W. Teh. 2006. A fast learning algorithm for deep belief nets. *Neural computation*, 18(7): 1527–1554.

S. Hochreiter and J. Schmidhuber. 1997. Long short-term memory. *Neural computation*, 9(8): 1735–1780.

K. Holkar and L. M. Waghmare. 2010. An overview of model predictive control. *International Journal of control and automation*, 3(4): 47–63.

P. Houlden, S. LaTour, L. Walker, and J. Thibaut. 1978. Preference for modes of dispute resolution as a function of process and decision control. *Journal of Experimental Social Psychology*, 14(1): 13–30.

L. Hu, B. Wilder, A. Yadav, E. Rice, and M. Tambe. 2018. Activating the "breakfast club": Modeling influence spread in natural-world social networks. International Foundation for Autonomous Agents and Multiagent Systems, Stockholm, Sweden.

S. Huang and S. Ontañón. 2020. A closer look at invalid action masking in policy gradient algorithms. *arXiv preprint arXiv:2006.14171*.

A. Z. Huq. 2020. A right to a human decision. *Va. L. Rev.*, 106: 611.

C. Ilvento. 2020. Metric learning for individual fairness. In *Symposium on Foundations of Responsible Computing*.

A. Ilyas, S. Santurkar, D. Tsipras, L. Engstrom, B. Tran, and A. Madry. 2019. Adversarial examples are not bugs, they are features. In *Advances in Neural Information Processing Systems*.

Information Technology Industry Council, 2021. ITI's Global AI Policy Recommendations. https://www.itic.org/documents/artificial-intelligence/ITI_GlobalAIPrinciples_032321_v3.pdf.

INRIX, 2022. Inrix traffic. https://inrix.com/.

I. Ioannidis and A. Grama. Jan. 6-9 2003. An efficient protocol for Yao's millionaires' problem. In *Hawaii International Conference on System Sciences (HICSS-36)*, pp. 205–210. Waikoloa Village, Hawaii.

M. Jain, J. Tsai, J. Pita, C. Kiekintveld, S. Rathi, M. Tambe, and F. Ordónez. 2010. Software assistants for randomized patrol planning for the lax airport police and the federal air marshal service. *Interfaces*.

M. Jain, D. Korzhyk, O. Vaněk, V. Conitzer, M. Pěchouček, and M. Tambe. 2011. A double oracle algorithm for zero-sum security games on graphs. In *International Conference on Autonomous Agents and Multiagent Systems*, pp. 327–334. Citeseer.

H. Jaldell. 2017. How important is the time factor? saving lives using fire and rescue services. *Fire Technology*, 53(2): 695–708.

H. Ji and R. Grishman. 2008. Refining event extraction through cross-document inference. In *Annual Meeting of the Association for Computational Linguistics*, pp. 254–262.

A. Jobin, M. Ienca, and E. Vayena. 2019. The global landscape of ai ethics guidelines. *Nature machine intelligence*, 1(9): 389–399.

W. Joe and H. C. Lau. 2020. Deep reinforcement learning approach to solve dynamic vehicle routing problem with stochastic customers. In *Conference on Automated Planning and Scheduling (ICAPS)*, volume 30, pp. 394–402.

J. Roach, 2018. Microsoft improves facial recognition to perform well across all skin tones. The AI Blog. https://blogs.microsoft.com/ai/gender-skin-tone-facial-recognition-improvement/.

S. C. Joshua and N. J. Garber. 1990. Estimating truck accident rate and involvements using linear and poisson regression models. *Transportation Planning and Technology*, 15(1): 41–58.

P. P. Jovanis and H.-L. Chang. 1986. Modeling the relationship of accidents to miles traveled. *Transportation Research Record*, 1068: 42–51.

L. H. Kaack, P. L. Donti, E. Strubell, G. Kamiya, F. Creutzig, and D. Rolnick. 2022. Aligning artificial intelligence with climate change mitigation. *Nature Climate Change*, 12(6): 518–527.

D. Kalimeris, Y. Singer, K. Subbian, and U. Weinsberg. 2018. Learning diffusion using hyperparameters. In *International Conference on Machine Learning*, pp. 2420–2428.

M. E. Kaminski. 2021. The right to explanation, explained. In *Research handbook on information law and governance*, pp. 278–299. Edward Elgar Publishing.

M. E. Kaminski. 2023. Regulating the risks of ai. *BUL Rev.*, 103: 1347.

A. Kanervisto, C. Scheller, and V. Hautamäki. 2020. Action space shaping in deep reinforcement learning. In *2020 IEEE conference on games (CoG)*, pp. 479–486. IEEE.

M. Kantarcıoğlu and C. Clifton. June 2 2002. Privacy-preserving distributed mining of association rules on horizontally partitioned data. In *The ACM SIGMOD Workshop on Research Issues on Data Mining and Knowledge Discovery (DMKD'02)*, pp. 24–31. Madison, Wisconsin. http://www.bell-labs.com/user/minos/DMKD02/Papers/kantarcioglu.pdf.

M. Kantarcıoğlu and C. Clifton. Sept. 2004. Privacy-preserving distributed mining of association rules on horizontally partitioned data. *IEEE TKDE*, 16(9): 1026–1037. http://ieeexplore.ieee.org/iel5/69/29187/01316832.pdf?isnumber=29187&prod=JNL&arnumber=1316832&arnumber=1316832&arSt=+1026&ared=+1037&arAuthor=Kantarcioglu%2C+M.%3B+Clifton%2C+C.

H. Kargupta, S. Datta, Q. Wang, and K. Sivakumar. 2003. On the privacy preserving properties of random data perturbation techniques. In *ICDM '03*, pp. 96–106. Melbourne, FL, USA.

M. Kearns, S. Neel, A. Roth, and Z. S. Wu. 2018. Preventing fairness gerrymandering: Auditing and learning for subgroup fairness. In *International Conference on Machine Learning*, pp. 2564–2572.

O. Kehinde, R. Abdul, B. Afolabi, P. Vir, C. Namblard, A. Mukhopadhyay, and A. Adereni. 2024. Deploying adviser: Impact and lessons from using artificial intelligence for child vaccination uptake in nigeria. In *Proceedings of the AAAI Conference on Artificial Intelligence*, volume 38, pp. 22185–22192.

J. A. Kelly, D. A. Murphy, K. J. Sikkema, T. L. McAuliffe, R. A. Roffman, L. J. Solomon, R. A. Winett, S. C. Kalichman, and T. C. H. P. R. Collaborative. 1997. Randomised, controlled, community-level HIV-prevention intervention for sexual-risk behaviour among homosexual men in US cities. *The Lancet*, 350(9090): 1500–1505.

D. Kempe, J. Kleinberg, and É. Tardos. 2003. Maximizing the spread of influence through a social network. In *Proceedings of the ninth ACM SIGKDD international conference on Knowledge discovery and data mining*, pp. 137–146. ACM.

W. Kempton and J. Tomić. 2005. Vehicle-to-grid power fundamentals: Calculating capacity and net revenue. *Journal of Power Sources*, 144(1): 268–279.

S. K. Keneally, M. J. Robbins, and B. J. Lunday. 2016. A markov decision process model for the optimal dispatch of military medical evacuation assets. *Health Care Management Science*, 19(2): 111–129.

O. Kesten. 2010. School choice with consent. *The Quarterly Journal of Economics*, 125(3): 1297–1348.

C. Kiekintveld, V. Lisỳ, and R. Píbil. 2015. Game-theoretic foundations for the strategic use of honeypots in network security. In *Cyber Warfare: Building the Scientific Foundation*, pp. 81–101. Springer.

N. Kilbertus, M. Rojas Carulla, G. Parascandolo, M. Hardt, D. Janzing, and B. Schölkopf. 2017. Avoiding discrimination through causal reasoning. In *Neural Information Processing Systems*.

D. A. Kim, A. R. Hwong, D. Stafford, D. A. Hughes, A. J. O'Malley, J. H. Fowler, and N. A. Christakis. 2015. Social network targeting to maximise population behaviour change: a cluster randomised controlled trial. *The Lancet*, 386(9989): 145–153.

P. Kim and R. Durrie. 2025. Ai ethics, law, and policy. *Law, and Policy (June 11, 2025). Washington University in St. Louis Legal Studies Research Paper*, (25-06): 03.

P. T. Kim. 2016. Data-driven discrimination at work. *Wm. & Mary L. Rev.*, 58: 857.

P. T. Kim. 2022. Race-aware algorithms: Fairness, nondiscrimination and affirmative action. *Cal. L. Rev.*, 110: 1539.

D. P. Kingma and J. Ba. 2014. Adam: A method for stochastic optimization. *arXiv preprint arXiv:1412.6980*.

J. Kleinberg, S. Mullainathan, and M. Raghavan. 2016. Inherent trade-offs in the fair determination of risk scores. *arXiv preprint arXiv:1609.05807*.

J. Kleinberg, S. Mullainathan, and M. Raghavan. 2017. Inherent trade-offs in the fair determination of risk scores. In *Innovations in Theoretical Computer Science Conference*.

V. A. Knight, P. R. Harper, and L. Smith. 2012. Ambulance allocation for maximal survival with heterogeneous outcome measures. *Omega*, 40(6): 918–926.

M. J. Kochenderfer. 2015. *Decision Making Under Uncertainty: Theory and Application*. MIT press.

D. Korzhyk, Z. Yin, C. Kiekintveld, V. Conitzer, and M. Tambe. 2011. Stackelberg vs. nash in security games: An extended investigation of interchangeability, equivalence, and uniqueness. *Journal of Artificial Intelligence Research*, 41: 297–327.

M. Kosinski, D. Stillwell, and T. Graepel. 2013. Private traits and attributes are predictable from digital records of human behavior. *Proceedings of the national academy of sciences*, 110(15): 5802–5805.

A. Krause, H. B. McMahan, C. Guestrin, and A. Gupta. 2008. Robust submodular observation selection. *Journal of Machine Learning Research*, 9(Dec): 2761–2801.

A. Krizhevsky, I. Sutskever, and G. E. Hinton. 2012. Imagenet classification with deep convolutional neural networks. In *Advances in neural information processing systems*, pp. 1097–1105.

Y. Kuang, M. Hu, R. Dai, and D. Yang. 2017. A collaborative decision model for electric vehicle to building integration. *Energy Procedia*, 105: 2077–2082.

A. Kumar et al. 2020. Mixed-integer linear programming for energy management in smart grids: A review. *Renewable and Sustainable Energy Reviews*, 130: 109953.

B. Le Gallic and A. Cox. 2006. An economic analysis of illegal, unreported and unregulated (iuu) fishing: Key drivers and possible solutions. *Marine Policy*, 30(6): 689–695.

N. Leader-Williams and E. Milner-Gulland. 1993. Policies for the enforcement of wildlife laws: the balance between detection and penalties in luangwa valley, zambia. *Conservation Biology*, 7(3): 611–617.

Y. LeCun, L. Bottou, Y. Bengio, and P. Haffner. 1998. Gradient-based learning applied to document recognition. *Proceedings of the IEEE*, 86(11): 2278–2324.

Y. LeCun, Y. Bengio, and G. Hinton. 2015. Deep learning. *Nature*, 521(7553): 436–444.

M. Lecuyer, V. Atlidakis, R. Geambasu, D. Hsu, and S. Jana. 2019. Certified robustness to adversarial examples with differential privacy. In *IEEE Symposium on Security and Privacy*.

M. K. Lee, A. Jain, H. J. Cha, S. Ojha, and D. Kusbit. 2019. Procedural justice in algorithmic fairness: Leveraging transparency and outcome control for fair algorithmic mediation. *ACM Conference on Human-Computer Interaction*, 3(CSCW): 1–26.

K. LeFevre, D. J. DeWitt, and R. Ramakrishnan. 2005. Incognito: efficient full-domain k-anonymity. In *SIGMOD '05: Proceedings of the 2005 ACM SIGMOD international conference on Management of data*, pp. 49–60. ACM, New York, NY, USA. ISBN 1-59593-060-4. .

K. LeFevre, D. J. DeWitt, and R. Ramakrishnan. 2006. Mondrian multidimensional k-anonymity. In *ICDE '06: Proceedings of the 22nd International Conference on Data Engineering*, p. 25. IEEE Computer Society, Washington, DC, USA. ISBN 0-7695-2570-9. .

M. A. Lemons and C. A. Jones. 2001. Procedural justice in promotion decisions: using perceptions of fairness to build employee commitment. *Journal of Managerial Psychology*, 16(4): 268–281.

J. Letchford and Y. Vorobeychik. 2013. Optimal interdiction of attack plans. In *International Conference on Autonomous Agents and Multiagent Systems*, pp. 199–206.

S. Levine and V. Koltun. 17–19 Jun 2013. Guided policy search. In S. Dasgupta and D. McAllester, eds., *Proceedings of the 30th International Conference on Machine Learning*, volume 28 of *Proceedings of Machine Learning Research*, pp. 1–9. PMLR, Atlanta, Georgia, USA. https://proceedings.mlr.press/v28/levine13.html.

B. Li and Y. Vorobeychik. 2018. Evasion-robust classification on binary domains. *ACM Transactions on Knowledge Discovery from Data*.

C. Li, J. Wang, Z. Niu, J. Yao, and X. Zeng. 2021a. A spatial-temporal gated attention module for molecular property prediction based on molecular geometry. *Briefings in Bioinformatics*, 22(5): bbab078.

J.-Q. Li. 2014. Transit bus scheduling with limited energy. *Transportation Science*, 48(4): 521–539.

L. Li, H. K. Lo, and F. Xiao. 2019. Mixed bus fleet scheduling under range and refueling constraints. *Transportation Research Part C: Emerging Technologies*, 104: 443–462.

M. Li, A. Zareian, Q. Zeng, S. Whitehead, D. Lu, H. Ji, and S.-F. Chang. 2020. Cross-media structured common space for multimedia event extraction. *arXiv preprint arXiv:2005.02472*.

N. Li, T. Li, and S. Venkatasubramanian. 2007. t-closeness: Privacy beyond k-anonymity and l-diversity. In *ICDE '07*, pp. 106–115. IEEE, Istanbul, Turkey.

S. Li, Z. Yan, and C. Wu. 2021b. Learning to delegate for large-scale vehicle routing. *Advances in Neural Information Processing Systems*, 34: 26198–26211.

N. Lichtlé, E. Vinitsky, M. Nice, B. Seibold, D. Work, and A. M. Bayen. 2022. Deploying traffic smoothing cruise controllers learned from trajectory data. In *2022 International Conference on Robotics and Automation (ICRA)*, pp. 2884–2890. IEEE.

T. P. Lillicrap et al. 2015. Continuous control with deep reinforcement learning. *arXiv preprint arXiv:1509.02971*.

Y. Lindell and B. Pinkas. 2002. Privacy preserving data mining. *Journal of Cryptology*, 15(3): 177–206. http://www.research.ibm.com/people/l/lindell//id3_abs.html.

M. Linkie, D. J. Martyr, A. Harihar, D. Risdianto, R. T. Nugraha, Maryati, N. Leader-Williams, and W. Wong. 2015. Editor's choice: Safeguarding sumatran tigers: evaluating effectiveness of law enforcement patrols and local informant networks. *Journal of Applied Ecology*.

G. Litjens, T. Kooi, B. E. Bejnordi, A. A. A. Setio, F. Ciompi, M. Ghafoorian, J. A. van der Laak, B. van Ginneken, and C. I. Sánchez. 2017. A survey on deep learning in medical image analysis. *arXiv preprint arXiv:1702.05747*.

M. L. Littman. 1994. Markov games as a framework for multi-agent reinforcement learning. In *International Conference on Machine Learning*, pp. 157–163.

F. Liu, R. Sen, J. P. Talusan, A. Pettet, A. Kandel, Y. Suzue, A. Mukhopadhyay, and A. Dubey. 2025. Reinforcement learning-based approach for vehicle-to-building charging with heterogeneous agents and long term rewards. In *Proceedings of the 24th International Conference on Autonomous Agents and Multiagent Systems*, AAMAS '25, p. 1345–1353. International Foundation for Autonomous Agents and Multiagent Systems, Richland, SC. ISBN 9798400714269.

S. Liu, X. Wang, L. Zhao, B. Li, W. Hu, J. Yu, and Y. Zhang. 2021. 3dcann: a spatio-temporal convolution attention neural network for eeg emotion recognition. *IEEE Journal of Biomedical and Health Informatics*.

W. Liu, Y. Wen, Z. Yu, and M. Yang. 2016. Large-margin softmax loss for convolutional neural networks. In *Proceedings of The 33rd International Conference on Machine Learning*, pp. 507–516.

W. Liu, Y. Wen, Z. Yu, M. Li, B. Raj, and L. Song. 2017. Sphereface: Deep hypersphere embedding for face recognition. In *Proceedings of the IEEE Conference on Computer Vision and Pattern Recognition*, pp. 212–220.

D. Lord, S. P. Washington, and J. N. Ivan. 2005. Poisson, poisson-gamma and zero-inflated regression models of motor vehicle crashes: Balancing statistical fit and theory. *Accident Analysis & Prevention*, 37(1): 35–46.

M. Lowalekar, P. Varakantham, and A. Kumar. 2016. Robust influence maximization. In *Proceedings of the 2016 International Conference on Autonomous Agents & Multiagent Systems*, pp. 1395–1396.

D. Lowd and C. Meek. 2005. Adversarial learning. In *ACM SIGKDD International Conference on Knowledge Discovery in Data Mining*, pp. 641–647.

H. Lund et al. 2017. Smart energy and smart energy systems. *Energy*, 137: 556–565.

X. Ma, Y. He, X. Luo, J. Li, M. Zhao, B. An, and X. Guan. Jul 2018. Camera placement based on vehicle traffic for better city security surveillance. *IEEE Intelligent Systems*, 33(4): 49–61. ISSN 1941-1294. http://dx.doi.org/10.1109/MIS.2018.223110904. .

Z. Ma, D. S. Callaway, and I. A. Hiskens. 2013. Optimal charging control of electric vehicles in smart grid: A survey. *Renewable and Sustainable Energy Reviews*, 28: 575–588.

Z. Ma, X. Chang, Z. Xu, N. Sebe, and A. G. Hauptmann. 2017. Joint attributes and event analysis for multimedia event detection. *IEEE Transactions on Neural Networks and Learning Systems*, 29(7): 2921–2930.

A. Machanavajjhala, J. Gehrke, D. Kifer, and M. Venkitasubramaniam. 2006. l-diversity: Privacy beyond k-anonymity. In *ICDE '06*, p. 24. IEEE Computer Society, Atlanta, GA, USA.

A. Madry, A. Makelov, L. Schmidt, D. Tsipras, and A. Vladu. 2018. Towards deep learning models resistant to adversarial attacks. In *International Conference on Learning Representations*.

M. J. Maher and I. Summersgill. 1996. A comprehensive methodology for the fitting of predictive accident models. *Accident Analysis & Prevention*, 28(3): 281–296.

F. L. Mannering and C. R. Bhat. 2014. Analytic methods in accident research: Methodological frontier and future directions. *Analytic methods in accident research*, 1: 1–22.

MapZen, 2023. Valhalla. https://github.com/valhalla.

R. McCormack and G. Coates. 2015. A simulation model to enable the optimization of ambulance fleet allocation and base station location for increased patient survival. *European Journal of Operational Research*, 247(1): 294–309.

R. D. McKelvey and T. R. Palfrey. 1995. Quantal response equilibria for normal form games. *Games and economic behavior*.

H. B. McMahan, E. Moore, D. Ramage, S. Hampson, et al. 2016. Communication-efficient learning of deep networks from decentralized data. *arXiv preprint arXiv:1602.05629*.

A. McNamara, J. Smith, and E. Murphy-Hill. 2018. Does acm's code of ethics change ethical decision making in software development? In *Proceedings of the 2018 26th ACM joint meeting on european software engineering conference and symposium on the foundations of software engineering*, pp. 729–733.

A. Medley, C. Kennedy, K. O'Reilly, and M. Sweat. 2009. Effectiveness of peer education interventions for HIV prevention in developing countries: a systematic review and meta-analysis. *AIDS Education and Prevention*, 21(3): 181–206.

S. Mehrabi, S. Sohn, D. Li, J. J. Pankratz, T. Therneau, J. L. S. Sauver, H. Liu, and M. Palakal. 2015. Temporal pattern and association discovery of diagnosis codes using deep learning. In *2015 International conference on healthcare informatics*, pp. 408–416. IEEE.

Meteostat, 2020. Historical weather and climate data. https://meteostat.net/en Raw data: NOAA, Deutscher Wetterdienst.

A. Meyerson and R. Williams. 2004. On the complexity of optimal k-anonymity. In *Proceedings of the 23rd ACM SIGACT-SIGMOD-SIGART Symposium on Principles of Database Systems (PODS 2004)*. ACM Press, Paris, France.

S.-P. Miaou and H. Lum. 1993. Modeling vehicle accidents and highway geometric design relationships. *Accident Analysis & Prevention*, 25(6): 689–709.

R. Miotto, L. Li, B. A. Kidd, and J. T. Dudley. 2016. Deep patient: An unsupervised representation to predict the future of patients from the electronic health records. *Scientific reports*, 6: 26094.

S. Mitchell, E. Potash, S. Barocas, A. D'Amour, and K. Lum. 2021. Algorithmic fairness: Choices, assumptions, and definitions. *Annual Review of Statistics and its Application*, 8(1): 141–163.

T. M. Moerland, J. Broekens, A. Plaat, C. M. Jonker, et al. 2023. Model-based reinforcement learning: A survey. *Foundations and Trends in Machine Learning*, 16(1): 1–118.

M. Mohammadi, A. Al-Fuqaha, S. Sorour, and M. Guizani. 2018. Deep learning for iot big data and streaming analytics: A survey. *IEEE Communications Surveys & Tutorials*, 20(4): 2923–2960.

S.-M. Moosavi-Dezfooli, A. Fawzi, and P. Frossard. 2016. Deepfool: a simple and accurate method to fool deep neural networks. In *Proceedings of the IEEE conference on computer vision and pattern recognition*, pp. 2574–2582.

W. D. Moreto. 2015. Introducing intelligence-led conservation: bridging crime and conservation science. *Crime Science*, 4(1): 15.

M. H. Morton, A. Dworsky, J. L. Matjasko, S. R. Curry, D. Schlueter, R. Chávez, and A. F. Farrell. 2018. Prevalence and correlates of youth homelessness in the United States. *Journal of Adolescent Health*, 62(1): 14–21.

A. Mukhopadhyay. 2019. *Robust Incident Prediction, Resource Allocation and Dynamic Dispatch*. PhD thesis, Vanderbilt University.

A. Mukhopadhyay, Y. Vorobeychik, A. Dubey, and G. Biswas. 2017. Prioritized allocation of emergency responders based on a continuous-time incident prediction model. In *International Conference on Autonomous Agents and MultiAgent Systems*, pp. 168–177.

A. Mukhopadhyay, Z. Wang, and Y. Vorobeychik. 2018. A decision theoretic framework for emergency responder dispatch. In *International Conference on Autonomous Agents and MultiAgent Systems*, pp. 588–596.

A. Mukhopadhyay, G. Pettet, C. Samal, A. Dubey, and Y. Vorobeychik. 2019. An online decision-theoretic pipeline for responder dispatch. In *International Conference on Cyber-Physical Systems*, pp. 185–196. ISBN 978-1-4503-6285-6. .

A. Mukhopadhyay, G. Pettet, S. M. Vazirizade, D. Lu, A. Jaimes, S. El Said, H. Baroud, Y. Vorobeychik, M. Kochenderfer, and A. Dubey. 2022. A review of incident prediction, resource allocation, and dispatch models for emergency management. *Accident Analysis & Prevention*, 165: 106501.

Y. Mundlak. 1978. On the pooling of time series and cross section data. *Econometrica: journal of the Econometric Society*, pp. 69–85.

S. P. Nageshrao, J. Jacob, and S. Wilkins. 2017. Charging cost optimization for EV buses using neural network based energy predictor. *IFAC-PapersOnLine*, 50(1): 5947–5952.

V. Nair, K. Prakash, M. Wilbur, A. Taneja, C. Namblard, O. Adeyemo, A. Dubey, A. Adereni, M. Tambe, and A. Mukhopadhyay. 2022. Adviser: Ai-driven vaccination intervention optimizer for increasing vaccine uptake in nigeria. *International Joint Conference on Artificial Intelligence (IJCAI)*.

M. Naor and B. Pinkas. Jan. 7-9 2001. Efficient oblivious transfer protocols. In *Proceedings of SODA 2001 (SIAM Symposium on Discrete Algorithms)*. Washington, D.C.

H. Narasimhan, D. C. Parkes, and Y. Singer. 2015. Learnability of influence in networks. In *Advances in Neural Information Processing Systems*, pp. 3186–3194.

F. Nargesian, A. Asudeh, and H. Jagadish. 2021. Tailoring data source distributions for fairness-aware data integration. *Proceedings of the VLDB Endowment*, 14(11): 2519–2532.

National Emergency Number Association, 2019. 9-1-1 statistics. https://www.nena.org/page/911Statistics.

National HCH Council, 2012. HIV/AIDS among persons experiencing homelessness. In Focus Quarterly Research Review.

National Institute of Standards and Technology, 2023. Artificial Intelligence Risk Management Framework (AI RFM 1.0). https://nvlpubs.nist.gov/nistpubs/ai/NIST.AI.100-1.pdf.

National Institute of Standards and Technology, 2024. Artificial Intelligence Risk Management Framework: Generative Artificial Intelligence Profile. https://nvlpubs.nist.gov/nistpubs/ai/NIST.AI.600-1.pdf.

G. L. Nemhauser, L. A. Wolsey, and M. L. Fisher. 1978. An analysis of approximations for maximizing submodular set functions–i. *Mathematical programming*, 14(1): 265–294.

T. H. Nguyen, R. Yang, A. Azaria, S. Kraus, and M. Tambe. 2013. Analyzing the effectiveness of adversary modeling in security games. In *AAAI*.

T. H. Nguyen, K. Cho, and R. Grishman. 2016. Joint event extraction via recurrent neural networks. In *Proceedings of the 2016 Conference of the North American Chapter of the Association for Computational Linguistics: Human Language Technologies*, pp. 300–309.

A. R. L. S. P. M. J. W. C. S. Nicholas R. Jennings, Peyman Faratin. 2001. Automated negotiation: Prospects, methods and challenges. *Group Decision and Negotiation*, 10: 199–215.

Office of Transportation and Air Quality. June 2019. Fast facts: U.S. transportation sector greenhouse gas emissions 1990–2017. Technical Report EPA-420-F-19-047, U.S. Environmental Protection Agency. https://nepis.epa.gov/Exe/ZyPDF.cgi?Dockey=P100WUHR.pdf.

The Leadership Conference on Civil and Human Rights, 2020. Principles for Hiring Assessment Technologies. civil-rights-principles-for-hiring-assessment-technologies/.

E. L. Paluck, H. Shepherd, and P. M. Aronow. 2016. Changing climates of conflict: A social network experiment in 56 schools. *Proceedings of the National Academy of Sciences*, 113(3): 566–571.

S. Panda and Y. Vorobeychik. 2017. Near-optimal interdiction of factored mdps. In *Conference on Uncertainty in Artificial Intelligence*.

S. Panda and Y. Vorobeychik. 2018. Scalable initial state interdiction for factored mdps. In *International Joint Conference on Artificial Intelligence*.

A. Pande and M. Abdel-Aty. 2006. Assessment of freeway traffic parameters leading to lane-change related collisions. *Accident Analysis & Prevention*, 38(5): 936–948. ISSN 0001-4575. .

J. Pang, J. Wang, Z. Zhu, Y. Yao, C. Qian, and Y. Liu. 2024. Fairness without harm: An influence-guided active sampling approach. In *Neural Information Processing Systems*, pp. 61513–61548.

N. Papernot, P. McDaniel, S. Jha, M. Fredrikson, Z. B. Celik, and A. Swami. 2016. The limitations of deep learning in adversarial settings. In *2016 IEEE European Symposium on Security and Privacy (EuroS&P)*, pp. 372–387. IEEE.

O. M. Parkhi, A. Vedaldi, and A. Zisserman. 2015. Deep face recognition. In *Proceedings of the British Machine Vision Conference (BMVC)*, pp. 41.1–41.12.

Partnership on AI. Partnership on AI: Our Tenets. https://partnershiponai.org/about/#tenets.

T. Paul and H. Yamada. 2014. Operation and charging scheduling of electric buses in a city bus route network. In *17th International IEEE Conference on Intelligent Transportation Systems (ITSC)*, pp. 2780–2786. IEEE.

S. Pavia, D. Rogers, A. Sivagnanam, M. Wilbur, D. Edirimanna, Y. Kim, P. Pugliese, S. Samaranayake, A. Laszka, A. Mukhopadhyay, and A. Dubey. 2024. Deploying mobility-on-demand for all by optimizing paratransit services. *International Joint Conference on Artificial Intelligence (IJCAI)*.

B. S. Pay, J. R. Merrick, and Y. Song. 2019. Stochastic network interdiction with incomplete preference. *Networks*, 73(1): 3–22.

F. Perrotta, T. Parry, and L. C. Neves. 2017. Application of machine learning for fuel consumption modelling of trucks. In *2017 IEEE International Conference on Big Data (Big Data)*, pp. 3810–3815. IEEE.

G. Pettet, A. Mukhopadhyay, M. Kochenderfer, and A. Dubey. 2020a. Hierarchical planning for resource allocation in emergency response systems. *arXiv preprint arXiv:2012.13300*.

G. Pettet, A. Mukhopadhyay, M. Kochenderfer, Y. Vorobeychik, and A. Dubey. 2020b. On algorithmic decision procedures in emergency response systems in smart and connected communities. In *International Conference on Autonomous Agents and Multiagent Systems*, pp. 1046–1054.

J. Pita, M. Jain, J. Marecki, F. Ordóñez, C. Portway, M. Tambe, C. Western, P. Paruchuri, and S. Kraus. 2008. Deployed armor protection: the application of a game theoretic model for security at the los angeles international airport. In *AAMAS: industrial track*.

J. Pouget-Abadie and T. Horel. 2015. Inferring graphs from cascades: A sparse recovery framework. *arXiv preprint arXiv:1505.05663*.

Project-OSRM, 2022. Open source routing machine. https://project-osrm.org/.

M. L. Puterman. 1994. *Markov Decision Processes: Discrete Stochastic Dynamic Programming*. Wiley-Interscience.

M. L. Puterman. 2014. *Markov decision processes: discrete stochastic dynamic programming*. John Wiley & Sons.

M. Rabin. 1981. How to exchange secrets by oblivious transfer. Technical Report TR-81, Aiken Computation Laboratory, Harvard University.

M. Raghavan and P. T. Kim. 2024. Limitations of the "four-fifths rule" and statistical parity tests for measuring fairness. *Geo. L. Tech. Rev.*, 8: 93.

A. Rajkomar, E. Oren, K. Chen, A. M. Dai, N. Hajaj, M. Hardt, P. J. Liu, X. Liu, J. Marcus, M. Sun, et al. 2018. Scalable and accurate deep learning with electronic health records. *npj Digital Medicine*, 1(1): 18.

P. Rajpurkar, A. Y. Hannun, M. Haghpanahi, C. Bourn, and A. Y. Ng. 2017. Cardiologist-level arrhythmia detection with convolutional neural networks. *arXiv preprint arXiv:1707.01836*.

D. Ravi, C. Wong, B. Lo, and G. Z. Yang. 2016. Deep learning for human activity recognition: A resource efficient implementation on low-power devices. In *IEEE International Conference on Wearable and Implantable Body Sensor Networks*, pp. 71–76.

D. Ravì, C. Wong, F. Deligianni, M. Berthelot, J. Andreu-Perez, B. Lo, and G.-Z. Yang. 2017. Deep learning for health informatics. *IEEE journal of biomedical and health informatics*, 21(1): 4–21.

P. J. Reny. 2022. Efficient matching in the school choice problem. *American Economic Review*, 112(6): 2025–2043.

C. Revelle and K. Hogan. 1989. The maximum reliability location problem and α-reliable p-center problem: Derivatives of the probabilistic location set covering problem. *Annals of Operations Research*, 18(1): 155–173.

E. Rice, W. Monro, A. Barman-Adhikari, and S. D. Young. 2010. Internet use, social networking, and HIV/AIDS risk for homeless adolescents. *Journal of Adolescent Health*, 47(6): 610–613.

E. Rice, A. Barman-Adhikari, N. G. Milburn, and W. Monro. 2012. Position-specific HIV risk in a large network of homeless youths. *American Journal of Public Health*, 102(1): 141–147. https://doi.org/10.2105/AJPH.2011.300295. . PMID: 22095350.

E. Rice, A. Yoshioka-Maxwell, R. Petering, L. Onasch-Vera, J. Craddock, M. Tambe, A. Yadav, B. Wilder, D. Woo, H. Winetrobe, et al. 2018. Piloting the use of artificial intelligence to enhance hiv prevention interventions for youth experiencing homelessness. *Journal of the Society for Social Work and Research*, 9(4): 551–573.

N. Richards and W. Hartzog. 2018. The pathologies of digital consent. *Wash. UL Rev.*, 96: 1461.

N. Richards, A. Serwin, and T. Blake. 2022. Understanding american privacy. In *Research Handbook on Privacy and Data Protection Law*, pp. 60–72. Edward Elgar Publishing.

C. Riviere, P. Lauret, J.-F. Ramsamy Manicom, and Y. Page. 2006. A Bayesian neural network approach to estimating the energy equivalent speed. *Accident Analysis and Prevention*, 38(2): 248–259. ISSN 0001-4575. .

F. Rosenblatt. 1957. *The perceptron, a perceiving and recognizing automaton Project Para.* Cornell Aeronautical Laboratory.

A. Rosenfeld and S. Kraus. 2017. When security games hit traffic: Optimal traffic enforcement under one sided uncertainty. In *IJCAI*, pp. 3814–3822.

A. E. Roth and M. Sotomayor. 1990. *Two-sided Matching: A Study in Game-Theoretic Modelling and Analysis*, volume 18 of *Econometric Society Monographs*. Cambridge University Press, Cambridge England.

D. E. Rumelhart, G. E. Hinton, R. J. Williams, et al. 1988. Learning representations by back-propagating errors. *Cognitive modeling*, 5(3): 1.

SafeGraph, 2023. Safegraph data documentation. https://docs.safegraph.com/docs.

R. Salakhutdinov and G. Hinton. 2009. Deep boltzmann machines. In *Artificial Intelligence and Statistics*, pp. 448–455.

M. Salazar, F. Rossi, M. Schiffer, C. H. Onder, and M. Pavone. 2018. On the interaction between autonomous mobility-on-demand and public transportation systems. In *2018 21st International Conference on Intelligent Transportation Systems (ITSC)*, pp. 2262–2269. IEEE.

D. Santos, Z. Kokkinogenis, J. F. de Sousa, D. Perrotta, and R. J. Rossetti. 2016. Towards the integration of electric buses in conventional bus fleets. In *2016 IEEE 19th International Conference on Intelligent Transportation Systems (ITSC)*, pp. 88–93. IEEE.

T. Sayed and F. Rodriguez. 1999. Accident prediction models for urban unsignalized intersections in british columbia. *Transportation Research Record: Journal of the Transportation Research Board*, (1665): 93–99.

D. Schiff, J. Borenstein, J. Biddle, and K. Laas. 2021. Ai ethics in the public, private, and ngo sectors: A review of a global document collection. *IEEE Transactions on Technology and Society*, 2(1): 31–42.

R. T. Schirrmeister, J. T. Springenberg, L. D. J. Fiederer, M. Glasstetter, K. Eggensperger, M. Tangermann, F. Hutter, W. Burgard, and T. Ball. 2017. Deep learning with convolutional neural networks for eeg decoding and visualization. *Human brain mapping*, 38(11): 5391–5420.

A. Schlenker, O. Thakoor, H. Xu, F. Fang, M. Tambe, L. Tran-Thanh, P. Vayanos, and Y. Vorobeychik. 2018a. Deceiving cyber adversaries: A game theoretic approach. In *AAMAS*.

A. Schlenker, O. Thakoor, H. Xu, F. Fang, M. Tambe, L. Tran-Thanh, P. Vayanos, and Y. Vorobeychik. 2018b. Deceiving cyber adversaries: A game theoretic approach. In *International Conference on Autonomous Agents and MultiAgent Systems*, pp. 892–900.

J. A. Schneider, A. N. Zhou, and E. O. Laumann. 2015. A new HIV prevention network approach: sociometric peer change agent selection. *Social Science & Medicine*, 125: 192–202.

F. Schroff, D. Kalenichenko, and J. Philbin. 2015. Facenet: A unified embedding for face recognition and clustering. In *Proceedings of the IEEE Conference on Computer Vision and Pattern Recognition*, pp. 815–823.

Scikit-learn Developers. Sklearn.tree.decisiontreeregressor. https://scikit-learn.org/stable/modules/generated/sklearn.tree.DecisionTreeRegressor.html, Accessed: May 31st, 2020.

T. Séjourné, S. Samaranayake, and S. Banerjee. 2018. The price of fragmentation in mobility-on-demand services. *Proceedings of the ACM on Measurement and Analysis of Computing Systems*, 2(2): 1–26.

R. Sen, Y. Zhang, F. Liu, J. P. Talusan, A. Pettet, Y. Suzue, A. Mukhopadhyay, and A. Dubey. 2025. Online decision-making under uncertainty for vehicle-to-building systems. In *Proceedings of the ACM/IEEE 16th International Conference on Cyber-Physical Systems (with CPS-IoT Week 2025)*, ICCPS '25. Association for Computing Machinery, New York, NY, USA. ISBN 9798400714986. https://doi.org/10.1145/3716550.3722024. .

Y. Senarath, A. Mukhopadhyay, S. Vazirizade, H. Purohit, S. Nannapaneni, and A. Dubey. 2021. Practitioner-centric approach for early incident detection using crowdsourced data for emergency services. In *International Conference on Data Mining (to appear)*, pp. 22–31.

M. Sharif, S. Bhagavatula, L. Bauer, and M. K. Reiter. 2016a. Accessorize to a crime: Real and stealthy attacks on state-of-the-art face recognition. In *ACM SIGSAC Conference on Computer and Communications Security*, pp. 1528–1540. ACM.

M. Sharif, S. Bhagavatula, L. Bauer, and M. K. Reiter. 2016b. Accessorize to a crime: Real and stealthy attacks on state-of-the-art face recognition. In *Proceedings of the 2016 ACM SIGSAC Conference on Computer and Communications Security*, p. 1528–1540. Association for Computing Machinery, New York, NY, USA. ISBN 9781450341394.

T. A. Sheldon. 2000. Estimating treatment effects: real or the result of chance? *Evidence-Based Nursing*, 3(2): 36–39.

Z. R. Shi, A. D. Procaccia, K. S. Chan, S. Venkatesan, N. Ben-Asher, N. O. Leslie, C. Kamhoua, and F. Fang. 2020. Learning and planning in the feature deception problem. In *International Conference on Decision and Game Theory for Security*, pp. 23–44.

M. B. Short, A. B. Pitcher, and M. R. D'Orsogna. 2013. External conversions of player strategy in an evolutionary game: A cost-benefit analysis through optimal control. *European Journal of Applied Mathematics*, 24(1): 131–159.

F. Silva and D. Serra. 2008. Locating emergency services with different priorities: the priority queuing covering location problem. *Journal of the Operational Research Society*, 59(9): 1229–1238.

R. Sioshansi. 2011. *Smart Grid: Integrating Renewable, Distributed & Efficient Energy*. Academic Press.

A. Sivagnanam, A. Ayman, M. Wilbur, P. Pugliese, A. Dubey, and A. Laszka. February 2021. Minimizing energy use of mixed-fleet public transit for fixed-route service. In *35th AAAI Conference on Artificial Intelligence (AAAI)*, pp. 14930–14938.

A. Sivagnanam, S. U. Kadir, A. Mukhopadhyay, P. Pugliese, A. Dubey, S. Samaranayake, and A. Laszka. July 2022. Offline vehicle routing problem with online bookings: A novel problem formulation with applications to paratransit. In *31st International Joint Conference on Artificial Intelligence (IJCAI)*, pp. 3933–3939.

J. C. Smith and Y. Song. 2020. A survey of network interdiction models and algorithms. *European Journal of Operational Research*, 283(3): 797–811.

M. Smith and J. Humphreys. 2015. *The Poaching Paradox: Why South Africa's 'Rhino Wars' Shine a Harsh Spotlight on Security and Conservation.* Ashgate Publishing Company.

C. Smutz and A. Stavrou. 2012. Malicious pdf detection using matadata structural features. In *Annual Computer Security Applications Conference*, pp. 239–248.

D. Solove. 2015. The growing problems with the sectoral approach to privacy law. *Privacy+ Security Blog: Teach Privacy. Link: https://teachprivacy.com/problems-sectoral-approach-privacy-law*.

D. J. Solove. 2013. Introduction: Privacy self-management and the consent dilemma. *Harvard law review*, 126(7): 1880–1903.

E. Sortomme and M. A. El-Sharkawi. 2011. Optimal scheduling of vehicle-to-grid energy and ancillary services. *IEEE Transactions on Smart Grid*, 3(1): 351–359.

N. Šrndic and P. Laskov. 2014. Practical evasion of a learning-based classifier: A case study. In *IEEE Symposium on Security and Privacy*, pp. 197–211.

Stan Development Team, 2023. RStan: the R interface to Stan. https://mc-stan.org/. R package version 2.21.8.

State of California, 2018. California Consumer Privacy Act of 2018.

State of California, 2020. California Privacy Rights Act of 2020.

State of Colorado, 2021. An Act Concerning Additional Protection of Data Relating to Personal Privacy. https://leg.colorado.gov/bills/sb21-190.

State of Utah, 2022. Utah Consumer Privacy Act. https://le.utah.gov/~2022/bills/static/SB0227.html.

State of Virginia, 2022. Virginia Consumer Data Protection Act. https://law.lis.virginia.gov/vacode/title59.1/chapter53/.

R. E. Stern, S. Cui, M. L. Delle Monache, R. Bhadani, M. Bunting, M. Churchill, N. Hamilton, H. Pohlmann, F. Wu, B. Piccoli, et al. 2018. Dissipation of stop-and-go waves via control of autonomous vehicles: Field experiments. *Transportation Research Part C: Emerging Technologies*, 89: 205–221.

Y. Sun, Y. Chen, X. Wang, and X. Tang. 2014a. Deep learning face representation by joint identification-verification. In *Advances in Neural Information Processing Systems*, pp. 1988–1996.

Y. Sun, X. Wang, and X. Tang. 2014b. Deep learning face representation from predicting 10,000 classes. In *Proceedings of the IEEE Conference on Computer Vision and Pattern Recognition*, pp. 1891–1898.

Z. Sun, P. Kairouz, A. T. Suresh, and H. B. McMahan. 2019. Can you really backdoor federated learning? *arXiv preprint arXiv:1911.07963*.

O. Sundstrom and C. Binding. 2012. Flexible charging optimization for electric vehicles considering distribution grid constraints. *IEEE Transactions on Smart Grid*, 3(1): 26–37.

J. Sunshine and T. R. Tyler. 2003. The role of procedural justice and legitimacy in shaping public support for policing. *Law & Society Review*, 37(3): 513–548.

R. S. Sutton and A. G. Barto. 2018. *Reinforcement Learning: An Introduction.* MIT Press.

L. Sweeney. 2002. k-anonymity: a model for protecting privacy. *International Journal on Uncertainty, Fuzziness and Knowledge-based Systems*, 10(5): 557–570.

C. Szegedy, W. Zaremba, I. Sutskever, J. Bruna, D. Erhan, I. Goodfellow, and R. Fergus. 2014. Intriguing properties of neural networks. In *International Conference on Learning Representations.*

Y. Taigman, M. Yang, M. Ranzato, and L. Wolf. 2014. Deepface: Closing the gap to human-level performance in face verification. In *Proceedings of the IEEE Conference on Computer Vision and Pattern Recognition*, pp. 1701–1708.

J. P. Talusan, R. Sen, A. Pettet, A. Kandel, Y. Suzue, L. Pedersen, A. Mukhopadhyay, and A. Dubey. 2024. Optimus: Discrete event simulator for vehicle-to-building charging optimization. In *2024 IEEE International Conference on Smart Computing (SMARTCOMP)*, pp. 223–230. .

M. Tambe. 2011. *Security and game theory: algorithms, deployed systems, lessons learned.* Cambridge University Press.

M. Tambe, B. Wilder, and F. Fang. 2023. *AI for Social Impact.* Open-Source.

K.-L. Tan, B. Carminati, E. Ferrari, and C. Jianneng. 2008. Castle: A delta-constrained scheme for k-anonymizing data streams. In *ICDE '08*, pp. 1376–1378. Cancún, México.

Q. Tang and J. Yu. 2014. A new perspective on kesten's school choice with consent idea. *Journal of Economic Theory*, 154: 543–561.

Y. Tang, X. Xiao, and Y. Shi. 2014. Influence maximization: Near-optimal time complexity meets practical efficiency. In *Proceedings of the 2014 ACM SIGMOD International Conference on Management of Data*, pp. 75–86.

K. Tanguy, M. R. Dubois, K. L. Lopez, and C. Gagné. 2016. Optimization model and economic assessment of collaborative charging using vehicle-to-building. *Sustainable Cities and Society*, 26: 496–506.

H. Technologies, 2022. Here traffic. https://www.here.com/.

O. Thakoor, M. Tambe, P. Vayanos, H. Xu, C. Kiekintveld, and F. Fang. 2019. Cyber camouflage games for strategic deception. In *International Conference on Decision and Game Theory for Security*, pp. 525–541.

The White House, 2022. Blueprint for an AI Bill of Rights. https://bidenwhitehouse.archives.gov/ostp/ai-bill-of-rights/.

The White House, 2025. Removing Barriers to American Leadership in Artificial Intelligence. https://www.whitehouse.gov/presidential-actions/2025/01/removing-barriers-to-american-leadership-in-artificial-intelligence/.

J. W. Thibaut and L. Walker. 1975. *Procedural justice: A psychological analysis*. L. Erlbaum Associates.

N. Tomašev, J. Cornebise, F. Hutter, S. Mohamed, A. Picciariello, B. Connelly, D. C. Belgrave, D. Ezer, F. C. van der Haert, F. Mugisha, et al. 2020. AI for social good: unlocking the opportunity for positive impact. *Nature Communications*, 11(1): 1–6.

L. Tong, B. Li, C. Hajaj, C. Xiao, N. Zhang, and Y. Vorobeychik. 2019. Improving robustness of ml classifiers against realizable evasion attacks using conserved features. In *USENIX Security Symposium*.

L. Tong, Z. Chen, J. Ni, W. Cheng, D. Song, H. Chen, and Y. Vorobeychik. June 2021. Facesec: A fine-grained robustness evaluation framework for face recognition systems. In *Proceedings of the IEEE/CVF Conference on Computer Vision and Pattern Recognition (CVPR)*, pp. 13254–13263.

J. Topf and F. Ramm, 2020. Geofabrik. http://www.geofabrik.de/.

C. Toregas, R. Swain, C. ReVelle, and L. Bergman. 1971. The location of emergency service facilities. *Operations Research*, 19(6): 1363–1373.

A. Torfi and E. A. Fox. 2020. Corgan: Correlation-capturing convolutional generative adversarial networks for generating synthetic healthcare records. In *The Thirty-Third International Flairs Conference*.

R. Tublitz and S. Lawrence. 2014. Public assessing east palo alto's fitness improvement training zone program. *The Chief Justice Earl Warren Institute on Law and Social Policy Research Brief*.

W. Tushar, T. K. Saha, C. Yuen, D. B. Smith, H. V. Poor, and T. Morstyn. 2018. Grid interactive electric vehicles: A review of vehicle-to-grid and vehicle-to-building technologies. *Renewable and Sustainable Energy Reviews*, 91: 59–73.

T. R. Tyler. 2003. Procedural justice, legitimacy, and the effective rule of law. *Crime and Justice*, 30: 283–357.

T. R. Tyler. 2006. Psychological perspectives on legitimacy and legitimation. *Annual Review of Psychology*, 57: 375–400.

T. R. Tyler and Y. J. Huo. 2002. *Trust in the law: Encouraging public cooperation with the police and courts.* Russell Sage Foundation.

T. Unterthiner, A. Mayr, G. Klambauer, and S. Hochreiter. 2015. Toxicity prediction using deep learning. *Computer Science*, 3(8).

J. Urban and M. Kaminski. 2019. The right to contest ai. *Berkeley Tech L. J.*, 34: 189–218.

U.S. Congress, 1970. Fair Credit Reporting Act.

U.S. Congress, 1974. Family Educational Rights and Privacy Act of 1974.

U.S. Congress, 1996. Health Insurance Portability and Accountability Act of 1996.

U.S. Congress, 2008. Genetic Information Nondiscrimination Act of 2008.

U.S. District Court, 2010. Carroll v. City of Mount Vernon.

U.S. Eighth Circuit Court of Appeals, 1997. Duffy v. Wolle.

U.S. Second Circuit Court of Appeals, 2013. Maraschiello v. City of Buffalo Police Dept.

U.S. Seventh Circuit Court of Appeals, 2005. Rudin v. Lincoln Land Community College.

U.S. Seventh Circuit Court of Appeals, 2006. Mlynczak v. Bodman.

US State AI Governance Legislation Tracker. International Association of Privacy Professionals. https://iapp.org/resources/article/us-state-ai-governance-legislation-tracker/.

US State Privacy Legislation Tracker., 2025. US State Privacy Legislation Tracker. https://iapp.org/resources/article/us-state-privacy-legislation-tracker/.

U.S. Supreme Court, 1971. Griggs v. Duke Power Co.

U.S. Supreme Court, 1973. McDonnell Douglas Corp. v. Green.

U.S. Supreme Court, 1975. Albemarle Paper Co. v. Moody.

U.S. Supreme Court, 1977. Dothard v. Rawlinson.

U.S. Supreme Court, 1986a. Wygant v. Jackson Bd. of Educ.

U.S. Supreme Court, 1986b. Local No. 93, Intern. Association of Firefighters, AFL-CIO C.L.C. v. City of Cleveland.

U.S. Supreme Court, 2009. Ricci v. DeStefano.

U.S. Supreme Court, 2023. Students for Fair Admissions, Inc. v. President and Fellows of Harvard College.

K. Vaccaro, K. Karahalios, D. K. Mulligan, D. Kluttz, and T. Hirsch. 2019. Contestability in algorithmic systems. In *Conference on Computer Supported Cooperative Work and Social Computing*, pp. 523–527.

T. W. Valente and P. Pumpuang. 2007. Identifying opinion leaders to promote behavior change. *Health Education & Behavior*, 34(6): 881–896.

A. Vaswani, N. Shazeer, N. Parmar, J. Uszkoreit, L. Jones, A. N. Gomez, L. Kaiser, and I. Polosukhin. 2017. Attention is all you need. *Advances in neural information processing systems*, 30.

S. M. Vazirizade, A. Mukhopadhyay, G. Pettet, S. E. Said, H. Baroud, and A. Dubey. 2021. Learning incident prediction models over large geographical areas for emergency response systems. *arXiv preprint arXiv:2106.08307*.

S. Verma, A. Mate, K. Wang, N. Madhiwalla, A. Hegde, A. Taneja, and M. Tambe. 2023. Restless multi-armed bandits for maternal and child health: Results from decision-focused learning. In *Conference on Autonomous Agents and Multiagent Systems (AAMAS)*, pp. 1312–1320.

Y. Vorobeychik and M. Pritchard. 2020. Plan interdiction games. In *Adaptive Autonomous Secure Cyber Systems*, pp. 159–182. Springer.

Y. Vorobeychik, B. An, and M. Tambe. 2012. Adversarial patrolling games. In *2012 Association for the Advancement of Artificial Intelligence Spring Symposium Series*.

Y. Vorobeychik, B. An, M. Tambe, and S. Singh. 2014. Computing solutions in infinite-horizon discounted adversarial patrolling games. In *International Conference on Automated Planning and Scheduling*.

S. Wachter, B. Mittelstadt, and L. Floridi. 2017. Why a right to explanation of automated decision-making does not exist in the general data protection regulation. *International data privacy law*, 7(2): 76–99.

G. Wang, X. Xie, F. Zhang, Y. Liu, and D. Zhang. 2018a. bCharge: Data-driven real-time charging scheduling for large-scale electric bus fleets. In *2018 IEEE Real-Time Systems Symposium (RTSS)*, pp. 45–55.

Q. Wang and W. Chen. 2017. Improving regret bounds for combinatorial semi-bandits with probabilistically triggered arms and its applications. In *Advances in Neural Information Processing Systems*, pp. 1161–1171.

R. Wang, F. M. Harper, and H. Zhu. 2020. Factors influencing perceived fairness in algorithmic decision-making: Algorithm outcomes, development procedures, and individual differences. In *CHI Conference on Human Factors in Computing Systems*, pp. 1–14.

S. Wang, Y. Zhong, and E. Wang. 2019. An integrated gis platform architecture for spatiotemporal big data. *Future Generation Computer Systems*, 94: 160–172.

X. Wang, B. An, M. Strobel, and F. Kong. 2018b. Catching captain jack: Efficient time and space dependent patrols to combat oil-siphoning in international waters. In *Proceedings of the AAAI Conference on Artificial Intelligence*, volume 32.

Y. Wang, D. Zhang, L. Hu, Y. Yang, and L. H. Lee. 2017. A data-driven and optimal bus scheduling model with time-dependent traffic and demand. *IEEE Transactions on Intelligent Transportation Systems*, 18(9): 2443–2452.

Y. Wen, K. Zhang, Z. Li, and Y. Qiao. 2016. A discriminative feature learning approach for deep face recognition. In *European Conference on Computer Vision*, pp. 499–515. Springer.

Z. Wen, B. Kveton, M. Valko, and S. Vaswani. 2017. Online influence maximization under independent cascade model with semi-bandit feedback. In *Advances in neural information processing systems*, pp. 3022–3032.

P. J. Werbos. 1974. Beyond regression: New tools for prediction and analysis in the behavioral sciences. *Doctoral Dissertation, Applied Mathematics, Harvard University, MA*.

S. Wickramanayake and H. D. Bandara. 2016. Fuel consumption prediction of fleet vehicles using machine learning: A comparative study. In *2016 Moratuwa Engineering Research Conference (MERCon)*, pp. 90–95. IEEE.

M. Wilbur, A. Ayman, A. Sivagnanam, A. Ouyang, V. Poon, R. Kabir, A. Vadali, P. Pugliese, D. Freudberg, A. Laszka, et al. 2020. Impact of covid-19 on public transit accessibility and ridership. *Transportation Research Record*, p. 03611981231160531.

M. Wilbur, A. Mukhopadhyay, S. Vazirizade, P. Pugliese, A. Laszka, and A. Dubey. September 2021a. Energy and emission prediction for mixed-vehicle transit fleets using multi-task and inductive transfer learning. In *2021 European Conference on Machine Learning and Principles and Practice of Knowledge Discovery in Databases (ECML PKDD)*, pp. 502–517.

M. Wilbur, P. Pugliese, A. Laszka, and A. Dubey. May 2021b. Efficient data management for intelligent urban mobility systems. In *Proceedings of the Workshop on Data-Driven and Intelligent Cyber-Physical Systems (DI-CPS'21)*, pp. 22–26.

M. Wilbur, S. U. Kadir, Y. Kim, G. Pettet, A. Mukhopadhyay, P. Pugliese, S. Samaranayake, A. Laszka, and A. Dubey. May 2022. An online approach to solve the dynamic vehicle routing problem with stochastic trip requests for paratransit services. In *13th ACM/IEEE International Conference on Cyber-Physical Systems (ICCPS)*, pp. 147–158.

B. Wilder. 2018. Equilibrium computation and robust optimization in zero sum games with submodular structure. In *Thirty-Second AAAI Conference on Artificial Intelligence*.

B. Wilder, A. Yadav, N. Immorlica, E. Rice, and M. Tambe. 2017. Uncharted but not uninfluenced: Influence maximization with an uncertain network. In *Proceedings of the 16th Conference on Autonomous Agents and MultiAgent Systems*, pp. 1305–1313. International Foundation for Autonomous Agents and Multiagent Systems.

B. Wilder, N. Immorlica, E. Rice, and M. Tambe. 2018a. Maximizing influence in an unknown social network. In *Thirty-Second AAAI Conference on Artificial Intelligence*.

B. Wilder, L. Onasch-Vera, J. Hudson, J. Luna, N. Wilson, R. Petering, D. Woo, M. Tambe, and E. Rice. 2018b. End-to-end influence maximization in the field.

R. J. Williams and D. Zipser. 1989. A learning algorithm for continually running fully recurrent neural networks. *Neural computation*, 1(2): 270–280.

E. Wong and Z. Kolter. 2018. Provable defenses against adversarial examples via the convex outer adversarial polytope. In *International conference on machine learning*, pp. 5286–5295.

E. Wong, L. Rice, and J. Z. Kolter. 2020. Fast is better than free: Revisiting adversarial training. In *International Conference on Learning Representations*.

R. K. Wood. 1993. Deterministic network interdiction. *Mathematical and Computer Modelling*, 17(2): 1–18.

A. Woodruff, S. E. Fox, S. Rousso-Schindler, and J. Warshaw. 2018. A qualitative exploration of perceptions of algorithmic fairness. In *CHI Conference on Human Factors in Computing Systems*, pp. 1–14.

J. R. Wright and K. Leyton-Brown. 2014. Level-0 meta-models for predicting human behavior in games. In *Proceedings of the fifteenth ACM conference on Economics and computation*, pp. 857–874. ACM.

J. Wu, C. Kamhoua, M. Kantarcioglu, and Y. Vorobeychik. 2021. Learning generative deception strategies in combinatorial masking games. In *International Conference on Decision and Game Theory for Security*, pp. 98–117.

T. Wu, L. Tong, and Y. Vorobeychik. 2020. Defending against physically realizable attacks on image classification. In *8th International Conference on Learning Representations (ICLR)*.

N. Wulan, W. Wang, P. Sun, K. Wang, Y. Xia, and H. Zhang. 2020. Generating electrocardiogram signals by deep learning. *Neurocomputing*, 404: 122–136.

WWF, 2015. Developing an approach to community-based crime prevention. http://zeropoaching.org/pdfs/Community-based-crime%20prevention-strategies.pdf.

X. Xiao and Y. Tao. 2006. Anatomy: simple and effective privacy preservation. In *VLDB '06: Proceedings of the 32nd international conference on Very large data bases*, pp. 139–150. VLDB Endowment, Seoul, Korea.

X. Xiao and Y. Tao. 2008. Output perturbation with query relaxation. *PVLDB*, 1(1): 857–869.

W. Xu, Y. Qi, and D. Evans. 2016a. Automatically evading classifiers: A case study on PDF malware classifiers. In *Network and Distributed System Security Symposium*.

Y. Xu, F. Pan, and L. Tong. 2016b. Dynamic scheduling for charging electric vehicles: A priority rule. *IEEE Transactions on Automatic Control*, 61(12): 4094–4099.

Z. Xu, S. Wang, F. Zhu, and J. Huang. 2017. Seq2seq fingerprint: An unsupervised deep molecular embedding for drug discovery. In *ACM International Conference on Bioinformatics, Computational Biology,and Health Informatics*, pp. 285–294.

A. Yadav, L. S. Marcolino, E. Rice, R. Petering, H. Winetrobe, H. Rhoades, M. Tambe, and H. Carmichael. 2015. Preventing hiv spread in homeless populations using psinet. In *Twenty-Seventh IAAI Conference*.

A. Yadav, H. Chan, A. Jiang, E. Rice, E. Kamar, B. Grosz, and M. Tambe. 2016a. Pomdps for assisting homeless shelters–computational and deployment challenges. In *Autonomous Agents and Multiagent Systems: AAMAS 2016 Workshops, Visionary Papers, Singapore, Singapore, May 9-10, 2016, Revised Selected Papers*, pp. 67–87. Springer.

A. Yadav, H. Chan, A. Xin Jiang, H. Xu, E. Rice, and M. Tambe. 2016b. Using social networks to aid homeless shelters: Dynamic influence maximization under uncertainty. In *Proceedings of the 2016 International Conference on Autonomous Agents & Multiagent Systems*, pp. 740–748. International Foundation for Autonomous Agents and Multiagent Systems.

A. Yadav, L. S. Marcolino, E. Rice, R. Petering, H. Winetrobe, H. Rhoades, M. Tambe, and H. Carmichael. 2016c. Psinet: assisting hiv prevention amongst homeless youth by planning ahead. *AI magazine*, 37(2): 47–62.

A. Yadav, H. Chan, A. X. Jiang, H. Xu, E. Rice, R. Petering, and M. Tambe. 2017a. Using social networks to raise hiv awareness among homeless youth. *IBM Journal of Research and Development*, 61(6): 4–1.

A. Yadav, H. Chan, A. X. Jiang, H. Xu, E. Rice, and M. Tambe. 2017b. Maximizing awareness about hiv in social networks of homeless youth with limited information. In *IJCAI*, pp. 4959–4963.

A. Yadav, B. Wilder, E. Rice, R. Petering, J. Craddock, A. Yoshioka-Maxwell, M. Hemler, L. Onasch-Vera, M. Tambe, and D. Woo. 2017c. Influence maximization in the field: The arduous journey from emerging to deployed application. In *Proceedings of the 16th conference on autonomous agents and multiagent systems*, pp. 150–158.

A. Yadav, R. Noothigattu, E. Rice, L. Onasch-Vera, L. Soriano Marcolino, and M. Tambe. 2018a. Please be an influencer? contingency-aware influence maximization. In *Proceedings of the 17th International Conference on Autonomous Agents and MultiAgent Systems*, AAMAS '18, p. 1423–1431. International Foundation for Autonomous Agents and Multiagent Systems, Richland, SC.

A. Yadav, R. Noothigattu, E. Rice, L. Onasch-Vera, L. Soriano Marcolino, and M. Tambe. 2018b. Please be an influencer?: Contingency-aware influence maximization.

A. Yadav, B. Wilder, E. Rice, R. Petering, J. Craddock, A. Yoshioka-Maxwell, M. Hemler, L. Onasch-Vera, M. Tambe, and D. Woo. 2018c. Bridging the gap between theory and practice in influence maximization: Raising awareness about hiv among homeless youth. In *IJCAI*, pp. 5399–5403.

S. Yan, Y. Xiong, D. Lin, and X. Tang. 2018. Spatial temporal graph convolutional networks for skeleton-based action recognition. pp. 7444–7452.

R. Yang, F. Ordonez, and M. Tambe. 2012. Computing optimal strategy against quantal response in security games. In *AAMAS*.

R. Yang, A. X. Jiang, M. Tambe, and F. Ordonez. 2013. Scaling-up security games with boundedly rational adversaries: A cutting-plane approach. In *International Joint Conference on Artificial Intelligence*.

A. C. Yao. 1982. Protocols for secure computation. In *Proceedings of the 23rd IEEE Symposium on Foundations of Computer Science*, pp. 160–164. IEEE.

A. C. Yao. 1986. How to generate and exchange secrets. In *Proceedings of the 27th IEEE Symposium on Foundations of Computer Science*, pp. 162–167. IEEE.

Z. Yao, Z. Zhu, and Y. Chen. 2017. Atrial fibrillation detection by multi-scale convolutional neural networks. In *Information Fusion (Fusion), 2017 20th International Conference on*, pp. 1–6. IEEE.

Z. Yao, J. Li, Z. Guan, Y. Ye, and Y. Chen. 2020. Liver disease screening based on densely connected deep neural networks. *Neural Networks*, 123: 299–304.

Z. Yao, Q. Xu, Y. Chen, Y. Tu, H. Zhang, and Y. Chen. 2021. Internet traffic forecasting using temporal-topological graph convolutional networks. In *2021 International Joint Conference on Neural Networks (IJCNN)*, pp. 1–8. IEEE.

Z.-J. Yao, J. Bi, and Y.-X. Chen. 2018. Applying deep learning to individual and community health monitoring data: A survey. *International Journal of Automation and Computing*, 15(6): 643–655.

S. Yasmin, N. Eluru, C. R. Bhat, and R. Tay. 2014. A latent segmentation based generalized ordered logit model to examine factors influencing driver injury severity. *Analytic methods in accident research*, 1: 23–38.

R. Ying, R. He, K. Chen, P. Eksombatchai, W. L. Hamilton, and J. Leskovec. 2018. Graph convolutional neural networks for web-scale recommender systems. pp. 974–983.

J. M. Young, M. J. Hollands, J. Ward, and C. J. Holman. 2003. Role for opinion leaders in promoting evidence-based surgery. *Archives of Surgery*, 138(7): 785–791.

S. D. Young and E. Rice. 2011. Online social networking technologies, HIV knowledge, and sexual risk and testing behaviors among homeless youth. *AIDS and Behavior*, 15(2): 253–260.

H. Yu, X. Li, R. M. Murray, S. Ramesh, and C. J. Tomlin. 2018. *Safe, autonomous and intelligent vehicles*. Springer.

R. Yu and M. Abdel-Aty. 2014. Analyzing crash injury severity for a mountainous freeway incorporating real-time traffic and weather data. *Safety Science*, 63: 50–56. ISSN 0925-7535. .

Y. Zeng, E. Lu, and C. Huangfu. 2018. Linking artificial intelligence principles. *arXiv preprint arXiv:1812.04814*.

F. Zhang, P. Chan, B. Biggio, D. Yeung, and F. Roli. 2015. Adversarial feature selection against evasion attacks. *IEEE Transactions on Cybernetics*.

Q. Zhang, X. Chen, Q. Zhan, T. Yang, and S. Xia. 2017. Respiration-based emotion recognition with deep learning. *Computers in Industry*, 92: 84–90.

T. Zhang, H. Lin, B. Xu, L. Yang, J. Wang, and X. Duan. 2021. Adversarial neural network with sentiment-aware attention for detecting adverse drug reactions. *Journal of Biomedical Informatics*, 123: 103896.

Y. Zhang and G. Augenbroe. 2018. Optimal demand charge reduction for commercial buildings through a combination of efficiency and flexibility measures. *Applied Energy*, 221: 180–194.

B. Zhou, L. Wu, X. Zhang, L. Cheng, and C. Long. 2016. Peak load shaving and valley filling of building energy consumption using electric vehicles. *Applied Energy*, 183: 123–132.

G.-J. Zhou, D.-F. Xie, X.-M. Zhao, and C. Lu. 2020. Collaborative optimization of vehicle and charging scheduling for a bus fleet mixed with electric and traditional buses. *IEEE Access*, 8: 8056–8072.

L. Zhu, F. Guo, R. Krishnan, and J. W. Polak. 2018. The use of convolutional neural networks for traffic incident detection at a network level. In *Transportation Research Board Annual Meeting*.

Index

About the Editors

Dr. Ayan Mukhopadhyay is an Assistant Professor of Computer Science in School of Computing, Data Sciences, and Physics at William & Mary, where he directs the Robust and Adaptive Intelligence Laboratory. His research focuses on developing scalable and adaptive algorithmic methods for decision-making under uncertainty in large cyber-physical systems such as transportation, healthcare, and emergency response. Ayan's work has won best paper awards at multiple top-tier venues, such as IJCAI, ICCPS, INFORMS, ICLR's AI for Good Workshop, and the Google Research AI for Good program. Before his current role, he was a post-doctoral researcher at Stanford University. He holds a doctorate in Computer Science from Vanderbilt University. His doctoral dissertation on scalable algorithmic approaches for semi-Markovian decision processes was nominated for the IFAAMAS Victor Lesser Distinguished Dissertation Award.

Dr. Yevgeniy Vorobeychik is a Professor of Computer Science and Engineering in Washington University in St. Louis. His research focuses on game-theoretic modeling of security and privacy, adversarial machine learning, algorithmic and behavioral game theory, incentive design, optimization, agent-based modeling, complex systems, network science, and epidemic control. He was an assistant professor of computer science and biomedical informatics at Vanderbilt University from 2013 until 2018, and a principal research scientist at Sandia National Laboratories from 2010 until 2013. Between 2008 and 2010 he was a post-doctoral research associate at the University of Pennsylvania Computer and Information Science department. He holds a doctorate in Computer Science from the University of Michigan.

Professor Vorobeychik received an NSF CAREER award in 2017 and was invited to give an IJCAI-16 early career spotlight talk. He was nominated for the 2008 ACM Doctoral Dissertation Award and received honorable mention for the 2008 IFAAMAS Distinguished Dissertation Award.

For Product Safety Concerns and Information please contact our
EU representative GPSR@taylorandfrancis.com Taylor & Francis
Verlag GmbH, Kaufingerstraße 24, 80331 München, Germany